THE FIRST PAPERBACK COLLECTION
OF GREAT FILM SCENES
FROM THE ORIGINAL SCRIPTS.

Here is a unique opportunity to develop your acting talent by playing some of the greatest scenes ever written for two actors. Whether you are a professional or amateur, an actor of stage, screen or television, you can now perform roles never before available in print, all from the original film screenplays. Each scene has been carefully chosen to display the widest range of dramatic ability, for both men and women.

With over 70 scenes in all—from classic comedy to high drama—you will not find another collection like it anywhere.

FILM SCENES FOR ACTORS

THE ACTOR'S SCENEBOOK edited by Michael Schulman and
Eva Mekler

AUDITION by Michael Shurtleff

BRIAN'S SONG by William Blinn

THE EFFECTS OF GAMMA RAYS ON MAN-IN-THE-MOON
MARIGOLDS by Paul Zindel

50 GREAT SCENES FOR STUDENT ACTORS edited by Lewy
Olfson

FILM SCENES FOR ACTORS by Joshua Karton

FOOL FOR LOVE & OTHER PLAYS by Sam Shepard

FOR COLORED GIRLS WHO HAVE CONSIDERED SUICIDE
WHEN THE RAINBOW IS ENUF by Ntozake Shange

INHERIT THE WIND by Jerome Lawrence and Robert E. Lee

THE MIRACLE WORKER by William Gibson

MODERN AMERICAN SCENES FOR STUDENT ACTORS
edited by Wynn Handman

THE MOUSETRAP AND OTHER PLAYS by Agatha Christie

THE NIGHT THOREAU SPENT IN JAIL by Jerome Lawrence
and Robert E. Lee

SAM SHEPARD: SEVEN PLAYS by Sam Shepard

FILM SCENES
FOR
ACTORS

Edited by Joshua Karton

BANTAM BOOKS

TORONTO • NEW YORK • LONDON • SYDNEY • AUCKLAND

FILM SCENES FOR ACTORS
A Bantam Book / March 1983

Bantam Books are published by Bantam Books, Inc. Its trademark, consisting of the words "Bantam Books" and the portrayal of a rooster, is Registered in U.S. Patent and Trademark Office and in other countries. Marca Registrada. Bantam Books, Inc., 666 Fifth Avenue, New York, New York 10103.

PRINTED IN THE UNITED STATES OF AMERICA

O   0 9 8 7 6 5 4

Contents

Introduction

Seventy scenes from the movies have been collected here for the same reason that play scenes have long been anthologized: to supply the studying actor's need for well-written scenes. Even if and when actors act for pay, they continue to take class; the demand for new material is endless.

Most people who study acting today see many more movies than they see plays. I don't know anyone who would say that this is good, but the situation does exist, and along with it, the continually growing desire for an anthology of film scenes. It is from the characters and images of the movies that we have chosen so much of ourselves: how we talk, walk, dress and dance; how we meet, love and leave one another. But even if the plays of the theater were the more familiar of the two, access to screenplay scenes is still essential. We've moved far from the time when even the most enlightened film reviewer ignored the script or the screenwriter. It is now recognized that without the script, there would be nothing *up there*. Much of what has been written for the screen offers us the richest caliber of dramatic writing. This collection, then, is not a nostalgic survey of star turns or Great Moments from the Movies, but rather a long-overdue addition to the actor's working library of scenes from some of the world's best known dramatic literature.

The first criterion of selection was that a given scene be excerpted from a screenplay not based on a play script. Beyond that, it could be original or based on a novel, short story, magazine article—anything. An adaptation of a play script offers material that can be found elsewhere; even when the adaptation's dialogue and construction differ from the play's, the characters, and the situations in which they encounter one another, are already in print somewhere. The object here was to concentrate on scenes not previously available to the acting student.

The shortest scenes in the collection run approximately three and a half minutes—which is long for most movie scenes. A scene in a film is not the structural equivalent of a scene in a play. The rhythmic dynamic of film, which according to one theory corresponds to the human heartbeat, usually involves several shots and "scenes" to fulfill the dramatic event which constitutes a play "scene." Most scenes of continuous action between two characters in a film will not run more than two and a half pages; the rule of thumb for screen time is that one page of script equals roughly one minute of running time. (This is a hazy rule, however, depending on how the dialogue and description are distributed on the page; see Sample Scripts, pages 463 to 467, for facsimiles of different forms in which filmscripts may be found.)

The first movie script that I read for this anthology was *Wuthering Heights*. I sped through in search of the thrilling part when Cathy dies in Heathcliff's arms and he begs her ghost to drive him mad if he must live on this earth without her. Great stuff, but it all took place in three-quarters of a page with three other characters running in and out of the action. The scripts of so many films revealed their best loved scenes to be only moments; it is in our hearts and minds that the montage of these moments has crystallized into what we now recall as "a great scene."

A scene's action, to be wholly profitable for study, must transpire fully within the "live" circumstances of the acting studio. Therefore no scenes are included here that hinge upon intercutting or special effects for their dramatic value. There are no brilliant telephone conversations which would require the actors not to look at one another the whole time, and no scenes requiring the immediate presence of erupting volcanoes, departing trains, or huge crowds. Sometimes a scene contains details that may serve the actor's understanding of the scene but are not to be played; these details have been enclosed in brackets. For example, the screenwriters' descriptions of the characters' "prior moments"—the where, when and what of a character's life just before the scene begins—are included wherever possible, but appear in brackets.

The scenes were chosen without any eye toward training the actor in the specifics of film acting. Certainly there are significant differences in acting for a camera and acting for a live audience; the voice, for example, must be trained for the theater in a way not necessary for film or video. On the other hand, I never knew an actor who had to take diving or flying lessons for a part in a play. An actor onstage will never be directed, as Garbo was, to "think nothing" for a close-up. An actor in a film need not memorize the entire part for a single performance. But because films are seldom shot in sequence, the actor in a film must usually piece together the arc of the character's development from little bits all out of order, playing one moment—which results from an earlier moment—before *that* earlier moment has even been played.

In a scene study class you do not adjust your performance technique to reach the second balcony any more than you try to act on a horse with a Steadi-cam chasing you. The work of the class is the essential challenge of the craft: to bring your own life to someone else's language and, without changing that language, to make it your own.

One living character from the written page, however, does not a scene make. The scene is fulfilled by the actor who creates his or her character *inside a relationship with the other character in the scene*. Your "objective" in a scene is to effect a change in the behavior of the other character—this is what makes a scene playable. It is not uncommon to see a young actor missing this point. He's the earnest fellow ostensibly working on his Stanley Kowalski from Tennessee William's *A Streetcar Named Desire*, but in his heart-of-hearts—that region from which all great performance emanates—he is working on his Marlon Brando. Or she is ostensibly working on Eleanor of Aquitaine from James Goldman's *The Lion in Winter*, but her real goal is to be just as wonderful as Katharine Hepburn. The opportunity for this kind of error in these movie scenes is so immediate that the lesson cannot be avoided. Actors play characters, not other actors. If you want to play an actor who formerly played the character, then your objective in the scene has nothing to do with your scene-partner's character. Rather than searching for that human exchange or connection with the other living person on the stage, you are playing to yourself, to a dream or notion of yourself. "The purpose of playing," Hamlet tells us, "whose end both at the first and now, was and is, to hold, as 'twere, the mirror up to nature"—not up to one's own face in the hope of finding one's favorite movie star. Playing Marlon Brando instead of Terry Malloy in the taxicab scene from *On*

the Waterfront makes for an unachievable objective that
scuttles the scene. (Unless, of course, the actor playing your
brother Charley suddenly exclaims, "My God! You know who
you remind me of?!")

When the real but undeclared objective in a scene is "to be
Marilyn Monroe" or "to be Al Pacino," the actor is idling
on the non-active, existential verb "to be." As Robert Levitt
pointed out when he taught acting at the American Conservatory
Theatre, existential verbs are not for actors—they are for the
gods, lovers, and idiots who exist in some private and sus-
pended animation. Because the scenes in this collection are
well-written, the characters in them are all striving for some
emotional possibility which can only be achieved through
interaction with the other character. In fact, it is the event
of this interaction that constitutes the crux of what is called
"a playable scene."

Almost all of the films excerpted in this volume have been
seen all over the world, yet almost none of the scripts are
easy to locate. The notes to the scenes attempt to provide as
much character and plot information as space allows. The
source appendix will tell you whether the screenplay has
been published; if you can possibly locate it in print, it is
essential to read it in its entirety as is the rule when working
on play scenes. What we remember from seeing the movie is
just a drop from the dense sea of specifics in which character life is born. If you are working on one scene from a
section that offers other scenes from the same film, read all of
the scenes; the information within them can not be picked up
from the connecting notes.

When these scenes are brought into class, they don't look
or sound any different from play scenes. But to those in
the audience, they can *feel* different—subtly and powerfully
different. I think this has something to do with the distinctly
different senses of time in which the two art forms are
usually experienced. In live theater, the actors are present,
real, three dimensional. Both actors and audience are awake
to what has just happened and what will happen next.
Watching a film, on the other hand, has been likened
to dreaming, because in the on-going stream of images
the present tense becomes enveloping. Any given moment
is intensified by its isolation from even the most immediate
past and future, which are off the screen and therefore
invisible. The live-playing of these film scenes brings together

the forward-moving sense of "real time" and the surrounding sense of "film time." And the convergence of the two can feel as startling for the audience as waking up from a dream to find that it's actually happening.

—JOSHUA KARTON
Los Angeles, October 1981

FILM SCENES
FOR
ACTORS

Frank Capra's IT HAPPENED ONE NIGHT

A Columbia Pictures presentation. Producer, Harry Cohn. Director, Frank Capra. Screenplay by Robert Riskin. Based on the novelette *Night Bus* by Samuel Hopkins Adams. Photography, Joseph Walker. Film Editor, Gene Havlick. Art Director, Stephen Gosson. Sound, Edward Bernds. Musical Director, Louis Silvers. Running time, 105 minutes. 1934.

CAST

PETER WARNE	Clark Gable
ELLIE ANDREWS	Claudette Colbert
ALEXANDER ANDREWS	Walter Connolly
SHAPELEY	Roscoe Karns
KING WESTLEY	Jameson Thomas
DANKER	Alan Hale
BUS DRIVER	Ward Bond
BUS DRIVER	Eddie Chandler
LOVINGTON	Wallis Clark
HENDERSON	Harry Bradley
REPORTER	Charlie Brown
THIRD AUTO CAMP OWNER	Harry Holman
HIS WIFE	Maidel Turner
ZEKE	Arthur Hoyt
ZEKE'S WIFE	Blanche Frederici
STATION ATTENDANT	Irving Bacon

Peter and Ellie define two characters in a certain type of male/female confrontation which was to become a staple of American films. Fate has thrown them together on the road.

He is a newspaper reporter who won't stop until he gets the whole story, even though he has just had another fight with his editor and quit again because he's just been fired again. On the outside, Peter is snappy and hearty and tough; on the inside, he's a boy scout with a deeply romantic dream. While he knows his way around and his talk sounds cynical, his feelings are not. Ellie, on the other hand, comes from so much money that her arrogance is really ignorance of the world in which most everybody else has had to live. She has inherited, along with her wealth, a fineness of mind, high temper, health and beauty, and a fierceness of loyalty and determination that won't let her stop until she learns the truth about herself. They take each other down a peg so that they can fall in love, and when they do, after much contest, they're happy ever after.

It Happened One Night opens as Ellie has eloped against her father's wishes. He kidnaps her and imprisons her on the family yacht until he can buy an annulment. She jumps overboard, swims ashore to Miami where she hocks her wristwatch, and boards a bus for New York where she expects her playboy husband to be waiting. She sits in Peter's seat, which he has left momentarily. When he returns, he exudes such self-confidence in informing her of her mistake that she's offended and won't budge. He's alternately amused and put out by her high-hatted ways; he enjoys her spirit and enjoys watching it tested. When Ellie meets obstacles beyond her control, such as having her money stolen, he enjoys helping her out. Because she's trying to be independent, this only offends her more. When she finally starts to recognize his worth, it's his turn to be offended. He pretends to both of them that his interest is merely professional—she is the escaped heiress and he is the reporter and they'll leave it at that. Of course, they don't.

In the scene below, a bridge on the road has been washed out by a storm and the bus passengers have had to put up at a motel for the night.

[DYKE'S AUTO CAMP. ELLIE stands alone on the porch of a small bungalow, sheltered from the rain. Over her head is a sign reading: "OFFICE—Dyke Auto Co.—P. D. Dyke, Prop." She looks about her restlessly, giving the impression that she has been waiting for someone. Suddenly she is attracted by something and gazes in its direction. Then, as seen by ELLIE in a long view, there appears, about twenty yards away, a small cabin, lighted on the inside; and from it PETER emerges accompanied by a man—presumably MR. DYKE. We cannot hear what is being said; from their movements, however, it is apparent that an exchange of money is taking place. DYKE waves his hand in departure and starts toward ELLIE. At the same time, PETER calls to her.

PETER: (*shouting*) Hey! Come on! We're all set. (*Saying which he enters the cabin.*)

ELLIE hesitates a moment, then starts toward the cabin. Now she is hurrying across the open space. En route she passes DYKE.

DYKE: (*as they pass*) Good evening. Hope you and your husband rest comfortably.

ELLIE keeps on running, but suddenly she stops dead and looks back at DYKE, following which a close-up of ELLIE shows her eyes opening wide with astonishment. Her impulse is to call DYKE back, to make him repeat what he said—to make certain she heard him correctly. But DYKE is gone, and she turns and glances thoughtfully in the direction of the cabin. Then slowly the corners of her mouth screw up in an attitude of cynicism. So that's it, is it! He has given her no previous evidence of being "on the make"; yet now, with the first opportunity—. Her thoughts, however, are interrupted by PETER'S voice:

PETER'S VOICE: Well, Brat—what do you say!

As she doesn't stir, there appears a close view of PETER standing in the doorway of the cabin, looking toward ELLIE.

PETER: (*impatiently*) Come on! Come on! What are you going to do? Stand there all night? (*He disappears inside.*)

For a long moment, ELLIE is lost in speculation as to how to proceed. Then, tossing her head defiantly, with her lips set grimly, she starts toward the cabin until she reaches it, stops in the doorway and peers in. As she does this, there is a view of the inside of the cabin, as seen by her at the door. Except for two cots on either side of the room, a few sticks of cane furniture, a small table upon which stands an oil burner for cooking, the place is barren. At the moment PETER is attaching a clothes line across the center of the room. His suitcase is already open.—] And now ELLIE steps inside, surveying the place contemptuously. But PETER, with his back to her, is oblivious of her presence; and as he works, he hums his favorite melody. ELLIE finally breaks the silence.

ELLIE: (*sarcastically*) Darn clever, these Armenians.

PETER: (*seen close as he turns*) Yeah. Yeah, it's a gift. (*But he finishes his hammering and turns to his suitcase.*)

ELLIE: (*seen with Peter*) I just had the unpleasant sensation of hearing you referred to as my husband.

PETER: (*carelessly*) Oh, I forgot to tell you. I registered as Mr. and Mrs. (*The matter-of-fact way in which he says this causes her eyebrows to lift.*)

ELLIE: Oh, you did? What am I expected to do—leap for joy?

PETER: I kind of half expected you to thank me.

ELLIE: Your ego is colossal.

PETER: (*blithely*) Yeah. Yeah, not bad. How's your's?

There is silence for a moment, and PETER proceeds with the unpacking of his suitcase. As she watches him, ELLIE'S mood changes from one of anger to that of sarcasm.

ELLIE: (*appearing in a close-up, her face disdainful*) Compared to you, my friend Shapeley's an amateur. (*Sharply*) Whatever gave you an idea you can get away with this! You're positively the most conceited—

PETER'S VOICE: (*interrupting*) Hey, wait a minute! (*Appearing beside her*) Let's get something straightened out right now. If you've got any peculiar ideas that I'm interested in you, forget it. You're just a headline to me.

ELLIE: (*frightened*) A headline? You're not a newspaper man, are you?

PETER: Chalk up one for your side. Now listen, you want to get to King Westley, don't you? All right, I'm here to help you. What I want is your story, exclusive. A day-to-day account. All about your mad flight to happiness. I need that story. Just between you and me I've got to have it.

ELLIE: Now isn't that just too cute? There's a brain behind that face of yours, isn't there? You've got everything nicely figured out, for yourself, including this.

PETER: This? Oh, that's a matter of simple mathematics. These cabins cost two bucks a night and I'm very sorry to inform you, wifey dear, but the family purse won't stand for our having separate establishments. (*He goes back to the business of laying out his things.*)

ELLIE: (*starting to leave*) Well, thank you. Thank you very much, but—you've been very kind. (*But the rain outside causes her to hesitate.*)

PETER: Oh, yeah? It's all right with me. Go on out in the storm, but I'm going to follow you, see? Yeah. And if you get tough I'll just have to turn you over to your old man right now. Savvy? Now that's my whole plot in a nutshell. A simple story for simple people. Now if you behave yourself, I'll see that you get to King Westley; if not, I'll just have to spill the beans to papa. Now which of these beds do you prefer? This one? All right.

While he speaks he has taken the extra blanket from the cot and hung it over the clothes line. This manages to divide the room in half.

A close view at the door shows ELLIE watching him with interest.

ELLIE: (*sarcastically*) That, I suppose, makes everything— uh—quite all right.

PETER: (*the previous scene returning*) Oh, this?—I like privacy when I retire. I'm very delicate in that respect. Prying eyes annoy me. (*He has the blanket spread out now.*) Behold the walls of Jericho! Maybe not as thick as the ones that Joshua blew down with his trumpet, but a lot safer. You see, I have no trumpet. (*Taking out pajamas*) Now just to show you my heart's in the right place, I'll give you my best pair of pajamas.

He flings them over to her, and she catches them and throws them on her cot. Throughout the scene she hasn't budged from the door, but PETER now prepares to undress.

PETER: Do you mind joining the Israelites?

ELLIE: You're not really serious about this, are you?

PETER: (*seen at close range, going about the job of undressing very diffidently*) All right, don't join the Israelites. Perhaps you're interested in how a man undresses. (*And he hangs his coat over the chair.*) Funny thing about that. Quite a study in psychology. No two men do it alike. (*Now his shirt is coming off.*)

A close view of ELLIE shows her standing stubbornly.

PETER'S VOICE: I once knew a chap who kept his hat on until he was completely undressed. (*Chuckling*) Made a comical picture. . . .

As a scene includes both of them, PETER spreads his shirt over his coat.

PETER: Years later his secret came out. He wore a toupee.

He lights a cigarette diffidently while she remains brazenly watching him, her eyes flashing defiantly.

PETER: I have an idiosyncracy all my own. You'll notice my coat came first—then the tie—then the shirt—now, according to Hoyle, the pants should come next. But that's where I'm different. (*He bends over.*) I go for the shoes first. After that I—

ELLIE: (*unable to stand it any longer*) Smart Aleck!

And thoroughly exasperated, she goes behind the blanket, and plops on the cot. She sits on the edge, debating what to do, feeling herself trapped. Her impulse is to leave, if only to show this smart Aleck he's not dealing with a child, and she rises impetuously and moves to the window.

A close view at the window shows her looking out. The downpour has not abated one bit, and the heavy raindrops clatter against the window pane in a sort of challenge to ELLIE, whose jaw drops. She turns slowly back to the room, and as she does so her eyes light on the cot. It looks most inviting; after all, she hasn't had any rest for two nights. She falls on the cot again, her shoulders sagging wearily. Following this, the view reveals both sides of the blanket. PETER is already in his pajamas.

PETER: Still with me, Brat? (*There is no answer from* ELLIE.) Don't be a sucker. A night's rest'll do you a lot of good. Besides, you've got nothing to worry about. The Walls of Jericho will protect you from the big bad wolf.

A close view shows ELLIE glancing over at the blanket. Despite herself, the suggestion of a smile flits across her face.

ELLIE: You haven't got a trumpet by any chance, have you?

PETER gets the idea and smiles broadly.

PETER: No. Not even a mouth organ.

Pulling the covers back, he prepares to get into bed, humming as he does so.

PETER: (humming to himself)
Who's afraid of the big bad wolf—
The big bad wolf, the big bad wolf. (Louder)
She's afraid of the big bad wolf,
Tra-la-la-la-la—(He springs into bed.)

ELLIE smiles, and wearily she pulls her hat off her head. She sits this way a moment, thoughtfully; then, determined, she looks up.

ELLIE: Do you mind putting out the light?

PETER: Not at all. (He leans over and snaps it off.)

The room is thrown into darkness except for a stream of light coming in the window from the night-light outside the camp. Visible are PETER'S face and arms as he stares ceilingward, while on ELLIE'S side all we can see of her is her silhouette, except for such times as she gets in direct line with the window. There are glimpses of her as she moves around in the process of undressing, and we see, or rather sense, her dress dropping to the floor. She now stands in her chemise; this being white silk, it stands out more prominently against the darkness. She picks up the pajamas and backs into a corner, following which a close-up of her head and shoulders shows her glancing apprehensively toward PETER'S side of the room; and holding the pajamas in front of her with one hand, with the other she slips the strap off her shoulders. She flings her "slip" over the blanket.

PETER, on his side of the room, looks toward the blanket, and reacts to the "slip" coming into sight. Then other undergarments join the "slip" on the blanket.

PETER: (hoarsely) Do you mind taking those things off the walls of Jericho? (A pause) It's tough enough as it is.

ELLIE'S VOICE: Oh, excuse me. (*And we see the underthings flipped off the blanket.*)

ELLIE'S side of the room appears, showing her crawling quickly into bed, pulling the covers over her and glancing apprehensively in PETER'S direction—following which a close view shows PETER being very conscious of her proximity. The situation is delicate and dangerous; the room is atingle with sex. He turns his gaze toward the blanket. The view moves to the blanket, remaining on it a moment. It is a frail barrier! The view then moves back to PETER, whose eyes are still on the blanket, his face expressionless. A close view of ELLIE, next, shows that she, too, has her eyes glued on the blanket, a little fearfully. She turns her head and gazes at the ceiling for a moment. Then suddenly her eyes widen—and she sits up abruptly.

ELLIE: (*seriously*) Oh, by the way—what's your name?

PETER: (*seen close; turning his head toward her*) What's that?

ELLIE: (*both sides of the blanket coming into view*) Who are you?

PETER: Who, me? Why, I'm the whippoorwill that cries in the night. I'm the soft morning breeze that caresses your lovely face.

ELLIE: (*interrupting*) You've got a name, haven't you?

PETER: Yeah. I got a name. Peter Warne.

ELLIE: Peter Warne? I don't like it.

PETER: Don't let it bother you. You're giving it back to me in the morning.

ELLIE: (*flopping back on her pillow as she mumbles*). Pleased to meet you, Mr. Warne. . . .

PETER: The pleasure is all mine.

There is silence between them for a few seconds.

PETER: I've been thinking about you.

ELLIE'S VOICE: Yes?

PETER: You've had a pretty tough break at that. Twice a Missus and still unkissed.

ELLIE doesn't like the implication, and glares in his direction as PETER'S voice continues.

PETER'S VOICE: *(meaningly)* I'll bet you're in an awful hurry to get back to New York, aren't you?

ELLIE: *(hard)* Goodnight, Mr. Warne. *(She turns over.)*

PETER: Goodnight.

He also turns his head toward the wall, and the scene fades out.

Frank Capra's MR. SMITH GOES TO WASHINGTON

A Columbia Pictures presentation. Producer & Director, Frank Capra. Screenplay by Sidney Buchman. Based on the novel *The Gentleman from Montana* by Lewis R. Foster. Photography, Joseph Walker. Film Editors, Gene Havlick, Al Clark. Music, Dimitri Tiomkin. Musical Director, Morris Stoloff. Art Director, Lionel Banks. Assistant Director, Arthur S. Black. Second unit Director, Charles Vidor. Running time, 125 minutes. 1939.

CAST

CLARISSA SAUNDERS	Jean Arthur
JEFFERSON SMITH	James Stewart
SENATOR JOSEPH PAINE	Claude Rains
BOSS JIM JAYLOR	Edward Arnold
GOVERNOR HOPPER	Guy Kibbee
DIZ MOORE	Thomas Mitchell
CHICK MCGANN	Eugene Pallette
MA SMITH	Beulah Bondi
SENATE MAJORITY LEADER	H. B. Warner
PRESIDENT OF THE SENATE	Harry Carey
SUSAN PAINE	Astrid Allwyn
MRS. HOPPER	Ruth Donnelly
HIMSELF	H. V. Kaltenborn

When Senator Foley suddenly dies in office, the governor of his state appoints Jefferson Smith to finish out the remaining two months of Foley's term. Smith has no political experience. He is a naturalist, head of the Boy Rangers and editor of their publication *Boys' Stuff*, a local hero to the state's youth. Smith is so square, so idealistically ga-ga over the precepts of democracy, that the state's machine assumes it will have no trouble keeping him quietly sight-seeing during his brief stay in Washington, D. C. Reciting the phrases of Lincoln and Jefferson, which he knows by heart, Mr. Smith goes to Washington.

Senator Foley's secretary, Saunders, is described in the script as "a girl in her late twenties—pretty—and a shrewd, keen, abrupt creature." She is ashamed of two things—her first name, Clarissa, and the corruption of her boss. The political bigwigs flatter her with promises of more power and money if she will only stay on and babysit this hick for the next two months while they cram their Willet Creek Dam bill through Congress. Under dummy names, the machine has bought up the canyon surrounding Willet Creek. If the bill passes, the state will have to buy back the land for the construction of a bogus dam. Jefferson Smith must be kept ignorant and out of the way; Saunders is handed the job. Assuming that Jefferson's corny patriotism is just another shovelful of the local political hogwash she loathes, Saunders sets up a press conference to make a fool of him.

The Washington papers portray Jefferson as such a clown that he stalks into the press room and starts punching reporters' noses. There is a movement in the Senate to block his confirmation. Joseph Paine, a great friend of Jefferson's father in the early days of their careers as "the twin champions of lost causes," and now the other senator from Jefferson's state, comes to his defense. Jefferson's father was murdered while fighting a syndicate, and Jefferson reveres Paine, unaware that both Paine and the governor are under the thumb of the machine's Boss Taylor. Jefferson wants to leave Washington if all he can do is to discredit himself in his country's most respected chambers. But Paine suggests Jefferson learn the business of the Senate by writing and introducing his own bill for Jefferson's long-standing dream of a National Boys' Camp. What no one yet realizes is that the site of the proposed camp is the canyon surrounding Willet Creek.

The following two dialogues occur during the work session in which Jefferson drafts his bill. (They are bracketed to allow continuous playing of them as a single scene.) Saunders is assisting Jefferson, first with contempt, and then with a willingness to recognize, respect, and eventually partake of his idealism.

(The "Susan" referred to in the scene is Senator Paine's daughter on whom Jefferson has a highly visible crush. Later in the story, the machine uses her as a decoy to keep Jefferson ignorant of their shenanigans. Disgusted at the exploitation of Jefferson's vulnerability, Saunders gets drunk, quits her job, and reveals all to Jefferson. When he tries to expose the Willet Creek Dam fraud, the machine offers him a life in the Senate for his silence. But Jefferson says that "there just can't be any compromise with the inalienable rights like life and liberty. That's about the only thing I know for sure." The machine sets out with massive violence to crush him and the Boy Rangers. Saunders is the only one in Washington to stand by him and urge him to keep fighting—which he does in an heroic filibuster that climaxes in his collapse.)

JEFF'S PRIVATE OFFICE:

He enters, marching to his desk. SAUNDERS comes slowly toward him, after closing the door.

SAUNDERS: Go ahead—punch.

JEFFERSON: Punch?

SAUNDERS: I had a lot to do with that little press conference last night—

JEFFERSON: (*excitedly*) Well, then, I—I *thank* you, Miss Saunders! Nothing better could have happened—. Yes, *sir*, Miss Saunders, we're going right ahead with it!

SAUNDERS: We're going right ahead with—*what?*

JEFFERSON: Why, the Bill—the Bill—to make a National Boys' Camp. . . .

SAUNDERS: One moment, Senator. Do I understand you're going to present a *Bill?*

JEFFERSON: Sure! A Bill. Senator Paine and I decided it was the one way in the world I could make myself—

SAUNDERS: Pardon me. Senator Paine decided this *with* you?

JEFFERSON: Yes. Sure. It was his idea. *I* should have been the one to think of it—

SAUNDERS: My dear Senator, have you the faintest idea of what it takes to get a Bill passed?

JEFFERSON: I know—but you—you're going to help.

SAUNDERS: If I were *triplets,* I couldn't—. Look, Senator— let me give you a rough idea. A member has a Bill in mind—like you—a camp. Right?

JEFFERSON: Right.

SAUNDERS: Fine. Now, what does he do? He's got to sit down first and write it up. The where, when, why, how—and everything else. That takes time—

JEFFERSON: Oh, but this one is so simple.

SAUNDERS I see. *This* one is so simple—

JEFFERSON: And with your help—

SAUNDERS: Oh, yes. And *I'm* helping. Simple—and I'm helping. So we knock this off in record-breaking time of— let's say three or four days—

JEFFERSON: Oh, just a day—

SAUNDERS: A *day!*

JEFFERSON: Tonight.

SAUNDERS: Tonight. (*Controlling herself in a quiet burn*) Look—uh—I don't want to seem to be complaining, Senator—but in all civilized countries, there's an institution called *dinner—!*

JEFFERSON: (*laughing a little*) Oh—dinner. Yes. Well, I'm hungry, too. I thought—maybe—we could have something brought in—you know, like big executives who eat off trays. You see, we've got to light into this and get it going—

SAUNDERS: Uh-huh. Well, dinner comes in on trays. We're executives. And we light into this. It is dawn. Your Bill is ready. You go over there and introduce it—

JEFFERSON: How?

SAUNDERS: You get to your feet in the Senate and present it. Then you take the Bill and put it in a little box—like a letter box—on the side of the rostrum. Just hold it between thumb and forefinger and drop it in. Clerks read it and refer it to the right committee—

JEFFERSON: Committee, huh?

SAUNDERS: Committee.

JEFFERSON: Why?

SAUNDERS: That's how Congress—or any large body— is run. All work has to be done by committees.

JEFFERSON: Why?

SAUNDERS: Look—committees—small groups of Senators— have to sift a Bill down—look into it—study it—and report to the whole Senate. You can't take a Bill no one knows anything about and discuss it among ninety-six men. Where would you get?

JEFFERSON: Yes, I see that.

SAUNDERS: Good. Where are we?

JEFFERSON: Some committee's got it.

SAUNDERS: Yes. They give it to a *sub*committee, where they really give it a going over—hold hearings—call in people and ask questions—then report back to the bigger committee—where it's considered some more, changed, amended, or whatever. Days are going by, Senator. Days—weeks. Finally, they think it's quite a Bill. It goes over to the House of Representatives for debate and a vote. *But* it's got to wait its turn on the calendar—

JEFFERSON: Calendar?

SAUNDERS: That's the order of business. Your Bill has to stand *way* back there in line unless the Steering Committee decides it is important enough to be—

JEFFERSON: What's that?

SAUNDERS: What?

JEFFERSON: The Steering Committee.

SAUNDERS: (*depressed*) Do you really think we're getting anywhere?

JEFFERSON: Yes. Sure. What's a Steering Committee?

SAUNDERS: A committee of the majority party leaders. They decide when a Bill is important enough to be moved up toward the head of the list—

JEFFERSON: *This* is.

SAUNDERS: Pardon me—*this* is. Where are we now?

JEFFERSON: We're over in the House.

SAUNDERS: Yes. House. More amendments—more changes—
and the Bill goes back to the Senate—and *waits its turn
on the calendar again*. The Senate doesn't like what the
House did to the Bill. They make more changes. The
House doesn't like *those* changes. Stymie. So they ap-
point men from each house to go into a huddle called a
conference and battle it out. Besides that, all the lobby-
ists interested give cocktail parties for and against—government departments get in their two cents' worth—cabinet
members—budget bureaus—embassies. Finally, if the
Bill is alive after all this vivisection, it comes to a vote.
Yes, sir—the big day finally arrives. And— nine times
out of ten, they vote it down. (*Taking a deep breath*) Are
you catching on, Senator?

JEFFERSON: Yes. Shall we start on it right now—or order
dinner first?

SAUNDERS: (*mouth drops open*) Pardon?

JEFFERSON: I said—shall we get started *now* or—

SAUNDERS: (*weakly*) Yes—sure. Why not? (*Then, very tired*)
You don't mind if I take the time to get a pencil?

She turns mechanically and heads for the outer office.

JEFFERSON: (*calling after her—laughing in high spirits*) No!
Go right ahead, Miss Saunders.

SAUNDERS: Thanks very much.

JEFFERSON: And a *lot* of paper!

As JEFFERSON starts picking up the telegrams and reading
them avidly, SAUNDERS goes out.

* * *

[JEFF'S PRIVATE OFFICE—AT NIGHT—SAUNDERS and JEFFER-
SON. SAUNDERS is against one end of the desk with papers
before her; JEFFERSON, his coat off, is walking in circles—in
the throes of creating his bill. (Dinner trays, with empty
dinner dishes on them, are in evidence.)

JEFFERSON: (*in a brown study*)—that's the main idea, Miss Saunders. The United States Government isn't going to buy or build this camp—just lend us the money. You've made a note of that, huh?

SAUNDERS: Yes, Senator—*twice*.

JEFFERSON: (*walking circles*) Uh—have you?] (*Running his hand through his hair*) Did you ever have so much to say about something—you couldn't say it?

SAUNDERS: (*drily*) Try sitting down.

JEFFERSON: I did—and—and I got right up.

SAUNDERS: Now, let's get down to particulars. How big is this thing? Where is it to be? How many boys will it take care of? If they're going to buy it—how do they make their contributions? Your bill has to have all that in it—

JEFFERSON: And something else, too, Miss Saunders— the spirit of it—the idea—the—

In his walk, he has come to the window. He points out suddenly.

JEFFERSON: That's what's got to be in it.

She looks in that direction, and sees the lighted Capitol dome, as seen through the window—with JEFFERSON in the foreground.

JEFFERSON: (*pointing*). That.

SAUNDERS indicates that she sees the Dome, her eyebrows lifting a little.

SAUNDERS: (*quietly—with only a touch of sarcasm*) On paper?

JEFFERSON: (*still looking out of the window, not conscious of her cynical question*) I want to make that come to life— yes, and lighted up like that, too—for every boy in the land. Boys forget what their country means—just reading "land of the free" in history books. And they get to be men—and forget even more. Liberty is too precious to get buried in books, Miss Saunders. Men ought to hold it up in front of them—every day of their lives and say: "I am free—to think—to speak. My ancestors couldn't. I can. My children will."

And we see SAUNDERS looking at JEFFERSON with a new expression—listening rather raptly—then starting to make rapid notes.

JEFFERSON'S VOICE: The boys ought to grow up *remembering* that.

He breaks off—turns from the window—collecting himself out of a daze—and a little embarrassed.

JEFFERSON: Well—gosh—that—that isn't "particulars," is it?

SAUNDERS: But you've just taken care of the spirit all right.

JEFFERSON: Well, anyway, it's *something* like that— (*Then— impulsively*) And it *is* important. That—that Steering Committee has *got* to see it that way. And I'm sure Senator Paine will do all he can—(*Breaking off*) He's a fine man, Miss Saunders, isn't he? He knew my father, you know.

SAUNDERS: He did?

JEFFERSON: We need a lot like him—his kind of character— ideals.

SAUNDERS: (*dropping her head to the paper*) Uh—getting back to this, Senator—

JEFFERSON: Yes, yes—

SAUNDERS: Now, this camp is going to be out in your state, of course—

JEFFERSON: (*with enthusiasm*) About two hundred of the most beautiful acres that ever were! Mountains, prairie land, trees, streams! A paradise for boys who live in stuffy cities—(*Breaking off*) You don't know that country out there, do you, Miss Saunders?

SAUNDERS: No.

JEFFERSON: I've been over every foot of it. You couldn't have any idea. You'd have to see for yourself—(*gazing off, enraptured*)—the prairies—the wind leaning on the tall grass—

SAUNDERS is seen again, raptly watching him.

JEFFERSON'S VOICE: —lazy streams down in the meadows— and angry little midgets of water up in the mountains—

(*again seen, together with* SAUNDERS)—cattle moving down a slope against the sun—camp-fires—snowdrifts. . . . (*Breaking off*) Everybody ought to have *some* of that—*some* time in his life. My father taught me to see those things. He grew up with our state—an' he used to say to me, "Son, don't miss the wonders that surround you. Every tree, every sunset, every ant-hill and star is filled with the wonders of nature." He used to say, "Haven't you ever noticed how grateful you are to see daylight again after going through a dark tunnel?" "Well," he'd say, "open your eyes and always see life around you as if you'd just come out of a long tunnel." (*Then*) Where did *you* come from, Miss Saunders?

SAUNDERS: (*quietly*) Well—I guess I've been in that tunnel all my life.

JEFFERSON: You mean—here?

SAUNDERS: Baltimore. Pure city-dweller.

JEFFERSON: But you've had beautiful country all around you. You've just had to lift up your eyes!

SAUNDERS: City-dwellers never do that—for fear of what might drop *in* 'em.

JEFFERSON: (*observing her a second*) Have you always had to—work?

SAUNDERS: Since sixteen or so.

JEFFERSON: I take it your—your parents couldn't—uh—

SAUNDERS: No, they couldn't. Father was a doctor. The kind who placed ethics above collections. That speaks well for Father but it always left us kind of—(*Then*) Could we get on with this, Senator?

JEFFERSON: It hasn't been easy, has it?

SAUNDERS: No complaints.

JEFFERSON: But—I mean—for a woman—And—you've done awfully well—

SAUNDERS: Have I?

JEFFERSON: I never met anyone more—more intelligent—

or capable. I—I don't know where I'd be on this bill of
mine without your help—

SAUNDERS: I don't see where we are *with* it.

JEFFERSON: (*jumping*) No! Gosh! I better get moving here,
Miss Saunders—(*Suddenly*) Everybody else calls you just
plain "Saunders." Why can't I?

SAUNDERS: Go right ahead.

JEFFERSON: Saunders. That's better. (*Practicing*) Good morning, Saunders. Hello, Saunders. How's the bill coming,
Saunders—?

SAUNDERS: (*permitting herself a laugh*) Terrible, thank you.

JEFFERSON: Yeah. Yeah. Well, anyway, we've got "Saunders"
settled. Maybe that was my trouble all along. (*Rubbing
his hands*) Yes, *sir*. I'm all ready to go now—(*Then—
suddenly*) What's your *first* name?

SAUNDERS: Why?

JEFFERSON: Well—nobody calls you anything but Saunders.

SAUNDERS: I also answer to whistles.

JEFFERSON: You—you've *got* a first name, haven't you?

SAUNDERS: Look—I think we ought to skip it.

JEFFERSON: All right. Sure. Just curious. The picture popped
into my mind all of a sudden of a pump without a
handle—or something—

SAUNDERS: Well, if it's all the same to you—

JEFFERSON: (*kidding her*) I know. It's—Violet.

SAUNDERS: It *is* not!

JEFFERSON: Abigail.

SAUNDERS: No!

JEFFERSON: Letitia.

SAUNDERS: No!

JEFFERSON: Lena.

SAUNDERS: (*laughing*) No! Stop it!

JEFFERSON: I've got more. You better tell me.

SAUNDERS: You win. It's—Clarissa.

JEFFERSON: (*dashed down a little*) Clarissa. Oh. Uh-huh. (*Then*) Well, *Saunders*—let's go—

SAUNDERS: Now, *Susan*—that's really a pretty name—

JEFFERSON: (*rising to the bait*) Susan! Susan Paine—that's beautiful—

SAUNDERS: And a beautiful woman, too—don't you think?

JEFFERSON: Yes. The most beautiful I think I ever—gee— (*Catching himself—leaping into action*) Say— we're *never* going to finish this thing! Now, here we go, Saunders. I'm going to talk faster'n you can write—

JEFFERSON walks around rapidly. He is off at great speed now.

JEFFERSON: The location of this camp. About two hundred acres situated in Ambrose County—Terry Canyon—

SAUNDERS is seen busily writing down the facts.

JEFFERSON'S VOICE: —running about a quarter of a mile on either side of Willet Creek—

SAUNDERS: (*suddenly—sharply*) On either side of—*what?*

JEFFERSON pauses—a little astonished at her sharp question.

JEFFERSON: (*seen with* SAUNDERS *again*) Uh—Willet Creek. It's just a little stream—

SAUNDERS: In Terry Canyon?

JEFFERSON: You—don't know it, do you?

SAUNDERS: (*quickly*) No—

JEFFERSON: You couldn't. You've never been out there, you said.

SAUNDERS: (*quickly again*) No, I haven't. I guess I thought the name was familiar. (*Then*) By the way, you discussed with Senator Paine where the camp was to be situated and everything?

JEFFERSON: Well—no. I didn't. Why?

SAUNDERS: Nothing. I just wondered. No *reason* to take it up with him. (*Reading from pad*) "—about a quarter of a mile on either side of Willet Creek—"

JEFFERSON: (*picking up again*) Yeah. This land to be bought
   by contributions from the boys. You have that. Money to
   be—

SAUNDERS, writing, looks up at JEFFERSON from under her
brows with growing interest.

REBECCA

A Selznick International Production. Distributed by United Artists. Director, Alfred Hitchcock. Producer, David O. Selznick. Screenplay by Robert E. Sherwood & Joan Harrison. Adaptation, Philip MacDonald & Michael Hogan. Based on the novel *Rebecca* by Daphne Du Maurier. Director of Photography, George Barnes. Film Editor, Hal C. Kern. Music, Franz Waxman. Sets, Lyle Wheeler. Running time, 130 minutes. 1940.

CAST

MAXIM DE WINTER	Laurence Olivier
MRS. DE WINTER	Joan Fontaine
JACK FAVELL	George Sanders
MRS. DANVERS	Judith Anderson
MAJOR GILES LACY	Nigel Bruce
COLONEL JULYAN	C. Aubrey Smith
FRANK CRAWLEY	Reginald Denny
BEATRICE LACY	Gladys Cooper
ROBERT	Philip Winter
FRITH	Edward Fielding
MRS. VAN HOPPER	Florence Bates
CORONER	Melville Cooper
DR. BAKER	Leo G. Carroll

The script of *Rebecca* constantly designates shots to be made over the shoulders of the characters, so that we are always invisibly in the scene, watching. We are seeing through the eyes of Rebecca, whose presence, a year after her death in a boating accident, still dominates the lives of those who live in the great English country house Manderley. The widower, Maxim de Winter, is given to moods of deep blackness, assumed to erupt from the devastating loss of the brilliant, beautiful Rebecca.

The narrator of the film is the adoring young bride whom Maxim brings home to Manderley. We never learn her name; she is designated in the script as "I." Shy, gauche, and unsophisticated, she is no match for everyone's memory of Rebecca. Because Maxim becomes violent or withdrawn at any mention of Rebecca, "I" can never learn enough about his former marriage to alleviate her anguish of self-consciousness. When a telephone caller asks for Mrs. de Winter, "I"—who a month ago was working as a paid companion—cannot imagine that the caller means *her*; she apologizes that Mrs. de Winter has been dead for a year. "I" has no idea, until the scene below, why Maxim would want a wife who in every way seems inadequate to the splendors of his house and his lost love.

The third principal resident of Manderley is the housekeeper, Mrs. Danvers. As obsessed with Rebecca in death as she was in life, she keeps Rebecca's former bedroom filled with flowers and the bed linen fresh and waiting. She cannot forgive "I's" trespass into her holy shrine and sets out to destroy the intruder. (Eventually, she will torch Manderley rather than let Maxim and another wife live there.) When "I" decides to revive the gaiety of Manderley by giving one of the costume balls that used to be a tradition in the days of Rebecca, Mrs. Danvers tricks her into wearing the exact costume in which Rebecca had dazzled everyone last year. What "I" expects to be her triumph is instead her mortification as the guests stare in dumb horror at her entrance until Maxim explodes. With her hypnotic voice, Mrs. Danvers urges "I" to terminate her despair in suicide, but the spell is broken by the sudden wailing of sirens from a shipwreck. The diver who investigates also finds the boat in which Rebecca was drowned. The following morning, Maxim has still not come back from the shore, so "I" goes down to Rebecca's cottage in the cove in search of him.

THE BOATHOUSE COVE

She looks across to the cottage. In her face appears the recollection of everything the cottage means to her. Suddenly her attention is arrested as she sees the COTTAGE IN A MIST. A lamp is alight in the window of the cottage, and firelight throws flickering shadows on the window pane. Thereupon, we see her determinedly but nervously hurrying toward the cottage and opening the door.

THE COTTAGE

(viewed over "I's" shoulder in the doorway) She is confronted by the figure of MAXIM, sitting, gazing off into space.

MAXIM: *(without moving)* Hello—

"I" advances toward him (the view bringing them together), extremely worried. MAXIM is still in evening dress. His tails are stained with sea water, and generally he has a dishevelled look; but it is more than that—he has the air of a man who has come to the end of his tether.

"I": *(as she gets near him)* Maxim—you haven't had any sleep. *(After a moment; tenderly)* Have you forgiven me?

MAXIM: *(He comes out of his mood, looks at her fondly)* Forgiven you? What have I got to forgive you for?

"I": For last night—my stupidity about the costume.

MAXIM: Oh, that! I'd forgotten. I was angry with you, wasn't I?

"I": *(shyly)* Yes. *(There is a moment's silence. She looks at him pleadingly.)* Maxim, can't we start all over again? I don't ask that you should love me . . . I won't ask impossible things. I'll be your friend and companion . . . I'll be happy with that.

He rises, goes to her, pulls her to him very closely, his behaviour strangely tense. He looks at her strangely, takes her face between his hands and looks at her, tortured.

MAXIM: You love me very much, don't you? *(Dropping his hands from her shoulders)* But it's too late, my darling. . . . We've lost our little chance of happiness.

"I": *(frantically)* No, Maxim, no!

MAXIM: It's all over now. The thing's happened—the thing I've dreaded day after day, night after night.

The scene moves with them as they walk across the room. MAXIM seats himself, and she comes to him and kneels in front of him.

"I": Maxim, what're you trying to tell me?

MAXIM: Rebecca has won.

She looks at him, her worst fears realized: that he still loves Rebecca. After a moment, he speaks again.

MAXIM: Her shadow has been between us all the time— keeping us from one another. She knew that this would happen.

"I": (*gazing at him, speaking in stifled voice*) What are you saying?

MAXIM: They sent a diver down. He found another boat—

"I": (*interrupting, comfortingly, but somewhat relieved*) Yes, I know. Frank told me. Rebecca's boat. It's terrible for you. I'm so sorry.

MAXIM: The diver made another discovery. He broke one of the ports and looked into the cabin. There was a body in there.

She reacts sharply to this, bewildered at the tone of utter fatality with which MAXIM speaks.

"I": Then she wasn't alone. There was someone sailing with her and you have to find out who it was— that's it, isn't it, Maxim?

MAXIM: You don't understand. There was no one with her. (*A moment's pause while she looks at him*) It's Rebecca's body lying there on the cabin floor.

"I": No! No!

MAXIM: The woman that was washed up at Edgecombe— the woman that is now buried in the family crypt— that was not Rebecca. That was the body of some unknown woman, unclaimed, belonging nowhere. I identified it, but I knew it wasn't Rebecca. It was all a lie. *I* knew where Rebecca's body was! Lying on that cabin floor, on the bottom of the sea.

"I": (*terrified*) How did you know, Maxim?

MAXIM: Because—(*looking at her*) I put it there!

There is a tense pause.

MAXIM:　(*bitterly*) Would you look into my eyes and tell me that you love me now?

She cannot believe what she has heard. Involuntarily she draws a little apart from him, rises, and goes out of view for the moment. MAXIM sees she is stunned, overwhelmed, horrified by what he has told her. He rises and walks away.

As he does so, the scene moves up to a close-up of "I," and then we see MAXIM at close range:

MAXIM:　(*standing before fireplace, back to camera*) You see, I was right. It's too late.

"I" comes into the scene toward MAXIM, her heart jumping in quickened, sudden panic. MAXIM turns toward her and takes her in his arms.

"I":　No, it's not too late! (*She puts her arms around him*) You're not to say that! I love you more than anything in the world. . . . Please, Maxim, kiss me, please!

MAXIM:　No. It's no use. It's too late.

"I":　We can't lose each other now! We must be together— always! With no secrets, no shadows . . .

MAXIM:　We may only have a few hours, a few days.

"I":　(*pleadingly*) Maxim, why didn't you tell me before?

MAXIM:　I nearly did sometimes, but you never seemed close enough.

"I":　(*she pulls away, looks at him*) How could we be close when I knew you were always thinking of Rebecca? How could I even ask you to love me when I knew you loved Rebecca still?

MAXIM:　What are you talking about? What do you mean?

"I":　Whenever you touched me I knew you were comparing me to Rebecca. Whenever you looked at me, spoke to me, or walked with me in the garden, I knew you were thinking, "This I did with Rebecca—and this—and this. . . ."

MAXIM stares at her, bewildered, amazed, then turns slightly away.

"I": *(taking a step toward him)* Oh, it's true, isn't it?

MAXIM: *(amazed)* You thought I loved Rebecca? You thought that? I *hated* her!

"I" (seen in a close-up) is incredulous—with the dawning realization that all this time she has been mistaken in thinking MAXIM was in love with Rebecca. The view moves with MAXIM as he talks . . . speaking in an almost quiet, reflective voice.

MAXIM: Oh, I was carried away by her—enchanted by her, as everyone was. And when I was married, I was told I was the luckiest man in the world. She was so lovely—so accomplished—so amusing. "She's got the three things that really matter in a wife," everyone said—"breeding, brains and beauty." And I believed them—completely. But I never had a moment's happiness with her. *(with a bitter little laugh)* She was incapable of love, or tenderness, or decency.

There is exultation in "I's" face as she looks at him.

"I": *(seen fairly close; almost to herself)* You didn't love her? You didn't love her. . . .

The scene moves with MAXIM as he still paces. He lights a cigarette and puffs on it spasmodically as he continues to talk.

MAXIM: Do you remember that cliff where you first saw me in Monte Carlo? Well, I went there with Rebecca on our honeymoon. That was where I found out about her—four days after we were married. She stood there laughing, her black hair blowing in the wind, and told me all about herself—everything. *(bitterly; tensely)* Things I'll never tell a living soul. I wanted to kill her. It would have been so easy. Remember the precipice? I frightened you, didn't I? You thought I was mad. Perhaps I was. Perhaps I am mad. It wouldn't make for sanity, would it—living with the devil?

He comes to a halt and swings around to her. She looks up at him with deep compassion, as he continues, in desperate self-accusation.

MAXIM: "I'll make a bargain with you," she said. "You'd look rather foolish trying to divorce me now after four days of marriage, so I'll play the part of a devoted wife, mistress of your precious Manderley. I'll make it the most famous show place in England, if you like—and people will visit us and envy us and say we're the luckiest, happiest couple in the country. What a grand joke it will be— what a triumph" (*Walking to end of the couch and looking out the window*) I should never have accepted her dirty bargain, but I did. I was younger then and tremendously conscious of the family honor. (*He utters a short, bitter laugh.*) Family honor! And she knew that I'd sacrifice everything rather than stand up in a divorce court and give her away, admit that our marriage was a rotten fraud. (*Looking at her searchingly*) You despise me, don't you—as I despise myself. You can't understand what my feelings were, can you?

"I":   (*seen closer; with infinite tenderness*) Of course I can, darling. Of course I can.

MAXIM: (*as the scene moves with him*) Well, I kept the bargain—and so did she apparently. Oh, she played the game brilliantly. (*He sits on the end of the couch.*) But after a while, she began to grow careless. She took a flat in London and she'd stay away for days at a time. Then she started to bring her friends down here. I warned her, but she shrugged her shoulders: "What's it got to do with you?" she said. She even started on Frank—poor, faithful Frank. (*After a pause*) Then there was a cousin of hers—a man named Favell.

"I":   (*seen close*) Yes, I know him. He came the day you went to London.

MAXIM: (*sitting on couch*) Why didn't you tell me?

"I":   (*seen close*) I didn't like to. I thought it would remind you of Rebecca.

MAXIM: (*rising*) Remind me! As if I needed reminding! (*The view moves with him as he crosses in front of her.*) Favell used to visit her here in this cottage. I found out about it and I warned her that if he came here again I'd shoot them both. (*Facing her*) One night when I found that she'd come back quietly from London, I thought that Favell was with her—and I knew then that I couldn't stand this life of filth and deceit any longer. I decided to come down here and have it out with both of them. But she was alone. She was expecting Favell, but he hadn't come. She was lying on the divan—a large tray of cigarette stubs beside her.

The view moves over to the divan, showing the tea table and a portion of the divan with a tray of cigarette stubs on it as his voice comes over.

MAXIM'S VOICE: She looked ill—queer. Suddenly she got up—started to walk toward me.

The scene tilts up and moves around the room to the door, then to a fairly close view of MAXIM standing with his back to the door.

MAXIM: "When I have a child," she said, "neither you nor anyone else could ever prove it wasn't yours. You'd like to have an heir, wouldn't you, Max, for your precious Manderley?" And then she started to laugh. "How funny, how supremely, wonderfully funny! I'll be the perfect mother just as I've been the perfect wife, and no one will ever know. It ought to give you the thrill of your life, Max, to watch my son grow bigger day by day and to know that when you die, Manderley will be his." (His voice has sunk to a hoarse whisper.) She was face to face with me—one hand in her pocket, the other holding a cigarette. She was smiling, "Well, Max, what're you going to do about it? Aren't you going to kill me?" I suppose I went mad for a moment—I must have struck her. She stood staring at me.

The view moves down to the floor, indicating the place where Rebecca had stood.

MAXIM'S VOICE: She looked almost triumphant—and then she started toward me again, smiling. Suddenly she stumbled and fell.

The scene moves over to take in the ship's tackle on the floor.

MAXIM'S VOICE: When I looked down—ages afterwards it seemed—she was lying on the floor. She'd struck her head on a heavy piece of ship's tackle. I remember wondering why she was still smiling—and then I realized she was dead.

"I": (seen fairly close) But you didn't kill her—it was an accident!

MAXIM is standing in the center of the room, having backed away in horror from the spot where Rebecca had fallen.

MAXIM: Who would believe me? I lost my head. I just knew I had to do something—anything. (*We follow him to the window where he continues talking, his back turned.*) I carried her out to the boat. It was very dark. There was no moon. I put her in the cabin. When the boat seemed a safe distance from the shore, I took a spike and drove it again and again through the planking of the hull. I opened up the seacocks and the water began to come in fast. I climbed over into the dinghy and pulled away. I saw the boat heel over and sink. I pulled back into the cove—it started raining.

"I": (*coming to him*) Maxim, does anyone else know of this?

MAXIM: No, no one—except you and me.

"I": (*walking away from MAXIM*) We must explain it. It's got to be the body of someone you've never seen before.

MAXIM: No, they're bound to know her—her rings and bracelets—she always wore them—they'll identify her body—then they'll remember the other woman—the other woman buried in the crypt.

"I" turns and comes back to MAXIM, and embraces him.

"I": (*intelligent, mature, taking command of the situation*) If they find out it was Rebecca you must simply say that you made a mistake about the other body—that the day you went to Edgecombe you were ill, you didn't know what you were doing. Rebecca's dead, that's what we've got to remember! Rebecca's dead. She can't speak—she can't bear witness. She can't harm you any more. We're the only two people in the world that know, Maxim—you and I.

MAXIM: (*taking tight hold of her arms; desperately*) I told you once that I'd done a very selfish thing in marrying you. You can understand now what I meant. I've loved you, my darling—I shall always love you—but I've known all along that Rebecca would win in the end.

"I": (*putting her arms round him as if to shield him from everything; almost triumphantly she exclaims*) No—no! She hasn't won. No matter what happens now, she hasn't won!

Suddenly the telephone rings, startling the two. The view moves to the phone, covered with dust, on the table. MAXIM comes to the phone, and we see his hand pick up the receiver, as the scene tilts up to MAXIM with the receiver to his ear.

MAXIM: Hello—hel—oh—hello, Frank. Yes. Who? Colonel Julyan?

The view draws back, bringing "I" into the scene.

MAXIM: Yes, tell him I'll meet him there as soon as I possibly can. What? Oh, well, say we could talk about that when we're sure about the matter. Yes— (*he puts down the receiver*)

"I":   (*coming to him*) What's happened?

MAXIM: Colonel Julyan called—he's the Chief Constable of the County. He's been asked by the police to go to the mortuary. He wants to know if I could possibly have made a mistake about that other body.

The two of them stand looking at each other, the girl terrified as to what this may mean. MAXIM puts his arms around her as the scene dissolves.

CITIZEN KANE

A Mercury Production of an RKO Radio Pictures presentation. Director & Producer, Orson Welles. Screenplay by Herman J. Mankiewicz & Orson Welles. Photography, Gregg Toland. Film Editor, Robert Wise. Art Director, Van Nest Polglase. Associate Art Director, Perry Ferguson. Music, Bernard Herrmann. Special Effects, Vernon L. Walker. Running time, 119 minutes. 1941.

CAST

CHARLES FOSTER KANE	Orson Welles
JEDEDIAH LELAND	Joseph Cotten
SUSAN ALEXANDER KANE	Dorothy Comingore
KANE'S MOTHER	Agnes Moorehead
EMILY NORTON KANE	Ruth Warrick
JAMES W. GETTYS	Ray Collins
MR. CARTER	Erskine Sanford
MR. BERNSTEIN	Everett Sloane
THOMPSON, THE REPORTER	William Alland
RAYMOND, THE BUTLER	Paul Stewart
WALTER PARKS THATCHER	George Coulouris
SIGNOR MATISTI	Fortunio Bonanova
HEADWAITER	Gus Schilling
RAWLSTON	Philip Van Zandt
KANE, SR.	Harry Shannon
KANE'S SON	Sonny Bupp

"The Shooting Script" from *The Citizen Kane Book* © 1970 Bantam Books, Inc. Reprinted by permission of Bantam Books, Inc. and Martin Secker and Warburg, Ltd. All rights reserved.

32

"Other names are honored more than Charles Foster Kane's, more justly revered . . . but none of these so loved— hated— and feared, so often spoken—as Charles Foster Kane."

Kane comes barreling through the first part of the twentieth century with a particularly American blend of vigor, shamelessness, charm, and acquisitiveness. He is the American Kubla Khan, amassing an empire of newspapers and real estate, making kings and wars, enthroning himself at Xanadu, his fantastical pleasure dome chocked with actual castles, museums, and zoos. The only thing absent in Kane is a "person." He is an omnivorous appetite, buying and bullying his way into everything he wants—and finally losing it all.

Kane's impoverished mother, upon coming into a fortune, has given up the rearing of her child to the guardianship of the bank. After being expelled from all the best colleges, Kane takes over *The New York Inquirer* and, through extremely creative yellow journalism, parlays it into the wealthiest and most powerful publishing empire in the world. All the while Kane is piling fortune upon fortune, he fancies himself as the protector of the common man, buster of corporate trusts, teller of the truth to the people. He marries the President's niece and is about to win the election for governor of New York on the reform ticket, but a scandal involving his mistress throws him out of electoral politics. After Kane's death, Jed Leland, his best friend who'd been set up as drama critic on the *Inquirer* when Kane first took it over, says this of him:

"You want to know what I think of Charlie Kane? —Well—I suppose he had some private sort of greatness. But he kept it to himself. He never gave himself away. . . . He never gave anything away. He just . . . left you a tip. He had a generous mind. I don't suppose anyone ever had so many opinions. That was because he had the power to express them, and Charlie lived on power and the excitement of using it—But he didn't believe in anything except Charles Kane. . . . I was his oldest friend. As far as I was concerned he behaved like a swine. Not that Charlie ever was brutal. He just did brutal things. Maybe I wasn't his friend. If *I* wasn't, he never had one. Maybe I was what nowadays you call a stooge."

The scene below depicts the first meeting of Kane and Susan Alexander, the girl involved in the scandal which will ruin the election and who eventually becomes the second Mrs. Charles Foster Kane.

SCENE 1

EXTERIOR CORNER DRUGSTORE AND STREET ON THE WEST SIDE OF NEW YORK—NIGHT—1915

SUSAN, aged twenty-two, neatly but cheaply dressed, is leaving the drugstore. (It's about eight o'clock at night.) With a large, man-sized handkerchief pressed to her cheek, she is in considerable pain. A carriage crosses in front of the camera—passes—SUSAN continues down the street—CAMERA FOLLOWING her—encounters KANE—very indignant, standing near the edge of the sidewalk, covered with mud. She looks at him and smiles. He glares at her. She starts on down the street; turns, looks at him again, and starts to laugh.

KANE: (*Glowering*) It's not funny.

SUSAN: I'm sorry, mister—but you *do* look awful funny. (*Suddenly the pain returns and she claps her hand to her jaw*) Ow!

KANE: What's the matter with you?

SUSAN: Toothache.

KANE: Hmm! (*He has been rubbing his clothes with his handkerchief*)

SUSAN: You've got some on your face. (*Starts to laugh again*)

KANE: What's funny now?

SUSAN: You are. (*The pain returns*) Oh!

KANE: Ah ha!

SUSAN: If you want to come in and wash your face—I can get you some hot water to get that dirt off your trousers—

KANE: Thanks.

SUSAN starts, with KANE following her.

DISSOLVE

INTERIOR SUSAN'S ROOM—NIGHT—1915

SUSAN comes into the room, carrying a basin, with towels over her arm. KANE is waiting for her. She doesn't close the door.

SUSAN: *(By way of explanation)* My landlady prefers me to keep this door open when I have a gentleman caller. She's a very decent woman. *(Making a face)* Ow!

KANE rushes to take the basin from her, putting it on the chiffonier. To do this, he has to shove the photograph to one side with the basin. SUSAN grabs the photograph as it is about to fall over.

SUSAN: Hey, you should be more careful. That's my Ma and Pa.

KANE: I'm sorry. They live here too?

SUSAN: No. They've passed on. *(Again she puts her hand to her jaw)*

KANE: You poor kid, you are in pain, aren't you?

SUSAN can't stand it any more and sits down in a chair, bent over, whimpering a bit.

KANE: Look at me. *(She looks at him)* Why don't you laugh? I'm just as funny in here as I was on the street.

SUSAN: I know, but you don't like me to laugh at you.

KANE: I don't like your tooth to hurt, either.

SUSAN: I can't help it.

KANE: Come on, laugh at me.

SUSAN: I can't—what are you doing?

KANE: I'm wiggling both my ears at the same time. *(He does so)* It took me two solid years at the finest boys' school in the world to learn that trick. The fellow who taught me is now president of Venezuela. *(He wiggles his ears again and SUSAN starts to smile)* That's it.

SUSAN smiles very broadly—then starts to laugh.

                                                      DISSOLVE

INTERIOR SUSAN'S ROOM—NIGHT—1915

Close-up of a duck, camera pulls back, showing it to be a

shadowgraph on the wall, made by KANE, who is now in his shirt-sleeves.

SUSAN: *(Hesitatingly)* A chicken?

KANE: No. But you're close.

SUSAN: A rooster?

KANE: You're getting further away all the time. It's a duck.

SUSAN: A duck. You're not a professional magician, are you?

KANE: No. I've told you. My name is Kane—Charles Foster Kane.

SUSAN: I know. Charles Foster Kane. Gee—I'm pretty ignorant, I guess you caught on to that—

KANE: You really don't know who I am?

SUSAN: No. That is, I bet it turns out I've heard your name a million times, only you know how it is—

KANE: But you like me, don't you? Even though you don't know who I am?

SUSAN: You've been wonderful! I can't tell you how glad I am you're here, I don't know many people and—*(She stops)*

KANE: And I know too many people. Obviously, we're both lonely. *(He smiles)* Would you like to know where I was going tonight—when you ran into me and ruined my Sunday clothes?

SUSAN: I didn't run into you and I bet they're not your Sunday clothes. You've probably got a lot of clothes.

KANE: I was only joking! *(Pauses)* I was on my way to the Western Manhattan Warehouse—in search of my youth.

SUSAN is bewildered.

KANE: You see, my mother died too—a long time ago. Her things were put into storage out West because I had no place to put them then. I still haven't. But now I've sent for them just the same. And tonight I'd planned to make a sort of sentimental journey— and now—

KANE doesn't finish. He looks at SUSAN. Silence.

KANE: Who am I? Well, let's see. Charles Foster Kane was born in New Salem, Colorado in eighteen six— *(He stops on the word "sixty"—obviously a little embarrassed*) I run a couple of newspapers. How about you?

SUSAN: Me?

KANE: How old did you say you were?

SUSAN: (*Very bright*) I didn't say.

KANE: I didn't think you did. If you had, I wouldn't have asked you again, because I'd have remembered. How old?

SUSAN: Pretty old. I'll be twenty-two in August.

KANE: That's a ripe old age—What do you do?

SUSAN: I work at Seligman's.

KANE: Is that what you want to do?

SUSAN: I wanted to be a singer. I mean, I didn't. Mother did for me.

KANE: What happened to the singing?

SUSAN: Mother always thought—she used to talk about grand opera for me. Imagine!—Anyway, my voice isn't that kind. It's just—you know what mothers are like.

KANE: Yes.

SUSAN: As a matter of fact, I do sing a little.

KANE: Would you sing for me?

SUSAN: Oh, you wouldn't want to hear me sing.

KANE: Yes, I would. That's why I asked.

SUSAN: Well, I—

KANE: Don't tell me your toothache is bothering you again?

SUSAN: Oh, no, that's all gone.

KANE: Then you haven't any alibi at all. Please sing.

SUSAN, with a tiny ladylike hesitancy, goes to the piano and sings a polite song. Sweetly, nicely, she sings with a small, untrained voice. KANE listens. He is relaxed, at ease with the world.

SCENE 2

The scene below occurs immediately after the Kane newspapers have had to concede the gubernatorial election with the headline, "Kane Defeated—FRAUD AT POLLS!"

INTERIOR KANE'S OFFICE—"INQUIRER"—NIGHT—1916

KANE looks up from his desk as there is a knock on the door.

KANE: Come in.

LELAND enters.

KANE: (*Surprised*) I thought I heard somebody knock.

LELAND: (*A bit drunk*) I knocked. (*He looks at him defiantly*)

KANE: (*Trying to laugh it off*) Oh! An official visit of state, eh? (*Waves his hand*) Sit down, Jedediah.

LELAND: (*Sitting down angrily*) I'm drunk.

KANE: Good! It's high time—

LELAND: You don't have to be amusing.

KANE: All right. Tell you what I'll do. I'll get drunk, too.

LELAND: (*Thinks this over*) No. That wouldn't help. Besides, you never get drunk. (*Pauses*) I want to talk to you—about—about—(*He can't get it out*)

KANE: (*Looks at him sharply a moment*) If you've got yourself drunk to talk to me about Susan Alexander— I'm not interested.

LELAND: She's not important. What's much more important—(*He keeps glaring at* KANE)

KANE: (*As if genuinely surprised*) Oh! (*He gets up*) I frankly didn't think I'd have to listen to that lecture from you. (*Pauses*) I've betrayed the sacred cause of reform, is that it? I've set back the sacred cause of reform in this state twenty years. Don't tell me, Jed, *you*—

Despite his load, LELAND manages to achieve a dignity about the silent contempt with which he looks at KANE.

KANE: (*An outburst*) What makes the sacred cause of reform so sacred? Why does the sacred cause of reform have to be exempt from all the other facts of life? Why do the laws of this state have to be executed by a man on a white charger?

LELAND lets the storm ride over his head.

KANE: (*Calming down*) But, if that's the way they want it—they've made their choice. The people of this state obviously prefer Mr. Rogers to me. (*His lips tighten*) So be it.

LELAND: You talk about the people as though they belong to you. As long as I can remember you've talked about giving the people their rights as though you could make them a present of liberty—in reward for services rendered. You remember the workingman? You used to write an awful lot about the workingman. Well, he's turning into something called organized labor, and you're not going to like that a bit when you find out it means that he thinks he's entitled to something as his right and not your gift. (*He pauses*) And listen, Charles. When your precious underprivileged really do get together—that's going to add up to something bigger—than your privilege—and then I don't know what you'll do. Sail away to a desert island, probably, and lord it over the monkeys.

KANE: Don't worry about it too much, Jed. There's sure to be a few of them there to tell me where I'm wrong.

LELAND: You may not always be that lucky. (*Pauses*) Charlie, why can't you get to look at things less personally? Everything doesn't have to be between you and—the personal note doesn't always—

KANE: (*Violently*) The personal note is all there is to it. It's all there ever is to it. It's all there ever is to anything! Stupidity in our government—crookedness—even just complacency and self-satisfaction and an unwillingness to believe that anything done by a certain class of people can be wrong—you can't fight those things impersonally. (They're not impersonal crimes against the people.) They're being done by actual persons—with actual names and positions and—the right of the American people to their own country is not an academic issue, Jed, that you debate—and then the judges retire to return a verdict—and the winners give a dinner for the losers.

LELAND: You almost convince me, almost. The truth is, Charlie, you just don't care about anything except you. You just want to convince people that you love them so much that they should love you back. Only you want love on your own terms. It's something to be played your way—according to your rules. And if anything goes wrong and you're hurt—then the game stops, and you've got to be soothed and nursed, no matter what else is happening—and no matter who else is hurt!

They look at each other.

KANE: (*Trying to kid him into a better humor*) Hey, Jedediah!

LELAND is not to be seduced.

LELAND: Charlie, I wish you'd let me work on the Chicago paper—you said yourself you were looking for someone to do dramatic criticism there—

KANE: You're more valuable here.

There is silence.

LELAND: Well, Charlie, then I'm afraid there's nothing I can do but to ask you to accept—

KANE: (*Harshly*) All right. You can go to Chicago.

LELAND: Thank you.

There is an awkward pause. KANE opens a drawer of his desk and takes out a bottle and two glasses.

KANE: I guess I'd better *try* to get drunk, anyway. (KANE *hands* JED *a glass, which he makes no move to take*) But I warn you, Jedediah, you're not going to like it in Chicago. The wind comes howling in off the lake, and the Lord only knows if they've ever heard of lobster Newburg.

LELAND: Will a week from Saturday be all right?

KANE: (*Wearily*) Anytime you say.

LELAND: Thank you.

KANE looks at him intently and lifts the glass.

KANE: A toast, Jedediah—to love on *my* terms. Those are the only terms anybody knows—his own.

THE MALTESE FALCON

A Warner Bros. presentation. Director, John Huston. Executive Producer, Hal B. Wallis. Associate Producer, Henry Blanke. Screenplay by John Huston. Based on the novel *The Maltese Falcon* by Dashiell Hammett. Director of Photography, Arthur Edeson. Music, Adolph Deutsch. Film Editor, Thomas Richards. Dialogue Director, Robert Foulk. Assistant Director, Claude Archer. Art Director, Robert Haas. Sound Recorder, Oliver S. Garretson. Running time, 100 minutes. 1941.

CAST

SAM SPADE	Humphrey Bogart
BRIGID O'SHAUGHNESSY	Mary Astor
IVA ARCHER	Gladys George
JOEL CAIRO	Peter Lorre
LIEUTENANT DUNDY	Barton MacLane
EFFIE PERINE	Lee Patrick
KASPER GUTMAN	Sydney Greenstreet
DETECTIVE TOM POLHAUS	Ward Bond
MILES ARCHER	Jerome Cowan
WILMER COOK	Elisha Cook, Jr.
LUKE	James Birke
FRANK	Murray Alper
DISTRICT ATTORNEY BRYAN	John Hamilton
MATE OF THE *LA PALOMA*	Emory Parnell
CAPTAIN JACOBI	Walter Huston

The opening title of *The Maltese Falcon* reads:

> "In 1539 the Knight Templars of Malta paid tribute to Charles V of Spain by sending him a Golden Falcon encrusted from beak to claw with rarest jewels—but pirates seized the galley carrying this priceless token and the fate of the Maltese Falcon remains a mystery to this day."

Four hundred years later a stunning woman who calls herself Miss Wonderly comes to the San Francisco office of private investigators Miles Archer and Sam Spade. Her real name is Brigid O'Shaughnessy, and she is after the Maltese Falcon, but none of this will come out for quite a while. Every single thing she tells Spade and Archer is a lie. She wants them to follow a man named Floyd Thursby. Smitten by her beauty, Archer rushes to accommodate her, and before another day passes, both Thursby and Archer have been shot dead.

The police enjoy playing Spade for the scapegoat—maybe he killed Archer because of the affair Spade was known to be having with Archer's wife; or maybe he killed Thursby in revenge for his partner's death. Spade is contemptuous of the cops who keep pestering him. While he may be cynical of any of life's prizes, he nonetheless enjoys the game of it, and the police are dull and sloppy players. He recognizes Brigid for what she is, but the desperate ingenuity with which she plays her game fascinates him. It is his appreciation of her skill, as much as any need to clear his name or uncover Archer's murderer, that embroils him in the affair of the Maltese Falcon.

The Falcon is due to arrive in San Francisco, and Brigid plans to intercept it. While there has been no "rightful owner" since it was first stolen by pirates in 1539, its passage to America has been arranged by Kasper Gutman, an extremely polite, 300-pound fanatic whose life is consecrated to possessing the Falcon. To do his bidding, Gutman employs two highly exotic and disturbed personalities, both armed—Wilmer Cook and Joel Cairo. They are the ones who lead Spade to Gutman so that Spade can lead Gutman to Brigid and thereby to the Falcon.

When Brigid first comes to Spade and Archer's office, she

promises to be in her hotel lobby that night with Thursby so that the two detectives can get a look at him. Archer never makes it. After identifying his partner's body, Spade goes to the hotel, but Brigid has already checked out. The following day she calls, leaving the name of "LeBlanc" and a new address. In the first of the two scenes below, Spade has just arrived at this new address. In the scene, Brigid tells a whole new set of lies, which are not fully unmasked until the second of the two scenes. The second scene comes at the very end of the film, after the Falcon has just been unwrapped and discovered to be a fraud. With good-humored resignation, Gutman has excused himself to set out for Istanbul to continue his search for the real Falcon, leaving Brigid and Sam alone in the room.

(*Note:* Toward the end of the first scene, while Brigid is in the bedroom getting money, Spade quickly removes her key from her purse and pockets it. Then, at the end of the scene, he surprises her by holding up the key as he tells her that he'll let himself in. Although this "business" does not appear in the final draft of the script, it occurs in the film.)

SCENE 1

INTERIOR HALLWAY CORONET APARTMENTS—CLOSE SHOT—SPADE pressing the buzzer of Apartment 1001. MISS WONDERLY, in a belted green crepe dress, opens the door immediately. Her face is flushed. Her hair parted on the left side, sweeping back in loose waves over her right temple, is somewhat tousled.

SPADE: (*taking off his hat*) Good morning.

MISS WONDERLY: (*lowers her head—then in a hushed timid voice*) Come in, Mr. Spade.

INTERIOR LIVING ROOM

Several bags stand open on the floor. MISS WONDERLY and SPADE enter from the hall.

MISS WONDERLY: Everything is upside-down. I haven't even finished unpacking.

She lays his hat on a table, sits down on a walnut settee.

MISS WONDERLY: Sit down.

SPADE sits on a brocaded oval-backed chair, facing her. She looks at her fingers, working them together. Then:

MISS WONDERLY: Mr. Spade, I've a terrible, terrible confession to make.

He smiles a polite smile.

MISS WONDERLY: That—that story I told you yesterday was just—a story. (*she stammers, looks at him with miserable, frightened eyes*)

SPADE: Oh, that . . . (*lightly*) We didn't exactly believe your story Miss—Miss—What is your name, Wonderly or LeBlanc?

MISS WONDERLY: (*working her fingers again*) It's really O'Shaughnessy—Brigid O'Shaughnessy.

SPADE: We didn't exactly believe your story, Miss O'-Shaughnessy. We believed your two hundred dollars.

BRIGID: You mean? . . .

SPADE: I mean, that you paid us more than if you had been telling us the truth . . . (*blandly*) . . . and enough more to make it all right.

BRIGID: (*bites her lip*) Mr. Spade, tell me . . . (*her face becomes haggard, eyes desperate*) Am I to blame—for last night?

SPADE: You warned us that Thursby was dangerous. Of course, you lied to us about your sister and all—but that doesn't count. We didn't believe you. (*he shrugs his sloping shoulders*) I wouldn't say it was your fault.

BRIGID: (*very softly*) Thank you. (*she puts her hand to her throat*) Mr. Archer was so—so alive yesterday, so solid and hearty and . . .

SPADE: (*sharply*) Stop it! He knew what he was doing. Those are the chances we take.

BRIGID: Was—was he married?

SPADE: Yes, with ten thousand insurance, no children, and a wife who didn't like him.

BRIGID: Oh, please don't!

SPADE: (*shrugging again*) That's the way it was.

He glances at his watch, gets up.

SPADE: Anyway, there's no time for worrying about that now. (*nods his head toward the window*) Out there a flock of policemen and assistant district attorneys are running around with their noses to the ground.

BRIGID moves over on the sofa, making a place for him beside her—but SPADE remains standing.

BRIGID: (*her voice thin and tremulous*) Mr. Spade, do they know about me?

SPADE: Not yet. I've been stalling them until I could see you.

BRIGID: Do they have to know about me at all. I mean couldn't you somehow shield me so that I won't have to answer their questions?

SPADE: Maybe. But I'll have to know what it's all about.

She rises, puts a timid hand to his coat sleeve.

BRIGID: I can't tell you—I can't tell you now—later I will—when I can. You must trust me, Mr. Spade. Oh, I'm so alone and afraid! I've got nobody to help me if you won't help me. (*begging*) Be generous, Mr. Spade. You're brave. You're strong. You can spare me some of that courage and strength, surely. (*she drops to her knees, her hand touching his, clings pitifully*) Help me, Mr. Spade! I need help so badly. I've no right to ask you I know I haven't, but I do ask you. Help me!

SPADE empties his lungs with a long sighing exhalation.

SPADE: You won't need much of anybody's help. You're good. It's chiefly your eyes, I think, and that throb you get into your voice when you say things like "Be generous, Mr. Spade."

She jumps to her feet. Her face blanching painfully, but she holds her head erect and she looks SPADE straight in the eye.

BRIGID: (*voice chilled*) I deserve that. But—oh—The lie was in the way I said it and not at all in what I said. (*lips trembling slightly, but head still erect*) It's my own fault if you can't believe me now.

SPADE'S face darkens. He looks down at the floor.

SPADE: (*muttering*) Now you are dangerous.

BRIGID O'SHAUGHNESSY goes to the table, picks up his hat. She comes back and stands in front of him, holding the hat for him to take if he wishes. Her face is thin, haggard.

SPADE: (*looking at his hat*) Well, I'm afraid I'm—I'm not going to be able to be of much help to you if I haven't some idea of what it's all about. For instance, I've got to have some sort of line on your Floyd Thursby.

She puts his hat on the table, slips down onto the settee again.

BRIGID: I met him in the Orient. (*tracing with pointed fingers a figure eight on a sofa pillow*) We came here from Hong Kong last week. He had promised to help me. He took advantage of my dependence on him to betray me.

SPADE: Betray you how?

BRIGID O'SHAUGHNESSY shakes her head and says nothing.

SPADE: (*taking a new tack*) Why did you want him shadowed?

BRIGID: I wanted to learn how far he had gone, whom he was meeting. Things like that.

SPADE: Did he kill Archer?

BRIGID: (*surprised*) Yes, certainly. He had a Luger in his shoulder holster.

SPADE: Archer wasn't shot with a Luger.

BRIGID: Mr. Spade, you don't think I had anything to do with the death of Mr. Archer?

SPADE: Did you?

BRIGID: No.

SPADE: That's good.

BRIGID: Floyd always carried an extra revolver in his overcoat pocket.

SPADE: Why all the guns?

BRIGID: He lived by them. The story in Hong Kong is that he first came to the Orient as bodyguard to a gambler who had to leave the States—that the gambler had since disappeared, and that Floyd knew about his disappearance. I don't know. I do know that he always went heavily armed and that he never went to sleep without covering the floor around his bed with crumpled newspapers so nobody could come silently into his room.

SPADE: You picked a nice sort of playmate.

BRIGID: (*simply*) Only that sort could have helped me—if he had been loyal.

SPADE: (*pinching his lower lip between finger and thumb*) How bad a hole are you actually in?

BRIGID: (*the chill coming back into her voice*) As bad as could be.

SPADE: Physical danger?

BRIGID: I'm not heroic. I don't think there is anything worse than death!

SPADE: Then it's that?

BRIGID: It's that as surely as we're sitting here . . . (*she shivers*) . . . unless you help me.

SPADE releases his lower lip, runs his fingers through his hair.

SPADE: Who killed Thursby? Your enemies or his?

BRIGID puts a crumpled handkerchief to her mouth, speaks through it.

BRIGID: I don't know. His, I suppose. But I'm afraid . . . I don't know.

SPADE makes a growling animal noise in his throat.

SPADE: This is hopeless. I don't know what you want done. I don't even know if you know what you want done. (*he reaches for his hat*)

BRIGID: (*begging in a somewhat choked voice*) You won't go to the police?

SPADE: (*his voice loud with rage*) Go to them? (*puts his hat on his head, pulling it down tightly*) All I've got to do is stand still and they'll be swarming all over me. All right, I'll tell them all I know, and you'll have to take your chances.

The girl rises from the settee and stands very straight in front of him, holding her white, panic-stricken face high, though she cannot hold the twitching muscles of mouth and chin still.

BRIGID: You've been patient with me. You've tried to help
me. It's useless and hopeless, I suppose. (*she stretches
out her right hand*) I do thank you for what you have
done. —I—I'll have to take my chances.

SPADE makes the growling, animal noise in his throat again.
Then:

SPADE: (*abruptly*) How much money have you got?

The question startles her.

BRIGID: (*reluctantly*) I've about five hundred dollars left.

SPADE: Give it to me.

She hesitates, looking timidly at him. He makes an angry
gesture. She goes into her bedroom, returning almost immediately with a sheaf of paper in one hand. He takes the
money from her, counts it. Then:

SPADE: (*scowling*) There's only four hundred here.

BRIGID: (*meekly*) I had to keep some to live on. (*she raises
a hand to her breast*)

SPADE: (*brutally*) Can't you get any more?

BRIGID: No.

SPADE: You must have something you can raise money on.

BRIGID: I've some furs and a little jewelry.

SPADE: You'll have to hock them. (*he holds out his hand*)

BRIGID looks pleadingly at him. His eyes are hard and implacable. Slowly she puts her hand into the neck of her dress,
brings out a slender roll of bills, gives them to him. He
smooths the bills out, counts them, gives her back two of the
five bills, puts the others in his pocket.

SPADE: There you are. I'll be back as soon as I can with the
best news I can manage. I'll ring four times—long-short-
long-short—so you'll know it's me. And, oh, you needn't
bother to come to the door. I'll let myself in.

He leaves her standing in the center of the floor looking after
him with dazed blue eyes.

SCENE 2

INTERIOR LIVING ROOM—SPADE'S APARTMENT—DAY.
CLOSE SHOT SPADE AT TELEPHONE—SPADE takes the receiver off the hook and dials a number. BRIGID watches him, a slight frown on her face.

SPADE: (*into phone*) Hello. . . . Is Sergeant Polhaus there? . . . Yeah. . . . This is Sam Spade. (*he stares into space, waiting, then*) Hello, Tom. . . . Now listen. I've got something for you. . . . Here it is: Thursby and Jacobi were killed by a man named Wilmer Cook. . . . Yeah. He's about twenty years old, five feet six. In gray woolen suit, gray single-breasted overcoat and hat, shirt with soft attached collar and a light crepe silk tie. He's working for a man named Kasper Gutman. You can't miss Gutman. He must weigh three hundred pounds. . . . That fellow Cairo is in with them too. . . . Right. . . . They just left here for the Alexandria Hotel, but they're blowing town so you'll have to move fast. . . . I don't think they're expecting a pinch. . . . Watch yourself when you go up against the kid. . . . That's right. Very. Well, good luck, Tom.

SPADE slowly replaces the receiver on the prong. He fills his chest with air and exhales. His eyes are glittering between narrowed lids. He turns, takes three swift steps toward BRIGID O'SHAUGHNESSY. The girl, startled by the suddenness of his approach, lets her breath out in a little gasp. SPADE, face to face with BRIGID, looks at her hard of jaw and eye.

SPADE: Now, they'll talk when they're nailed—about us. We're sitting on dynamite. We've only got minutes to get set for the police. Give me all of it fast.

She starts to speak, hesitates, bites her lip. SPADE takes her by the shoulder, cries angrily:

SPADE: Talk.

BRIGID: (*uncertainly*) Where . . . shall . . . I . . . begin?

SPADE: The day you first came to my office. . . . Why did you want Thursby shadowed?

BRIGID: I told you, Sam, I suspected he was betraying me and I wanted to find out.

SPADE: That's a lie! You had Thursby hooked, and you knew
it, and you wanted to get rid of him before Jacobi came
with the loot so you wouldn't have to split it with him.
Isn't that so?

BRIGID lowers her eyes shamefacedly.

SPADE: What was your scheme?

BRIGID: (*timidly*) I thought that if he saw someone following
him, he might be frightened into going away.

SPADE: Miles wasn't clumsy enough to be spotted the first
night. You told Thursby he was being followed.

BRIGID: I told him. (*catches her breath, tortures her lower
lip.*) I told him . . . Yes . . . But please believe me,
Sam. I wouldn't have told him if I had thought Floyd
would kill him.

SPADE: (*interrupting*) If you thought he wouldn't kill Miles,
you were right, Angel.

BRIGID: (*her upraised face holds utter astonishment*) Didn't
he?

SPADE: Miles hadn't many brains, but he had too many years
experience as a detective to be caught like that—by a
man he was shadowing—up a blind alley with his gun
tucked away in his hip and his overcoat buttoned. (*he
takes his hand away from her shoulder, looks at her for
a long moment smiling, then:*) But he would have gone
up there with you, Angel. He was just dumb enough for
that. He'd have looked you up and down and licked his
lips and gone grinning from ear to ear. And then you
could have stood as close to him as you liked in the dark
and put a hole through him with the gun you had gotten
from Thursby that evening.

BRIGID shrinks back from him until the edge of the table stops
her.

BRIGID: (*staring with terrified eyes*) Don't—don't talk to me
like that, Sam. You know I didn't . . . you know—

SPADE: Stop it! (*he glances at the clock*) The police will be
blowing in any minute now. Talk!

BRIGID: (*puts the back of her hand to her forehead*) Oh,
why do you accuse me of such a terrible . . .?

SPADE: (*very low—impatient*) This isn't the spot for the school-girl act. The pair of us are sitting under the gallows.

He grasps her wrists forcing her to stand up straight in front of him. Her face becomes suddenly haggard.

SPADE: Why did you shoot him?

BRIGID: (*voice hushed and troubled*) I didn't mean to at first. I didn't really but when I saw that Floyd couldn't be frightened, I—I can't look at you and tell you this, Sam. (*she starts to sob, clings to him*)

SPADE: You thought Thursby would tackle him and one or the other of them would go down. If Thursby was the one, then you were rid of him. If it was Miles, then you could see that Thursby was caught and sent up for it. Isn't that right?

BRIGID: S—something—like—that.

SPADE: And when you found that Thursby didn't mean to tackle him, you borrowed the gun and did it yourself. Right?

She nods mutely.

SPADE: And when you heard Thursby was shot, you knew Gutman was in town! And you knew you needed another protector, somebody to fill Thursby's boots, so you came back to me.

She puts her hands up around the back of his neck pushing his head down until his mouth all but touches hers.

BRIGID: Yes, but—Oh, sweetheart, it wasn't only that. I would have come back to you sooner or later. From the very first instant I saw you I knew . . .

He puts his arms around her holding her tight to him.

SPADE: (*tenderly*) Well, if you get a good break, you'll be out of Tahatchapi in twenty years, and you can come back to me then.

She draws away from him slightly, throws her head far back to stare up at him, uncomprehending.

SPADE: (*tenderly*) I hope they don't hang you, Precious, by that sweet neck.

He puts his hand up and caresses her throat. In an instant

she is out of his arms back against the table crouching, both hands spread over her throat. Her face is wild-eyed, haggard. Her mouth opens and closes.

BRIGID: (*in a small parched voice*) You're not . . .? (*she can get no other words out*)

SPADE'S face is damp with sweat now. His mouth smiles and there are smile wrinkles around his glittering eyes.

SPADE: (*gently*) Yes, Angel, I'm going to send you over. The chances are you'll get off with life. That means if you're a good girl, you'll be out in twenty years. I'll be waiting for you. (*he clears his throat*) If they hang you, I'll always remember you.

BRIGID drops her hands, stands erect. Her face becomes smooth and untroubled except for the faintest of dubious glints in her eyes. She smiles back at him.

BRIGID: Don't, Sam. Don't say that—even in fun. Oh, you frightened me for a moment. I really thought—you do such wild and unpredictable things . . .

She breaks off, thrusts her head forward and stares deep into his eyes. The flesh around her mouth shivers and fear comes back into her eyes. She puts her hands to her throat again. SPADE laughs—his laugh is a croak.

SPADE: Now don't be silly. You're taking the fall.

BRIGID: (*takes a long, trembling breath*) You've been playing with me—only pretending you cared—to trap me like this. You didn't—care at all. You—don't—love me.

The muscles holding his smile stand out like wales.

SPADE: I won't play the sap for you.

BRIGID: (*tears come to her eyes*) You know it is not like that! You can't say that!

SPADE: You've never played square with me for half an hour at a stretch since I've known you.

BRIGID blinks her tears away, takes a few steps backward, stands looking at him, straight and proud.

BRIGID: You know, down deep in your heart you know that in spite of anything I've done, I love you.

He puts his hand back on her shoulder—the hand shakes and jerks.

SPADE: I don't care who loves who. I'm not going to play the sap for you. I won't walk in Thursby's—and I don't know how many others—footsteps. You killed Miles and you're going over for it.

She takes his hand from her shoulder, holds it close to her face.

BRIGID: Oh, how can you do this to me, Sam? Surely Mr. Archer wasn't as much to you as—

He is no longer smiling. He pulls his hand away from her. His wet face is set hard and deeply lined. His eyes burn madly.

SPADE: (hoarsely) Listen . . . This won't do any good. You'll never understand me, but I'll try once and then give it up. When a man's partner is killed, he's supposed to do something about it. It doesn't make any difference what you thought of him. He was your partner and you're supposed to do something about it. Then it happens we're in the detective business. Well, when one of your organization gets killed, it's bad business to let the killer get away with it—bad all around—bad for every detective everywhere.

BRIGID: You don't expect me to think that these things you're saying are sufficient reason for sending me to the . . .?

SPADE: Wait till I'm through. Then you can talk. I've no earthly reason to think I can trust you, and if I did this and got away with it, you'd have something on me you could use whenever you wanted to. Since I've got something on you, I couldn't be sure you wouldn't decide to put a hole in me some day. All those are on one side. Maybe some of them are unimportant. I won't argue about that. But look at the number of them. What have we got on the other side? All we've got is that maybe you love me and maybe I love you.

BRIGID: (whispers) You know whether you love me or not.

SPADE: Maybe I do.

He looks hungrily from her hair to her feet and up to her eyes again.

SPADE: I'll have some rotten nights after I've sent you over, but that'll pass. (*he takes her by the shoulders, bends her back leaning over her*) If all I've said doesn't mean anything to you, forget it and we'll make it just this. I won't because all of me wants to—regardless of consequences—and because you've counted on that with me the same as you counted on that with the others. . . . (*he takes his hands from her shoulders, lets them fall to his side*)

She puts her hands up to his cheeks, draws his face down toward her again.

BRIGID: Look at me and tell me the truth. Would you have done this to me if the Falcon had been real and you had been paid your money?

SPADE: Don't be too sure I'm as crooked as I'm supposed to be. That kind of reputation might be good business bringing in high priced jobs and making it easier to deal with the enemy.

She looks at him, saying nothing. SPADE moves his shoulders a little.

SPADE: But a lot of money would have been at least one more item on your side of the scales.

BRIGID: (*whispers*) If you loved me, you'd need nothing more on that side.

She puts her mouth to his slowly and is in his arms when the doorbell rings. Before he releases her, he calls:

SPADE: Come in.

CASABLANCA

A Warner Bros. presentation. Producer, Hal. B. Wallis. Director, Michael Curtiz. Screenplay by Julius J. Epstein, Philip G. Epstein, Howard Koch. Suggested by the unproduced play *Everybody Comes to Rick's* by Murray Burnett & Joan Alison. Director of Photography, Arthur Edeson. Film Editor, Owen Marks. Sound, Francis J. Scheid. Art Director, Carl Jules Weyl. Music, Max Steiner. Running time, 102 minutes. 1943.

CAST

RICK BLAINE	Humphrey Bogart
ILSA LUND	Ingrid Bergman
VICTOR LASZLO	Paul Henreid
CAPTAIN LOUIS RENAULT	Claude Rains
MAJOR STRASSER	Conrad Veidt
SENOR FARRARI	Sydney Greenstreet
UGARTE	Peter Lorre
CARL	S.Z. Sakall
YVONNE	Madeleine LeBeau
SAM	Dooley Wilson
BERGER	John Qualen
SASCHA	Leonid Kinskey
ANNINA BRANDEL	Joy Page
JAN BRANDEL	Helmut Dantine
PICKPOCKET	Curt Bois

To follow the refugee trail from Casablanca to Lisbon to the Americas—this is the dream of the thousands who pour into Casablanca during the early years of World War II. Everyone who comes through Casablanca comes to Rick's, described in the script as "an expensive and chic nightclub which definitely possesses an air of sophistication and intrigue." Rick Blaine, the owner, is a cool, detached, cynical American, who keeps repeating "I stick my neck out for nobody." But in 1935 he ran guns to Ethiopia, and in 1936 he fought with the Loyalists in Spain, and if he'd remained in Paris, where he was the day the Germans marched in, the Gestapo would have taken him. What changed? While in Paris, he fell in love with Ilsa Lund, and they were to leave Paris together, but as the train was pulling out he received a note from her that said she could not come and that they would never see each other again. And ever since then, he has covered over his grief with a deadpan mask and an alienated pose.

There is a teeming black market in Casablanca, and while visas are often bought and sold in Rick's, the boss, himself, remains aloof from any activity other than the running of his saloon. But two Letters of Transit fall into Rick's hands. They have been signed by the highest of authorities and cannot be rescinded or questioned. The letters were to be sold to the famous Resistance leader Victor Laszlo and his female companion, who have just arrived in Casablanca. The Nazis want both the letters and Laszlo, but because Casablanca is technically in unoccupied French territory, the Nazis must work through the local authority, the charmingly corrupt Captain Renault. Renault escorts the German major to Rick's to arrest the man with the letters. Rick, who has been given the letters for safekeeping, says nothing when the man is seized. After the place has quieted down, Victor Laszlo enters with his female companion—Ilsa Lund. Later that night, miserable and unstrung, Rick grimly wonders why, "of all the gin joints in all the towns in all the world, she walks into mine."

The German major has made it clear to Renault that Laszlo must not be allowed to get out of Casablanca. Renault makes certain that even the black market is closed to Laszlo and Ilsa. Their only hope are the Letters of Transit, which they learn are most probably in Rick's possession. Laszlo knows nothing of Ilsa's earlier relationship with Rick, and her feelings for Rick are still so strong that she doesn't want Laszlo to know. She goes to Rick herself and tries to explain what happened in Paris. He is too bitter to listen. The next day he tries to talk to her, but she has been so stung by the hate in his eyes that she doesn't want to deal with him. But when the

German major warns her that Laszlo's life is virtually over, she realizes that she has no choice but to somehow get the Letters of Transit.

RICK'S APARTMENT—DARK

The door is opened by RICK, letting in some light from the hall. A figure is revealed in the room. RICK lights a small lamp. There is ILSA facing him, her face white but determined. RICK pauses for a moment in astonishment.

RICK: How did you get in?

ILSA: The stairs from the street.

RICK: I told you this morning you'd come around, but this is a little ahead of schedule. (*With mock politeness*) Well, won't you sit down?

ILSA: (*as she takes the chair*) Richard, I had to see you.

RICK: So it's Richard again? We're back in Paris.

ILSA: Please . . .

RICK: (*lighting a cigarette*) Your unexpected visit isn't connected by any chance with the Letters of Transit? It seems as long as I have those letters I'll never be lonely.

ILSA: (*looking at him steadily*) You can ask any price you want, but you must give me those letters.

RICK: I went all through that with your husband. It's no deal.

ILSA: Well, I know how you feel about me, but I'm asking you to put your feelings aside for something more important.

RICK: Do I have to hear again what a great man your husband is? What an important Cause he's fighting for?

ILSA: It was your Cause, too. In your own way, you were fighting for the same thing.

RICK: I'm not fighting for anything anymore, except myself. I'm the only cause I'm interested in.

A pause, then ILSA deliberately takes a new approach.

ILSA: Richard, we loved each other once. If those days meant anything at all to you—

RICK: (*harshly*) I wouldn't bring up Paris if I were you. It's poor salesmanship.

ILSA: Please. Please listen to me. If you knew what really happened. If you only knew the truth—

RICK: (*cutting in*) I wouldn't believe you no matter what you told me. You'd say anything to get what you want.

ILSA: (*her temper flaring—scornfully*) You want to feel sorry for yourself, don't you? With so much at stake, all you can think of is your own feeling. One woman has hurt you, and you take your revenge on the rest of the world. You're a coward and a weakling! (*Breaking*) No. Oh, Richard, I'm sorry, I'm sorry but, but you, you are our last hope. If you don't help us, Victor Laszlo will die in Casablanca.

RICK: What of it? I'm going to die in Casablanca. It's a good spot for it. Now, if you— (*He stops short as he looks closely at Ilsa.*)

A close view shows ILSA holding a small revolver in her hand.

ILSA: All right. I tried to reason with you. I tried everything. Now I want those letters.

A close view discloses RICK as, for a moment, a look of admiration comes into his eyes. Then we see ILSA and RICK together.

ILSA: Get them for me!

RICK: I don't have to. (*Reaching into his inner pocket*) I got them right here. (*He has the letters in his hand.*)

ILSA: Put them on the table.

RICK: (*shaking his head*) No.

ILSA: For the last time, put them on the table.

RICK: If Laszlo and the Cause mean so much to you, you won't stop at anything . . . All right, I'll make it easier for you. Go ahead and shoot. You'll be doing me a favor.

ILSA, seen close, rises, still pointing the gun at RICK. Her finger rests on the trigger. It seems as if she is summoning nerve to press it. Then, suddenly, her hand trembles and the pistol falls to the table. She breaks up, covering her face with her hands. RICK walks into the scene and stands close to her. Suddenly, she flings herself into his arms.

ILSA: (almost hysterical) Richard, I tried to stay away. I thought I would never see you again . . . that you were out of my life. The day you left Paris, if you knew what I went through! If you knew how much I loved you . . . how much I still love you—

Her words are smothered as he presses her tight to him, kisses her passionately. She is lost in his embrace [as the scene fades out.

RICK'S APARTMENT fades in. Then, a little while later, there is a close view of a table before a couch. There is a bottle of champagne on the table and there are two half-filled glasses. We hear ILSA talking as the scene moves to her and RICK. She is gazing into space as she talks. RICK is listening intently, but not looking at her.

RICK: And then?]

ILSA: It wasn't long after we were married that Victor went back to Czechoslovakia. They needed him in Prague, but there the Gestapo were waiting for him. Just a two line item in the paper: "Victor Laszlo apprehended. Sent to concentration camp." I was frantic. For months I tried to get word. Then it came. He was dead, shot, trying to escape . . . (she pauses for a moment) I was lonely. I had nothing. Not even hope. (She puts her hand on his.) Then I met you.

RICK: Why weren't you honest with me? Why did you keep your marriage a secret?

ILSA: Oh, it wasn't my secret, Richard. Victor wanted it that way. Not even our closest friends knew about our marriage. That was his way of protecting me. I knew so much about his work, and if the Gestapo found out I was his wife, it would be dangerous for me and for those working with us.

RICK: Well, when did you first find out he was alive?

ILSA: Just before you and I were to leave Paris together. A friend came and told me that Victor was alive. They were hiding him in a freight car on the outskirts of Paris.

He was sick; he needed me. I wanted to tell you, but I, I didn't dare. I knew, I knew you wouldn't have left Paris, and the Gestapo would have caught you. So I—well, well you know the rest.

RICK: It's still a story without an ending. (*He looks at her directly*) What about now?

ILSA: Now? I don't know. I know that I'll never have the strength to leave you again.

RICK: And Laszlo?

ILSA: You'll help him now, Richard, won't you? You'll see that he gets out? (RICK *nods.*) And then he'll have his work. All the things that he's been living for.

There is a pause.

RICK: All except one. He won't have you.

ILSA: I can't fight it anymore. I ran away from you once. I can't do it again . . . Oh, I don't know what's right any longer. You'll have to think for both of us, for all of us.

RICK: (*taking her in his arms*) All right, I will . . . Here's looking at you, kid.

ILSA: (*in a whisper*) I wish I didn't love you so much. (*She draws his face down to hers.*)

ADAM'S RIB

A Metro-Goldwyn-Mayer presentation. Producer, Lawrence Weingarten. Director, George Cukor. Screenplay by Ruth Gordon & Garson Kanin. Music, Miklos Rozsa. Song "Farewell, Amanda" by Cole Porter. Director of Photography, George J. Folsey. Art Directors, Cedric Gibbons, William Ferrari. Film Editor, George Boemler. Sound, Douglas Shearer. Special Effects, A. Arnold Gillespie. Running time, 101 minutes. 1949.

CAST

ADAM BONNER	Spencer Tracy
AMANDA BONNER	Katharine Hepburn
DORIS ATTINGER	Judy Holliday
WARREN ATTINGER	Tom Ewell
KIP LURIE	David Wayne
BERYL CAIGHIN	Jean Hagen
OLYMPIA LAPERE	Hope Emerson
GRACE	Eve March
JUDGE REISER	Clarence Kolb
JULES FRIKKE	Emerson Tracy

Adam Bonner and Amanda Faring Bonner (Pinky and Pinkie to each other) are New York attorneys, he with the D.A.'s office and she as a partner in a private firm. There is such an agreeable mesh to their personalities that they are invigorated when they find themselves on opposite sides of a case. At first they are knocking their pencils onto the floor of the courtroom so they can lean down to send smiles and kisses to each other under the table. But soon the issues of the case challenge precepts fundamental to both of them and to their marriage.

A woman shot but did not kill her husband when she found him in the apartment and arms of his mistress. Adam's prosecution is based on the wife's actions—the illegality of what she did. Amanda's line of defense is that were the couple's roles reversed, the husband would get off, as the husband always has in similar cases, on the unwritten agreement that when a man breaks the law to save his home, it is seen as justifiable. Amanda demands that the wife is entitled to the same justice in the courts that a man receives, *whatever* that justice may be.

The trial is in progress, attracting such enormous press coverage that it is turning into a courtroom circus. After a rough day in court, the Bonners are at home, giving each other their customary massages.

(*Note:* The song which comes over the radio, "Farewell, Amanda," has been written by the Bonners' next-door neighbor, whom Amanda enjoys and whom Adam can barely stomach. Earlier in the script it has been established that when excited, Adam jumbles syllables: hence, his "diriculous" for "ridiculous." Double brackets indicate those parts of the original script that were not filmed; footnotes show additions in the completed film.)

INTERIOR, THE BONNER SITTING ROOM—FULL SHOT

The room is as we have seen it before. This time we are close enough to a wall to see a large watercolor of "Bonner Hill." An incongruous piece of furniture has been added to the room. This is a folding massage table now spread for work. On the table, face down, his middle covered by a towel, is ADAM. Beside the table, in the process of giving him an expert massage, is AMANDA. She wears pajama bottoms and a sweatshirt. Beside her, an end table has been moved into convenient position. It holds cold cream, alcohol, and almond oil. During the activity, ADAM and AMANDA carry on a fitful conversation, between gasps and grunts.[1]

ADAM: Hmmph!—but don't try to tell me—ho!—he's impar-

---

[1] In the film, this scene takes place in the bedroom, and Amanda is wearing a towel.

tial because—ow!—every time I look—ooh—up at him,
I can see him just—ho!

AMANDA: Quiet, please. It doesn't really—pah!—do you good
if you don't—wait a second—relax.

ADAM: I'm relaxed.

AMANDA: You're not. I can feel.

ADAM: So—can I.

AMANDA: You can?

She hits him a whacking smack.

[[ADAM: Hey!]]²

AMANDA: Testing. (*she massages the back of his neck*)

ADAM: Oh, thank you, thank you. I seem to need this more
and more every day.

AMANDA: You're aging fast, that's all.

ADAM: You can say that again.

AMANDA: All right, I will. You're aging fast, that's all.

ADAM: You're helping.

AMANDA: [[All right,]] done.

ADAM: Thanks.

As he gets off the table, the CAMERA SWINGS over toward
AMANDA, who dashes some alcohol into her hands and rubs
them together. Now she dries them and begins to remove
her sweatshirt. As she does so, she walks out of the SHOT and
ADAM, tying the sash of his robe, comes into her vacated
position. He turns the sheet on the rubbing table.

ADAM: Ought to be some news on. Want it?

AMANDA'S VOICE: If it's good news, yes.

ADAM: Try my best.

He goes to the radio, the CAMERA FOLLOWING—and turns it
on. He presses a button.

AMANDA: Why don't they have all the good news on one
station and all the bad news on another station, now why
wouldn't that be good?

---

²In the film, instead:
ADAM: Um—oow! What are you doing?

[[ADAM: Lie down.]][3]

He moves toward her, CAMERA FOLLOWING. The radio, warmed up now, sings out. The voice of one of the most popular singers in the land is singing his heart out, with volume and vitality. The song is "Farewell, Amanda." ADAM dives back to the radio and shuts it off. AMANDA'S gentle laugh is heard, off.

ADAM: [[I guess]] I got the station with the *bad* news.

He goes to the table. AMANDA lies there, face down, the towel across her. The CAMERA MOVES IN TO:

CLOSE TWO-SHOT—AMANDA AND ADAM

ADAM starts to give her her rubdown.

AMANDA: Getting awfully popular, Kip's song. I hear it everywhere.

ADAM: Me, too. I even hear it when it isn't playing.

AMANDA   (*softly singing*): "Farewell, Amanda, Adios, addio, adieu—"

ADAM moves out of the SHOT. AMANDA continues with a rather dreamy rendition of her song. Suddenly, from offscreen, we hear the sound of a solid flesh-on-flesh smack! AMANDA wheels over as the CAMERA RIDES IN TO:

[[EXTREME CLOSE-UP—AMANDA'S OUTRAGED FACE

AMANDA   (*a shriek*): Pinky!]]

MEDIUM SHOT—ADAM

He is getting some cold cream out of a jar preparatory to acting as AMANDA'S masseur. He looks over at her, innocence personified. (Throughout this scene ADAM tries to hold on to the two globs of cold cream in either hand. The difficulty of this is increased when he makes a forceful fist and the cold cream squooshes through his fingers.)

MEDIUM SHOT—AMANDA

She is off the table, pulling on her sweatshirt, her back to ADAM and the CAMERA. She looks over her shoulder at him, eyes flashing. ADAM comes to her, moving into the SHOT.

ADAM: Something the matter? (*a little pause*) Don't you want your rub? (*another pause*) What's the beef? You sore about a little slap?

---
[3]In the film, instead:

ADAM: Um. I guess nobody—ever thought of that—

AMANDA: No.

ADAM: Then what?

AMANDA (*her eyes narrowing*): You meant that, didn't you?
    You really meant it!

ADAM: No, I—

AMANDA: You did. I can tell. I know your touch. I can tell a
    slap from a slug.

ADAM: Okay, okay.

AMANDA: I'm not so sure it is. I'm not so sure I want to be
    subjected to typical—to instinctive—masculine—brutal-
    ity.

ADAM (*calming her*): Oh, now look.

He nearly drops some cold cream on the floor.

AMANDA (*rubbing her hip*): And it felt not only as though
    you meant it but also as though you thought you had a
    right to. I can tell.

ADAM: What have you got back there? Radar equipment?

AMANDA: You're really sore at me, aren't you?

ADAM (*with a measured beat*): Don't be diriculous. Ridic-
    ulous.

AMANDA (*pointing finger*): There! Proves it.

ADAM: [[All right then, I am. What about it?

AMANDA: Why are you?

ADAM: You know why.

AMANDA: Kip? Just because he's having fun?

ADAM: No. You. You having fun and in the wrong way.
    Down at the trial. You're shaking the tail of the law,
    Amanda—trying to—and I don't like it. I'm ashamed of you.

His words suddenly wound her. Tears well up in her eyes
and her throat catches.

AMANDA: You don't say.

ADAM: We've disagreed on plenty—that's okay. I try to see
    your point always, but I'm stumped now, baby.

AMANDA: You don't even try to see why I—if you respected
    my—

She can't go on. She's in tears.

ADAM: Oh, fine! Here we go. The old juice. Never fails, does it? Guaranteed heart-melter. A few female tears. Stronger than the strongest acid. Well, not this time. You can cry from now until the jury comes back in—it won't make you right and it won't win your silly case.

AMANDA   (*appealing*): Adam, please. Please understand.

ADAM: Nothing doing.

A pause. She sits down on the sofa and weeps. ADAM watches her for a moment, then speaks. Her tears succeed, as usual.

ADAM   (*softly*): You want your rubdown? (AMANDA *shakes her head. He comes a step closer*) You want a drink? (*She shakes her head again. He moves forward another step*) You want anything? (*She nods.* ADAM *comes closer still*) What?

She kicks him in the shin. He springs back with a cry.

AMANDA   (*quietly and in perfect control*): That. (*she rises*) Let's *all* be manly!]][4]

---

[4]In the film, instead:
ADAM: All right, all right, I am . . . sore. I am sore. What about it?
AMANDA: Why are you?
ADAM: You know why.
AMANDA: You mean Kip? Just because he's having a little fun?
ADAM: No. Because you're having a little fun. You're having the wrong kind of fun—down in that courtroom. You're shaking the law by the tail, and I don't like it. I'm ashamed of you, Amanda.
AMANDA: Is that so?
ADAM: Yes, that's so. We've had our little differences and I've always tried to see your point of view, but this time you've got me stumped, baby.
AMANDA: You haven't tried to see my point of view. You haven't even any respect for my, my, my—
ADAM: There we go, there we go, there we go—Oh, oh, here we go again. The old juice—Ah, guaranteed heart-melter. A few female tears—
AMANDA (*sobbing*): I can't help it—
ADAM: —stronger than any acid. But this time they won't work—
AMANDA: I didn't—
ADAM: You can cry from now until the time the jury comes in and it won't make you right and it won't win you that silly case.
AMANDA (*sobbing*): Adam! Please, please try to undersst-t- . . .
ADAM: Nothing doing—
AMANDA (*offscreen*): . . . t-tand.
ADAM: Ah, don't you want your rubdown? You want a drink?
AMANDA: No.
ADAM: Do you want anything? What, honey? (*she kicks him in the shin*)
ADAM: Ow!
AMANDA: Let's all be manly!

SUNSET BOULEVARD

A Paramount Pictures Corporation presentation. Producer, Charles Brackett. Director, Billy Wilder. Screenplay by Charles Brackett, Billy Wilder, D.M. Marshman, Jr. Director of Photography, John F. Seitz. Art Directors, Hans Dreier & John Meehan. Special Photographic Effects, Gordon Jennings, Farciot Edouart. Film Editor, Arthur Schmidt. Editorial Supervision, Doane Harrison. Sound, Harry Lindgren & John Cope. Music, Franz Waxman. Assistant Director, C.C. Coleman. Running time, 115 minutes. 1950.

CAST

JOE GILLIS	William Holden
NORMA DESMOND	Gloria Swanson
MAX VON MAYERLING	Erich von Stroheim
BETTY SCHAEFER	Nancy Olson
SHELDRAKE	Fred Clark
MORINO	Lloyd Gough
ARTIE GREEN	Jack Webb
UNDERTAKER	Franklyn Farnum
THEMSELVES	Cecil B. DeMille
	Hedda Hopper
	Buster Keaton
	Anna Q. Nilsson
	H.B. Warner
	Ray Evans
	Jay Livingston

Sunset Boulevard begins with the image of a dead body floating in a swimming pool. A voice-over narration identifies the body as "Just a movie writer with a couple of B pictures to his credit. The poor dope." Sounding amused and cynical, the narrator promises to tell us the real story of how the body, *his* body, ended up face down in that pool, before the press blows it all out of proportion.

The story Joe Gillis tells is already all out of proportion. It takes place in Hollywood. He's a screenwriter without money or work. The only agents who want him are from the finance company; they want his car back for failure to make payments. Driving along Sunset Boulevard one night, he sights them in his rearview mirror and ditches them by swerving into the driveway of what appears to be an abandoned mansion. It is grotesquely magnificent, built during the 1920s, in a Hollywood in love with its own revisions of reality. A relic from that time still lives in the house that her fame and fortune built. Hers was one of those fabulous faces on the silent screen, adored around the world, proposed to by princes. She believes that her fans have never forgiven her for leaving them alone in the dark of the movie theatre without her. For twenty years she has lived like Dickens' Miss Havisham, the clocks having stopped with the advent of the talking motion picture. She has no idea that the fan letters she still receives are all written by her obsessively protective butler Max, who also happened to be one of her greatest directors, as well as her first husband.

When Joe pulls his car into the driveway, the butler comes out of the house as if he were expecting Joe, who is informed that he is not properly dressed. Joe starts to explain who he is—or who he isn't—but Max cuts him short because "Madame is waiting." Joe shrugs and enters the mansion; Max sends him upstairs to meet Norma Desmond.

(*Note*: The size and condition of the mansion are vital given circumstances, and they must be created by the actors for themselves, even though a literal reproduction of the upstairs and the downstairs with their intensely ornate interiors is obviously impossible. The scene can be played continuously, beginning with Norma's summoning, "This way!" Joe's voice-over narrative is not to be played; it appears here to feed the actor's inner monologue. Although Max will not appear, his silent offstage presence is real and imminent to both Joe and Norma.)

[INTERIOR NORMA DESMOND'S ENTRANCE HALL

It is grandiose and grim. The whole place is one of those abortions of silent-picture days, with bowling alleys in the cellar and a built-in pipe organ, and beams imported from Italy, with California termites at work on them. Portieres are drawn before all the windows, and only thin slits of sunlight find their way in to fight the few electric bulbs which are always burning.

GILLIS starts up the curve of the black marble staircase. It has a wrought-iron rail and a worn velvet rope along the wall.

MAX   (*from below*): If you need help with the coffin call me.

The oddity of the situation has caught GILLIS'S imagination. He climbs the stairs with a kind of morbid fascination. At the top he stops, undecided, then turns to the right and is stopped by]

WOMAN'S VOICE: This way!

GILLIS swings around.

NORMA DESMOND stands down the corridor next to a doorway from which emerges a flickering light. She is a little woman. There is a curious style, a great sense of high voltage about her. She is dressed in black house pyjamas and black high-heeled pumps. Around her throat there is a leopard-patterned scarf, and wound around her head a turban of the same material. Her skin is very pale, and she is wearing dark glasses.

NORMA: In here. I put him on my massage table in front of the fire. He always liked fires and poking at them with a stick.

GILLIS enters the SHOT and she leads him into

NORMA DESMOND'S BEDROOM

It is a huge, gloomy room hung in white brocade which has become dirty over the years and even slightly torn in a few places. There's a great, unmade gilded bed in the shape of a swan, from which the gold has begun to peel. There is a disorder of clothes and negligees and faded photographs of old-time stars about.

In an imitation baroque fireplace some logs are burning. On the massage table before it lies a small form shrouded under a Spanish shawl. At each end on a baroque pedestal stands a three-branched candelabrum, the candles lighted.

NORMA: I've made up my mind we'll bury him in the garden. Any city laws against that?

GILLIS: I wouldn't know.

NORMA: I don't care anyway. I want the coffin to be white. And I want it specially lined with satin. White, or deep pink.

She picks up the shawl to make up her mind about the color. From under the shawl flops down a dead arm. GILLIS stares and recoils a little. It is like a child's arm, only black and hairy.

NORMA: Maybe red, bright flaming red. Gay. Let's make it gay.

GILLIS edges closer and glances down. Under the shawl he sees the sad, bearded face of a dead chimpanzee. NORMA drops back the shawl.

NORMA: How much will it be? I warn you—don't give me a fancy price just because I'm rich.

GILLIS: Lady, you've got the wrong man.

For the first time, NORMA really looks at him through her dark glasses.

GILLIS: I had some trouble with my car. Flat tire. I pulled into your garage till I could get a spare. I thought this was an empty house.

NORMA: It is not. Get out.

GILLIS: I'm sorry, and I'm sorry you lost your friend, and I don't think red is the right color.

NORMA: Get out.

GILLIS: Sure. Wait a minute—haven't I seen you—?

NORMA: Or shall I call my servant?

GILLIS: I know your face. You're Norma Desmond. You used to be in pictures. You used to be big.

NORMA: I *am* big. It's the pictures that got small.

GILLIS: I knew there was something wrong with them.

NORMA: They're dead. They're finished. There was a time when this business had the eyes of the whole wide world. But that wasn't good enough. Oh, no! They wanted the ears of the world, too. So they opened their big mouths, and out came talk, talk, talk . . .

GILLIS: That's where the popcorn business comes in. You buy yourself a bag and plug up your ears.

NORMA: Look at them in the front offices—the master minds! They took the idols and smashed them. The Fairbankses and the Chaplins and the Gilberts and the Valentinos. And who have they got now? Some nobodies—a lot of pale little frogs croaking pish-posh!

GILLIS: Don't get sore at me. I'm not an executive. I'm just a writer.

NORMA: You are! Writing words, words! You've made a rope of words and strangled this business! But there is a microphone right there to catch the last gurgles, and Technicolor to photograph the red, swollen tongue!

GILLIS: Ssh! You'll wake up that monkey.

NORMA: Get out!

GILLIS starts down the stairs.

GILLIS: Next time I'll bring my autograph album along, or maybe a hunk of cement and ask for your footprints.

He is halfway down the staircase when he is stopped by

NORMA: Just a minute, you!

GILLIS: Yeah?

NORMA: You're a writer, you said.

GILLIS: Why?

NORMA starts down the stairs.

NORMA: Are you or aren't you?

GILLIS: I think that's what it says on my driver's license.

NORMA: And you have written pictures, haven't you?

GILLIS: Sure have. The last one I wrote was about cattle rustlers. Before they were through with it, the whole thing played on a torpedo boat.

NORMA has reached him at the bottom of the staircase.

NORMA: I want to ask you something. Come in here.

She leads him into

THE HUGE LIVING ROOM

It is dark and damp and filled with black oak and red velvet furniture which looks like crappy props from the *Mark of Zorro* set. Along the main wall, a gigantic fireplace has been freezing for years. On the gold piano is a galaxy of photographs of NORMA DESMOND in her various roles. On one wall is a painting—a California Gold Rush scene, Carthay Circle school. (We will learn later that it hides a motion picture screen.)

One corner is filled with a large pipe organ, and as NORMA and GILLIS enter, there is a grizzly moaning sound. GILLIS looks around.

NORMA: The wind gets in that blasted pipe organ. I ought to have it taken out.

GILLIS: Or teach it a better tune.

NORMA has led him to the card tables which stand side by side near a window. They are piled high with papers scrawled in a large, uncertain hand.

NORMA: How long is a movie script these days? I mean, how many pages?

GILLIS: Depends on what it is—a Donald Duck or Joan of Arc.

NORMA: This is to be a very important picture. I have written it myself. Took me years.

GILLIS: (*looking at the piles of script*) Looks like enough for six important pictures.

NORMA: It's the story of Salome. I think I'll have DeMille direct it.

GILLIS: Uh-huh.

NORMA: We've made a lot of pictures together.

GILLIS: And you'll play Salome?

NORMA: Who else?

GILLIS: Only asking. I didn't know you were planning a comeback.

NORMA: I hate that word. It is a return. A return to the millions of people who have never forgiven me for deserting the screen.

GILLIS: Fair enough.

NORMA: Salome—what a woman! What a part! The Princess in love with a Holy Man. She dances the Dance of the Seven Veils. He rejects her, so she demands his head on a golden tray, kissing his cold, dead lips.

GILLIS: They'll love it in Pomona.

NORMA: (*taking it straight*) They will love it every place. (*she reaches for a batch of pages from the heap*) Read it. Read the scene just before she has him killed!

GILLIS: Right now? Never let another writer read your stuff. He may steal it.

NORMA: I am not afraid. Read it! [(*calling*) Max! Max!] (*to Gillis*) Sit down. Is there enough light?

GILLIS: I've got twenty-twenty vision.

[MAX has entered.

NORMA: Bring something to drink.

MAX: Yes, Madame.

He leaves. NORMA turns to GILLIS again.]

NORMA: I said sit down.

There is compulsion in her voice.

GILLIS looks at her and starts slowly reading.

[GILLIS' VOICE: Well, I had no pressing engagement, and she'd mentioned something to drink. . . . Sometimes it's interesting to see just how bad bad writing can be. This promised to go the limit. I wondered what a handwriting expert would make of that childish scrawl of hers. . . .

MAX comes in, wheeling a wicker tea wagon on which are two bottles of champagne and two red Venetian glasses, a box of zweiback, and a jar of caviar. NORMA sits on her feet, deep in a chair, a gold ring on her forefinger with a clip which holds a cigarette . . .

GILLIS' VOICE: Max wheeled in some champagne and some caviar. Later, I found out that Max was the only other person in that grim Sunset castle, and I found out a few other things about him . . . As for her, she sat coiled up like a watch spring, her cigarette clamped in a curious holder. I could sense her eyes on me from behind those dark glasses, defying me not to like what I read, or maybe begging me in her own proud way to like it. It meant so much to her . . .]

She gets up and forces on GILLIS another batch of script, goes back to her chair.

[SHOT OF THE CEILING. PAN DOWN TO THE MOANING ORGAN . . .

GILLIS' VOICE: It sure was a cozy set-up. That bundle of raw nerves, and Max, and a dead monkey upstairs, and the wind wheezing through that organ once in a while. Later on, just for comedy relief, the real guy arrived with a baby coffin . . .

PAN OVER TO THE ENTRANCE DOOR

MAX opens it, and a solemn-faced MAN in undertaker's clothes brings in a small coffin. (Through these shots the room has been growing duskier.)

GILLIS' VOICE: It was all done with great dignity. He must have been a very important chimp—the great grandson of King Kong, maybe.

DISSOLVE TO:

GILLIS, reading. The lamp beside him is now really paying its way in the dark room. A lot of the manuscript pages are piled on the floor around his feet. A half empty champagne glass stands on the arm of his chair.

GILLIS' VOICE: It got to be eleven. I was feeling a little sick at my stomach, what with that sweet champagne and that tripe I'd been reading—that silly hodgepodge of melodramatic plots. However, by then, I'd started concocting a little plot of my own . . .]

The CAMERA SLOWLY DRAWS BACK to include NORMA DESMOND sitting in the dusk, just as she was before. GILLIS puts down a batch of script. There is a little pause.

NORMA: (*impatiently*) Well?

GILLIS: This is fascinating.

NORMA: Of course it is.

GILLIS: Maybe it's a little long and maybe there are some repetitions . . . but you're not a professional writer.

NORMA: I wrote that with my heart.

GILLIS: Sure you did. That's what makes it great. What it needs is a little more dialogue.

NORMA: What for? I can say anything I want with my eyes.

GILLIS: It certainly could use a pair of shears and a blue pencil.

NORMA: I will not have it butchered.

GILLIS: Of course not. But it ought to be organized. Just an editing job. You can find somebody—

NORMA: Who? I'd have to have somebody I can trust. (*there is a pregnant pause*) When were you born—I mean what sign of the zodiac?

GILLIS: I don't know.

NORMA: What month?

GILLIS: December twenty-first.

NORMA: Sagittarius. I like Sagittarians. You can trust them.

GILLIS: Thank you.

NORMA: I want you to do this work.

GILLIS: Me? I'm busy. Just finished one script. I'm due on another assignment.

NORMA: I don't care.

GILLIS: You know, I'm pretty expensive. I get five hundred a week.

NORMA: I wouldn't worry about money. I'll make it worth your while.

GILLIS: Maybe I'd better finish reading it.

NORMA:	You'll read it tonight.

GILLIS:	It's getting kind of late—

NORMA:	(*out of nowhere*) Are you married, Mr.—?

GILLIS:	The name is Gillis. I'm single.

NORMA:	Where do you live?

GILLIS:	In Hollywood. The Alto Nido Apartments.

NORMA:	There's something wrong with your car, you said.

GILLIS:	There sure is.

NORMA:	(*calling*) Max! (*to* GILLIS) You're staying here.

GILLIS:	I am?

NORMA takes off her glasses.

NORMA:	Yes, you are. There's a room over the garage. Max!

The CAMERA MOVES towards NORMA'S face, right up to her staring eyes.

ALL ABOUT EVE

A Twentieth Century-Fox Film presentation. Producer, Darryl F. Zanuck. Director, Joseph L. Mankiewicz. Screenplay by Joseph L. Mankiewicz. Based on the story *The Wisdom of Eve* by Mary Orr. Director of Photography, Milton Krasner. Special Photographic Effects, Fred Sersen. Film Editor, Barbara McLean. Art Directors, Lyle Wheeler, George W. Davis. Music, Alfred Newman. Sound, W.D. Flick, Roger Heman. Running time, 138 minutes. 1950.

CAST

MARGO CHANNING	Bette Davis
EVE HARRINGTON	Anne Baxter
ADDISON DEWITT	George Sanders
KAREN RICHARDS	Celeste Holm
BILL SAMPSON	Gary Merrill
LLOYD RICHARDS	Hugh Marlowe
BIRDIE	Thelma Ritter
MISS CASWELL	Marilyn Monroe
MAX FABIAN	Gregory Ratoff
PHOEBE	Barbara Bates
AGED ACTOR	Walter Hampden

As the voice-over narrator tells us when the film opens,

> "Margo Channing is a star of the Theatre. She made her first stage appearance at the age of four, in *Midsummer Night's Dream*. She played a fairy and entered—quite unexpectedly—stark naked. She has been a star ever

since. Margo is a great Star. A true Star. She never was or will be anything less or anything else."

Margo has just turned forty, and she is having more than a hard time with the choice to "be anything less or anything else." She is in love with her director, Bill Sampson, and he with her. But as she has no idea who she really is beyond her public persona—what Joseph Mankiewicz calls the "identity-proxy" or "personality-substitute" or "ego-alias"—she cannot believe Bill really knows her either. Her stylish tantrums about her age have begun to wear thin on even her most devoted inner circle. Enter Eve Harrington, twenty years younger, and filled with insatiable ambition and talent. There isn't a lie Eve won't tell or a friend she won't betray in order to worm her way into Margo's world and finally into Margo's roles.

There is one person who is wise to Eve from the beginning—Addison De Witt, the drama critic and columnist. He is described as "not young, not unattractive, a fastidious dresser, sharp of eye and merciless of tongue. An omnipresent cigarette holder projects from his mouth like the sword of D'Artagnan." He describes himself as "essential to the Theatre—as ants to a picnic, as the boll weevil to a cotton field."

Margo is appearing in a play called *Aged in Wood*. She has promised the producer, Max Fabian, to help him out by reading with another actress, a protégé of Addison's, at the replacement audition for a supporting role. She breezes into the theatre lobby hours late. Addison informs her that Eve, to whom she is finally wise, has been named her understudy and has read in her place, mesmerizing the producer and playwright and director. Addison describes Eve's reading as "brilliant, vivid, something made of fire and music." Margo storms into the auditorium and onto the stage, creating an ugly row. The playwright slams out, exploding, "It's about time the piano realized it has not written the concerto." Only Bill is left on stage with Margo. He is peacefully smoking a cigarette as he lies on the bed which is part of the set.

SCENE 1

MARGO: (*quiet menace*) And you, I take it, are the Paderewski who plays his concerto on me, the piano? (BILL *waves his cigarette; he's noncommittal*) Where is Princess Fire-and-Music?

BILL: Who?

MARGO: The kid. Junior.

BILL: (*looks lazily*) Gone.

MARGO: I must have frightened her away.

BILL: I wouldn't be surprised. Sometimes you frighten me.

MARGO: (*paces up and down*) Poor little flower. Just dropped her petals and folded her tent . . .

BILL: Don't mix your metaphors.

MARGO: I'll mix what I like.

BILL: Okay. Mix.

MARGO: I'm nothing but a body with a voice. No mind.

BILL: What a body, what a voice.

MARGO: That ex-ship news reporter. No body, no voice, all mind!

BILL: The gong rang. The fight's over. Calm down.

MARGO: I will not calm down!

BILL: Don't calm down.

MARGO: You're being terribly tolerant, aren't you?

BILL: I'm trying terribly hard.

MARGO: Well, you needn't. I will not be tolerated. And I will not be plotted against!

BILL: Here we go . . .

MARGO: Such nonsense, what do you all take me for—little Nell from the country? Been my understudy for over a week without my knowing, carefully hidden no doubt—

BILL: (*sits up*) Now don't get carried away—

MARGO: (*going right on*) —shows up for an audition when everyone knew I'd be here . . . and gives a performance! Out of nowhere—gives a performance!

BILL: You've been all through that with Lloyd—

MARGO: The playwright doesn't make the performance—
and it doesn't just happen! And this one didn't— full of
fire and music and what-not, it was carefully rehearsed I
have no doubt, over and over, full of those Bill Sampson
touches!

BILL: I am sick and tired of these paranoiac outbursts!

MARGO: Paranoiac!

BILL: I didn't know Eve Harrington was your understudy
until half past two this afternoon!

MARGO: Tell that to Dr. Freud! Along with the rest of it . . .

She turns away. BILL grabs her, pulls her down on the bed.
He holds her down.

BILL: No, I'll tell it to you! For the last time, I'll tell it to
you. Because you've got to stop hurting yourself, and
me, and the two of us by these paranoiac tantrums!

MARGO: (*struggling*) That word again! I don't even know
what it means . . .

BILL: (*firmly*) It's about time you found out. I love you.
(MARGO *says* "*Ha!*") I love you. You're a beautiful and
intelligent woman— (MARGO *says* "*A body with a voice*")—
a beautiful and intelligent woman and a great actress—
(*he waits*. MARGO *says nothing*)—at the peak of her career. You have every reason for happiness—(MARGO *says*
"*Except happiness*")—every reason, but due to some
strange, uncontrollable, unconscious drive you permit
the slightest action of a kid—(MARGO *sneers* "*Kid!*")—kid
like Eve to turn you into an hysterical, screaming harpy!
Now once and for all, stop it!

MARGO seems quiet. He gets up. She sits up.

MARGO: It's obvious you're not a woman.

BILL: I've been aware of that for some time.

MARGO: Well, I am.

BILL: I'll say.

MARGO: Don't be condescending.

BILL: Come on, get up. I'll buy you a drink.

MARGO (*with dignity*): I admit I may have seen better days, but I am still not to be had for the price of a cocktail—like a salted peanut.

BILL: (*laughs*) Margo, let's make peace.

MARGO: The terms are too high. Unconditional surrender.

BILL: Just being happy? Just stopping all this nonsense about Eve—and Eve and me?

MARGO: It's not nonsense.

BILL: But if I tell you it is—as I just did. Were you listening to me? (MARGO *nods*) Isn't that enough?

MARGO: I wish it were.

BILL: Then what would be enough? (MARGO *doesn't answer*) If we got married?

MARGO: I wouldn't want you to marry me just to prove something.

BILL: You've had so many reasons for not wanting to marry me. . . . Margo, tell me what's behind all this.

MARGO: I—I don't know, Bill. Just a feeling, I don't know. . . .

BILL: I think you do know but you won't or can't tell me. (MARGO *doesn't say*) I said before it was going to be my last try, and I meant it. I can't think of anything else to do. I wish I could. (*a pause*) We usually wind up screaming and throwing things as the curtain comes down. Then it comes up again and everything's fine. But not this time. (*he takes a breath*) You know there isn't a playwright in the world who could make me believe this would happen between two adult people. Good-bye, Margo.

No word from her. He starts away.

MARGO: Bill . . . (*he stops*) . . . where are you going? To find Eve?

BILL (*smiles grimly*): That suddenly makes the whole thing believable.

He goes out. MARGO alone, sits for a moment sadly. Then she begins to cry. . . .

SCENE 2

Eve's conquest appears complete. She has managed to maneuver the sympathies of Margo's best friend, Karen Richards, to the point that Karen "helps" Margo miss a performance so that Eve can go on in her place. Eve has arranged for the press to be in full attendance, and she receives glowing notices. Eve has also won over Karen's husband Lloyd, the author of *Aged in Wood*. She tries to blackmail Karen into urging Lloyd to use Eve rather than Margo in his new play. When Margo decides to marry Bill and not to do the new play, the part goes to Eve.

The new play is now having its out-of-town opening in New Haven. Eve is triumphant but calm. She has captivated Lloyd so completely that he is going to leave Karen for her. She assumes she has exploited Addison to his fullest, because he has written several columns about her, but she has underestimated both Addison and his ambitions. It is four o'clock in the afternoon. Addison is escorting Eve back to her hotel room, where she will take a nap before tonight's opening. She invites Addison in for just a moment to tell him something.

(*Note:* The references to Eddie the pilot and the Schubert Theatre concern a sob story Eve had told everyone of how, as a war widow, she found herself stranded in San Francisco, how it was there that she first saw Margo perform at the Schubert Theatre, and how her life was changed by the experience.)

EVE'S SUITE—TAFT HOTEL—DAY

Old-fashioned, dreary and small. The action starts in the living room and continues to the bedroom.

ADDISON closes the door, crosses to a comfortable chair.

ADDISON: Suites are for expense accounts. Aren't you being extravagant?

EVE: Max is paying for it. He and Lloyd had a terrific row but Lloyd insisted . . . well. Can I fix you a drink?

She indicates a table elaborately stocked with liquor, glasses, etc. ADDISON'S eyebrows lift.

ADDISON: Also with the reluctant compliments of Max Fabian?

EVE: Lloyd. I never have any, and he likes a couple of drinks after we finish—so he sent it up . . .

ADDISON: Some plain soda. (EVE *starts to fix it*) Lloyd must be expecting a record run in New Haven.

EVE: That's for tonight. You're invited. We're having everyone up after the performance.

ADDISON: *We're?*

EVE: Lloyd and I.

She carries the soda to him, sits on an ottoman at his feet.

ADDISON: I find it odd that Karen isn't here for the opening, don't you?

He sips his soda and puts it away, carefully avoiding a look at EVE. As he looks back—

EVE: Addison . . .

ADDISON: (*blandly*) She's always been so fanatically devoted to Lloyd. I would imagine that only death or destruction could keep her—

EVE: (*breaks in*) Addison, just a few minutes ago. When I told you this would be a night to remember—that it would bring to me everything I wanted—

ADDISON: (*nods*)—something about an old road ending and a new one starting—paved with stars . . .

EVE: I didn't mean just the theatre.

ADDISON: What else?

EVE gets up, crosses to look out over the Common.

EVE: (*her back to him*) Lloyd Richards. He's going to leave Karen. We're going to be married.

For just a flash, ADDISON'S eyes narrow coldly, viciously. Then they crinkle into a bland smile.

ADDISON: So that's it. Lloyd. Still just the theatre after all . . .

EVE: (*turns, shocked*) It's nothing of the kind! Lloyd loves me, I love him!

ADDISON: I know nothing about Lloyd and his loves—I leave those to Louisa May Alcott. But I do know you . . .

EVE: I'm in love with Lloyd!

ADDISON: Lloyd Richards is commercially the most successful playwright in America—

EVE: You have no right to say such things!

ADDISON: —and artistically, the most promising! Eve dear, this is Addison.

EVE drops her shocked manner like a cape. Her face lights up—she crosses back to the ottoman.

EVE: Addison, won't it be just perfect? Lloyd and I—there's no telling how far we can go . . . he'll write great plays for me, I'll make them be great! (*as she sits*) You're the only one I've told, the only one that knows except Lloyd and me . . .

ADDISON: . . . and Karen.

EVE: She doesn't know.

ADDISON: She knows enough not to be here.

EVE: But not all of it—not that Lloyd and I are going to be married . . .

ADDISON: (*thoughtfully*) I see. And when was this unholy alliance joined?

EVE: We decided the night before last, before we came up here . . .

ADDISON: (*increasingly tense*) Was the setting properly romantic—the lights on dimmers, gypsy violins off stage?

EVE: The setting wasn't romantic, but Lloyd was. He woke me up at three in the morning, banging on my door—he couldn't sleep, he told me—he'd left Karen, he couldn't go on with the play or anything else until I promised to marry him . . . we sat and talked until it was light. He never went home . . .

ADDISON: You sat and talked until it was light . . .

EVE: (*meaningly*) We sat and talked, Addison. I want a run-of-the-play contract.

ADDISON: (*quietly*) There never was, there'll never be another like you.

EVE: (*happily*) Well, say something—anything! Congratulations, skoal—good work, Eve!

ADDISON rises slowly, to his full height. As EVE watches him, as her eyes go up to his, her smile fades—

ADDISON: (*slowly*) What do you take me for?

EVE: (*cautiously*) I don't know that I take you for anything . . .

ADDISON: (*moving away*) Is it possible—even conceivable— that you've confused me with that gang of backward children you've been playing tricks on? That you have the same contempt for me that you have for them?

EVE: I'm sure you mean something by that, Addison— but I don't know what.

ADDISON: Look closely, Eve, it's time you did. I am Addison De Witt. I am nobody's fool. Least of all—yours.

EVE: I never intended you to be.

ADDISON: Yes, you did. You still do.

EVE gets up, now.

EVE: I still don't know what you're getting at. Right now I want to take my nap. It's important that I—

ADDISON: (*breaks in*) —it's important right now that we talk. Killer to killer.

EVE: (*wisely*) Champion to champion.

ADDISON: Not with me, you're no champion. You're stepping way up in class.

EVE: Addison, will you please say what you have to say plainly and distinctly—and then get out so I can take my nap!

ADDISON: Very well, plainly and distinctly. Although I consider it unnecessary—because you know as well as I, what I am about to say . . . (*they are now facing each other*) Lloyd may leave Karen, but he will not leave Karen for you.

EVE: What do you mean by that?

ADDISON: More plainly and more distinctly? I have not come to New Haven to see the play, discuss your dreams, or to pull the ivy from the walls of Yale! I have come to tell you that you will not marry Lloyd—or anyone else— because I will not permit it.

EVE: What have you got to do with it?

ADDISON: Everything. Because after tonight, you will be-long to me.

EVE: I can't believe my ears . . .

ADDISON: A dull cliché.

EVE: Belong—to you? That sounds medieval—something out of an old melodrama . . .

ADDISON: So does the history of the world for the past twenty years. I don't enjoy putting it as bluntly as this, frankly I had hoped that you would, somehow, have known—have taken it for granted that you and I . . .

EVE: . . . taken it for granted? That you and I . . .

She smiles. Then she chuckles, then laughs. A mistake. ADDISON slaps her sharply across the face.

ADDISON: (*quietly*) Remember as long as you live, never to laugh at me. At anything or anyone else—but never at me.

EVE eyes him coldly, goes to the door, throws it open.

EVE: Get out!

ADDISON walks to the door, closes it.

ADDISON: You're too short for that gesture. Besides, it went out with Mrs. Fiske.

EVE: Then if you won't get out, I'll have you thrown out.

She goes to the phone.

ADDISON: Don't pick it up! Don't even put your hand on it.

She doesn't. Her back is to him. ADDISON smiles.

ADDISON: Something told you to do as I say, didn't it? That instinct is worth millions, you can't buy it, cherish it, Eve. When that alarm goes off, go to your battle stations.

He comes up behind her. EVE is tense and wary.

ADDISON: Your name is not Eve Harrington. It is Ger-trude Slescynski.

EVE: What of it?

ADDISON: It is true that your parents were poor. They still
are. And they would like to know how you are—and where.
They haven't heard from you for three years . . .

EVE: (*curtly*) What of it?

She walks away. ADDISON eyes her keenly.

ADDISON: A matter of opinion. Granted. It is also true that
you worked in a brewery. But life in the brewery was apparently not as dull as you pictured it. As a matter of fact
it got less and less dull—until your boss's wife had your
boss followed by detectives!

EVE: (*whirls on him*) She never proved anything, not a
thing!

ADDISON: But the $500 you got to get out of town brought
you straight to New York—didn't it?

EVE turns and runs into the bedroom, slamming the door.
ADDISON opens it, follows close after her . . . He can be
seen in the bedroom, shouting at EVE who is OFFSCREEN.

ADDISON: That $500 brought you straight to New York—
didn't it?

BEDROOM. EVE, trapped, in a corner of the room.

EVE: She was a liar, she was a liar!

ADDISON: Answer my question! Weren't you paid to get out
of town?

EVE throws herself on the bed, face down, bursts into tears.
ADDISON, merciless, moves closer.

ADDISON: There was no Eddie—no pilot—and you've never
been married! That was not only a lie, but an insult to
dead heroes and to the women who loved them . . .
(EVE, *sobbing, puts her hands over her ears*. ADDISON,
closer, pulls them away) San Francisco has no Schubert
Theatre, you've never been to San Francisco! That was a
stupid lie, easy to expose, not worthy of you . . .

EVE twists to look up at him, her eyes streaming.

EVE: I had to get in, to meet Margo! I had to say something, be somebody, make her like me!

ADDISON: She did like you, she helped and trusted you! You paid her back by trying to take Bill away!

EVE: That's not true!

ADDISON: I was there, I saw you and heard you through the dressing-room door!

EVE turns face down again, sobbing miserably.

ADDISON: You used my name and my column to black-mail Karen into getting you the part of "Cora"—and you lied to me about it!

EVE: (*into the bed*) No—no—no . . .

ADDISON: I had lunch with Karen not three hours ago. As always with women who want to find out things, she told more than she learned . . . (*he lets go of her hands*) . . . do you want to change your story about Lloyd beating at your door the other night?

EVE covers her face with her hands.

EVE: Please . . . please . . .

ADDISON gets off the bed, looks down at her.

ADDISON: That I should want you at all suddenly strikes me as the height of improbability. But that, in itself, is probably the reason. You're an improbable person, Eve, and so am I. We have that in common. Also a contempt for humanity, an inability to love or be loved, insatiable ambition—and talent. We deserve each other. Are you listening to me?

EVE lies listlessly now, her tear-stained cheek against the coverlet. She nods.

ADDISON: Then say so.

EVE: Yes, Addison.

ADDISON: And you realize—you agree how completely you belong to me?

EVE: Yes, Addison.

ADDISON: Take your nap, now. And good luck for tonight.

He starts out.

EVE: (*tonelessly*) I won't play tonight. (ADDISON *pauses*) I couldn't. Not possibly. I couldn't go on . . .

ADDISON: (*smiles*) Couldn't go on? You'll give the performance of your life.

He goes out. The CAMERA REMAINS on EVE'S forlorn, tearstained face. Her eyes close . . . she goes to sleep.

THE AFRICAN QUEEN

A Horizon Pictures-Romulus Production. Released through
United Artists Corporation. Producer, S.P. Eagle. Director,
John Huston. Screenplay by James Agee with John Huston.
Based on the novel *The African Queen* by C.S. Forester.
Director of Photography, Jack Cardiff. Second unit Photography, Ted Scaife. Film Editor, Ralph Kemplen. Special Effects, Cliff Richardson. Art Director, William Shingleton.
Music, Alan Gray. Assistant Director, Guy Hamilton. Technicolor. Running time, 105 minutes. 1951.

CAST

CHARLIE ALLNUTT	Humphrey Bogart
ROSE SAYER	Katharine Hepburn
BROTHER SAYER	Robert Morley
CAPTAIN	Peter Bull
FIRST OFFICER	Theodore Bikel
SECOND OFFICER	Walter Gotell
PETTY OFFICER	Gerald Onn
FIRST OFFICER	Peter Swansick
SECOND OFFICER	Richard Marner

The African Queen is a boat, described in the script as
"squat, flat-bottomed—thirty feet long. A tattered awning
roofs in six feet of her stern. Amidships stand her boiler and
engine. A stumpy funnel reaches up a little higher than the
awning."

The African Queen is the sole source of news and supplies
for an up-river African mission run by the very, very English

Acknowledgment is made to Sam Spiegel of Horizon Pictures for permission to
include the excerpts from *The African Queen* in this volume.

Brother Sayer and his sister Rose. World War I reaches the
Sayers' settlement when, without a word of warning, the
Germans burn it to the ground. Brother dies of shock at the
destruction of his life's work. The captain and owner of The
African Queen, Charlie Allnutt, helps bury Brother and vol-
unteers to conduct the spinster Rose out of the now-dangerous
German territory. Miss Sayer, however, has little interest in
safety. "Through her very genteelism and total unconcern for
what she is up against—an unawareness—we begin already
to sense her complete intrepidity."

Allnutt, with a Cockney mixture of pride and class defer-
ence, feels both inferior and superior to his odd passenger. In
physical contrast to Rose's starched primness, he is a grubby,
ratty little guy. After he politely seats her onboard, "he
pauses to light up a cigarette before going to work. He hangs
the cigarette inside his upper lip. This cigarette, dead or
alive, is a chronic fixture with Allnutt." Since Charlie's two-
man native crew fled when the Germans attacked, he must
teach Rose how to work the tiller so that he can keep the
engine fueled. He suggests that since the railway is in German hands, the two of them may have to hide out for a few
months on The African Queen, which he unthinkingly assures
her is more than comfortably stocked with cigarettes and gin.

SCENE 1

MOVING SHOT—THE LAUNCH

The boat crawls up a narrow tunnel of leaf and shade. (If
color photography is used, the SHOT would be startlingly juicy
and green—many shades of green reflected in rich brown
water.)

ALLNUTT comes leaping back over the cargo and shuts off the
engine; the propeller stops vibrating.

ALLNUTT dashes into the bow again. Just as the trees (SHOOT-
ING PAST ROSE and her interest in it) begin apparently to
move forward again as the current overcomes the boat's way,
he lets go the anchor with a rattling CRASH, and almost without
a jerk the launch comes to a standstill.

A great silence seems to close in on them—the silence of a
tropical river at noon. The only SOUND is the subdued rush

and gargle of the water. The sober air is filled with a strange
light—a green light.

ALLNUTT turns from his work at the anchor. He and ROSE
look about them and at each other, for a moment mysteri-
ously bemused by the stillness and by the beauty of the
place. The sudden quietness and the look of the place are
richly romantic; the two people are quieted by it, but they
are wholly unaware of any such potentiality between them.
They are just a couple of oddly assorted derelicts who hardly
even know each other, and don't care for what little they
know.

A pause.

ALLNUTT: So far so good. 'Ere we are safe an' sound, as you
      might say. (*he beams upon his surroundings*) Not too
      bad a spot, is it, Miss, to sit a war out in? All the
      comforts of 'ome, includin' runnin' water.

He laughs at his joke and is disappointed when ROSE does not
join him.

ROSE: I'm afraid, Mr. Allnutt, that what you suggest is quite
      impossible.

ALLNUTT: 'Ave you got any ideas? (*he takes a map out of his
      pocket and hands it to her*) 'Ere's a map, Miss. Show me
      the way out an' I'll take it.

ROSE opens the map and starts studying it.

ALLNUTT: (*after a while*) One thing sure; our men won't
      come up from the Congo, not even if they want to.
      They'd 'ave to cross the lake, and *nothin'* won't cross the
      lake while *The Louisa* is there.

ROSE: (*blankly*) *The Louisa?* What's that?

ALLNUTT: It's an 'undred-ton German steamer, Miss, and
      she's the boss o' the lake 'cause she's got a six-pounder.

ROSE: What's that?

ALLNUTT: A gun, Miss. The biggest gun in Central Africa.

ROSE: I see.

ALLNUTT: If it wasn't for *The Louisa*, there wouldn't be nothin'
      to it. The Germans couldn't last a month if our men
      could get across the lake . . . But all this doesn't get us

any nearer 'ome, does it, Miss? Believe me, if I could think wot we could do. . . .

ROSE: This river, the Ulanga, runs into the lake, doesn't it?

ALLNUTT: Well Miss, it does; but if you was thinkin' of goin' to the lake in this launch—well, you needn't think about it any more. We can't and that's certain.

ROSE: Why not?

ALLNUTT: Rapids, Miss. Cataracts and gorges. There's an 'undred miles of rapids down there. Why, the river's even got a different nyme where it comes out on the lake to what it's called up 'ere. It's the Bora down there. No one knew they was the same river until that chap Spengler—

ROSE: He got down it. I remember.

ALLNUTT: Yes, Miss, in a dugout canoe. 'E 'ad half a dozen Swahili paddlers. Map makin', 'e was. In fact, that's 'is map you're lookin' at. There's places where this ole river goes shootin' down there like out of a fire 'ose. We couldn't never get this ole launch through.

While he talks, ROSE begins to look restive and vague, as well as discouraged. By the time he is through, she has stood up, CAMERA WITH HER; she hardly hears him. She strolls a little aimlessly PAST THE CAMERA, which SWINGS TO CENTER HER BACK as she walks forward. As if half in her sleep, she sidesteps the engine.

REVERSE ANGLE—ROSE (SHOOTING FROM THE BOW) as ROSE sidesteps. She walks toward CAMERA into MEDIUM CLOSE UP, eyes glazing with dreamlike concentration. She sees something before and below her eye-level; stops, focusing on it.

CLOSE SHOT—(FROM ROSE'S ANGLE)—THE GELATINE CASES not marked or labeled as such.

ROSE'S VOICE: (OFFSCREEN) Mr. Allnutt—

MEDIUM CLOSE SHOT—ALLNUTT

ALLNUTT: Yes, Miss.

MEDIUM CLOSE SHOT—ROSE—(FROM ALLNUTT'S ANGLE)

ROSE: What did you say is in these boxes with the red lines on them?

MEDIUM CLOSE SHOT—ALLNUTT—(FROM ROSE'S ANGLE) lounging and lazy.

ALLNUTT: That's blastin' gelatine, Miss.

MEDIUM SHOT—ALLNUTT AND ROSE (SHOOTING FROM BOW)

ROSE: (*head towards him, away from* CAMERA) Isn't it dangerous?

ALLNUTT: Bless you, no, Miss, that's safety stuff, that is. It can get wet and not do any 'arm. If you set fire to it, it just burns. You can '*it* it wiv an 'ammer and it won't go off—at least I don't fink it will. It takes a detonator to set it off. I'll put it over the side if it worries you though.

ROSE: (*sharply, yet absently as she turns into* CAMERA) No. We may need it.

Allnutt keeps watching her idly, a little amused and very slightly contemptuous. She wanders away from the boxes, eyes downcast in thought, and pauses again.

ROSE: (*not looking up*) Mr. Allnutt—

ALLNUTT: Yeah?

INSERT—THE STEEL CYLINDERS IN BOTTOM OF BOAT

ROSE'S VOICE: (OFFSCREEN) And what are these queer long round things?

MEDIUM SHOT—THE BOW—(PAST ROSE—ON ALLNUTT)

ALLNUTT: Them's the oxygen and hydrogen cylinders, Miss. Ain't no good to *us*, though. Next time I shift cargo, I'll dump 'em.

CLOSER SHOT—ROSE

ROSE: (*sharply, yet still more subconsciously and quietly than before*) I wouldn't do that.

She keeps looking down at them, musingly, "subconsciously," while CAMERA CREEPS CLOSER to her.

ROSE: They look like—like torpedoes. (*"Torpedoes" is spoken over:*)

INSERT-CYLINDERS—a new and most deadly possible looking SHOT of the cylinders.

STILL CLOSER SHOT—ROSE. Slowly she raises her eyes from floor angle to normal; a wild light is dawning in her eyes.

ROSE: (*in the voice almost of a medium*) Mr. Allnutt— (*She turns very slowly towards him.*)

MEDIUM CLOSE SHOT—ALLNUTT—(FROM ROSE'S ANGLE)

ALLNUTT: (*a little bit smug*) I'm still right here, Miss, and on a thirty-foot boat there ain't much of any place else I could be.

MEDIUM CLOSE SHOT—ROSE—(FROM ALLNUTT'S ANGLE) walking slowly and somewhat portentously towards him.

ROSE: (*full of the wild light*) You're a machinist, aren't you? Wasn't that your position at the mine?

MEDIUM CLOSE SHOT—ALLNUTT—(FROM ROSE'S ANGLE) — CAMERA ADVANCING on him at ROSE'S pace, stopping, looking down, during his last six or eight words.

ALLNUTT: (*comfortably*) Yeah, kind of fixer. Jack of all trades and master o' none, like they say.

CLOSE SHOT—ROSE—(FROM ALLNUTT'S ANGLE), disconcertingly close.

ROSE: Could you make a torpedo?

ALLNUTT'S VOICE: Come again, Miss?

ROSE: Could you make a torpedo.

CLOSE SHOT—ALLNUTT

ALLNUTT: You don't really know what you're askin', Miss. It's this way, you see. A torpedo is a very complicated piece of machinery what with gyroscopes an' compressed air chambers an' vertical and horizontal rudders an' compensating weights. Why, a torpedo costs at least a thousand pounds to make.

He relaxes; his manner is "The State Rests."

SWING CAMERA to center ROSE, still perched on the gunwale.

ROSE: (*after a short pause; unperturbed*) But all those things, those gyroscopes and things, they're only to make it *go*, aren't they?

MEDIUM CLOSE SHOT—ALLNUTT—(NEUTRAL ANGLE)

ALLNUTT: Uh-huh. Go—and hit what it's goin' after.

ROSE—(AS BEFORE)

ROSE: *(at the height of her inventiveness; the words triumphant and almost stumbling out)* Well! We've got *The African Queen*.

She stands up with these words, CAMERA RISING with her, SHOOTING FROM A LITTLE BELOW; her eager eyes are constantly on ALLNUTT.

ROSE: If we put this—this blasting stuff—in the front of the boat here—and a—what did you say—deno—detonator there, why that would be a torpedo, wouldn't it?

CLOSE SHOT—ALLNUTT looking up at her, greatly amused, almost sardonically admiring her.

ROSE'S VOICE: Those cylinders. They could stick out over the end, with that gunpowder stuff in them and the detonator in the tips where the taps are.

ROSE—(AS BEFORE)

ROSE: Then if we ran the boat against the side of a ship, they'd—well, they'd go off, just like a torpedo. *(somewhat doubtfully, in a return to her submissive feminine habit)* Wouldn't they?

TWO SHOT—ROSE AND ALLNUTT

ALLNUTT: *(tremendously amused; gravely)* That might work. *(humoring her along, and a little taken in by his own fondness for makeshift)* Them cylinders'd do right enough. I could let the gas out of 'em and fill 'em up with the gelignite. I could fix up a detonator all right. Revolver cartridge'd do. *(warming up to it, as an impossible project)* Why, sure, we could cut 'oles in the bows of the launch, and 'ave the cylinders stickin' out through them, so's to get the explosion near the water. Might turn the trick. But what would 'appen to us? It would blow this ole launch and us and everything all to Kingdom come.

ROSE: I wasn't thinking that we should be in the launch. Couldn't we get everything ready and have a—what do you call it—a good head of steam up and point the launch toward the ship and then dive off before it hit? Wouldn't that do?

ALLNUTT: Might work, Miss. But what are we talkin' about, anyway. There ain't nothin' to torpedo. 'Cause *The African Queen's* the only boat on the river.

ROSE: Oh, yes there is.

ALLNUTT: Is what?

ROSE: Something to torpedo.

ALLNUTT: An' what's that, Miss?

ROSE: *The Louisa.*

ALLNUTT: (*on mention of The Louisa, a blank, silent stare of mock amazement. Then, patiently*) Don't talk silly, Miss. You can't do that. Honest you can't. I told you before we can't get down the river.

ROSE: Spengler did.

ALLNUTT: In a *canoe*, Miss!

ROSE looks stubborn.

ROSE: If a German did it, we can, too.

ALLNUTT: Not in no launch. We wouldn't 'ave a prayer.

ROSE: How do you know? You've never tried.

ALLNUTT: Never tried shootin' myself through the 'ead, neither. (*pause*) Trouble with you is, you just don't know nothin' about boats, or water.

A pause. They look at each other, ROSE much more fixedly and searchingly than ALLNUTT.

ROSE: In other words, you are refusing to help your country in her hour of need, Mr. Allnutt?

ALLNUTT: I didn't say that.

ROSE: Well then—!

ALLNUTT: (*sighs deeply*) 'Ave it your own way, Miss—only don't blame me, that's all.

ALLNUTT stands perplexed and inarticulate, his cigarette drooping from his upper lip. His wandering gaze strays from Rose's feet, up her white drill frock to her face; he starts slightly at her implacable expression.

ROSE: Very well, let's get started.

ALLNUTT: What! *Now*, Miss?

ROSE: (*impatiently*) Yes, now. Come along.

ALLNUTT: There isn't two hours of daylight left, Miss.

ROSE: We can go a long way in two hours.

ALLNUTT starts to speak; refrains; limps over to windlass and raises the anchor. ROSE watches him. CAMERA PANS after *The African Queen* as ALLNUTT backs her out into the channel, then turns her nose downstream.

SCENE 2

Charlie expects that the first rough waters will take some of the wind out of Rose's oblivious sails. He's wrong. She steers the tiller through the rapids of the Ulanga River and declares, "I'd never dreamed that any—any mere—ar—*physical* experience could be so—so stimulating." Her subtle class arrogance is epitomized by her calm insistence that they will take Charlie's boat past the armed German city of Shona. He gets drunk and insults her: " 'Oose boat *is* this any'ow? 'Oo asked *you* aboard? *Huh? Huh?* You crazy, psalm-singin' skinny old maid."

(*Note:* The course of dialogue in the following scenes allows for a single acting scene providing the actors condense the time dissolves into a single morning.)

EXTERIOR RIVER AND THE AFRICAN QUEEN—MEDIUM CLOSE SHOT—ALLNUTT

He is prostrate beside the engine in early morning sunlight. Except that his eyes are closed, he looks as if he had been dead for about a day.

Offscreen the harsh scraping of broken glass against wood and the happy shouts of early birds; also the quiet gurgling of river water.

For a few seconds, these sounds don't even register. Then they reach into him and he winces profoundly. (NOTE: Suddenly and painfully exaggerate all SOUNDS.) His dry mouth works a little. His eyelids twitch. The eyes open—and shut fast; light is painful to him.

OFFSCREEN (O.S.) the SOUND of a small avalanche of broken glass being thrown overside and hitting the water.

ROSE'S hand reaches down past the far side of his head and picks up an empty bottle and an almost empty bottle, and withdraws from SHOT. ALLNUTT registers vague awareness that someone is near, but doesn't open his eyes.

O.S. again painfully exaggerated, the SOUND of the gin case being dragged along the deck. His eyes still shut, ALLNUTT suffers intense pain. He opens his eyes, squeezes them tight shut (which hurts him badly), opens them again, and gazes up past CAMERA in listless, uncomprehending horror.

ROSE—(FROM HIS VIEWPOINT). She is in painfully bright, early sunlight, and she is wearing white. She has lifted the bottles and the case to the bench beside her. She kneels on the bench, aloof to the CAMERA. She tosses the empty bottle astern. She is on the verge of disposing of the gin in the nearly-empty bottle; on second thought she sniffs at it with mistrustful curiosity; her reaction indicates disgust with the smell, with Drink, and with ALLNUTT. She turns the bottle upside down and lets the contents pour overside into the river, and tosses the bottle contemptuously astern.

ALLNUTT—(SAME ANGLE AS BEFORE)—A LITTLE CLOSER. His eyes are bloodshot and are swimming with tears induced by the light. He doesn't quite take in what he sees.

ALLNUTT: (*a whimpering moan, pure misery; not for what he sees*) Oh. . . . Oh . . .!

ALLNUTT shuts his eyes. O.S the glug-glug-glugging of a full bottle. He looks again. He begins to comprehend and what he sees is, to him, terrible and almost unbelievable.

ALLNUTT: (*with deeper feeling but quietly; reacting now to what he sees*) Oh . . .!

O.S. the SOUND of another flung bottle hitting the water, and of another being opened. ALLNUTT, using all his strength, manages to lift his head from the floor. The effort is so exhausting and the pain so excruciating that he just lets it fall; the bang is even more agonizing. He licks his dry lips with his dry tongue and tries speaking.

ALLNUTT: (*in a voice like a crow*) Miss.

ROSE—(FROM HIS VIEWPOINT). She is emptying gin and pays him no attention.

ALLNUTT'S VOICE: *Miss?*

She pays him no attention except to turn the inverted bottle to absolute verticle.

ALLNUTT—(AS BEFORE)—A LITTLE CLOSER

ALLNUTT: Have pity, Miss! (*pause; sound of "glug-glug"* o.s.) Miss? (*"glug-glug"*) Oh, Miss, you don't know what you're doin'. . . . I'll perish without a hair o' the dog.

SOUND, O.S., of bottle hitting water.

ALLNUTT: (*continuing*) Ain't your property, Miss.

SOUND, O.S., of a new bottle being opened. CAMERA CREEPS CLOSER on ALLNUTT, whose eyes become those of a man in hell who knows, now, that his sentence is official, and permanent. With terrible effort, he lifts his head and shoulders.

MEDIUM CLOSE SHOT—ROSE—(NEUTRAL ANGLE)—NORMAL EX-POSURE. She is emptying gin. She hears the SOUNDS of ALLNUTT'S moving offscreen. Her hard face hardens still more. She glances toward him, continuing to pour.

MEDIUM SHOT—ALLNUTT—(FROM HER VIEWPOINT). He is with great pain and effort getting himself to his knees and his arms onto the side bench. It may seem for a moment that he is going to try to come at ROSE and make a struggle for it, but no: he now gets his knees to the bench and hangs his body far out over the gunwale and drinks ravenously of the muddy water. He overhangs so far that he is in clear danger of falling in.

ROSE—(SAME ANGLE AS BEFORE)—A LITTLE CLOSER. She is watching him. SOUNDS, O.S., of the gin emptying, and of his drinking. She is aware he may fall in and she doesn't care.

ALLNUTT—(AS BEFORE). He finishes drinking and tremulously pulls himself back, and turns, and collapses into a sitting position on the bench.

ROSE—(AS BEFORE). She is opening another bottle and casually watching him, and as casually looking away. She is piti-less, vengeful, contemptuous, and disgusted.

ALLNUTT—MEDIUM CLOSE SHOT—(NEUTRAL ANGLE). His head hangs between his knees; his hands hang ape-like beside his ankles. After a little he is able to lift his head. He props his temples between his hands and his elbows on his knees. He is so weak that one elbow slips, letting his head fall with a nasty jolt and a whimper of anguish. He sets himself more carefully solid and gazes ahead of him at the floor.

ALLNUTT: Oh . . .!

ROSE—(AS BEFORE). She ignores him completely; she lays the flap back from some canned meat.

ALLNUTT—(AS BEFORE). He gets out and fumblingly lights a cigarette; his hands are shaky. He takes a deep drag and it gives him a dreadful fit of coughing. He glances toward her piteously.

ROSE—(AS BEFORE). She is slicing bread; she ignores him. His coughing is loud, O.S.

ALLNUTT—(AS BEFORE). Recovered from his spasms, he timidly tries a lighter drag. This time he can taste it. It tastes foul. He puts it out, carefully, for later use, takes one look at it, and disconsolately tosses it overside. He looks again toward ROSE. He looks away again. He sighs deeply and buries his face in his hands.

O.S. their SOUND abnormally sharp, the birds are singing like mad.

DISSOLVE TO

MEDIUM SHOT—ROSE—(MID-AFTERNOON). She is sitting on a side-bench in the shade of the awning, calmly reading her Bible. She is in a clean white dress, exactly like the one she wore yesterday. Not a hair is out of place in her tight hair-do. Her bare feet are crossed demurely at the ankles. She sits up straight. She looks very cool, considering the weather.

PULL BACK, bringing in her day's work: up past her left, pinned to the edge of the awning, hang her newly-laundered dress and undergarments, full of sunlight. There are a few ineradicable streaks of grease in the dress. On the bench to her right, her sewing-basket and some evidently finished sewing chores.

O.S. the steady gurgling of river water among the tree roots of the bank; the nervous scraping of a razor.

FORMAL SHOT—THE ENGINE. It looks much cleaner than ever before. (Same SOUNDS O.S.) The CAMERA IS RISING as the SHOT OPENS. It soon brings in ALLNUTT'S head, past the engine, very hot-looking in strong sunlight. He is shaving.

SLOW PANNING DETAIL. A welter of wet footprints and splashed, soapy deck, ALLNUTT'S clean bare heels glistening high in the

SHOT as he stands shaving. CAMERA TILTS and brings in a drowned sliver of soap. ALLNUTT'S filthy clothes, a wet and arrestingly filthy towel.

Same SOUNDS O.S., razor-scraping a little UP.

Past the back of ALLNUTT'S head on his close reflection in a small mirror, hung from a funnel-stay; past that, ROSE.

ALLNUTT is shaving; ROSE, in background, is reading. It is painful to take off as much beard as ALLNUTT has been carrying, and he is not a man who takes pain easily; but he does his best to keep his reactions private, and by now he is nearly through. He is whistling softly against his teeth, and frowning at his reflected work with the concentration of a surgeon. He knows, however, that he is visible to ROSE, and unwisely keeps glancing toward her (she never looks up once); thanks to this, he lets the razor slip.

ALLNUTT: Ow . . . cut myself.

He glances sharply at ROSE to see if she has taken any notice. She does not glance up. ALLNUTT resents this bitterly. He finishes shaving, and strokes his smooth cheeks with satisfaction. ROSE turns a page. With a Rembrandt's patience and concern, he perfects, with his comb, the ideal coiffure, with an artistic quiff along the forehead. His eyes go vain. He treats himself, in reflection, to his idea of what the Lord of Creation should look like. Then he glances toward ROSE, who keeps on reading. His look is aloof, miles above her.

CLOSE UP—ROSE

SOUND, O.S., of ALLNUTT'S entrance past the engine. She does not glance up, but her eyelids flicker.

ALLNUTT—(PAST ROSE). He walks a couple of steps towards her in the brilliant sunlight, swaggering a little. Then he stands still, the Stag at Eve, looking at her with a certain high contempt. He is obviously challenging response and recognition. He gets none.

ALLNUTT: (after a pause; scornfully) Huh!

He walks in under the shade of the awning and into MEDIUM CLOSE UP—(CAMERA SWINGING PAST AND OPPOSITE ROSE). As he sits down. After another silence, he decides on a new approach. He arranges his face to express high good humor.

ALLNUTT: (*brightly*) Well, Miss, 'ere we are, everything ship-shape, like they say.

PULL AWAY to TWO SHOT of ROSE and ALLNUTT, as he awaits her reaction. No answer.

ALLNUTT: (*continuing*) Great thing to 'ave a lyedy aboard, with clean 'abits. Sets me a good example. A man alone, 'e gets to livin' like a bloomin' 'og. (*no answer*) Then, too, with me, it's always—put things orf. Never do todye wot ya can put orf till tomorrer. (*he chuckles and looks at her, expecting her to smile. Not a glimmer from ROSE*) But you: business afore pleasure, every time. Do yer pers'nal laundry, make yerself spic an' span, get all the mendin' out o' the way, an' *then*, an' *hone-ly then*, set down to a nice quiet hour with the *Good*-Book. (*he watches for something; she registers nothing*) I tell you, it's a model for me, like. An inspiration. I ain't got that ole engine so clean in years; inside an' out, Miss. Just look at 'er, Miss! She practically sparkles. (ROSE *evidently does not hear him*) Myself, too. Guess you ain't never 'ad a look at me without whiskers an' all cleaned up, 'ave you, Miss? (*no look*) Freshens you up, too; if I only 'ad clean clothes, like you. (*huh-uh*) Now you: why you could be at 'igh tea. (*no recognition from ROSE*) 'Ow 'bout some tea, Miss, come to think of it? Don't you stir; I'll get it ready.

ROSE does not stir. ALLNUTT is running low. A little silence, now. He watches her read.

ALLNUTT: (*continuing*) 'Ow's the book, Miss? (*no answer*) Not that I ain't read it, some—that is to say, me ole lyedy read me stories out of it. (*no answer; pause*) 'Ow 'bout readin' it out loud, eh, Miss? (*silence*) I'd like to 'ave a little spiritual comfort m'self. (*silence; he flares up*) An' you call yerself a Christian! (*silence*) You 'ear me, Miss. (*silence*) Don't yer? (*silence; a bright cruel idea. Louder, leaning to her*) Don't yer? (*silence. Suddenly, at the top of his lungs*) HUH??

EXTREME CLOSE UP—ROSE. In spite of herself she flinches; but swiftly controls it.

LONG SHOT—FROM OTHER SIDE OF THE RIVER. A half mile of

hot, empty water, then jungle, silent on a dream of heat. On the far side the tiny boat and the two infinitesimal passengers.

After two seconds, ALLNUTT'S "IIUII?" is heard.

EXTREME CLOSE UP—ROSE. In her face are victory, cruelty, and tremendous secret gratification: a Jocasta digesting her young.

The ECIIO comes. Over it—

                                                                   CUT TO

EXTREME CLOSE UP—ALLNUTT. A second, further echo comes, and dies.

ALLNUTT: *(yelling) Heyy!!*

Watchful, listening, he walks out of SIIOT; CAMERA LOWERS to ROSE, whose quiet, pitiless eyes—wholly unamused—follow him secretly. The ECIIO returns to her; she resumes reading.

TWO SIIOT—FAVORING ALLNUTT (PAST ROSE). He wanders all over the boat, CAMERA ALWAYS CENTERING him, always sifting past the statue-like reader. He barks like a dog; he yowls like a tomcat; he roars like a lion; he bleats like a goat; he crows like a rooster. Finally he sickens of it and walks back past her to his old seat at right angles to her.

MEDIUM CLOSE SIIOT—ALLNUTT as he sits. Clearly now he is going to try silent decorum, in imitation of her. He crosses his ankles in imitation, and settles his hands in his lap, and even holds his head primly, watching her. But something itches him under the arm and he scratches—first covertly and insufficiently, then to his heart's content. His exertions have worked up quite a sweat; the midges of late afternoon convene enthusiastically about his head. He looks bitterly toward ROSE.

MEDIUM CLOSE SIIOT—ROSE. There isn't a bug near her. Taking her time, she finishes the last page and, not hurrying, but without pause, starts right in on *Genesis*.

SWING CAMERA, losing ROSE, bringing ALLNUTT into CLOSE-UP. He hates her and the Good Book.

PULL AWAY into TWO SIIOT—of ROSE and ALLNUTT. After a few moments of silent, motionless tableau, ALLNUTT hating, ROSE reading, he speaks.

ALLNUTT: Feller *takes* a drop too much once in a while. T's only yoomin nyture.

CLOSE UP—ALLNUTT—NEUTRAL ANGLE. He is watching her; the last of his staying-power is dissolving.

MEDIUM CLOSE SHOT—ROSE—(FROM HIS VIEWPOINT). She is stirring her tea and now she drinks some.

ALLNUTT—CLOSE SHOT—(NEUTRAL ANGLE). He is watching her and thorough despair is in his eyes, and unconsciously his head begins to shake a little.

ROSE—(AS BEFORE). Now she is eating bread and canned meat.

ALLNUTT—(AS BEFORE). He stops shaking his head and just looks.

ALLNUTT: (*quietly*) All right, Miss. You win.

CLOSER SHOT—ROSE—(AS BEFORE). She meets his eyes, immediately, but says nothing.

ALLNUTT—(FROM HER ANGLE)

ALLNUTT: (*accepting utter defeat*) Down the river we go.

He turns to the engine.

TWO SHOT—ROSE AND ALLNUTT

ROSE: (*quietly*) Have some breakfast, Mr. Allnutt.

He is so moved by this line that he is on the verge of tears.

ROSE: Or, no. Get up steam. Breakfast can wait.

He reacts with the quiet hopelessness of a slave; one beaten look at her, gets to his feet and walks towards CAMERA and engine, filling SCREEN.

ON THE WATERFRONT

A Horizon Pictures Production. Released through Columbia Pictures. Producer, Sam Spiegel. Director, Elia Kazan. Screenplay by Budd Schulberg, based upon his original story. Suggested by articles, "Crime on the Waterfront" by Malcolm Johnson. Director of Photography, Boris Kaufman. Art Director, Richard Day. Film Editor, Gene Milford. Music, Leonard Bernstein. Sound, James Shields. Assistant Director, Charles H. Maguire. Running time, 101 minutes. 1954.

CAST

TERRY MALLOY	Marlon Brando
FATHER BARRY	Karl Malden
JOHNNY FRIENDLY	Lee J. Cobb
CHARLEY MALLOY	Rod Steiger
"KAYO" DUGAN	Pat Henning
EDIE DOYLE	Eva Marie Saint
"POP" DOYLE	John Hamilton
GLOVER	Leif Erickson
BIG MAC	James Westerfield
TRUCK	Tony Galento
TILLIO	Tami Mauriello
TOMMY	Thomas Handley
MRS. COLLINS	Anne Hegira

Terry Malloy is described as a "powerful-chested good-looking Irish roughneck in his late 20's." In a short career as a boxer, he made it all the way to Madison Square Garden. Now he works on the waterfront of New York's harbor and takes affectionate care of pigeons on the roof of his tenement apartment. Both his boxing career and his waterfront career have been managed by his older brother Charley. Charley is smart in a way that Terry isn't. He wears beautifully tailored suits and is in the inner circle of Johnny Friendly, who's got all the money on the docks. That money wasn't on Terry the night of his fight at the Garden; he was told to lose. It was the one night of his life when Terry Malloy *knew* that he had a winner inside himself. So when people call him a bum, Terry doesn't say anything: it's how he survives in the waterfront world as Friendly's lowest privileged flunkie. "I don't know nothing. I didn't see nothing. I ain't saying nothing."

Johnny Friendly owns the waterfront union and runs it with an openly brutal corruption. Men pay off their bosses in order to work. But more men are sold a day's work than there are jobs available, and the bosses enjoy watching the laborers fight it out. The Friendly racket is under investigation, but the day before the lead witness is to testify, Friendly has him killed. The witness' name was Joey Doyle, and he was set up by his unknowing friend, Terry Malloy.

Joey's sister Edie tries to find out the truth about her brother's death. She challenges Father Barry, the parish priest, to stand up in his faith. He opens his church to those who'll tell the truth about Friendly. He takes Jesus right out to the men on the waterfront, promising them that Christ stands alongside each and every one of them. They're crawling to a monster they can destroy if they'll only tell the truth. Edie also starts questioning Terry about Joey, and before they know it they are falling in love with each other. For Johnny Friendly's purposes, Terry is coming under too many influences, doing too much thinking. When Terry is being courted too successfully by the Crime Commission, Friendly cracks down.

There is no place for Terry to hide. Everybody is terrified of Friendly's reprisals: even if they weren't, the waterfront's binding code of honor forbids ratting. When it looks as if Terry is backing away into the arms of the Crime Commission, Friendly sends Charley to fetch Terry and escort him to his death.

(*Note*: Many visual circumstances must be made specific if the two actors playing Charley and Terry are to make the cab ride real to themselves. The scene should be brought into class with a present, but silent, cabbie, and all three actors should know the itinerary of the ride.)

INTERIOR TAXICAB—EVENING—NEW YORK BACKGROUND

Charley and Terry have just entered the cab.

TERRY: Gee, Charley, I'm sure glad you stopped by for me. I needed to talk to you. What's it they say about blood, it's—*(falters)*

CHARLEY: *(looking away coldly)* Thicker than water.

[DRIVER: *(gravel voice without turning around)* Where to?]

CHARLEY: 437 River Street.

TERRY: River Street? I thought we was going to the Garden.

CHARLEY: I've got to cover a bet there before we go over. Anyway, it gives us a chance to talk.

TERRY: *(good-naturedly)* Nothing ever stops you from talking, Charley.

CHARLEY: The grapevine says you picked up a subpoena.

TERRY: *(non-committal. Sullen)* That's right.

CHARLEY: *(watching for his reaction)* Of course the boys know you too well to mark you down for a cheese eater.

TERRY: Mm—Hmm.

CHARLEY: You know, the boys are getting rather interested in your future.

TERRY: Mm—hmm.

CHARLEY: They feel you've been sort of left out of things, Terry. They think it's time you had a few little things going for you on the docks.

TERRY: A steady job and a few bucks extra, that's all I wanted.

CHARLEY: Sure, that's all right when you're a kid, but you'll be pushing thirty pretty soon, slugger. It's time you got some ambition.

TERRY: I always figured I'd live longer without it.

CHARLEY: Maybe.

TERRY looks at him.

CHARLEY: There's a slot for a boss loader on the new pier we're opening up.

TERRY: (*interested*) Boss loader!

CHARLEY: Ten cents a hundred pounds on everything that moves in and out. And you don't have to lift a finger. It'll be three—four hundred a week just for openers.

TERRY: And for all that dough I don't do nothing?

CHARLEY: Absolutely nothing. You do nothing and you say nothing. You understand, don't you, kid?

TERRY: (*struggling with an unfamiliar problem of conscience and loyalties*) Yeah—yeah—I guess I do—but there's a lot more to this whole thing than I thought, Charley.

CHARLEY: You don't mean you're thinking of testifying against—(*turns a thumb in toward himself*)

TERRY: I don't know—I don't know! I tell you I ain't made up my mind yet. That's what I wanted to talk to you about.

CHARLEY: (*patiently, as to a stubborn child*) Listen, Terry, these piers we handle through the local—you know what they're worth to us? You don't think cousin Mickey'd jeopardize a set-up like that for one rubber-lipped . . .

TERRY: (*simultaneous*) Don't say that!

CHARLEY: (*continuing*)—ex-tanker who's walking on his heels—?

TERRY: Don't say that!

CHARLEY: What the hell!!!

TERRY: I could have been better! I could have been better!

CHARLEY: Listen, that isn't the point. The point is—there isn't much time, kid.

TERRY: (*desperately*) I tell you, Charley, I haven't made up my mind!

CHARLEY: Make up your mind, kid, I beg you, before we get to 437 River Street . . .

TERRY: (*stunned*) 437—that isn't where Gerry G . . .?

CHARLEY nods solemnly. TERRY grows more agitated.

TERRY: Charley . . . you wouldn't take me to Gerry G . . .?

CHARLEY continues looking at him. He does not deny it. They stare at each other for a moment. Then suddenly TERRY starts out of the cab. CHARLEY pulls a pistol. TERRY is motionless, now, looking at CHARLEY.

CHARLEY: Take the boss loading, kid. For God's sake. I don't want to hurt you.

TERRY: (*hushed*) Charley . . . Charley . . .

CHARLEY: (*genuinely*) I wish I didn't have to do this, Terry.

TERRY eyes him, beaten. CHARLEY leans back and looks at TERRY strangely. TERRY raises his hands above his head, somewhat in the manner of a prize fighter mitting the crowd. The image nicks CHARLEY'S memory.

TERRY: Yeah . . .

CHARLEY: (*gently*) What do you weigh these days, slugger?

TERRY: (*shrugs*) —eighty-seven, eighty-eight. What's it to you?

CHARLEY: (*nostalgically*) Gee, when you tipped one seventy-five you were beautiful. You should've been another Billy Conn. That skunk I got to manage you brought you along too fast.

TERRY: It wasn't him! (*years of abuse crying out in him*) It was you, Charley. You and Mickey. Like the night the two of you's come in the dressing room and says, 'Kid, this ain't your night—we're going for the price on Wilson.' *It ain't my night*. I'd of taken Wilson apart that night! I was ready—remember the early rounds throwing them combinations. So what happens—This bum Wilson he gets the title shot—outdoors in the ball park! —and what do I get—a couple of bucks and a one-way ticket to Palookaville. (*more and more aroused as he relives it*) It was you, Charley, You was my brother. You should of looked out for me. Instead of making me take them dives for the short end money.

CHARLEY: I always had a bet down for you. You saw some money.

TERRY: (*agonized*) See! You don't understand! I could've been a contender. I could've had class and been somebody. Real class. Instead of a bum. It was you, Charley.

CHARLEY takes a long, fond look at TERRY. Then he glances quickly out the window.

MEDIUM SHOT—WATERFRONT—NIGHT. From CHARLEY'S angle. A gloomy light reflects the street numbers— 433—435—

CLOSE ON CHARLEY AND TERRY—INTERIOR CAB—NIGHT

TERRY: It was you, Charley . . .

CHARLEY: (*turning back to* TERRY, *his tone suddenly changed*) Okay—I'll tell him I couldn't bring you in. Ten to one they won't believe it, but—go ahead, blow. Jump out, quick, and keep going . . . and God help you from here on in.

LONGER ANGLE—CAB—NIGHT as TERRY jumps out. A bus is just starting up a little further along the street.

EXTERIOR RIVER STREET—MEDIUM LONG SHOT—NIGHT. Running, TERRY leaps onto the back of the moving bus.

INTERIOR CAB—RIVER STREET—NIGHT

CHARLEY: (*to* DRIVER *as he watches* TERRY *go*) Now take me to the Garden.

THE GODDESS

A Columbia Pictures presentation of a Carnegie Productions Inc., production. Producers, Paddy Chayefsky, Milton Perlman. Director, John Cromwell. Screenplay by Paddy Chayefsky. Special Supervision, George Justin. Photography, Arthur J. Ornitz. Film Editor, Carl Lerner. Music, Virgil Thomson. Art Director, Edward Haworth. Sound, Ernest Zatorsky. Assistant Director, Charles H. Maguire. Running time, 105 minutes. 1958.

CAST

EMILY ANN FAULKNER, RITA SHAWN	Kim Stanley
DUTCH SEYMOUR	Lloyd Bridges
THE MOTHER	Betty Lou Holland
THE AUNT	Joan Copeland
THE UNCLE	Gerald Hiken
EMILY ANN (AGE 8)	Patty Duke
THE BOY	Burt Brinkerhoff
JOHN TOWER	Steve Hill
THE MINISTER	Gerald Petrarca
HILLARY	Joyce Van Patten
JOANNA	Joanna Linville
BURT HARRES	David White
LESTER BRACKMAN	Bert Freed
MRS. WOOLSY	Margaret Brayton
MR. WOOLSY	Werner Klemperer
THE SECRETARY	Elizabeth Wilson
THE DAUGHTER	Gail Haworth

The Goddess is a psychological case study of what has come to
be accepted as a modern archetype—the tragic movie star.
Rita Shawn is the name of the celluloid figment of the public's imagination. Emily Ann Faulkner is the real name of this
woman with no real self. What she has, in lieu of a personality, is an "availability" that radiates off the screen more powerfully than beauty. Desperate to love and be loved, but feeling
herself incapable of either, Emily follows her dream of being
a movie star (as distinct from an actress) straight through to the
crack-up. The years following the release of *The Goddess* saw
the suicides and collapses of the very actresses whom the
character seemed to delineate; so the components of Emily/
Rita's emotional development feel to us now almost too simple,
too familiar, too true. But what they are, really, is definitive.

Emily's teenage mother never wanted her and tried to
pawn her off on relatives. What Emily learns from her mother
about loving an infant is how to scream "shut up . . . leave
me alone." These are the words she will repeat to her own
unwanted baby after she marries a self-destructive G. I.
before she herself has reached twenty. In high school, Emily
is the girl who "puts out" because she is afraid that if she
doesn't, she won't have dates. She pursues the ambition of
becoming a movie star by going to Hollywood, where she
accepts the casting couch as her only avenue to success.

She struggles through a second marriage to an ex-professional
athlete many years her senior. Again, she wants above all else
to love him and be loved by him, but she is completely
devoid of the sense of inner self upon which to anchor such a
longing. At the obligatory parties, she's the girl with the
constant smile who is always restless, distracted, looking around
the room for something or someone outside herself to fill the
hollowness within. She truly believes, "If I was a star, then
everybody would like me." She dissolves into a monsoon of
moods, one moment wanting to flee Hollywood with her
husband, the next moment raging that he is trying to destroy
her chances for fame. Years later, having achieved the success, completely dependent upon alcohol and pills, she will
be told gently by her first husband, "You needed me, but you
never loved me. You never knew what love was. Whoever
taught it to you?"

The following scene takes place while Emily/Rita is recuperating at her Monterey Spanish-style house in Bel Air from a nervous breakdown she has had on the set. Her mother, who years ago traded in her own lost dreams for an implacable religious fanaticism, has come to California to visit her daughter. Although the mother has made it clear that she will only stay for a few months, Emily/Rita has decided that she has come to live with her, just as she had read years ago in a fan magazine that Ginger Rogers' mother lived with her daughter in a big house in Beverly Hills.

INTERIOR—RITA'S HOME—UPSTAIRS LANDING.

FULL SHOT of RITA coming to the top of the carpeted stairway, pausing a moment to look down the length of the corridor to her left.

REVERSE SHOT at the far end of the corridor. We can see into what seems to be a darkened bedroom—dark, that is, in relation to the brightness of the other rooms. Her mother is sitting, dressed as she was before, in a stiff armchair, reading her Bible. After a moment, RITA moves down the corridor to her mother.

EXTERIOR—THE MOTHER'S BEDROOM—ACROSS-THE-SHOULDER SHOT over RITA'S shoulder to her mother.

RITA: How do you feel, Ma?

THE MOTHER: Oh, everything's just fine. This is about the biggest house I think I ever saw.

RITA: I guess you could put Mrs. Phillips' house on Union Street which she was so arrogant about right inside that living room.

THE MOTHER: I guess you could.

RITA: I made inquiries about an Adventist congregation here in Los Angeles, and there is one. I'll drive you down there tomorrow.

THE MOTHER: Fine, because I do not want to miss Friday-night Sabbath.

RITA moves into the room, silently padding to the opposing wall, and sits down on a second soft chair.

RITA: You go on with your praying, Ma. I'll just sit here.

THE MOTHER, who has already turned her attention back to her Bible, her lips moving silently, smiles briefly even as she prays. For a long, long moment the room is hushed and still between the two women—the older woman by the window, softly murmuring over the Scriptures, the younger woman huddled in the far-corner soft chair watching her with wide eyes.

RITA: (*Suddenly*) I make four thousand dollars a week. Did I ever tell you that, Ma? You know what the studio got for me when they lent me out to Columbia for that Cary Grant picture? A quarter of a million dollars, but they got me on that staff contract, so all I got was my four thousand a week. Did you see the latest *Film Daily* listings? Well, I'm in the top eight in *Film Daily* box-office ratings. Do you know the kind of business my last picture, *Stardust Girl*, did on opening day in New York? We opened at the Roxy in New York, and we did fourteen thousand dollars, and that was a house record for an opening day. We did a boff one hundred and fifty-eight thousand for the week. What do you think of your little girl now?

THE MOTHER: Well, that's very nice.

RITA: What are you reading, Ma?

THE MOTHER: (*Looks briefly at her Bible, then turns to her daughter and recites amiably from memory*) "And ye shall know that I am the Lord, when I have opened your graves, O my people, and brought you up out of your graves, and shall put my Spirit in you, and ye shall live, and I shall place you in your own land; then shall ye know that I the Lord have spoken it, and performed it, saith the Lord."

Tears well in RITA'S eyes as she stares at her mother.

RITA: I'm so glad you came, Ma, because I was like to go crazy just wandering around this house all by myself.

THE MOTHER: I meant to come the day I read in the papers about your nervous breakdown, but the doctor—

RITA: (*The words pour out of her*) I don't know what's the matter with me. I have these black moods when I'm like to kill myself. I'm really like to kill myself. I had this nervous breakdown. They tell me I began to scream right on the set about this cat. Somebody had brought a cat on the set, and I just began to scream to take it away from me. And I love cats. I got these two big Siamese— you seen them. But my nerves were at the breaking point. I'd been drinking heavily. I confess to the sin of drinking. Oh, my God, I was arrested twice for drunken driving. I just feel, Ma, I'm losing all control of myself. I feel I'm going crazy. Sometimes I wake up in the morning, I don't know what I done the night before, and I feel I'm going right out of my mind. I can't bear to be alone. I can't bear it. I've taken men home with me who I didn't rightly know for more than an hour because I can't bear to be alone at night. I wake up in the middle of the night in a sweat and my heart pounding, and I've gone down and awakened my servants and made them sit with me till morning. Life just seems unbearable to me. I need you, Ma. I need you to be here with me because I'm like to go insane. I feel I'm going insane.

THE MOTHER: We are all put on this earth to suffer.

RITA: I'm going to take care of you. Wherever I go. I'm going to take you with me. You will always be at my side.

THE MOTHER: I spoke to you on the phone last week, and I hung up, and I turned to Elliot Wainwright, who is an elder, and to your aunt, who was sitting there, and I said, "Riches and fame mean nothing, for here is my daughter, the envy of her generation, who like to cry her heart out over the phone. She is a lost soul, and all the glory of her life is just vanity. King Solomon had all the wealth of the world, and queens of mighty nations rode miles of sand and desert to see him, and what did he say but 'It is all vanity.' I said, "My daughter is approaching her cataclysm. She has lived a life of sin and torment. She has borne the mark of the beast upon her. And surely she will be redeemed just as all men shall be redeemed from the curse as his corpse molders back to his mother earth."

She stands, stares at her daughter, her eyes wide with fervent intensity, but her words are gentle.

THE MOTHER: Wipe away the red stains of sin and clothe
yourself in dignity. Your body is the temple of the Holy
Spirit, and you must keep yourself in modesty. Let
righteousness into you, honey. Open your soul, open
your arms, and just let Jesus Christ in you. Don't hold
back a thought. Just let Him fill your body and your
soul, and ye shall be transported into Peace and Love.
(*Her eyes are closed now as she experiences something of
the rapture she describes*) O Lord, O Lord, I yield
myself without reservation, and I feel the sweet, sweet
warmth and peace.

In the corner soft chair, RITA sits hunched, bent almost
double, stirred by some physical anguish she has never felt
before. Her face is contorted with pain, her eyes clenched
shut, her knuckles white as her hands grip each other.

RITA: (*Muttering*) I feel Him near me. I feel Him near me.

THE MOTHER: Without reservation. Ye must open your heart
and your soul.

RITA: Oh, my God, my God!

THE MOTHER: Without reservation . . .

RITA: Oh, my God, My God!

THE MOTHER: Life is pain and sin and torment, and Jesus
Christ absolves you, and there ain't no pain, and there
ain't no sin, and there ain't no torment because your
body is filled with His eternal love and His eternal
compassion. Just open your arms and let Christ come
in to every part of you.

Suddenly RITA falls from her contorted position on the soft
chair onto the thickly carpeted floor, falling softly on her
knees, her back bent in an arch of trembling and supplica-
tion. She is sobbing, rather from the extraordinary exhilara-
tion that suffuses her than from a sense of pain. Her eyes are
open, brimming with tears, and she stares through the wet
film of her tears at the carpet before her. Her MOTHER
regards her with deep and gentle compassion. She pads
quietly to her daughter's bent figure and strokes her hair. She
kneels down beside her and begins to pray quietly. RITA
suddenly clutches at her MOTHER, and the two women hold
each other in passionate embrace.

SOME LIKE IT HOT

A Mirisch Company presentation of an Ashton Productions Picture. Released through United Artists Corporation. Producer & Director, Billy Wilder. Associate Producers, Doane Harrison & I.A.L. Diamond. Screenplay by Billy Wilder & I.A.L. Diamond. Suggested by a story by R. Thoeren & M. Logan. Photography, Charles Lang, Jr. Film Editor, Arthur Schmidt. Art Director, Ted Haworth. Music, Adolph Deutsch. Assistant Director, Sam Nelson. Running time, 120 minutes. 1959.

CAST

SUGAR KANE	Marilyn Monroe
JOE/JOSEPHINE	Tony Curtis
JERRY/DAPHNE	Jack Lemmon
SPATS COLUMBO	George Raft
MULLIGAN	Pat O'Brien
OSGOOD FIELDING III	Joe E. Brown
BONAPARTE	Nehemiah Persoff
SWEET SUE	Joan Shawlee
SIG POLIAKOFF	Billy Gray
TOOTHPICK	George E. Stone
BIENSTOCK	Dave Barry
SPATS HENCHMEN	Mike Mazurki
	Harry Wilson
NELLIE	Barbara Drew
DOLORES	Beverly Wills

Some Like it Hot is a slapstick roller coaster ride that careens through murder, corruption, terror, hunger, and unemployment. The outside world of the two male protagonists is so predatory that the only way to survive is to enter into the disguise of drag, and to take sanctuary in an all-female band. The film opens in Chicago in 1929. A hearse loaded with boot-leg booze is being chased by the police right up to the front door of Mozarella's Funeral Parlor, a front for a speakeasy. The password of Spats Columbo's private club is "I've come to grandma's funeral." Behind the mortuary's sliding panels, the "mourners" are served only coffee: "Scotch coffee, Canadian coffee, sour mash coffee." Almost everything in *Some Like It Hot* is a front for something else and gets turned inside out. The only thing that survives the anarchy is love, and even that gets quite a twisting.

Joe and Jerry are musicians in the speakeasy band. They are in threadbare tuxedos, and as they play, Jerry pesters Joe about whether tonight is the night they'll get paid. They owe everybody, including the landlord. Joe wants to take their wages and bet it all at the dog races, assuring Jerry that even if they lose, they've got these jobs for a long time to come. But the police, tipped off by the informer Toothpick Charlie, raid the establishment, and Jerry and Joe have to beat a fast getaway. They make the rounds of all the music booking agencies but there isn't any work. It's a bitterly cold February 14, and they have to hock their overcoats. Joe wants to hock his saxophone and Jerry's bass fiddle and put it all on a sure thing in the dog races, but Jerry refuses: "We're up the creek and you want to hock the paddle!"

They enter Sig Poliakoff's agency. The secretary, Nellie Weinmeyer, was stood up by Joe last week, so she gets even by telling the two of them that a sax and a fiddle are just what Sig is looking for, and they should march right in. What she doesn't mention is that the musicians are needed for an all-female band, Sweet Sue and her Society Syncopators. Sufficiently avenged, Nellie loans them her car to take them out to a one-night-stand St. Valentine's Day Dance. When Joe and Jerry go to collect the car from the garage, there is a poker game in progress and one of the players is Toothpick Charlie. Suddenly a saloon car barrels into the garage carrying Columbo and his armed henchmen, and everyone is mowed down except Jerry and Joe who've hidden behind Nellie's car. They are detected, but Spats and Company have to flee the approaching police sirens; they resolve to track down Joe and Jerry later.

The two musicians arrive at the train station disguised as "Josephine" (Joe) and "Daphne" (Jerry). As they are boarding the train that will take Sue's "girls" to their engagement at the Seminole-Ritz Hotel in Florida, Sugar and her ukulele walk by. "What can we say about Sugar except that she is the dream girl of every red-blooded American male who ever read *College Humor*?" Once on the train, Joe and Jerry try to affect a particularly ladylike demeanor to avoid detection, declaring themselves graduates of the Sheboygen Conservatory of Music. As females, Joe and Jerry have a few new rules and behaviors to learn. Every time "Daphne" gets out of line, "Josephine" yanks her back, which keeps jostling Jerry's padding loose from its pinnings. Hobbling to the Ladies Room in their first pairs of heels so that "Daphne" can rearrange himself, the two of them startle Sugar, who is inside, sneaking a drink. Sugar explains that "All the girls drink—but I'm the one that gets caught. That's the story of my life. I always get the fuzzy end of the lollipop." Later, during the rehearsal, while Sugar is playing and singing, her flask comes tumbling out. Since liquor and men are the two things Sue strictly forbids, and since one more infraction for Sugar will mean dismissal, "Daphne" says the flask is hers. She is forgiven as the ignorant newcomer.

Tucked into his berth for the night, "Daphne" is visited by a grateful Sugar. Jerry is smitten and, barely able to keep his disguise, he merrily agrees when Sugar offers to get some party fixings. Word of a party goes up and down the aisle. The noise of thirteen girls all crammed and partying in "Daphne's" berth finally awakens "Josephine" who has been asleep in the berth below. Sugar has pulled a cake of ice from beneath the water cooler and hands it to "Josephine," telling her to come along to the Ladies Room where they'll chop it up for cocktails.

SCENE 1

INTERIOR WOMEN'S LOUNGE—NIGHT

SUGAR comes in, followed by JOSEPHINE with the cake of ice.

SUGAR: (*pointing to sunken washbowl*) Put it here.

JOE: (*dropping the ice in the bowl*) Sugar, you're going to get yourself into a lot of trouble.

SUGAR: Better keep a lookout.

JOE crosses to the curtain, peers out. SUGAR, using the handle of the metal brush, starts to chop ice into the upturned cymbal.

JOE: If Bienstock catches you again—What's the matter with you, anyway?

SUGAR: I'm not very bright, I guess.

JOE: I wouldn't say that. Careless, maybe.

SUGAR: No—just dumb. If I had any brains, I wouldn't be on this crummy train with this crummy girls' band.

JOE: Then why did you take this job?

SUGAR: I used to sing with *male* bands. But I can't afford it any more.

JOE: Afford it?

SUGAR: Have you ever been with a male band?

JOE: Me?

SUGAR: That's what I'm running away from. I worked with six different ones in the last two years. Oh, brother!

JOE: Rough?

SUGAR: I'll say.

JOE: You can't trust those guys.

SUGAR: I can't trust myself. The moment I'd start with a new band—bingo!

JOE: Bingo?

SUGAR: You see, I have this *thing* about saxophone players.

JOE: (*abandoning his lookout post*) Really?

SUGAR: Especially tenor sax. I don't know what it is, but they just curdle me. All they have to do is play eight

bars of "Come to Me My Melancholy Baby"— and my
spine turns to custard, and I get goose-pimply all over—
and I come to them.

JOE: That so?

SUGAR: (*hitting her head*) Every time!

JOE: (*nonchalantly*) You know—*I* play tenor sax.

SUGAR: But you're a girl, thank goodness.

JOE: (*his throat drying up*) Yeah.

SUGAR: That's why I joined this band. Safety first. Anything
to get away from those bums.

JOE: (*drier yet*) Yeah.

SUGAR: (*hacking the ice viciously*) You don't know what they're
like. You fall for them and you love 'em— you think it's
going to be the biggest thing since the Graf Zeppelin—
and the next thing you know they're borrowing money
from you and spending it on other dames and betting the
horses—

JOE: You don't say?

SUGAR: Then one morning you wake up and the saxophone
is gone and the guy is gone, and all that's left behind is a
pair of old socks and a tube of toothpaste, all squeezed
out.

JOE: Men!

SUGAR: So you pull yourself together and you go on to the
next job, and the next saxophone player, and it's the
same thing all over again. See what I mean? —not very
bright.

JOE: (*looking her over*) Brains aren't everything.

SUGAR: I can tell you one thing—it's not going to happen to
me again. Ever. I'm tired of getting the fuzzy end of the
lollipop.

[OLGA bursts in through the curtains.

OLGA: Ice! What's keeping the ice? The natives are getting
restless.

JOE hands her the cymbal piled with ice.

JOE: How about a couple of drinks for us?

OLGA: Sure.

She scoots out. JOE and SUGAR are alone again.]

SUGAR: You know I'm going to be twenty-five in June?

JOE: You are?

SUGAR: That's a quarter of a century. Makes a girl think.

JOE: About what?

SUGAR: About the future. You know—like a husband? That's why I'm glad we're going to Florida.

JOE: What's in Florida?

SUGAR: Millionaires. Flocks of them. They all go south for the winter. Like birds.

JOE: Going to catch yourself a rich bird?

SUGAR: Oh, I don't care *how* rich he is—as long as he has a yacht and his own private railroad car and his own toothpaste.

JOE: You're entitled.

SUGAR: Maybe you'll meet one too, Josephine.

JOE: Yeah. With money like Rockefeller, and shoulders like Johnny Weismuller—

SUGAR: I want mine to wear glasses.

JOE: Glasses?

SUGAR: Men who wear glasses are so much more gentle and sweet and helpless. Haven't you ever noticed?

JOE: Well, now that you've mentioned it—

SUGAR: They get those weak eyes from reading—you know, all those long columns of tiny figures in the Wall Street Journal.

[OLGA is back again, carrying two Manhattans in paper cups on the cymbal. She hands them the drinks, starts to refill the cymbal with ice.

OLGA: That bass fiddle—wow! She sure knows how to throw a party!

She dashes out. JOE looks after her, worriedly.]

SUGAR: (*raising cup*) Happy days.

JOE: *(lifting his cup)* I hope this time you wind up with the *sweet* end of the lollipop.

They drink. JOE studies her like a cat studying a canary.

SCENE 2

Sweet Sue and her Society Syncopators have arrived at the Seminole-Ritz, described as a "sprawling gingerbread structure [that] basks in the warm Florida sun, fanned by towering palm trees and lulled by waves breaking lazily on the exclusive beach frontage." "Daphne" is spotted by Osgood Fielding III, a millionaire in his late fifties. "Daphne" does his best to discourage Osgood, but every vigorous rebuff only heightens Osgood's infatuation. Meanwhile, Joe has decided to make true Sugar's dream, which she has confessed to "Josephine," of meeting a millionaire who wears glasses. He steals the band manager's suitcase and eyeglasses. While "Daphne" and Sugar play with the other girls in the waves, Joe strolls onto the beach. "He is wearing Bienstock's blazer (crest and eight gold buttons), flannel slacks (bell-bottom), a silken scarf, a yachting cap, and the glasses (which blur his vision considerably). In his hand he carries a rolled-up copy of the *Wall Street Journal*. He looks off towards the ocean."

[The girls, SUGAR and JERRY among them, are standing in a wide circle, tossing the beach ball around and chanting rhythmically: "I love coffee, I love tea, how many boys are stuck on me? One, two, three, four, five—"

There is a wild throw over SUGAR'S head, in the direction of JOE'S chair.] SUGAR turns and runs after the ball to retrieve it.

This is exactly what JOE has been waiting for. As the ball comes rolling past, he unfolds the *Wall Street Journal*, pretends to be reading it. Just as SUGAR runs by, JOE extends his foot a couple of inches—enough to trip her and send her sprawling to the sand.

JOE: *(lowering paper; Cary Grant by now)* Oh, I'm terribly sorry.

SUGAR: My fault.

JOE: *(helping her up)* You're not hurt, are you?

SUGAR: I don't think so.

JOE: I wish you'd make sure.

SUGAR: Why?

JOE: Because usually, when people find out who I am, they get themselves a wheel chair and a shyster lawyer, and sue me for a quarter of a million dollars.

SUGAR: Well, don't worry. I won't sue you—no matter who you are.

JOE: (*returning to chair*) Thank you.

SUGAR: Who *are* you?

JOE: Now, really—

[JERRY and the other girls are looking off toward SUGAR, waiting for the ball.

JERRY: Hey, Sugar—come on.]

SUGAR picks up the ball.

JOE: (*blasé*) So long.

He buries himself behind the *Wall Street Journal* again. SUGAR hesitates for a second, then throws the ball back to the girls. She steps closer to JOE, peers around the paper, studying him.

SUGAR: Haven't I seen you somewhere before?

JOE: (*without looking up*) Not very likely.

SUGAR: Are you staying at the hotel?

JOE: Not at all.

SUGAR: Your face *is* familiar.

JOE: Possible you saw it in a newspaper—or magazine— *Vanity Fair*—

SUGAR: That must be it.

JOE: (*waving her aside*) Would you mind moving just a little? You're blocking my view.

SUGAR: Your view of what?

JOE: They run up a red-and-white flag on the yacht when it's time for cocktails.

SUGAR: (*snapping at the bait*) You have a yacht?

She turns and looks seaward at half-a-dozen yachts of different sizes bobbing in the distance.

SUGAR: (*continuing*) Which one is yours—the big one?

JOE: Certainly not. With all that unrest in the world, I don't think anybody should have a yacht that sleeps more than twelve.

SUGAR: I quite agree. Tell me, who runs up that flag— your wife?

JOE: No, my flag steward.

SUGAR: And who mixes the cocktails—your wife?

JOE: No, my cocktail steward. Look, if you're interested in whether I'm married or not—

SUGAR: I'm not interested at all.

JOE: Well, I'm not.

SUGAR: That's very interesting.

JOE resumes reading the paper. SUGAR sits on the sand beside his chair.

SUGAR: How's the stock market?

JOE: (*lackadaisically*) Up, up, up.

SUGAR: I'll bet just while we were talking, you made like a hundred thousand dollars.

JOE: Could be. Do you play the market?

SUGAR: No—the ukulele. And I sing.

JOE: For your own amusement?

SUGAR: Well—a group of us are appearing at the hotel. Sweet Sue and Her Society Syncopators.

JOE: You're society girls?

SUGAR: Oh, yes. Quite. You know—Vassar, Bryn Mawr— we're only doing this for a lark.

JOE: Syncopators—does that mean you play that fast music— jazz?

SUGAR: Yeah. Real hot.

JOE: Oh. Well, I guess some like it hot. But personally, I prefer classical music.

SUGAR: So do I. As a matter of fact, I spent three years at the Sheboygan Conservatory of Music.

JOE: Good school! And your family doesn't object to your career?

SUGAR: They do indeed. Daddy threatened to cut me off without a cent, but I don't care. It was such a bore—coming-out parties, cotillions—

JOE: —Inauguration balls—

SUGAR: —opening of the Opera—

JOE: —riding to hounds—

SUGAR: —and always the same Four Hundred.

JOE: You know, it's amazing we never ran into each other before. I'm sure I would have remembered anybody as attractive as you.

SUGAR: You're very kind. I'll bet you're also very gentle—and helpless—

JOE: I beg your pardon?

SUGAR: You see, I have this theory about men with glasses.

JOE: What theory?

SUGAR: Maybe I'll tell you when I know you a little better. What are you doing tonight?

JOE: Tonight?

SUGAR: I thought you might like to come to the hotel and hear us play.

JOE: I'd like to—but it may be rather difficult.

SUGAR: Why?

JOE: (*his eyes on the pail with the shells*) I only come ashore twice a day—when the tide goes out.

SUGAR: Oh?

JOE: It's on account of the shells. That's my hobby.

SUGAR: You collect shells?

JOE: (*taking a handful of shells from the pail*) Yes. So did my father and my grandfather—we've all had this passion for shells—that's why we named the oil company after it.

SUGAR: *(wide-eyed)* *Shell Oil?*

JOE: Please—no names. Just call me Junior.

SCENE 3

Osgood has insisted that he will pick up "Daphne" after the
band closes the show and whisk her onto his yacht for a
midnight supper. He has let all the crew off for the night. Joe
talks Jerry into keeping Osgood on shore so that *he* can whisk
Sugar onto the yacht and make her think it is his own. Since
he's never been on the boat before, and since he can barely
see in the glasses, Joe stumbles around at first, but eventually
he and Sugar locate the salon which is all set up for supper.
After the following scene, the return of Spats and his goons
into the action leads to more chase and disguise. Eventually
Joe and Sugar get together, Jerry reveals himself to Osgood,
and Osgood is so bowled over that he doesn't even seem to
mind.

INTERIOR SALON OF YACHT—NIGHT

It's a very elegant layout—mahogany paneling, shelves of
trophies, a stuffed marlin on the wall, a luxurious couch with
a table for two set up beside it. On the table are lit candles,
cold pheasant under glass, and champagne in a silver ice
bucket.

JOE and SUGAR come in, and as JOE takes his cap off, SUGAR
looks around, dazzled.

SUGAR: It's exquisite—like a floating mansion.

JOE: It's all right for a bachelor.

SUGAR: *(stopping by the stuffed marlin)* What a beautiful
    fish.

JOE: Caught him off Cape Hatteras.

SUGAR: What is it?

JOE: Oh—a member of the herring family.

SUGAR: A herring? Isn't it amazing how they get those big
    fish into those little glass jars?

JOE: They shrink when they're marinated.

During this, he has opened the champagne, filled a couple of glasses.

JOE: Champagne?

SUGAR: I don't mind if I do.

JOE: (*toasting her*) Down the hatch—as we say at sea.

SUGAR: Bon voyage.

As she sips the drink, she glances at the shelves of trophies.

SUGAR: Look at all that silverware.

JOE: Trophies. You know—skeet shooting, dog breeding, water polo . . .

SUGAR: Water polo—isn't that terribly dangerous?

JOE: I'll say. I had two ponies drowned under me.

SUGAR: Where's your shell collection?

JOE: Yes, of course. Now where could they have put it? (*looking under the couch*) On Thursdays, I'm sort of lost around here.

SUGAR: What's on Thursdays?

JOE: It's the crews' night off.

SUGAR: You mean we're alone on the boat?

JOE: Completely.

SUGAR: You know, I've never been completely alone with a man before—in the middle of the night—in the middle of the ocean.

JOE: Oh, it's perfectly safe. We're well-anchored—the ship is in shipshape shape—and the Coast Guard promised to call me if there are any icebergs around.

SUGAR: It's not the icebergs. But there are certain men who would try to take advantage of a situation like this.

JOE: You're flattering me.

SUGAR: Well, of course, I'm sure you're a gentleman.

JOE: Oh, it's not that. It's just that I'm—harmless.

SUGAR: Harmless—how?

JOE: Well, I don't know how to put it—but I have this thing about girls.

SUGAR: What thing?

JOE: They just sort of leave me cold.

SUGAR: You mean—like frigid?

JOE: It's more like a mental block. When I'm with a girl, it does nothing to me.

SUGAR: Have you tried?

JOE: Have I? I'm trying all the time.

He casually puts his arms around her, kisses her on the lips, lets go of her again.

JOE: See? Nothing.

SUGAR: Nothing at *all*?

JOE: Complete washout.

SUGAR: That makes me feel just awful.

JOE: Oh, it's not *your* fault. It's just that every now and then Mother Nature throws somebody a dirty curve. Something goes wrong inside.

SUGAR: You mean you can't fall in love?

JOE: Not any more. I *was* in love once—but I'd rather not talk about it. (*takes the glass bell off the cold cuts*) How about a little cold pheasant?

SUGAR: What happened?

JOE: I don't want to bore you.

SUGAR: Oh, you couldn't possibly.

JOE: Well, it was in my freshman year at Princeton— there was this girl—her name was Nellie—her father was vice-president of Hupmobile—she wore glasses, too. That summer we spent our vacation at the Grand Canyon— we were standing on the highest ledge, watching the sunset—suddenly we had an impulse to kiss—I took off my glasses—she took off her glasses—I took a step toward her—she took a step toward me—

SUGAR: (*hand flying to mouth*) Oh, no!

JOE: Yes. Eight hours later they brought her up by mule—I gave her three transfusions—we had the same blood type—Type O—it was too late.

SUGAR: Talk about sad.

JOE: Ever since then—(*indicating heart*)—numb—no feelings. Like my heart was shot full of novocaine.

SUGAR: You poor, poor boy.

JOE: Yes—all the money in the world—but what good is it? (*holding out serving plate*) Mint sauce or cranberries?

SUGAR: How can you think about food at a time like this?

JOE: What else is there for me? (*tears off leg of pheasant*)

SUGAR: Is it that hopeless?

JOE: (*eating*) My family did everything they could—hired the most beautiful French upstairs maids—got a special tutor to read me all the books that were banned in Boston—imported a whole troupe of Balinese dancers with bells on their ankles and those long fingernails—what a waste of money!

SUGAR: Have you ever tried American girls?

JOE: Why?

She kisses him—pretty good, but nothing spectacular.

SUGAR: Is *that* anything?

JOE: (*shaking his head*) Thanks just the same.

He resumes nibbling on the pheasant leg, sits on the couch.

SUGAR: Maybe if you saw a good doctor . . .

JOE: I have. Spent six months in Vienna with Professor Freud—flat on my back—(*stretches out on the couch, still eating*)—then there were the Mayo Brothers—and injections and hypnosis and mineral baths—if I weren't such a coward, I'd kill myself.

SUGAR: Don't talk like that. I'm sure there must be *some* girl *some* place that could—

JOE: If I ever found a girl that *could*—I'd marry her like that.

He snaps his fingers. The word "marriage" makes something snap inside SUGAR, too.

SUGAR: Would you do me a favor?

JOE: What is it?

SUGAR: I may not be Dr. Freud or a Mayo Brother or one of those French upstairs girls—but could I take another crack at it?

JOE: (*blasé*) All right—if you insist.

She bends over him, gives him a kiss of slightly higher voltage.

SUGAR: Anything this time?

JOE: I'm afraid not. Terribly sorry.

SUGAR: (*undaunted*) Would you like a little more champagne? (*proceeds to refill glasses*) And maybe if we had some music—(*indicating lights*)—how do you dim these lights?

JOE: Look, it's terribly sweet of you to want to help out— but it's no use. (*pointing*) I think the light switch is over there—(SUGAR *dims lights*)—and that's the radio. (SUGAR *switches it on*) It's like taking somebody to a concert when he's tone deaf.

By this time there is only candlelight in the salon, and from the radio comes soft music—"Stairway to the Stars." SUGAR crosses to the couch with two champagne glasses, hands one to JOE, sits beside him. JOE drinks down the champagne, and SUGAR hands him the *second* glass. He drains that, too.

SUGAR: You're not giving yourself a chance. Don't fight it. Relax. (*she kisses him again*)

JOE: (*shaking his head*) It's like smoking without inhaling.

SUGAR: So inhale!

This kiss is the real McCoy. As they stay locked in each other's arms—

[WIPE TO:

INTERIOR ROADHOUSE—NIGHT

It is small, dark, and practically deserted. The Cuban band is playing "La Cumparsita." Among the dancers on the floor are OSGOOD and JERRY easily the most stylish couple in the joint. JERRY has the flower tucked in his cleavage. As they tango—

OSGOOD: Daphne . . .

JERRY: Yes, Osgood?

OSGOOD: You're leading again.

JERRY: Sorry.

They tango on.

WIPE BACK TO:]

INTERIOR SALON OF CALEDONIA—NIGHT

JOE and SUGAR are still in the same embrace. The radio music continues. Finally they break.

SUGAR: (*waiting for the verdict*) Well—?

JOE: I'm not quite sure. Try it again.

She does. As they break, she looks at him—the suspense is unbearable.

JOE: (*trying to diagnose it*) I got a funny sensation in my toes—like somebody was barbecuing them over a slow flame.

SUGAR: Let's throw another log on the fire.

Another kiss.

JOE: I think you're on the right track.

SUGAR: I must be—because your glasses are beginning to steam up.

She kisses him again.

[WIPE TO:

INTERIOR ROADHOUSE—NIGHT

OSGOOD and JERRY have now got the tango by the throat. JERRY is dancing with his back to the CAMERA, and as OSGOOD whips him around, we see that JERRY has the flower clamped between his teeth. They reverse positions again, and OSGOOD grabs the flower between *his* teeth.

WIPE BACK TO:]

INTERIOR SALON OF CALEDONIA—NIGHT

The radio is still on, and JOE and SUGAR are just coming out of their last kiss. JOE removes his glasses, which are now completely fogged up.

JOE: I never knew it could be like this.

SUGAR: Thank you.

JOE: They told me I was kaputt—finished—washed up— and now you're making a chump out of all those experts.

SUGAR: Mineral baths—now really!

JOE: Where did you learn to kiss like that?

SUGAR: Oh, you know—Junior League—charity bazaars—I used to sell kisses for the Milk Fund.

They kiss again.

JOE: (*going, going, gone*) Tomorrow, remind me to send a check for a hundred thousand dollars to the Milk Fund.

She doesn't have to kiss him any more—he takes over now.

THE MISFITS

A Seven-Arts Production released through United Artists Corporation. Producer, Frank E. Taylor. Director, John Huston. Screenplay by Arthur Miller. Based on a story by Arthur Miller. Photography, Russell Metty. Film Editor, George Tomasini. Art Directors, Stephen Grimes, William Newberry. Music, Alex North. Second unit Director, Tom Shaw. Second unit Photography, Rex Wimpy. Sound, Philip Mitchell, Charles Grenzbach. Assistant Directors, Carl Beringer, John Gaudioso. Running time, 124 minutes. 1961.

CAST

GAY LANGLAND	Clark Gable
ROSLYN TABER	Marilyn Monroe
PERCE HOWLAND	Montgomery Clift
ISABELLE STEERS	Thelma Ritter
GUIDO DELINNI	Eli Wallach
OLD MAN IN BAR	James Barton
CHURCH LADY	Estelle Winwood
ROSLYN'S HUSBAND	Kevin McCarthy
YOUNG BOY IN BAR	Dennis Shaw
CHARLES STEERS	Philip Mitchell
OLD GROOM	Walter Ramage
YOUNG BRIDE	Peggy Barton
FRESH COWBOY IN BAR	J. Lewis Smith
SUSAN (AT RAILROAD STATION)	Marietta Tree
BARTENDER	Bobby LaSalle
MAN IN BAR	Ryall Bowker
AMBULANCE ATTENDANT	Ralph Roberts

The action of *The Misfits* transpires principally in three locations. The first is Reno, Nevada, a center for two of civilization's most uniquely human procedures—gambling and divorce. The second is the wild and harshly beautiful surrounding country, where up in the hills mustangs still run free. The third location is somewhere in between. It is here that Guido Delinni almost finished building his dream house, but abandoned it when his wife suddenly died. He loans the house to Roslyn Taber, who has come to Reno to get a divorce. She begins to live there with Gay Langland, a friend of Guido and a true cowboy, a man who only feels at home in the outlying wilderness, roping mustangs and living free of wages. When Gay comes into town, it's to sell the horses, escort the divorcees, and attend the rodeos.

The fact that the house is midway between the civilization and the wilderness and the fact that it is borrowed are both significant. Roslyn and Gay want love, but each also wants freedom. The ways in which they've seen men and women try to live together are unacceptable to them. Neither of them can "belong" to anyone. Gay says, "Nobody I ever met, and nobody I ever said good-bye to, ever owed me anything."

When Gay's strength is pitted against a wild horse, he feels himself alive and free in the natural orders and struggles of life. Miller writes that "a calm seems to exude from him, an absence of uncertainty which has the quality of kindness." For Roslyn, there is nothing kind, natural, or free in the hunting or killing of the animal life with which she feels such close affinity. She is a woman of swift transitions from sudden tears to sunrise-wide smiles, whose own kindness is closely linked to her uncertainties. "There is even a suggestion of trepidation in her," Guido says, "but above all she seems to be moving into a newness." Both Gay's age and the dwindling mustang population mean that he, too, must enter into a new phase of his life. Roslyn and Gay sense that they need each other, but they don't know *how* to need another person. This is just what they are starting to learn in the scenes below.

SCENE 1

[We open on another area; not the former valley where the highway runs, but up in the hills, and the sun is newly risen, the light brightening as we watch. At first the scene is pastoral, all beauty. Now we tilt down to discover the conflict and rapacity beneath; we come closeup upon a rabbit emerging from under a sage bush. A shadow passes over it and tilting up we catch a hawk floating in the air above. Cut to a butterfly lighting on a branch; then to a chameleon near it. The chameleon's tongue flicks, the butterfly is taken. Even now birds nearby are making a racket. We cut to a nest full of fledglings, the parent bird agitated. It suddenly takes off. We shoot up. Three or four birds are diving at the soaring hawk, bothering him to drive him off.

The screaming of these birds accompanies the camera, at first it cuts back to the fledglings, then pans across bushes and discovers GUIDO'S house close by. An open window faces us—this is the side of the house. We cut to the window and look in, the screaming of the birds continuing.]

Over the window sill we discover ROSLYN asleep alone in the bed. The screaming seems to be tensing her sleeping face; her fists are closing. The shot widens as the door opens and GAY, fully dressed, stands in the doorway looking down at her. From his viewpoint now, the camera runs its fingers along the outlines of her body under the sheet. Beside her head is his pillow, still dented. The picture of GUIDO and his wife is gone from over the bed, only the book remaining.

His face is almost inspired with lust and desire. He happens to catch his image in the mirror over the bureau. He smooths back his rumpled hair, but the gesture is transformed—he tautens the skin of his neck, as though for a moment he felt the ending of his youth. But as though to dispel this dark thought, he quickly goes from the mirror to her bedside and sits on his heels, his face a foot away from hers. Now, again, his eyes glide over her, and he shows the feeling of one who is both happy and troubled by the question of his possessing a wonder.

While outside, the racket of the birds rises to a crescendo, he moves his face in and kisses her. She instantly draws away, awakening. And then she stares at him.

GAY: Welcome to the country.

ROSLYN: (*Softly*) Hi!—I almost forgot where I was for a minute.

GAY: Well I didn't! I never knew a woman to look better in the morning than she does at night. (ROSLYN *softly laughs*. He *kisses her gently, then* . . .) How in the world did any man ever let you go?

ROSLYN: (*Shrugs. And with a certain faint guilt* . . .) Not all of them exactly let me. . . . I'm a pretty good runner if I have to. Boy, I'm hungry!

GAY: Come on out, I got a surprise.

He walks out of the room. She sits up, her face showing a pleasurable anticipation, and she starts out of bed.

We cut to GAY at the stove turning over some eggs in a pan. Near him is a kitchen table set for two. He turns and sees . . .

ROSLYN in a terry cloth robe emerging from the bedroom doorway. She looks about in surprise.

ROSLYN: You been *cleaning*?

He smiles in reply.

She moves, sees the table set, the breakfast sizzling on the stove; in a vase a few wild flowers. Something outside the door catches her eye. She looks and sees the mop standing in the empty pail among the weeds. Now she turns to him. She is moved by his need for her. She hurries toward him at the stove.

ROSLYN: Here, let me cook!

GAY: Just sit down, it's all done.

He dishes out eggs for both of them, sits opposite her. She stares at him. He starts eating.

ROSLYN: You always do this?

GAY: (*Denying*) Uh-uh. First time for me.

ROSLYN: Really and truly?

GAY nods; his having gone out of himself is enough. She starts eating.

ROSLYN: Ooo! It's delicious!

She eats ravenously. He watches with enjoyment.

GAY: You really go all out in everything, don't you. Even the way you eat. I like that. Women generally pick.

In reply she smiles and almost nods. She returns to eating. Their mutual satisfaction in the food is important; we dwell on it for a moment. With a full mouth . . .

ROSLYN: The air makes you hungry, doesn't it!

He laughs softly. Now he is sipping his coffee. He lights a cigarette, always trying to sound her. She eats like one who has starved. Now she stops for a breath.

ROSLYN: I love to eat! (*Happily she looks around at the room*) I'd never know it was the same house. It even smells different!

Suddenly she goes around the table and kisses his cheek.

ROSLYN: You like me, huh.

He draws her down to his lap, kisses her on the mouth, holds her with his head buried in her. She pats his neck, but we see an uneasiness on her face mixed with her happiness. He relaxes his hold. She gets up, walks to the doorway, looks out at the endless hills, the horizon.

ROSLYN: I can see what you mean—there *is* something here. It feels like a new start . . . maybe it's because it's so bare. (*Slight pause*) Birds must be brave, y'know?—to live alone. And when it gets dark? Whereas they're so small, y'know? (*She smiles to him from the doorway*) You think I'm crazy?

GAY: (*Denying*) Uh-uh. I'm glad to see you like it here.

ROSLYN: Don't most women?

GAY: It never bothered me if they didn't.

ROSLYN: You're a kind man.

GAY: I ain't kiddin' you.

She respects his seriousness, and turns back to look out again. For a moment we see her from his viewpoint, golden in the sunlight. We see the mixture of yearning and mystification in his eyes as he sips his coffee and smokes.

GAY: You seen a lot, haven't you?

ROSLYN:　Yes.

GAY:　So've I. I never see anybody like you, though.

ROSLYN:　Why?

GAY:　I don't know—you got respect for a man.

ROSLYN:　(*She turns to him in the doorway*) Don't most women?

GAY:　Uh-uh. You the first woman hasn't told me her husband wasn't much of a man.

ROSLYN:　And what do you say?

GAY:　Nothin' much. Cowboy's supposed to be dumb, y'know. They come out here from all the states—all kinds—stenographers, social register women with chauffeurs and maids, college teachers, all kinds. And they find a cowboy, and if they think he's stupid enough, they'll say and do all the things they didn't dare in New York and Chicago and St. Louis. And it's pitiful.

ROSLYN:　Why is it pitiful?

GAY:　Because they don't amount to nothin'. Try to remember them and all that comes to mind is . . . a hairbrush and a suitcase. They got no respect for themselves, y'know? Or for anybody else. You have. And I appreciate it. I ain't kiddin' you either.

ROSLYN:　(*Slight pause*) Thanks. I mean thanks for not laughing at me.

He looks at her mystified.

ROSLYN:　People do, you know. I don't know why.

GAY:　I could guess why.

ROSLYN:　Why?

GAY:　Well . . . people are mostly kiddin'—even when they ain't kiddin'. But you—even when you're kiddin' you ain't kiddin'. What you got to do is put it on a little bit, and you could go places. It's only a game, y'know—and you takin' it like it's serious. People always laugh at that.

ROSLYN:　Is it a game to you?

GAY:　Well, I don't mix much—and when I do, I just let 'em

talk. I mean I'm friendly, but I ain't *with* them. (*He gets up*) Let's go outside—sun is warm by now.

He helps her to hop down to the ground, and he takes her hand and they walk through the weeds, reflecting. They come to the lumber pile and sit on it.

GAY: Y'know, Roslyn, I don't think I've known a woman I'd grieve about if she left. I've always enjoyed sayin' good-bye. But there's somethin' about you—I don't know what—I'd be lonesome. For a long time.

ROSLYN: I'm glad. (*She kisses his cheek*) Where do you usually live out here?

GAY: I got a sleepin' bag in my truck. I stay over Guido's house, sometimes. I don't need much.

ROSLYN: You ever see your children?

GAY: Couple times a year. They come to the rodeos when they know I'm gonna be in them. I'm a pretty good roper, y'know.

ROSLYN: My mother had a son by her first husband, but I never met him. And you know?—(*Laughs*) I feel lonesome for him sometimes.

GAY: My daughter's about your size now. (*He sighs*) Time sure flies. (*With a quickened urgency*) . . . I hope you stay a good long time. Will ya?

ROSLYN: (*Sensing his tightening grasp on her*) I don't know. I . . . (*Her eye falls on something in the grass*) Say! Could we use that for a step?

GAY walks over and picks up a cinder block.

GAY: Just might at that.

He goes the few yards to the front door and sets the block under it.

GAY: There now!

ROSLYN: Let me try it!

She hurries and runs up the step into the house, then turns and hops down.

ROSLYN: It's perfect! I can come in and I can go out!

Suddenly, her simple enthusiasm moves him, and he laughs and lifts her, cradling her in his arms.

GAY: Sometimes, you're like a little baby girl!

She laughs, his feeling warming her.

ROSLYN: You're a dear man!

She kisses his neck as he walks up the step, carrying her into the house, both of them laughing with joy.

                                                            DISSOLVE.

SCENE 2

We open on a vast shot of Pyramid Lake, an endless water surrounded by abrupt lavalike hills, bare of vegetation or sign of human interference, the sky cloudless, featureless. Now, panning we discover ROSLYN'S car parked at the shore, and beside it. GAY, sitting on a blanket, drying his arms and chest with a towel. He is looking toward the water.

We shoot the water and out of it ROSLYN surfaces, laughing. She stands now, rising out of the water, glistening in the sun, breathing deeply, looking at the almost astounded admiration in GAY'S face.

GAY: (*Of her beauty*) I just never saw anything like it!

She bursts out laughing as he comes onto the beach, bends and kisses his head.

ROSLYN: Let's run! I love to run!

GAY: Lemme catch my breath!

She dashes away, trotting along the beach. We hold on him for a moment; he almost shakes his head with wonder. His dog is sitting beside him, watching her too.

We truck with her as she runs. Now she throws out her arms as though embracing an invisible world, and then as she is slowing, GAY runs into the shot and devours her lips, and she laughs. And now they stroll along the shore, back toward the car, catching their breaths.

They come to the blanket. She sprawls onto it, still wet. She looks up at him, smiling in knowledge of his need for her. He slowly comes down beside her. Lays his head in the pit of her arm. Silence.

ROSLYN: (*Softly, her face to the sky*) There's no sound at all!

He doesn't move. She turns her head.

We shoot the mute, barren hills along the opposite shore, the bare lake.

ROSLYN: In Chicago, everybody's busy. (*Pause*) Those hills are funny—you keep waiting for them to do something. (*She laughs*) I hope Guido isn't mad—I mean he doesn't come around.

GAY: (*He sits up now*) He's probably just sleepin'.

ROSLYN: For two weeks?!

GAY: That's what he mostly does—sleep and read comic books. Why would he be mad?

ROSLYN: Well, it's his house. And I think he kind of liked me.

GAY: Women don't mean much to Guido.

ROSLYN: Really? Why?

GAY: I don't know. He never got over that wife dyin'. That's what he says, anyway.

ROSLYN: I don't know. You can never tell about people. I've known men . . . so-called happily married, y'know? And the night before their wedding they were calling me up. I mean *calling me up*.

GAY: Well . . . I could understand that.

ROSLYN: But what were they getting married for?

GAY: (*Looks at her for a moment—a little incredulously*) You think there's got to be a reason for everything, don't you?

ROSLYN: I don't know. Maybe I do.

GAY: Let me tell you something. I never heard a complaint out of my wife. Come home one night, find her in a car with a fella. Turned out to be one of my real old friends. Cousin of mine, matter of fact.

ROSLYN: Oh, poor Gay!

GAY: Nobody can figure that out. And I've give up tryin'.

ROSLYN: Then what do you do?

GAY: Only thing you *can* do—roll with it. 'Cause there's nothin' you can change, Honey.

ROSLYN: (*From out of her own vision*) But what if it's so terrible you have to change it?

GAY: Then you get out. Like you got out.

ROSLYN: But when you get out enough times, Gay, it isn't enough. I mean there's got to be more to it than just getting out all the time. Although . . . I used to go to restaurants, y'know?—and I danced in places—you ever see the husbands and wives sitting there?—not talking to each other, looking around?—I mean *looking*.

GAY: I guess you believe in true love, don't you?

ROSLYN: I don't know . . . I never saw it, but . . . what good is it if nobody really cares? You know what I mean?—I mean, I'm not *curious* any more. And once you're not curious, what is there to go on? You know what I mean? It's kind of sad, and boring.

GAY: I'll swear to that. (*He sits up, facing the lake*) I tell you something. I never told it to anybody.

ROSLYN: I won't tell! . . . Gee, it's nice to talk to you, Gay! (*She sits up beside him*)

GAY: It's a funny thing. I've hated every woman I ever been with. Afterwards. (*He turns to her, a little shy grin*) And I'm known for just the opposite. Now that's a funny thing, ain't it?

ROSLYN: Why is that?

GAY: I don't know! That's why you keep surprisin' me. I can't get enough of you, and I think I never will . . . And I don't know just what to do about it.

ROSLYN: Why must you do something?

GAY: (*For the first time he appears afraid and humorless*) 'Cause I can't stand the idea of losing you. (*Pause*) What would I have to do for you to marry me?

ROSLYN: Oh, Gay . . . you wouldn't want to marry anybody! But I'm glad you feel that way. (*She laughs, kisses him*) You'll get tired of me!

She gets up suddenly with a stone in her hand and now she winds up and throws it high into the water. It falls with a little splash. She looks around across the long borders of the lake. Suddenly she yells . . .

ROSLYN: Hello!! (*She turns back to him where he sits*) You want to do something? Let's yell!

GAY: (*With a strained laugh*) What for!

ROSLYN: I don't know, I just thought of it! (*She rushes to him and pulls him to his feet*) Come on, it'll relax you! Nobody can hear us! In the whole world! Come on, one, two, three . . .!

She yells, and he, abashed, joins her but not with full voice.

ROSLYN: Louder! Come on, Gay, let go!

Once more they both yell. He joins now with fuller voice. And he laughs with her. And they yell again across the empty lake, and we come in close on their faces, calling into the emptiness.

LAWRENCE OF ARABIA

A Horizon Pictures (G.B.) Ltd. Production released through Columbia Pictures. Producer, Sam Spiegel. Director, David Lean. Screenplay by Robert Bolt. Music, Maurice Jarre. Director of Photography, F.A. Young. Production Designer, John Box. Art Director, John Stoll. Assistant Director, Roy Stevens. Film Editor, Anne Coates. Sound Editor, Winston Ryder. Sound, Paddy Cunningham. Second unit Directors, Andre Smagghe, Noel Howard. Second unit Photography, Skeets Kelly, Nicholas Roeg, Peter Newbrook. Super Panavision-70. Technicolor. Running time, 221 minutes. 1962.

CAST

LAWRENCE	Peter O'Toole
PRINCE FEISAL	Alec Guinness
AUDA ABU TAYI	Anthony Quinn
GENERAL ALLENBY	Jack Hawkins
TURKISH BEY	Jose Ferrer
COLONEL BRIGHTON	Anthony Quayle
MR. DRYDEN	Claude Rains
JACKSON BENTLEY	Arthur Kennedy
GENERAL MURRAY	Donald Wolfit
SHERIF ALI IBN EL KHARISH	Omar Sharif

Two of the scenes which appear below are between T. E. Lawrence and his commanding officer General Allenby. Both scenes take place in the offices of the British Army, first in Cairo and then in Jerusalem, during the years of the First World War when Lawrence was leading the Arabs in military campaigns against the Turks. These Lawrence-Allenby meetings are described by one of their associates as "a little clash of temperaments. . . . One of them's half mad. And the other—wholly unscrupulous." In both scenes Lawrence doesn't know which way to turn: he's begging Allenby to remove him from Arabia, and at the same time he's demanding that Allenby send him back with more guns, more money. In Arabia, Lawrence does the impossible. Mortal enemies from warring tribes unite behind him and follow where he leads. History is riding with him, and the momentum surges Lawrence far beyond the English codes of conduct which he cherishes. He discovers and slakes his thirst for pain and glory—and is repulsed by his satisfaction. In the desert (which he loves, he says enigmatically, because it is *clean*), Lawrence comes alive so fully that he comes apart.

The Arabs have made him first a prince (El Aurens, a Sherif of the Beni Wejh) and then a kind of prophet. He leads them on camels and horses, with guns and swords. They want to take Akaba, which the British said was too strongly defended by the Turks. Yes, but defended from *sea* attack with guns locked into immovable stones. That no one has yet been able to cross the Nefud desert to attack Akaba from behind, from land side, does not mean no one can. Ali Ibn el Kharish, the Sherif of the Harith, warns Lawrence that no one should try. After Lawrence tries and succeeds, taking Ali and fifty of Ali's men with him, Ali admits that truly, for some men, nothing is written.

Akaba is only a stop on the way to Damascus, which has been held for centuries by the Ottoman Turks. The Arabs want Arabia for the Arabs, but they are so traditionally divided amongst themselves that they cannot fight together against a common enemy. The unifying presence of Lawrence amongst the Arab tribes allows them to stop killing each other and to kill the Turks instead. Lawrence is also able to get them heavier forms of artillery from the British to match what is being supplied to the Turks by the Germans. On the other side of the world, England and Germany are at war. The British army, personified in the two scenes by Allenby, is exploiting both Lawrence and the Arabs to secure their own power in the Mideast. After World War I, the English and French will divide the land between themselves, and Lawrence is admonished not to pretend he didn't know that this would be the outcome.

It's a strange crucible that Lawrence forges for himself. He's in Arabia for the Arabs, and he's in Arabia for the English. Amidst the English civility, he makes a prickly buffoon of himself, but beneath his clenched pose there is a grace of wit that allows him to challenge the Arabs by turning dares into compliments. While still drawing maps in Cairo, before the army ever sends him out, Lawrence irritates his superior into grumbling, "I can't make out whether you're bloody bad-mannered or just half-witted." Lawrence answers, "I have the same trouble sir." The principal chronicler of his adventures, the newspaperman Bentley, says at Lawrence's funeral, "It was my privilege to know him and make him known to the world; he was a scholar, a poet, and a mighty warrior. . . . He was also the most shameless exhibitionist since Barnum and Bailey." Lawrence, himself, suggests the key: "The trick . . . is in not minding if it hurts."

In this first scene, Lawrence has returned from Akaba to Cairo to get the guns and gold he has promised the Arabs, but he wishes not to return himself, frightened by his own appetite for bloodshed.

(*Note:* Although the last beat of the scene cannot be played because it requires other actors, it should be carefully studied for the insight it lends to the Allenby-Lawrence relationship. It would also be of enormous value for the actor working on the character of Lawrence to study some maps of the area in which Lawrence moved. First, because Lawrence himself was a mapmaker, and second, because the actor ought to know just what it is that his character has crawled across, ridden to, and fought for.)

SCENE 1

INTERIOR GENERAL ALLENBY'S OFFICE

CLOSE SHOT (CS) ALLENBY. He is seated at his desk in the office previously occupied by MURRAY. Most of the furniture has been changed together with pictures and other ornamentation. On the wall behind him hangs a calendar depicting month by month a bucolic England which is no longer, and probably never was. The office now has an airy atmosphere with everything in apple-pie order. ALLENBY is a footballer, burly and fit; a gentleman, erect and self-respecting; a General Officer who has thoroughly assimilated power, shrewd, commanding, daring, and humble. He is reading with quiet concentration a personal dossier. His tone is flat, with no trace of comment, as if it might be a shopping list he is checking.

ALLENBY: . . . undisciplined, unpunctual, untidy.

The CAMERA TRACKS and PANS very slowly off ALLENBY towards the opposite side of his desk. [In the background we can see seated DRYDEN (nearest CAMERA) and BRIGHTON.]

ALLENBY: . . . several languages . . . knowledge of music . . . literature . . . (*he browses*)

The CAMERA comes to rest on a CS OF LAWRENCE, still in Arab clothes. He looks across the desk at ALLENBY cautiously. On the otherwise vacant desk we see three photographs. These are a rugby team, an English gentlewoman with a discreet dependent face and a single link of pearls, and a bonny child on a New Forest pony in front of a country house.

ALLENBY: Knowledge of . . . knowledge of . . .

CS ALLENBY. He looks up and it is impossible to tell from his expression or his voice whether he is satirical.

ALLENBY: You're an interesting man, there's no doubt about it.

[CS DRYDEN and BRIGHTON. BRIGHTON gives a quick glance at DRYDEN. DRYDEN feels the look but does not respond.]

CS ALLENBY and LAWRENCE. ALLENBY closes the dossier and puts it on the desk. Then he speaks, not hectoringly, not even sharply, but very much in the tone of a good barrister eliciting facts.

ALLENBY: Who told you to take Akaba?

LAWRENCE: Nobody.

ALLENBY: —Sir.

He says this after a pause and rather quietly, without a shade of personal indignation, not insisting on his own rights but gently indicating that the courtesies are to be observed. It shows a concern not for his own privileges but as it were a fatherly concern lest LAWRENCE should by his behaviour let himself down.

LAWRENCE: —Sir.

ALLENBY now turns sideways to LAWRENCE and commences a sort of forensic examination, his tone being light, quick and dispassionate. Now the pace goes ding-dong between them.

ALLENBY: Then why did you?

LAWRENCE: Akaba's important.

ALLENBY: Why is it important?

LAWRENCE: It's the Turkish route to the Canal.

ALLENBY: Not any more. They're coming through Beersheba.

LAWRENCE: I know. But we've gone forward to Gaza.

ALLENBY: So?

LAWRENCE: So that left Akaba behind your right.

ALLENBY: True.

LAWRENCE: And it will be further behind your right when you go for Jerusalem.

ALLENBY: Am I going for Jerusalem?

LAWRENCE: Yes.

ALLENBY considers this for a second or two quite immobile, and it seems that he might be angry.

[CS BRIGHTON and DRYDEN. DRYDEN glances at BRIGHTON, who is too pent-up with his own thoughts to notice.]

CS ALLENBY over LAWRENCE. After a moment's consideration ALLENBY smiles gently and quickly, and then dismissing the smile, faces LAWRENCE, and leaning forward looks at him full of keen interest.

ALLENBY: Very well. Akaba behind my right.

LAWRENCE: It threatened El Arish *and* Suez.

ALLENBY: Anything else?

CLOSE UP (CU) LAWRENCE.

LAWRENCE: Yes. Akaba's linked with Medina.

ALLENBY: (OFFSCREEN) You think we should shift them out of Medina now?

LAWRENCE: No. I think we should leave them there.

CU ALLENBY. He looks at LAWRENCE for a second or two, then relaxes, swivels his chair, and adopts the tone of a mere equal.

ALLENBY: You acted without orders you know.

CS LAWRENCE AND ALLENBY. LAWRENCE smiles.

LAWRENCE: Shouldn't Officers "use their initiative at all times"?

ALLENBY: Not really . . . It's awfully dangerous, Lawrence.

LAWRENCE: Yes, I know.

ALLENBY: Already?

LAWRENCE: Yes.

ALLENBY: (*suddenly brisk*) I'm promoting you Major . . .

LAWRENCE: I don't think that's a very *good* idea.

ALLENBY: I didn't ask you. I want you to go back and (*deliberately searches for the most banal phrase*)—carry on the good work.

LAWRENCE: No thank you, sir.

ALLENBY: Why not?

CS LAWRENCE over ALLENBY. Now we see LAWRENCE utterly in the grip of his contradictions. His face works and he twists slowly about in his chair as he gropes for words.

LAWRENCE: Well I . . . erm . . . It'—erm . . . let's see now . . . I—killed—two people.

And now it comes with a convulsive rush.

LAWRENCE: I mean two Arabs. One was a boy—this was (*in a tone of surprise*) yesterday . . . I led him into a quicksand . . . the other was a man—that was, oh let me see—before Akaba anyway—I had to execute him with my pistol . . . there was something about it I didn't like.

ALLENBY: (*watching him carefully*) Well naturally.

LAWRENCE: (*staring into* ALLENBY'S *face*) No. Something else.

CU ALLENBY.

ALLENBY: I see. (*He looks away—he is uncomfortable*) Well that's all right; let it be a warning.

CU LAWRENCE. He is looking at ALLENBY almost hungrily. His hands are beginning to shake.

LAWRENCE: No. Something else.

ALLENBY: (OFFSCREEN) What then?

LAWRENCE: (*after a pause*) I enjoyed it.

CU ALLENBY'S face is aged and gloomy. He comprehends. Glances at LAWRENCE, and with an almost physical effort slaps a mask of conventional ignorance and disbelief on his features.

CU LAWRENCE. He drops his eyes and tries to control his hands which are now shaking violently. [He suddenly becomes aware of the presence of:

CU DRYDEN AND BRIGHTON. DRYDEN is watching LAWRENCE with a deep look of pity and admiration. BRIGHTON'S face is frozen in horror and astonishment.]

ALLENBY: (OFFSCREEN) Rubbish. Rubbish and nerves. You're tired.

LONG SHOT (LS) ALLENBY has wheeled round in his chair to face LAWRENCE. He now stands up.

ALLENBY: What d'you mean by coming in here dressed like that? Amateur dramatics?

LAWRENCE has thrown himself back in his chair, very upright under this onslaught of calculated vulgarity, has retreated right back into the fastness of his glacial nature. His eyes flash contemptuously.

LAWRENCE: Oh yes sir. Entirely.

ALLENBY: (*holds out his hand*) Let me see that—hat—or whatever it is.

He takes the kafia and argyl, examining them with apparent interest.

ALLENBY: Fascinating gear they wear. How d'you think I'd look in this [Harry?

BRIGHTON: (*stiffly*) Damn ridiculous, sir.]

ALLENBY: (*looking at LAWRENCE and handing it back quietly*) Here, you keep it.

LAWRENCE: (*taking it slowly*) What I'm trying to say is . . . I . . . I don't think I'm fit for it?

ALLENBY: (*briskly*) Really? [What do you think, Dryden?

DRYDEN: Before he did it, sir, I'd have said it couldn't be done.

DRYDEN'S praise is evidently of no great value to LAWRENCE.

ALLENBY: Brighton?

LAWRENCE: (*wryly*) Oh, I know what he thinks.

BRIGHTON: (*standing to attention to emphasise that he speaks officially*) I think you should recommend a decoration, sir. I don't think it matters what his motives were. 'Twas a brilliant bit of soldiering.

BIG CU LAWRENCE. MUSIC, English theme, softly commences. The effect of BRIGHTON'S words upon LAWRENCE is almost of a declaration of love.

BIG CU ALLENBY. He watches LAWRENCE covertly for a moment or two, then raises his eyes towards the door.

ALLENBY: (*bawling*) Sergeant Major!

LS. There is an immediate answering roar from without.

ALLENBY: Let's have a drink.

DRYDEN: (*a little surprised*) Thank you, sir.

ALLENBY: No, no, downstairs.

DRYDEN and BRIGHTON are surprised—this rugger tough act is not usual—but they catch on.

BRIGHTON: Very good, sir.

The door flies open. A veteran REGIMENTAL SERGEANT MAJOR stands to attention. THE MUSIC is gathering strength.

RSM: Sir!

ALLENBY: You heard about this, Sergeant Major? (*indicating* LAWRENCE)

RSM: Yes, Sir!

ALLENBY: What do you think about it?

RSM: Bloody marvellous, sir. (*to* LAWRENCE) Well done sir.

LAWRENCE smiles hopelessly, and swallows.

ALLENBY: Thank you Sergeant Major.

RSM: (*roars*) Sir. (*and goes*)

ALLENBY: (*boisterous*) Come on then!

DRYDEN AND BRIGHTON take their cue.

CS: MUSIC CUTS ABRUPTLY. LAWRENCE and ALLENBY. LAWRENCE, though he knows he is lost, must register his protest, then slowly—rises from his chair.

LAWRENCE: (*rather bitterly into* ALLENBY'S *face*) You're a clever man, sir.

ALLENBY: (*he has the courage and takes the trouble to answer this personally, not officially*) No, but I know a good thing when I see one. That's fair, surely?]

SCENE 2

This scene, again between Lawrence and Allenby, occurs after Lawrence has allowed himself to be picked up by the Turkish governor and tortured. In the previous months, Lawrence has led crazed raids, screaming "No prisoners" and killing everything in the path of his command.

MEDIUM SHOT (MS) THE TERRACE OUTSIDE ALLENBY'S OFFICE.

LAWRENCE is seated in a chair. ALLENBY leaning against a pillar, his bottom on the terrace railing.

ALLENBY: . . . Yes. Well you've had a glimpse of the pit.

LAWRENCE: No, a glimpse of sanity. (*hard*) And I'm not going back.

There is a short pause. LAWRENCE'S eyes are on the GENERAL'S epaulettes. ALLENBY notices the look, glances at his crowns and crossed swords, and begins to unbutton his jacket.

ALLENBY: You won't go mad, Lawrence. (*quite indifferently*) You've got an iron mind.

LAWRENCE: (*grimly*) Oh no. (*but he is pleased*)

ALLENBY: Oh yes. And here's another thing. When you ask for "common humanity" you're crying for the moon. Common humanity's the one thing you can't have.

LAWRENCE: There's nothing else.

ALLENBY: (*mildly*) There is, for one man every hundred years or so.

LAWRENCE: (*sceptical, but we can just see the poison beginning to work*) Me?

ALLENBY: (*taking off his jacket*) Yes, I think so. (*Again he is careful to keep his voice matter-of-fact, as though this were some small technical judgment he had just made.*)

ALLENBY puts his jacket over the back of an empty chair, and from this point on he adopts the tone used between equals and friends, and friends of such long standing that they can even afford to be brusque. He regards his jacket, chuckling a little ruefully.

ALLENBY: Isn't that funny, I feel quite naked.

He busies himself collecting cigar, cutter, matches from the table.

ALLENBY: And that's the difference. I'm a leader because someone pins crowns on me. You're a leader, (*shrugs*) because God made you one I suppose. There's nothing you can do about it.

ALLENBY sits and seems totally preoccupied with the condition of his cigar. LAWRENCE does not answer but looks at him suspicious, flattered, comforted, above all longing to accept the paternal embrace that seems to be offered.

ALLENBY: (*quite idly*) You write poems don't you?

LAWRENCE: Yes.

ALLENBY: Any good?

LAWRENCE: No. Bad.

ALLENBY: (*nods sympathetically*) Hard luck.

LAWRENCE is a little amused and quite surprised by the degree of understanding ALLENBY assumes.

LAWRENCE: It's not a matter of luck.

ALLENBY: 'Course it is. (*he settles back comfortably*) I grow dahlias myself.

Apparently on impulse he takes from the table a photo of his house and offspring. He peers at it, pointing out a patch of cabbagy flowers in the background.

ALLENBY: There.

Together they study the photo. ALLENBY never looks once at his victim, seems innocently absorbed in the subject of the conversation. He pauses as he replaces the photo, and smiles.

ALLENBY: That's my lad. You must come and see us, afterwards.

LAWRENCE: (*he hesitates cautiously, but says*) I'd like to.

And it is almost like a physical object he has handed to ALLENBY—the keys of his citadel.

ALLENBY: I've got good soil, good compost, I buy good plants. And I'm a conscientious gardener. But I don't have the luck to be a good one. So (*he grins*) I'm a gardening sort of general. Most generals are. But there have been poet generals. Xenophon was one. Hannibal . . . Nelson was the last. I think you're another . . .

LAWRENCE: (*his tone sceptical but his smile tremulous and reproachful*) Nelson, and me?

He is asking ALLENBY to be merciful.

ALLENBY: Yes.

LAWRENCE: That's an extraordinary thing to say to a man.

ALLENBY: Not to an extraordinary man it isn't.

LAWRENCE: (*thrusting it away from him*) No. No.

ALLENBY: (*remorselessly matter-of-fact*) You must know it?

LAWRENCE: (*almost desperately*) No!

ALLENBY: (*in his cunning adopts a tone of irritation*) Look, Lawrence, I've taken those things off— (*rubs his shoulder*) —and I *don't* feel happy without them. I believe your name will be a household word when you'd have to go to the War Museum to find who Allenby was.

He makes this statement very deliberate. His voice now becomes low, confidential, but very steady; it is temptation incarnate.

CLOSE UP (CU) LAWRENCE.

ALLENBY: (OFFSCREEN) You are the most extraordinary man I ever met.

LAWRENCE: (*quick and low*) —leave me alone—

ALLENBY: (OFFSCREEN *quick and sharp*) —What?

LAWRENCE: (*quick and low*) —Leave me alone.

CLOSE SHOT (CS) ALLENBY over LAWRENCE. After a pause, ALLENBY shrugs, and the CAMERA PANS with him as he rises and moves away with feigned hostility, turning his back looking out over the garden, the very image of a disappointed father.

ALLENBY: That's a feeble thing to say. No wonder your poetry's bad.

CU LAWRENCE looks at ALLENBY'S back longingly. He hesitates and is lost. He prevaricates:

LAWRENCE: I know I'm not *ordinary* . . .

ALLENBY: (OFFSCREEN, *short*) That's not what I'm saying.

Suddenly LAWRENCE'S immobility flies apart. He is thrown about in his chair by muscular stresses—much as a man might respond to a thumbscrew—and he cries out:

LAWRENCE: All right I'm extraordinary! I'm extraordinary!

His tone in saying this is as though he were saying, "All right I've got cancer!" A tone of desperate lament . . . But then abruptly having accepted it, he freezes again and looking at ALLENBY he says in a very different tone quietly mocking, from a superior knowledge.

LAWRENCE: What of it?

CU ALLENBY. He is now looking at LAWRENCE, but has not yet caught the reversal of their positions.

ALLENBY: (*gravely and kindly*) Not many people *have* a destiny. Lawrence. A terrible thing for a man, to funk it, if he has.

MS ALLENBY walks back towards his chair.

LAWRENCE: (*almost smiling with a little cold smile*) Are you speaking from experience?

ALLENBY: (*caught in mid-air—he sits*) No.

LAWRENCE: You're guessing then.

ALLENBY is nonplussed and begins to be uneasy. LAWRENCE says in a deadly voice

LAWRENCE: Suppose you're *wrong*.

ALLENBY: (*briskly scrambles over his unease*) Why suppose that? We both know I'm right.

LAWRENCE: Yes.

ALLENBY: After all, it's—

LAWRENCE interrupts him rising from his chair and walking a few paces along the terrace where he stands in an archway his back to the GENERAL.

LAWRENCE: I said, yes.

ALLENBY watches him, cautiously. He turns. He addresses ALLENBY quite politely but not looking at him, as though he were a subordinate.

LAWRENCE: April the 16th.

ALLENBY: Yes. Can you do it. I'll give you a lot of money.

LAWRENCE: (*still not looking*) Artillery?

ALLENBY: I can't.

LAWRENCE: (*now looking at him*) They won't be coming for money, the best of them. They'll be coming for Damascus. (*very steadily*) Which I'm going to give them.

CS ALLENBY looking up at LAWRENCE from his chair. He blinks, but recovers immediately.

ALLENBY: That's all I want.

CS LAWRENCE.

LAWRENCE: All you want is someone holding down the Turkish Right. But I'm going to give them Damascus. We'll get there before you do. And when they've got it, they'll keep it.

CS ALLENBY.

LAWRENCE: (OFFSCREEN) You can tell the politicians to burn their bit of paper, now.

ALLENBY: (*spuriously boisterous*) Fair enough!

CS LAWRENCE. He looks away from ALLENBY and speaks almost idly, throwing his pearls for ALLENBY to pick up if he can.

LAWRENCE: "Fair." What's "fair" got to do with it? It's going to *happen* . . . (*looking at him again, quite brisk and matter of fact*) I *shall* want quite a lot of money.

ALLENBY: (OFFSCREEN) All there is!

LAWRENCE: Not that much.

He leaves the courtyard and walks towards the CAMERA, looming up in the frame against the background of a fresco on the wall.

LAWRENCE: The best of them won't come for money.

He is now in CU. His lip quivers slightly and his eyes glow.

LAWRENCE: They'll come for me . . .

SCENE 3

This scene, between the journalist Bentley and the elegant, pragmatic Prince Feisal, takes place just after Lawrence has returned from Cairo to Akaba. Bentley has followed to cover Lawrence's campaigns.

INTERIOR FEISAL'S QUARTERS IN AKABA

Almost stripped of furnishings. In the foreground, FEISAL is examining BENTLEY'S card. In background, BODYGUARDS carry out some more camel bags. A SERVANT places a metal coffee set conveniently to hand by a window embrasure with a seat in it. FEISAL hands back the card. BENTLEY says, wagging the card before putting it away

BENTLEY: The *Chicago Courier* is my own particular paper, but my work is syndicated throughout America.

FEISAL: I understood so from your letter. I am glad we effected our meeting, Mr. Bentley.

He gestures and they both sit in the embrasure. The window overlooks the courtyard. FEISAL smiles:

FEISAL: Now . . .?

BENTLEY: Where can I find Major Lawrence?

FEISAL: (*the smile going*) Is that what you have come for?

BENTLEY: (*covering up*) Not altogether sir, no . . .

FEISAL: (*dry*) Well you will find Major Lawrence with *my* army Mr. Bentley.

BENTLEY: That's what I meant sir. Where will I find your army?

FEISAL: I don't know.

BENTLEY stares.

FEISAL: Last week they were near El Ghira.

BENTLEY: (*incredulous horror*) Ghira!

FEISAL: (*smiling*) Oh yes. I fear you have a long journey. Can you ride a camel?

BENTLEY: I've never tried.

FEISAL: Take a mule. If I were you I should try Buldulla. Avoid Malaal—the Turks are there.

BENTLEY: In Malaal now? They move fast.

FEISAL: They do. But not so fast as we do you will find. (*he hesitates, then says*) Myself, I am going to Cairo, as you know.

BENTLEY: (*looks up from his pad; he has caught the change of tone instantly*) Yes.

FEISAL: There is work for me there of a different kind.

BENTLEY: Yes.

FEISAL feels it is now BENTLEY'S turn, and keeps silent. BENTLEY amplifies his last word.

BENTLEY: I understand that you've been given no artillery.

FEISAL: That is so.

BENTLEY: You're handicapped.

FEISAL: (*deprecatingly*) It . . . restricts us to small things.

BENTLEY: It's intended to.

There can be no mistaking this. FEISAL addresses him very directly:

FEISAL: Do you know General Allenby?

BENTLEY: Watch out for Allenby. A slim customer.

FEISAL: (*inclines politely*) Excuse me?

BENTLEY: A clever man.

FEISAL: (*the scholar for a moment*) "Slim customer"; very good. (*to* BENTLEY) I shall certainly "watch out for" him. (*he considers, then says:*) You are being very . . . sympathetic, Mr. Bentley.

BENTLEY: (*with that curious sincere insincerity of the newshawk on the job*) Your Highness, we Americans were once a Colonial people. We *naturally* sympathize with *any* people *anywhere* who are struggling for their freedom.

FEISAL doesn't even pretend to consider this as a serious motive.

FEISAL: Very gratifying.

BENTLEY: (*laughs, a genuine impulsive laugh of sheer amusement and appreciation*) Also, my interests are the same as yours, sir. You want your story told. I badly want a story to tell.

FEISAL: (*is amused and approving in his turn*) Ah. Now you are "talking turkey" are you not?

And now they are both amused, and surprised to find how well they are getting on together, each in his own way being a shrewd man and liking shrewdness in others. FEISAL rises swiftly from his chair and walks about a little, cheerful.

FEISAL: Well, Mr. Bentley, I will give you a guide. And a letter. And before I leave here . . . (*he breaks off and consults a fine gold watch, pursing his lips*) . . . Ah which must be presently . . . I will have some facts and figures put on paper for you. You will find that we have done many things, small but many. You know of course that we are destroying the Turkish railways . . .

BENTLEY: (*head bent, scribbling*) Yes, sir. Major Lawrence is in charge of all this is he?

FEISAL: (*pauses and looks at the bent head with some coldness*) My army is made up of Tribes. The Tribes are led by the Tribal leaders.

BENTLEY: *(looks up; insistently)* Your people do think very highly of Major Lawrence though?

FEISAL: *(sharply)* Yes. *(he goes to the window and looks out)* And rightly. In this country, Mr. Bentley, the man who gives victory in battle is prized . . . *(sadly)* beyond every other man . . . *(he is silent for a moment and then murmurs, mindless of the repetition)* Myself I am going to Cairo . . . *(abstractedly he returns and sits, facing BENTLEY. His eye lights upon the pad and this draws his attention back from his own thoughts)* One figure I can give you from my head; because it never leaves my head. Since starting this campaign four months ago we have lost thirty-seven wounded, one hundred and fifty-six dead.

BENTLEY is scribbling this down but does a horrified double take.

FEISAL: You remark the disproportion between our dead and wounded.

BENTLEY: *(wondering, even awed)* Yes; four times as many.

FEISAL: That is because those too badly wounded to bring away, we ourselves kill. We leave no wounded for the Turks.

BENTLEY: *(gently)* You mean . . .?

FEISAL: I mean we leave no wounded for the Turks. *(more moderately)* In their eyes we are not soldiers but rebels. And rebels, wounded or whole, are not protected by the Geneva Code and are treated . . . harshly.

BENTLEY: How harshly?

FEISAL: More harshly than I hope you can imagine.

BENTLEY: I see.

FEISAL: Our own prisoners, Mr. Bentley, are taken care of, until the British can relieve us of them, according to the Code. I should like you to notice that.

BENTLEY: *(scribbling)* I do, sir. *(off-hand again)* Is that the influence of Major Lawrence?

This time FEISAL's eyes snap with a direct anger and jealousy.

FEISAL: Why should you suppose so?

BENTLEY: (*a bit thrown at thus receiving for the first time the full impact of Royal personality*) Well I . . . it's just . . . I heard in Cairo, that the Major has a . . . horror of bloodshed.

FEISAL: That is exactly so. With Major Lawrence, mercy is a passion. With me it is merely good manners. *You* may judge which motive is the more reliable. (*he half pulls out the watch again*) And now perhaps . . .

BENTLEY: (*rising immediately*) Sure. Thank you, sir. (*he moves away towards the door*) D'you think you'll be able to manage the letter and . . .

FEISAL: (*quiet reproof*) I will do everything that I have said, Mr. Bentley.

BENTLEY, a bit rebuffed, nods smiling and goes to the doorway where he is arrested by:

FEISAL: *If* . . .(BENTLEY *turns.*) You will tell me *truly* the nature of your interest in my people, and in Major Lawrence.

FEISAL is serious, but BENTLEY grins disarmingly, like a boy caught out.

BENTLEY: It's very simple, sir. I'm looking for a hero.

FEISAL: (*is amused*) Indeed? You do not seem a romantic man?

BENTLEY: Oh no. (*again the "sincerity"*) But certain influential men back home believe the time has come for America to add her weight to the . . . the patriotic struggle against Germany . . . and Turkey. Now, I have been sent to find material which will show our people that this war is . . . (*he hesitates*)

FEISAL: Enjoyable?

BENTLEY: Hardly that, sir. But to show it in its more adventurous aspects. After all your Highness, war does wear such an aspect. Nobody deplores it more than . . .

FEISAL is looking out of the window again. He interrupts flatly.

FEISAL: You are looking for a figure who will draw your
country towards war?

BENTLEY: *(simply; hence with some dignity)* All right, yes.

FEISAL: Aurens is your man.

DR. STRANGELOVE, OR: HOW I LEARNED TO STOP WORRYING AND LOVE THE BOMB

A Hawk Films, Ltd. Production. Released through Columbia Pictures. Producer & Director, Stanley Kubrick. Associate Producer. Victor Lyndon. Screenplay by Stanley Kubrick, Terry Southern, Peter George. Based on the novel *Red Alert* by Peter George. Photography, Gilbert Taylor. Film Editor, Anthony Harvey. Production Designer, Ken Adam. Art Director, Peter Murton. Special Effects, Wally Veevers. Music, Laurie Johnson. Sound, John Cox. Running time, 94 minutes. 1963.

CAST

GROUP CAPTAIN LIONEL MANDRAKE	Peter Sellers
PRESIDENT MUFFLEY	Peter Sellers
DR. STRANGELOVE	Peter Sellers
GENERAL "BUCK" TURGIDSON	George. C. Scott
GENERAL JACK D. RIPPER	Sterling Hayden
COLONEL "BAT" GUANO	Keenan Wynn
MAJOR T.J. "KING" KONG	Slim Pickens
AMBASSADOR DE SADESKY	Peter Bull
LIEUTENANT LOTHAR ZOGG, BOMBADIER	James Earl Jones
MR. STAINES	Jack Dreley
LIEUTENANT H.R. DIETRICK	Frank Berry
LIEUTENANT W.D. KIVEL, NAVIGATOR	Glenn Beck

CAPTAIN G.A. "ACE" OWENS,
   CO-PILOT   Shane Rimmer
LIEUTENANT B. GOLDBERG,
   RADIO OPERATOR   Paul Tamarin
GENERAL FACEMAN   Gordon Tanner
ADMIRAL RANDOLPH   Robert O'Neil
MISS SCOTT   Tracy Reed

The opening narration of *Dr. Strangelove* explains "Operation Dropkick":

> "America's Strategic Air Command maintains a large force of B-52 bombers airborne twenty-four hours a day. Each B-52 can deliver a nuclear bomb-load of fifty megatons, equal to sixteen times the total explosive force of all the bombs and shells used by all the armies in World War II. Based in America, the Airborne Alert Force is deployed from the Persian Gulf to the Arctic Ocean but they have one geographical factor in common. They are all two hours from their targets inside Russia."

Operation Dropkick is set in motion by General Ripper, the Base Commander of Burpleson Air Force Base. He is acting under Plan R, "an emergency war plan in which a lower echelon Commander may order nuclear retaliation after a sneak attack if the normal chain of command has been disrupted." There has been no sneak attack, but General Ripper is convinced that one day there *will* be. He decides to save the Free World by getting the "Commies" before they get him. He telephones Group Captain Mandrake, an Englishman on the Exchange Officer Program, who is in the control tower. He instructs Mandrake to put the base on Red Alert, which includes trusting no one, despite the uniform he may be wearing, unless you know him personally, and firing on anything approaching within two hundred yards of the base. So that the Russians cannot plant false radio transmissions, Ripper instructs Mandrake to have all radios confiscated and to lock all radio communications to the B-52's into a special code preceded by a special prefix.

Ripper has effectively sealed the base against any interference and set into motion the end of the world. In the War

Room, the President of the United States tries to calm down the Soviet Premier to no avail. The President finally decides to send the 23rd Airborne Division, seven miles away from Burpleson, to attack and penetrate Burpleson, locate General Ripper, and reverse Operation Dropkick. It is too late. The final image of *Dr. Strangelove's* black, black comedy is that of the mushroom-shaped cloud.

The following scene occurs when Mandrake realizes that something is seriously wrong and approaches Ripper with the facts in which Ripper has no interest.

(*Note:* While bullets needn't be coming through the windows, the sound of firing guns is essential to the action of the scene.)

SCENE 1

INTERIOR HALL—LONG SHOT (LS)—MANDRAKE*

walks down corridor, exits into RIPPER'S Office.

INTERIOR RIPPER'S OFFICE—MEDIUM SHOT (MS) RIPPER back to camera sitting at desk. MANDRAKE enters through door BACK-GROUND (BG). He walks forward to stand facing camera in MS.

MANDRAKE: Excuse me sir, something rather interesting's just cropped up. Listen to that—music, civilian broadcasting. I think these fellows in the Pentagon have given us some sort of exercise to test our readiness. Personally, I think it's taking things a bit too far. Our fellows will be inside Russian radar cover in about twenty minutes. You listen to that, choc-a-bloc full of stations all churning it out. Huh.

RIPPER: Mandrake?

MANDRAKE: Yes, sir.

RIPPER: I thought I issued instructions for all radios on this base to be impounded.

MANDRAKE: Well, you did indeed, sir, and I was in the process of impounding this very one when I happened to switch it on—

---

*These scenes are excerpted from the continuity script, not from the shooting script. (Please see the source appendix at the end of this volume for an explanation of these terms.) The actor must view the action— which has not been written by the screenwriter— only as a guideline, and not as the screenwriter's stage directions.

RIPPER gets up and walks BG to door, MANDRAKE follows him. RIPPER closes door and locks it, returns to FOREGROUND (FG) to sit at desk. MANDRAKE follows him and stands once more in front of desk.

MANDRAKE: —I thought to myself, "Our fellows hitting Russian radar cover in twenty minutes dropping all their stuff, I'd better tell you because if they do it'll cause a bit of a stink, what?"

RIPPER: Group Captain. The Officer Exchange Programme does not give you any special prerogatives to question my orders.

MANDRAKE: Well, I, I realize that, sir, but I thought you'd be rather pleased to hear the news. After all, well, let's face it, we, we don't want to start a nuclear war unless we really have to, do we?

RIPPER: Please sit down. And turn that thing off.

MANDRAKE: Yes, sir. Eh, what about the planes sir? Surely we must issue the recall code immediately.

RIPPER: Group Captain, the planes are not going to be recalled. My attack orders have been issued and the orders stand.

MANDRAKE: Well, if you'll excuse me saying so, sir, that would be to my way of thinking rather, a rather odd way of looking at it. You see, if a Russian attack was in progress we would certainly not be hearing civilian broadcasting.

RIPPER lights a cigar.

RIPPER: Are you certain of that, Mandrake?

MANDRAKE: Yes, I'm absolutely positive, sir.

RIPPER: And what if it is true?

MANDRAKE: Well, I'm afraid I'm still not with you, sir; because, I mean, if a Russian attack was not in progress then your use of Plan-R, in fact, your orders to the entire Wing . . . oh! . . well, I would say, sir, that there was something dreadfully wrong somewhere.

RIPPER: Now why don't you just take it easy Group Captain and please make me a drink of grain alcohol and rainwater and help yourself to whatever you like.

MANDRAKE salutes.

MANDRAKE: General Ripper, sir. As an officer in Her Majesty's Air Force, it is my clear duty under the present circumstances to issue the recall code upon my own authority and bring back the Wing.
If you'll excuse me, sir . . .

MANDRAKE walks BG to door, finds it locked and tries another door BG Left. He turns to RIPPER.

MANDRAKE: . . . I'm afraid sir I must ask you for the key and the recall code. Have you got them handy, sir?

RIPPER: I told you to take it easy, Group Captain. There's nothing anybody can do about this thing now. I'm the only person who knows the three letter code group.

MANDRAKE goes to desk.

MANDRAKE: Then I must insist sir, that you give them to me.

CLOSE SHOT (CS) Low Angle RIPPER smoking.

CS High Angle RIPPER'S hand lifts file from desk to reveal revolver.

CS Low Angle MANDRAKE reacting to revolver. He looks up toward RIPPER.

MANDRAKE: Do I take it, sir, that you are threatening a brother officer with a gun?

RIPPER: Mandrake. I suppose it never occurred to you that while we're chatting here so enjoyably, a decision is being made by the President and the Joint Chiefs in the War Room at the Pentagon. When they realize there is no possibility of recalling the Wing, there will be only one course of action open. Total commitment, Mandrake. Do you recall what Clemenceau once said about war?

MANDRAKE: Eh, eh, no, I don't think I do sir—eh, no.

RIPPER: He said war was too important to be left to the generals. When he said that, fifty years ago, he might have been right. But today war is too important to be left to politicians. They have neither the time, the training or the inclination for strategic thought. I can no longer sit back and allow Communist infiltration, Communist subversion and the international Communist conspiracy to sap and impurify all of our precious bodily fluids.

FIRING HEARD OUTSIDE

MS MANDRAKE on settee, RIPPER enters Right and sits next to him putting his arm on his shoulder.

RIPPER: Mandrake.

MANDRAKE: Yes Jack?

RIPPER: Have you ever seen a Commie drink a glass of water?

MANDRAKE: Well, no, I, I can't say I have, Jack.

RIPPER: Vodka. That's what they drink, isn't it? Never water?

MANDRAKE: Well, I, I believe that's what they drink Jack, yes.

RIPPER: On no account will a Commie ever drink water, and not without good reason.

MANDRAKE: Oh, eh, yes. I, um, can't quite see what you're getting at, Jack.

RIPPER: Water. That's what I'm getting at, water. Mandrake, water is the source of all life. Seven-tenths of this earth's surface is water. Why, do you realize that seventy per- cent of you is water?

MANDRAKE: Uh, uh, Good Lord!

RIPPER: And as human beings you and I need fresh pure water to replenish our precious bodily fluids.

MANDRAKE: Yes.

RIPPER: Are you beginning to understand?

MANDRAKE: Yes.

RIPPER: Mandrake. Mandrake have you never wondered why I drink only distilled water, or rainwater—and pure-grain alcohol?

MANDRAKE: Well, it did occur to me Jack, yes.

RIPPER: Have you ever heard of a thing called fluorida- tion? Fluoridation of water?

MANDRAKE: Eh, yes, I, I have heard of that Jack, yes . . . yes.

RIPPER: Well, do you know what it is?

MANDRAKE: No, no I don't know what it is, no.

RIPPER: Do you realize that fluoridation is the most mon-
    strously conceived and dangerous Communist plot we
    have ever had to face? . . .

SOUND OF BULLETS

MEDIUM LONG SHOT (MLS) High Angle RIPPER & MANDRAKE
on settee.

CAMERA SHOOTING from behind. Bullets shattering windows
BG.

LS Windows as bullets shatter them.

MLS High Angle RIPPER & MANDRAKE on settee. RIPPER gets
up and moves BG to windows. MANDRAKE lies down on settee
FG.

RIPPER: Two can play at that game soldier.

MS RIPPER'S desk as bullets hit it. RIPPER BG at windows.

Bullets hit light above desk, it falls, and goes out.

RIPPER: That's nice shooting soldier.

CAMERA PANS Right with him in LS as he crosses to corner of
room to pick up bag, including MANDRAKE on settee FG.
RIPPER picks up bag and walks Right to exit Right as CAMERA
TRACKS IN to MS MANDRAKE on settee.

RIPPER enters Left carrying bag which he puts on table as he
stands in MLS. He struggles to free machine gun barrel from
bag, pulls it out and moves Right, CAMERA PANNING with
him, to put it on his desk. He returns to bag, CAMERA PAN-
NING Left with him.

RIPPER: Mandrake, come here.

MCS MANDRAKE on settee.

MANDRAKE: Are you calling me Jack?

RIPPER: Come over here and help me with this belt.

MANDRAKE: I, er . . .

MLS RIPPER pulling belt of cartridges from bag. CAMERA PANS
Right with him as he moves to desk.

MANDRAKE: . . . I haven't had much experience you know, with those sort of machines, Jack. I've only ever pressed a button in my old Spitfire.

RIPPER: Mandrake, in the name of Her Majesty and the Continental Congress, come here and feed me this belt, boy.

MCS MANDRAKE on settee.

MANDRAKE: Jack. I'd love to come, but what's happened you see, the string in my leg's gone.

RIPPER: The what?

MANDRAKE: The string. I never told you, but you see . . . a gammy leg . . . oh, gone, shot off.

MLS RIPPER at desk mounting machine gun.

RIPPER: Mandrake. Come over here, the Red coats are coming. Come on.

SOUND OF FIRING & SHATTERING GLASS. LS Wall as Pictures are hit by bullets.

SOUND OF FIRING. MLS RIPPER with machine gun, MANDRAKE holding ammunition. They move across floor and start firing through window. TRACK IN & HOLD MS.

MS High Angle RIPPER & MANDRAKE crouched against wall. Window shatters BG. Papers fall around them.

LS MANDRAKE & RIPPER crouched against wall. They turn and crawl toward CAMERA going to exit FG Left.

RIPPER: Stay with me, Mandrake.

LS RIPPER & MANDRAKE crawling round corner of desk. RIPPER stops, crouching behind desk. MANDRAKE crawls to his side Right. TILT UP slightly as he half-stands and fires machine gun through window.

RIPPER: All right, Mandrake, now feed me, feed me, boy.

SOUND OF FIRING. MS RIPPER firing machine gun.

LS RIPPER firing machine gun. MANDRAKE lying on ground beside him. RIPPER crouches beside MANDRAKE. FIRING STOPS. TILT DOWN. RIPPER lowers machine gun and takes cigar out of mouth.

MANDRAKE: Hah-hah, Jack, don't you think we'd be better off in some other part of the room away from all this flying glass?

RIPPER: No, no, no, we're okay here.

MANDRAKE: Ha-ha-ha-ha.

RIPPER: Mandrake, do you realize that in addition to fluoridating water, why, there are studies under way to fluoridate salt, flour, fruit juices, soup, sugar, milk . . . ice-cream, ice-cream, Mandrake . . . children's ice-cream.

CS High Angle MANDRAKE.

MANDRAKE: Good Lord!

MS High Angle RIPPER & MANDRAKE on floor.

RIPPER: You know when fluoridation first began?

MANDRAKE: Eh, no, I don't know.

RIPPER: 1946. 1946, Mandrake. How does that coincide with your post-war Commie conspiracy . . .

MS Alternative Angle MANDRAKE & RIPPER on floor.

RIPPER: . . . huh? Incredibly obvious, isn't it? A foreign substance is introduced into our precious bodily fluids without the knowledge of the individual and certainly without any choice. That's the way your hard-core Commie works.

MANDRAKE: Mm, Jack, Jack, listen, tell me, tell me, Jack, when did you first become, well, develop this theory?

MS High Angle RIPPER & MANDRAKE on floor.

RIPPER: Well, I—er—I first became aware of it, Mandrake, during the physical act of love.

MANDRAKE: Huh.

RIPPER: Yes, a—er—a profound sense of fatigue, a feeling of emptiness followed.

CS RIPPER.

RIPPER: Luckily, I—I was able to interpret these feelings correctly. Loss of essence.

CS High Angle MANDRAKE.

MANDRAKE: Heh.

CS RIPPER.

RIPPER: I can assure you that it has not recurred, Mandrake. Women, er, women sense my power and they seek the life essence. I do not avoid women, Mandrake . . .

MANDRAKE: No.

RIPPER: But I—I do deny them my essence.

CS High Angle MANDRAKE.

MANDRAKE: Yes—er—yes—er—yes.

SOUNDS OF FIRING.

MS RIPPER kneeling on floor, holding machine gun.

RIPPER: My boys must have surrendered.

MANDRAKE: Well there it is, eh-eh. Now Jack, listen, while there's still time, I beg you, let's recall the Wing . . .

RIPPER stands up, TILT UP. He walks BG to sit down. TRACK IN.

RIPPER: Those boys were like my children, Mandrake. Now they've let me down.

MANDRAKE: No, no . . .

MLS High Angle MANDRAKE lying on the floor. He gets up and walks over to RIPPER. PAN Left.

MANDRAKE: . . . Jack, not a bit of it. No, I'm sure they all gave their very best, and I'm equally sure they all died thinking of you, every man-Jack of them, eh, Jack.

CS Low Angle RIPPER.

MANDRAKE: Supposing a bit of water has gone off, eh? And certainly one can never be too sure about those sort of things—but you look at me now, do I look all rancid and clotted? You look at me, Jack. Eh? Look, eh? And I drink a lot of water, you know. I'm what you might call a water man, Jack—that's what I am. And I can swear to you, my boy . . .

MLS RIPPER & MANDRAKE sitting.

MANDRAKE: . . . swear to you, that there's nothing wrong with my bodily fluids. Not a thing, Jackie. Eh, eh.

RIPPER: Mandrake, were you ever a prisoner of war?

MANDRAKE: Well, Jack, the time's running very . . . What?

RIPPER: Were you ever a prisoner of war?

MANDRAKE: Er, yes, I was as a matter of fact, yes I was.

RIPPER: Did they torture you?

MANDRAKE: Er. Yes, they did. I was tortured by the Japanese, Jack, if you must know. Not a pretty story.

RIPPER: Well, what happened?

MANDRAKE: Oh, well, I don't know, Jack. It's difficult to think of under these conditions, but, well, what happened was—they . . .

MCS RIPPER & MANDRAKE sitting.

MANDRAKE: . . . they got me on the old Rangoon-Inchinana railway. I was laying train lines for the bloody Japanese puff-puffs, eh.

RIPPER: No, I mean, when they tortured you, did you talk?

MANDRAKE: Oh. No, no, I, well, I don't think they wanted me to say anything, it was just their way of having a bit of fun, the swines. The strange thing is they make such bloody good cameras.

CS Low Angle RIPPER, smoking cigar.

RIPPER: You know those clowns outside are going to give me a pretty good going over in a few minutes, for the code.

MCS RIPPER & MANDRAKE on settee.

MANDRAKE: Yes. Yes, well you may have, eh, you may have quite a point there, Jack, yes.

CU Low Angle RIPPER, smoking cigar.

RIPPER: I don't know how well I could stand up under torture.

MANDRAKE: Well, of course, the answer to that is, boy, no one ever does. And my advice to you, Jack, is to give me the code now, and if those devils come back and try any rough stuff, we'll fight 'em together, boy, like we did just now on the floor, eh.

MCS RIPPER & MANDRAKE on settee.

MANDRAKE:　You with the old gun and me with the belt and the ammo, feeding you, Jack. Feed me, you said, and I was feeding you, Jack.

CU Low Angle RIPPER smoking cigar.

RIPPER:　You know, Mandrake, I happen to believe in a life after this one and I know I'll have to answer for what I've done. I think I can.

MANDRAKE:　Yes, we . . . of course you can, yes of course you can. You can.

MLS RIPPER getting up from settee, MANDRAKE sitting.

MANDRAKE:　I'm a religious man myself, you know Jack, I believe in all that sort of thing and I'm hoping you know, Jack. You've dropped your gun, Jack . . .

RIPPER moves BG and takes off jacket. MANDRAKE follows him taking his jacket. PAN Right slightly with them, TRACK IN.

MANDRAKE:　. . . Yes, you know what I'm hoping—no, no here, Jack, let me take that for you, I'll take that for you . . . Jack, and—er—you know what I'm hoping, Jack, I'm hoping you're going to give me the code, boy, that's what I'm hoping . . .

PAN Right as they move to Bathroom door. RIPPER enters Bathroom and is seen in bath on mirror as he disappears through doorway. MANDRAKE stands outside.

MANDRAKE:　. . . And—er—oh, you're going to have a little wash and brush up are you? What a good idea. Always did wonders for a man that, Jack, a wash and brush up—water on the back of the neck. Makes you feel marvellous. That's what we need, Jack, water on the back of the neck and the code. Now, now supposing I play a little guessing game with you, Jack boy. I'll try and guess—

RIPPER closes door.

MANDRAKE:　I'll try and guess what the code is . . .

SOUND OF GUN SHOT from inside Bathroom as RIPPER commits suicide. MANDRAKE struggles to open door.

SCENE 2

The following scene occurs after Ripper's suicide, when a soldier from the 23rd Airborne Division finally breaks through into Ripper's office and finds the English Mandrake insisting on a highly implausible (but nonetheless true) story.

(*Note:* Again, while something like the destruction of the Coca-Cola machine can happen offstage, the *sounds* of attack and firing are essential.)

INTERIOR RIPPER'S OFFICE—CU Sheet of paper with writing "PEACE ON EARTH, PURITY OF ESSENCE." ZOOM back to CS of paper including MANDRAKE'S fingers.

MS MANDRAKE reacting. MS Office door. It opens to reveal GUANO who approaches holding gun.

GUANO: Put your hands over your head.

MANDRAKE: What the devil do . . .

MLS High Angle MANDRAKE standing behind RIPPER'S desk FG.

MANDRAKE: . . . you think you're doing, shooting your way in here. Who are you?

MS GUANO in doorway with gun.

GUANO: I said, put your hands over your head.

MLS High Angle MANDRAKE behind desk.

GUANO: What kind of suit do you call that, fella?

MANDRAKE: What do you mean, suit? This happens to be an R.A.F. uniform, sir, and I am Group Captain Lionel Mandrake. I am General Ripper's Executive Officer.

MS GUANO in doorway.

GUANO: Where's General Ripper?

MLS High Angle MANDRAKE behind desk.

MANDRAKE: He's dead, in the bathroom.

MS GUANO in doorway.

GUANO: Where's the bathroom?

MANDRAKE: Next to you.

PAN Right with GUANO as he moves to bathroom door. He pushes open door and looks inside. He whistles.

MANDRAKE: Look I don't know what sort of stupid game . . .

MLS High Angle MANDRAKE behind desk.

MANDRAKE: . . . this is you're playing, but I've got a very good idea what the recall code is and I have to get in touch with SAC headquarters immediately.

MCS GUANO with gun. PAN Right as he moves forward to include LS MANDRAKE behind desk.

GUANO: I said put your hands over your head and keep them there. Go on. Got any witnesses?

MANDAKE: Witnesses? What are you talking about, witnesses? He shot himself.

MCS GUANO.

GUANO: While he was shaving, huh?

MS MANDRAKE behind desk.

MANDRAKE: Now look, Colonel Bat Guano, if that really is your name, may I tell you that I have a very, very good idea, I think, I hope, I pray, what the recall code is. It's some sort of recurrent theme he kept repeating. It's a variation of Peace on Earth or Purity of Essence. E.O.P., O.P.E., it's one of those.

GUANO: Put your hands up . . .

MCS GUANO.

GUANO: . . . on top of your head. Start walking.

MS MANDRAKE behind desk.

MANDRAKE: Don't you know that General Ripper went as mad as a bloody March Hare and sent the whole of Wing to attack the Soviets. Don't you know that?

MCS GUANO.

GUANO: What are you talking about?

MS MANDRAKE behind desk.

MANDRAKE: I'll tell you what I'm talking about. I am going to pick up this red telephone which is connected to SAC, and I hope . . . (*He picks up receiver.*) . . . Blast, blast, shot away, I expect, by one of your men during this ridiculous fighting. Right. (*He puts down receiver. He picks up receiver of telephone* FOREGROUND Left.)

MCS GUANO.

GUANO: All right, Charlie, I've been wasting too much time on you. I've got a lot of wounded men outside. Start walking.

LS MANDRAKE exits into Corridor from RIPPER'S Office, followed by GUANO. MANDRAKE walks down Corridor into MS and halts.

GUANO: The other way.

MANDRAKE: Where are you taking me?

GUANO: To the main gate.

MANDRAKE: Colonel, Colonel, I must know what you think has been going on here.

GUANO: You want to know what I think?

MANDRAKE: Yes.

GUANO: I think you're some kind of deviated prevert. I think General Ripper found out about your preversion and that you were organizing some kind of mutiny of preverts. Now move.

MANDRAKE walks forward, GUANO following. TRACK BACK.

GUANO: On top of that I don't know anything about any planes attacking Russia. All I was told to do was get General Ripper on the 'phone with the President of the United States.

They stop again. MANDRAKE turns to face GUANO BG.

MANDRAKE: Now, just one second—you just said the President.

GUANO: What about the President?

MANDRAKE: Now the President wants to speak to General Ripper, doesn't he? Now, General Ripper is dead, is he not? I am General Ripper's Executive Officer, so the President will bloody well want to speak to me, won't he? There's a telephone box over there and the line may be open.

CS GUANO.

GUANO: You want to talk to the President of the United States?

MANDRAKE: I don't want to talk to him Colonel, I've got to talk to him, and I can assure you if you don't put that away and stop this stupid nonsense . . .

MCS MANDRAKE.

MANDRAKE: . . . the court of Enquiry on this will give you such a pranging, you'll be lucky if you end up wearing the uniform of a bloody toilet attendant!

CS GUANO.

GUANO: Okay . . .

MCS High Angle MANDRAKE.

GUANO: . . . go ahead. Try and get the President of the United States on the 'phone.

PAN Right as MANDRAKE moves BG to phone box. GUANO enters FG Left as MANDRAKE goes inside box. TRACK IN with GUANO who stands outside. Hold MS. GUANO pushes open door of phone box.

GUANO: If you try any of your preversions in there, I'll blow your head off.

MCS Low Angle MANDRAKE in phone box. He puts coin in and lifts receiver, dials number.

MANDRAKE: Operator? This is Group Captain Lionel Mandrake. I'm speaking from Burpelson Air Force Base. Look, something very urgent has come up and I want you to place an emergency person to person call with President Merkin Muffley in the Pentagon, Washington, D.C.

CS GUANO.

MANDRAKE: Eh, eh, Burpelson 39180.

MCS Low Angle MANDRAKE.

MANDRAKE: No. I'm perfectly serious, operator. The President, yes, the President of the United States. Oh. I'm sorry I haven't got enough change. Um, eh, could you make this a collect call, operator?

CS GUANO.

MCS Low Angle MANDRAKE.

SOUND OF JET PLANE FLYING OVERHEAD.

MANDRAKE: Just one second operator. They won't accept the call. Have you got 55 cents?

CS GUANO.

GUANO: Well, you don't think I go into combat with loose change in my pocket, do you?

MCS Low Angle MANDRAKE.

MANDRAKE: Operator? Look, eh, eh, is it possible to make this an ordinary, an ordinary trunk call? Well, what do you call it—you know, eh, oh, eh, station to station? Oh, blast. I'm still twenty cents short. Um, um. Operator, hold on for one, one, er, um, er, shan't keep you a second. Colonel! . . . that Coca-Cola machine—I want you to shoot the lock off it . . . there may be some change in there.

CS GUANO. He turns head and looks off Left. MS Coca-Cola machine, Staircase BG.

GUANO: That's private property.

MCS Low Angle MANDRAKE.

MANDRAKE: Colonel, can you possibly imagine what is going to happen to you, your frame outlook, way of life and everything, when they learn that you have obstructed a telephone call to the President of the United States?

CS GUANO.

MANDRAKE: Can you imagine? Shoot it off! Shoot . . .

MCS Low Angle MANDRAKE.

MANDRAKE: . . . with a gun—that's what the bullets are for . . .

MS GUANO entering Right, Coca-Cola machine Left.

MANDRAKE: . . . you twit!

GUANO: Okay. I'll get your money for you, but if you don't get the President of the United States on that 'phone, do you know what's going to . . .

MCS Low Angle MANDRAKE.

GUANO　. . . happen to you?

MANDRAKE:　What?

MS GUANO, machine Left.

GUANO:　You're going to have to answer to the Coca-Cola
　　Company. (*He fires.*)

CS Coca-Cola machine. Barrel of gun FG Right. SOUND OF
FIRING BULLET INTO MACHINE. TILT DOWN to opening, money
flying down.

MCS GUANO bending down in front of machine, to catch
money. Jet of Coca-Cola sprays from machine into his face.

THE PRODUCERS

A Joseph E. Levine presentation of an Embassy Pictures release. Producer, Sidney Glazier. Director, Mel Brooks. Screenplay by Mel Brooks. Associate Producer, Jack Grossberg. Director of Photography, Joe Coffey. Film Editor, Ralph Rosenbloom. Production Designer, Chuck Rosen. Choreographer, Alan Johnson. Assistant Directors, Mike Hertzberg, Martin Danzig. Color. Running time, 88 minutes. 1966.

CAST

MAX BIALYSTOCK	Zero Mostel
LEO BLOOM	Gene Wilder
FRANZ LIEBKIND	Kenneth Mars
"HOLD ME, TOUCH ME"	
OLD LADY	Estelle Winwood
EVA BRAUN	Renee Taylor
ROGER DE BRIS	Christopher Hewett
ULLA	Lee Meredith
CARMEN GIYA	Andreas Voutsinas
LSD	Dick Shawn

How to describe Max Bialystock? An endlessly needy, cunning, 250-pound infant? A Yiddish-Flamenco runaway vacuum cleaner? An arrogant auto wreck? An explosive breaking of extroverted wind? Max's behavior starts where flamboyant outrageousness leaves off. He is an extremely unsuccessful New York theatrical producer whose face wears an habitual expression of "despair and disgust" because he has cornered the market on flops. This is not the face he shows to the succession of little old ladies who puff up the dilapidated staircase to his office, each one bringing a check to finance Max's productions. A framed portrait of each little old lady is pulled from Max's "Investors File" just before one of these geriatric rendezvous and set out to look like a part of the office's permanent decor.

As the current benefactress (filed under "Hold Me, Touch Me!) is kissing away the wound she has just inflicted on Max's hand in a particularly bouncy romp, an accountant named Leo Bloom enters. Although he has an appointment to do Max's books, he is shooed out. While waiting in the hall, Bloom finds the building's landlord crouched in ambush to grab the check out of Max's hand the moment "Hold Me, Touch Me!" is escorted out the door. Victorious, the landlord shrugs that "He who signs a lease, must pay rent." Max cries, "Murderer! Thief! . . . Oh Lord, hear my plea. Destroy him. . . ." On the way downstairs, the landlord advises God, "Don't pay attention. He's crazy."

It is Leo Bloom who will inadvertently inspire Max's Master Plan of capitalizing a sure-to-fail abomination entitled *Springtime for Hitler* at far above what it will actually cost to produce; the production can be declared a loss to the investors and to the Internal Revenue Service off one set of books, while Max will be able to abscond with the surplus unused funds. The following scene begins out in the hallway just after the landlord has grabbed the check out of Max's injured hand.

CUT BACK TO BIALYSTOCK.

He turns to re-enter his office.

BIALYSTOCK: (biting his knuckle) Nnnnn. That hurt. (he sighs) I'll have to make another call.

He starts in and stops. He notices BLOOM.

BIALYSTOCK: (*to* BLOOM, *quietly*) Have you been there all this time?

BLOOM nods.

BIALYSTOCK: And did you see and hear everything?

BLOOM nods.

BIALYSTOCK: Then what do you have to say for yourself?

BLOOM: Uh . . . uh . . . ooooooops?

BIALYSTOCK: (*shouts*) Who are you? What do you want? Why are you loitering in my hallway. Speak, dummy, speak! Why don't you speak?

BLOOM: Scared. Can't talk.

BIALYSTOCK: All right. Get a hold of yourself. Take a deep breath, let it out slowly and tell me who you are.

BLOOM: (*breathes deeply. Words tumble from his mouth as he exhales*) I'm Leo Bloom, I'm an accountant, I'm from Whitehall and Marks, I was sent here to do your books and I'm terribly sorry I caught you with the old lady. (*he has run out of breath*)

BIALYSTOCK: "Caught you with the old lady." Come in, Mr. Tact.

CUT TO OFFICE. They enter.

BLOOM enters timorously. He doesn't know quite where to go. He looks to BIALYSTOCK for guidance. BIALYSTOCK studies BLOOM curiously from head to toe.

BIALYSTOCK: So you're an accountant, eh?

BLOOM: (*timidly*) Yes sir.

BIALYSTOCK: Then *account* for yourself! Do you believe in God? Do you believe in gold? Why are you looking up old lady's dresses? Bit of a pervert, eh?

BLOOM, who has been quaking under the assault, reaches into his pocket and takes out the tattered corner of an old blue baby blanket. He twists the blue blanket nervously in his hands.

BLOOM: Sir, I . . .

BIALYSTOCK: Never mind. Never mind. Do the books. They're in that desk over there. Top drawer.

BLOOM dutifully goes to desk. Opens top drawer and begins removing books.

BIALYSTOCK: How dare you condemn me without knowing all the facts.

BLOOM: But sir, I'm not condemn . . .

BIALYSTOCK: Shut up. I'm having a rhetorical conversation. (*to himself*) How humiliating. Max Bialystock. Max Bialystock.

BIALYSTOCK suddenly wheels and shouts at BLOOM.

BIALYSTOCK: You know who I used to be? Max Bialystock! The King of Broadway! Six shows running at once. Lunch at Delmonico's. Two hundred dollar suits. Look at me. Look at me now! I'm wearing a cardboard belt!

He rips the belt off and holds it in the air.

BIALYSTOCK: I used to have thousands of investors begging, pleading, to put their money into a Max Bialystock production.

He picks up the picture on desk ("Hold Me, Touch Me") takes it over to open cabinet filled with similar pictures.

BIALYSTOCK: Look at my investors now. Voila! (*gestures at pictures*) Hundreds of little old ladies stopping off at Max Bialystock's office to grab a last thrill on the way to the cemetery.

He puts picture back in its place. Looks toward BLOOM.

CUT TO BLOOM. He is obviously touched by the great man's dilemma.

CUT TO BIALYSTOCK.

BIALYSTOCK: You have exactly ten seconds to change that disgusting look of pity into one of enormous respect. One . . . Two . . .

CUT TO BLOOM. He is really trying to change his expression.

CUT TO BIALYSTOCK.

BIALYSTOCK: Do the books! Do the books!

CUT TO BLOOM. He is greatly relieved.

BLOOM: (*sighing*) Yes, sir. Thank you.

He plunges into his work.

CUT TO BIALYSTOCK. He goes to window, looks out.

BIALYSTOCK: (*to himself*) Window's so filthy, can't tell if it's day or night out there.

He wipes window with his cuff. Looks at window. No good.

Looks at his grimy cuff. Grimaces. From his desk he takes the remains of a cardboard container of coffee and sloshes it against the window. He wipes with his tie. He looks over his shoulder at BLOOM to see if he is watching. BLOOM is watching. Their eyes meet. BLOOM'S eyes retreat. BIALYSTOCK victoriously turns away and looks out the window down into the street.

CAMERA—SHOT OF STREET. BIALYSTOCK'S POINT OF VIEW. A white Rolls Royce slowly makes its way up the block.

BIALYSTOCK: (*voice over as camera follows Rolls*) Look at that. A white Rolls Royce. That's it baby, when you got it, flaunt it.

BLOOM: (OFFSCREEN) Koff, koff . . . ahem, ahem . . . harrumph . . .

BIALYSTOCK: I assume you are making those cartoon noises to attract my attention. Am I correct in my assumption, you fish-faced enemy of the people?

BLOOM is wounded.

BIALYSTOCK: I have hurt your feelings.

BLOOM nods.

BIALYSTOCK: Good what is it?

BLOOM: Sir, may I speak to you for a minute?

BIALYSTOCK: (*looking at his watch*) Go! You have fifty-eight seconds.

BLOOM: Well, sir, it seems . . .

BIALYSTOCK: (*interrupting*) You have forty-eight seconds left. Hurry. Hurry.

BLOOM: (*speedily*) In looking at your books, I've discovered that . . .

BIALYSTOCK: (*interrupting*) Twenty-eight seconds, hurry, hurry, you're using up your time.

In his anxiety, BLOOM unconsciously reaches into his pocket, takes out the old blue blanket and nervously strokes his cheek with it.

BLOOM: Mr. Bialystock, I cannot function under these conditions.

BIALYSTOCK curiously eyes the blanket.

BLOOM: You're making me extremely nervous.

BIALYSTOCK: What is that? A handkerchief?

BLOOM quickly begins to put away his blue blanket.

BLOOM: It's nothing . . . nothing.

Quick as a flash, BIALYSTOCK reaches over and snatches it out of BLOOM'S hand.

BIALYSTOCK: If it's nothing, why can't I see it?

BLOOM leaps up in hot pursuit of his blanket.

BLOOM: (*shrieking in panic*) My blanket. Give me my blue blanket.

BIALYSTOCK, taken aback, hurriedly gives the blanket back to BLOOM.

BIALYSTOCK: Here, don't panic.

BLOOM: (*clutching his blanket*) I'm sorry . . . I don't like people touching my blue blanket. It's not important. It's a minor compulsion. I can deal with it if I want to. It's just that I've had it ever since I was a baby and . . . and . . . I find it very comforting.

He kisses it and shoves it into his pocket.

BIALYSTOCK: (*to himself*) They come here. They all come here. How do they find me?

BLOOM: (*recovering his dignity*) Mr. Bialystock . . .

BIALYSTOCK: Yes, Prince Mishkin, what can we do for you?

BLOOM: This is hardly a time for levity. I've discovered a serious error here in the accounts of your last play.

BIALYSTOCK moves around the desk to examine the ledger.

BIALYSTOCK: Where? What?

BLOOM: According to the backer's list you raised $60,000. But the show you produced only cost fifty-eight thousand. There's two thousand dollars unaccounted for.

BIALYSTOCK: I went to a Turkish bath, who cares? The show was a flop. What difference does it make?

BLOOM: It makes a great deal of difference. That's fraud. If they found out, you could go to prison.

BIALYSTOCK: Why should they find out? It's only two thousand dollars. Bloom, do me a favor, move a few decimal points around. You can do it. You're an accountant. The word 'count' is part of your title.

BLOOM: *(aghast)* But that's cheating!

BIALYSTOCK: It's not cheating . . . It's charity. Bloom, look at me . . . *look at me*! I'm drowning. Other men sail through life. Bialystock has struck a reef. Bloom, I'm going under. I am being sunk by a society that demands success, when all I can offer is failure. Bloom, I'm reaching out to you. Don't send me to jail. Help! Help!

During BIALYSTOCK'S last speech, BLOOM unconsciously reaches into his pocket, takes out the blue blanket and rubs it across his cheek.

BLOOM: Oh dear, oh dear, oh dear, oh dear.

BIALYSTOCK: *(faintly)* Help!

BLOOM: All right. I'll do it. I'll do it.

BIALYSTOCK: Thank you, Bloom. I knew I could con you.

BLOOM: Oh, it's all right . . . wha?

BIALYSTOCK: Nothing. Nothing. Do it. Do it.

BLOOM: *(Poring over the accounts)* Now let's see, two thousand dollars. That isn't much. I'm sure I can hide it somewhere. After all, the department of internal revenue isn't interested in a show that flopped.

BIALYSTOCK: Yes. Right. Good thinking. You figure it out. I'm tired. I'm gonna take a little nap. *(crossing to couch)* Wake me if there's a fire.

He hurls himself down on to the couch.

CAMERA MOVES IN TO TIGHT SHOT OF BLOOM.

BLOOM: Now let's see, if we add these figures, we get . . .

CAMERA MOVES INTO CLOSE-UP OF BLOOM'S FINGER swiftly moving down long column of figures. He comes to the end and immediately writes total below.

BACK TO TIGHT SHOT OF BLOOM. He compares pages.

BLOOM: *(musing to himself)* Heh, heh, heh, amazing. It's absolutely amazing. But under the right circumstances, a producer could make more money with a flop than he could with a hit.

QUICK CUT TO BIALYSTOCK'S SLEEPING FACE. His eyes pop open.

CUT BACK TO BLOOM.

BLOOM: Yes. Yes. It's quite possible. If he were certain the show would fail, a man could make a fortune.

CUT TO BIALYSTOCK. By now he is halfway across the room, his whole being tingling with alertness. He moves to BLOOM'S desk and hovers over him, waiting expectantly for more information. But BLOOM is lost in his work, unaware that BIALYSTOCK is hanging on his every word.

BIALYSTOCK: Yes???

BLOOM looks up. He is startled to see BIALYSTOCK'S face so close to his own.

BLOOM: (*at a loss*) Yes, what?

BIALYSTOCK: What you were saying. Keep talking.

BLOOM: What was I saying?

BIALYSTOCK: You were saying that under the right circumstances, a producer could make more money with a flop than he could with a hit.

BLOOM: (*smiling*) Yes, it's quite possible.

BIALYSTOCK: You keep saying that, but you don't tell me how. *How* could a producer make more money with a flop than with a hit?

BLOOM, slightly exasperated, puts his pencil down and faces BIALYSTOCK. He speaks to BIALYSTOCK as a teacher would a student.

BLOOM: It's simply a matter of creative accounting. Let us assume, just for the moment, that you are a dishonest man.

BIALYSTOCK: Assume away!

BLOOM: Well, it's very easy. You simply raise more money than you really need.

BIALYSTOCK: What do you mean?

BLOOM: You've done it yourself, only you did it on a very small scale.

BIALYSTOCK: What did I do?

BLOOM: You raised two thousand more than you needed to produce your last play.

BIALYSTOCK: So what? What did it get me? I'm wearing a cardboard belt.

BLOOM: Ahhhhhh! But that's where you made your error. You didn't go all the way. You see, if you were *really* a bold criminal, you could have raised a million.

BIALYSTOCK: But the play only cost $60,000 to produce.

BLOOM: Exactly. And how long did it run?

BIALYSTOCK: One night.

BLOOM: See? You could have raised a million dollars, put on a sixty thousand dollar flop and kept the rest.

BIALYSTOCK: But what if the play was a hit?

BLOOM: Oh, you'd go to jail. If the play were a hit, you'd have to pay off the backers, and with so many backers there could *never* be enough profits to go around, get it?

BIALYSTOCK: Aha, aha, aha, aha, aha, aha!! So, in order for the scheme to work, we'd have to find a sure fire flop.

BLOOM: What scheme?

BIALYSTOCK: What scheme? Your scheme, you bloody little genius.

BLOOM: Oh, no. No. No. I meant no scheme. I merely posed a little, academic accounting theory. It's just a thought.

BIALYSTOCK: Bloom, worlds are turned on such thoughts!

BIALYSTOCK starts moving in on BLOOM.

BIALYSTOCK: Don't you see, Bloom. Darling, Bloom, glorious Bloom, it's so simple. Step one: We find the worst play in the world—a sure flop. Step two: I raise a million dollars—there's a lot of little old ladies in this world. Step three: You go back to work on the books. Phoney lists of backers—one for the government, one for us. You can do it, Bloom, you're a wizard. Step four: We open on

Broadway and before you can say 'step five' we close on Broadway. Step six: We take our million dollars and fly to Rio de Janiero.

BIALYSTOCK grabs BLOOM in his arms and begins to lead him in a wild tango around the room.

BIALYSTOCK: (*sings*) "Ah, Rio, Rio by the seao, meo, myo, meo . . ."

BLOOM: (*afraid of the scheme, afraid of the dance, afraid of* BIALYSTOCK) Mr. Bialystock. No. Wait. Please. You're holding me too tight. I'm an honest man. You don't understand.

BIALYSTOCK: (*leading* BLOOM *as he talks*) No, Bloom, *you* don't understand. This is fate, this is destiny. There's no avoiding it.

At this point, BIALYSTOCK sweeps BLOOM into an elaborate dip.

BLOOM: (*the back of his head practically touching the floor*) Mr. Bialystock, not more than five minutes ago, against my better judgment, I doctored your books. That, sir is the ultimate extent of my riminal life.

BIALYSTOCK raises his fists to the heavens in despair. BLOOM, experiencing a definite lack of support, goes crashing to the floor.

BIALYSTOCK: OOOOOHH! OOOOOHH! OOOOOHH! OO-OOOHH! I WANT THAT MONEY!

CAMERA ON BLOOM as he lies stricken on the floor.

BLOOM: (*to himself*) Oh, I fell on my keys. (*he shifts slightly to make himself more comfortable*) I've got to get out of here.

BIALYSTOCK: (*angrily hovering over* BLOOM) You miserable, cowardly, wretched little caterpillar. Don't you ever want to become a butterfly? Don't you want to spread your wings and flap your way to glory?

BIALYSTOCK flaps his arms like a huge predatory bird.

BLOOM: (*his eyes widened in terror*) You're going to jump on me.

BIALYSTOCK stares at him incredulously.

BLOOM: You're going to jump on me. I know you're going to jump on me—like Nero jumped on Poppea.

BIALYSTOCK: (*nonplussed*) What???

BLOOM: (*by now he is shrieking*) Poppea. She was his wife. And she was unfaithful to him. So he got mad and he jumped on her. Up and down, up and down, until he squashed her like a bug. Please don't jump on me.

BIALYSTOCK: (*shouting and jumping up and down next to* BLOOM) *I'm not going to jump on you!*

BLOOM: (*rolling away in terror*) Aaaaaaaaaa!

BIALYSTOCK: (*hoisting* BLOOM *to his feet*) Will you get a hold on yourself.

BLOOM: (*up on his feet and running for cover*) Don't touch me! Don't touch me!

He runs to a corner of the room. Trapped! He turns.

BIALYSTOCK: What are you afraid of? I'm not going to hurt you! What's the matter with you?

BLOOM: I'm hysterical. I'm having hysterics. I'm hysterical. I can't stop. When I get like this, I can't stop. I'm hysterical.

BIALYSTOCK rushes to the desk, picks up a carafe of water and sloshes its contents into BLOOM'S face.

BLOOM: I'm wet! I'm wet! I'm hysterical and I'm wet!

BIALYSTOCK in a desperate move to stop BLOOM'S hysterics, slaps him across the face.

BLOOM: (*holding his face*) I'm in pain! And I'm wet! And I'm still hysterical!

BIALYSTOCK raises his hand again.

BLOOM: No! No! Don't hit. It doesn't help. It only increases my sense of danger.

BIALYSTOCK: What can I do? What can I do? You're getting *me* hysterical.

BLOOM: Go away from me. You frighten me. (*he indicates the sofa*) Sit over there.

BIALYSTOCK sits on the sofa.

BIALYSTOCK: (*exasperated*) Okay. I'm way over here. Is that better?

BLOOM: It's a little better, but you still look angry.

BIALYSTOCK: How's this? (*he smiles sweetly*)

BLOOM: Good. Good. That's nice. That's very nice. I think I'm coming out of it now. Yes. Yes. I'm definitely coming out of it. Thank you for smiling. It helped a great deal.

BIALYSTOCK: (*for want of something sensible*) Well, you know what they say, "Smile and the world smiles with you." Heh, heh. (*to himself*) The man should be in a straight jacket. (*to* BLOOM) Feeling better?

BLOOM: Much, thank you. But I *am* a little lightheaded. Maybe I should eat something. Hysterics have a way of severely depleting one's blood sugar, you know.

BIALYSTOCK: They certainly do. They certainly do. Come, let me take you to lunch.

BLOOM: That's very kind of you, Mr. Bialystock, but I . . .

BIALYSTOCK: (*interrupting*) Nonsense, nonsense, my dear boy. I lowered your blood sugar, the least I could do is raise it a little.

BLOOM looks at him suspiciously.

BIALYSTOCK: And I promise you faithfully, I won't discuss that silly scheme to make a million dollars anymore.

BIALYSTOCK dons his cape and "Belasco" hat. From a rack he selects a gold-topped walking stick. He goes to door, opens it, and with a grand flourish, motions BLOOM to precede him.

BIALYSTOCK: Avanti!

BLOOM graciously complies. They exit.

THE GRADUATE

A Joseph E. Levine presentation of an Embassy Pictures release. Producer, Lawrence Turman. Director, Mike Nichols. Screenplay by Calder Willingham & Buck Henry. Based on the novel *The Graduate* by Charles Webb. Director of Cinematography, Robert Surtees. Film Editor, Sam O'Steen. Production Designer, Richard Sylbert. Sound, Jack Solomon. Songs, Paul Simon; sung by Simon & Garfunkel. Additional Music, Dave Grusin. Assistant Director, Don Kranze. Panavision, Technicolor. Running time, 105 minutes. 1967.

CAST

MRS. ROBINSON	Anne Bancroft
BENJAMIN BRADDOCK	Dustin Hoffman
ELAINE ROBINSON	Katharine Ross
MR. BRADDOCK	William Daniels
MRS. BRADDOCK	Elizabeth Wilson
MR. ROBINSON	Murray Hamilton
CARL SMITH	Brian Avery
MR. MAGUIRE	Walter Brooke
MR. MCCLEERY	Norman Fell
LADY #2	Elizabeth Fraser
MRS. SINGLEMAN	Alice Ghostley
ROOM CLERK	Buck Henry
MISS DE WITT	Marion Lorne

Benjamin Braddock, just graduated from college with honors, has returned to the upper-middle-class home of his parents. Benjamin is worried about his future. The film takes place in the 1960s, just prior to the years of great violence on America's college campuses; so, from everyone's points of view, both Ben's past and future can be expected to remain affluent, comfy and dull. This disturbs him.

One of the guests at the graduation party that his parents have thrown for him suggests that he devote his future to plastics, but Ben's first definite plans involve going up to his room and lying down. Mrs. Robinson, one of his parents' oldest friends who has known Ben all his life, comes into his bedroom and more or less insists that Benjamin drive her home, as her husband has already left with their car. Then she insists, coolly but firmly, that Benjamin accompany her into the house until she switches on the lights.

(*Note:* The following scene involves moving up and down stairs and in and out of a few rooms. In a more limited space, the scene can be played effectively if Mrs. Robinson moves offstage when she is in the bathroom, and if Benjamin moves offstage when he goes to retrieve her purse.)

SCENE 1

INTERIOR ROBINSON HALL AND SUN-ROOM— NIGHT.

MRS. ROBINSON: Would you mind walking ahead of me to the sun porch. I feel funny about coming into a dark house.

BEN: But it's light in there now.

MRS. ROBINSON: Please.

BEN turns and walks down the hall. They enter sun-room.

MRS. ROBINSON: What do you drink? Bourbon?

BEN: Look, Mrs. Robinson—I drove you home. I was glad to do it. But I have some things on my mind. Can you understand that?

MRS. ROBINSON: (*She nods*.) Yes.

BEN: All right, then.

MRS. ROBINSON: What do you drink?

He looks at her.

MRS. ROBINSON: Benjamin—I'm sorry to be this way, but I don't want to be alone in this house.

BEN: Why not?

MRS. ROBINSON: Please wait till my husband gets home.

BEN: When is he coming back?

MRS. ROBINSON: I don't know. (*She pours herself a drink.*) Drink?

BEN: No.

She hands him a drink. There is a pause.

BEN: Are you always this much afraid of being alone?

MRS. ROBINSON: Yes.

BEN: Well, why can't you just lock the doors and go to bed?

MRS. ROBINSON: I'm very neurotic.

She turns on the phonograph. SOUND OF PHONOGRAPH.

MRS. ROBINSON: May I ask you a question?

BEN looks at her.

MRS. ROBINSON: What do you think of me?

BEN: What do you mean?

MRS. ROBINSON: You've known me nearly all of your life. You must have formed some opinion.

BEN: Well—I've always thought that you were a very—nice— person.

MRS. ROBINSON: Did you know I was an alcoholic?

BEN: What?

MRS. ROBINSON: Did you know that?

BEN: Look—I think I should be going—

MRS. ROBINSON: Sit down, Benjamin.

BEN: Mrs. Robinson—if you don't mind my saying so— this conversation is getting a little strange. Now I'm sure that Mr. Robinson will be here any minute and—

MRS. ROBINSON: No.

BEN: What?

MRS. ROBINSON: My husband will be back quite late.

They look at each other. BEN is half-standing.

MRS. ROBINSON: He should be gone for several hours.

She takes a step toward him. He puts his hand up and retreats around the other side of the chair.

BEN: Oh my God.

MRS. ROBINSON: Pardon?

BEN: Oh no, Mrs. Robinson, oh no.

MRS. ROBINSON: What's wrong?

BEN: Mrs. Robinson, you didn't—I mean you didn't expect—

MRS. ROBINSON: What?

BEN: I mean—you didn't really think that I would do something like that.

MRS. ROBINSON: Like what?

BEN: What do you think?

MRS. ROBINSON: Well I don't know.

BEN: For God's sake, Mrs. Robinson, here we are, you've got me into your house. You give me a drink. You put on music, now you start opening up your personal life to me and tell me your husband won't be home for hours.

MRS. ROBINSON: So?

BEN: Mrs. Robinson—you are trying to seduce me.

There is a pause. She looks at him.

BEN: (weaker) Aren't you?

MRS. ROBINSON: Why no. I hadn't thought of it. I feel rather flattered that you—

BEN: Mrs. Robinson, will you forgive me for what I just said?

MRS. ROBINSON: It's all right.

BEN: It's not all right, it's the worst thing I've ever said to anyone.

MRS. ROBINSON: Sit down.

BEN: Please forgive me. Because I like you. I don't think of you that way. But I'm mixed up.

MRS. ROBINSON: All right. Now finish your drink.

BEN: Mrs. Robinson, it makes me sick that I said that to you.

MRS. ROBINSON: We'll forget it right now. Finish your drink.

BEN: What is wrong with me?

MRS. ROBINSON: Have you ever seen Elaine's portrait?

BEN: Her portrait?

MRS. ROBINSON: Yes.

BEN: No.

MRS. ROBINSON: We had it done last Christmas. Would you like to see it?

BEN: Very much.

We move with MRS. ROBINSON and BEN out of the sun-room, into the hall, up the stairs and along the hall to the doorway to ELAINE'S room.

INTERIOR ELAINE'S ROOM—NIGHT

BEN moves into the room and looks up at the portrait.

BEN: Elaine certainly is an attractive girl, isn't she?

In the background MRS. ROBINSON watches him.

BEN: (*looking at the portrait*) I don't remember her as having brown eyes.

MRS. ROBINSON: Benjamin?

BEN: Yes?

MRS. ROBINSON: Will you come over here a minute?

BEN: Over there?

MRS. ROBINSON: Yes.

BEN: Sure.

MRS. ROBINSON: Will you unzip my dress?

He steps back.

MRS. ROBINSON: I think I'll go to bed.

BEN: Oh. Well, goodnight.

MRS. ROBINSON: Won't you unzip my dress?

BEN: I'd rather not, Mrs. Robinson.

MRS. ROBINSON:　If you still think I'm trying to seduce you—

BEN:　No, I don't. But I just feel a little funny.

MRS. ROBINSON:　Benjamin—you've known me all your life.

BEN:　I know that. But I'm—

MRS. ROBINSON:　Come on.

She turns her back.

MRS. ROBINSON:　It's hard for me to reach.

BEN reaches forward and pulls the zipper down.

MRS. ROBINSON:　Thank you.

BEN:　Right.

BEN walks toward the door.

MRS. ROBINSON:　What are you so scared of?

BEN:　I'm not scared, Mrs. Robinson.

MRS. ROBINSON:　Then why do you keep running away?

BEN:　Because you're going to bed. I don't think I should be up here.

MRS. ROBINSON lets her dress fall to the floor.

MRS. ROBINSON:　Haven't you ever seen anybody in a slip before?

BEN:　Yes, I have—

He looks up at the portrait of ELAINE.

BEN:　But I just—Look—what if Mr. Robinson walked in right now?

MRS. ROBINSON:　What if he did?

BEN:　Well, it would look pretty funny, wouldn't it?

MRS. ROBINSON:　Don't you think he trusts us together?

BEN:　Of course he does. But he might get the wrong idea. Anyone might.

MRS. ROBINSON:　I don't see why. I'm twice as old as you are. How could anyone think—

BEN:　But they would! Don't you see?

MRS. ROBINSON: Benjamin—I'm not trying to seduce you. I wish you'd—

BEN: I know that. But please, Mrs. Robinson. This is difficult for me.

MRS. ROBINSON: Why is it?

BEN: Because I am confused about things. I can't tell what I'm imagining. I can't tell what's real. I can't—

MRS. ROBINSON: Would you like me to seduce you?

BEN: What?

MRS. ROBINSON: Is that what you're trying to tell me?

BEN: I'm going home now. I apologize for what I said. I hope you can forget it. But I'm going home right now.

BENJAMIN walks out of the door and down the hall. The CAMERA PUSHES with him to the door. We see the entire stairway and part of the downstairs hall. BEN gets to the stairs and starts down.

MRS. ROBINSON'S VOICE: Benjamin?

BEN: Yes.

MRS. ROBINSON'S VOICE: Will you bring up my purse before you go?

BEN: I have to go now. I'm sorry.

MRS. ROBINSON walks into the hall. Her back is to us. She is holding her dress in front of her.

MRS. ROBINSON: I really don't want to put this on again. Won't you bring it up?

BEN: Where is it?

MRS. ROBINSON: On that chair in the hall.

She walks out of the shot.

BEN: Mrs. Robinson?

MRS. ROBINSON'S VOICE: I'm in the bathroom.

BEN: Well here's the purse.

MRS. ROBINSON'S VOICE: Could you bring it up?

BEN: Well I'll hand it to you.

BEN starts back up the stairs.

BEN: Come to the railing and I'll hand it up.

MRS. ROBINSON'S VOICE: Benjamin—I am getting pretty tired of all this suspicion. Now if you won't do me a simple favor I don't know what.

BEN appears as he slowly climbs the stairs.

BEN: I'm putting it on the top step.

MRS. ROBINSON'S VOICE: For God's sake, Benjamin, will you stop acting that way and bring me the purse?

BEN gets to the top of the stairs, and starts slowly down the hall.

BEN: I'm putting it here by the door.

MRS. ROBINSON'S VOICE: Will you bring it in to me?

BEN: I'd rather not.

MRS. ROBINSON'S VOICE: All right. Put it in the room where we were.

BEN: Right.

INTERIOR ELAINE'S ROOM—NIGHT

BEN walks quickly into ELAINE'S room, crosses to the bed and puts the purse down. As he starts to turn back, he looks up at ELAINE'S portrait. There is a movement reflected in the glass of the portrait. He turns quickly. MRS. ROBINSON, naked, is shutting the door to the bedroom behind her.

BEN: Oh God.

She smiles.

BEN: Let me out.

She turns the lock on the door.

MRS. ROBINSON: Don't be nervous.

BEN: Get away from that door.

MRS. ROBINSON: I want to say something first.

BEN: Jesus Christ!

MRS. ROBINSON: Benjamin—I want you to know I'm available to you. If you won't sleep with me this time—

BEN: Oh my God.

MRS. ROBINSON: If you won't sleep with me this time, Benjamin, I want you to know you can call me up any time you want, and we'll make some kind of arrangement.

BEN: Let me out!

MRS. ROBINSON: Do you understand what I said?

BEN: Yes. Yes. Let me out!

MRS. ROBINSON: Because I find you very attractive and any time—

There is the SOUND of a CAR in the driveway outside. BEN leaps at the door, pushes MRS. ROBINSON aside, struggles with the lock, gets the door open, runs into the hall and down the stairs.

SCENE 2

Benjamin and Mrs. Robinson have now been meeting regularly at night in a room at the Taft Hotel. He passes the days by drinking beer as he drifts around his parents' swimming pool on an inflatable raft. His father wants to know just what was the point of those four years of hard work in college if he has no plans for graduate school or interest in any career. Ben wishes he knew the answer. His mother wants to know where he goes every night. Lying to her makes him miserable, particularly because she doesn't believe him when he says he just "drives around." When Ben arrives at the following rendezvous with Mrs. Robinson, he is struggling with his seriously eroding sense of self-worth.

   (*Note:* After this scene, Ben's parents insist that he date the Robinson's daughter, Elaine. They fall in love. When her parents try to separate them and push Elaine into a safe marriage to a fraternity type, Ben kidnaps her from the wedding with what appears to be her grateful approval.)

INTERIOR TAFT HOTEL ROOM—NIGHT—SHOT—BEN

MRS. ROBINSON'S hands are undoing his necktie. BEN is dressed as in previous scene, plus a jacket.

BEN: Wait a minute. (*he pushes her hand away*) Sit down a minute.

MRS. ROBINSON looks at him and raises her eyebrows.

BEN: Will you please sit down a minute.

MRS. ROBINSON walks to the bed and sits. She reaches down to take off a shoe.

BEN: Will you leave that shoe on for a minute. Please.

She straightens up.

BEN: Now—do you think we could say a few words to each other first this time?

MRS. ROBINSON: If you want.

BEN: Good. I mean are we dead or something?

MRS. ROBINSON: Well I just don't think we have much to say to each other.

BEN: All we ever do is come up here and throw off the clothes and leap into bed together.

MRS. ROBINSON: Are you tired of it?

BEN: I'm not. No. But do you think we could liven it up with a few words now and then?

MRS. ROBINSON: What do you want to talk about?

BEN: Anything. Anything at all.

MRS. ROBINSON: Do you want to tell me about some of your college experiences?

BEN: Oh my God.

MRS. ROBINSON: Well?

BEN: Mrs. Robinson. If that's the best we can do let's just get the goddamn clothes off and—

She reaches for her shoe.

BEN: Leave it on! Now we are going to do this thing. We are going to have a conversation. Think of another topic.

MRS. ROBINSON: How about art.

BEN: Art. That's a good subject. You start it off.

MRS. ROBINSON: You start it off. I don't know anything about it.

BEN: Oh.

MRS. ROBINSON: Don't you?

BEN: Yes I do. I know quite a bit about it.

MRS. ROBINSON: Go ahead then.

BEN: Art. Well what do you want to know about it.

She shrugs.

BEN: Are you interested more in modern art or more in classical art.

MRS. ROBINSON: Neither.

BEN: You're not interested in art?

MRS. ROBINSON: No.

BEN: Then why do you want to talk about it?

MRS. ROBINSON: I don't.

BEN nods and looks at the rug.

MRS. ROBINSON: Can I take off my clothes now?

BEN: No. Think of another topic. Tell me what you did today.

MRS. ROBINSON: Do you really want me to?

BEN: Yes I do.

MRS. ROBINSON: I got up.

BEN starts shaking his head.

MRS. ROBINSON: Do you want to hear it or not?

BEN: Yes. But you might try and spice it up with a little originality.

MRS. ROBINSON: I got up. I ate breakfast and went shopping. During the afternoon I read a novel.

BEN: What one?

MRS. ROBINSON: What?

BEN: What novel did you read?

MRS. ROBINSON: I don't remember.

BEN nods.

MRS. ROBINSON: Then I fixed supper for my husband and waited until—

BEN: There!

MRS. ROBINSON: What?

BEN: Your husband! Mrs. Robinson! There's something we could have a conversation about.

MRS. ROBINSON: Him?

BEN: I mean everything. I don't know anything about how you—how you work this. I don't know how you get out of the house at night. I don't know the risk involved.

MRS. ROBINSON: There isn't any.

BEN: There's no risk?

She shakes her head.

BEN: How do you get out of the house?

MRS. ROBINSON: I walk out.

BEN: You walk right out the door.

She nods.

BEN: What do you say to him?

MRS. ROBINSON: He's asleep.

BEN: Always?

MRS. ROBINSON: Benjamin, this isn't a very interesting topic.

BEN: Please. Now tell me. How do you know he won't wake up sometime and follow you.

MRS. ROBINSON: Because he takes sleeping pills. He takes three sleeping pills every night at ten o'clock.

BEN: But what about the noise from the car. What if—

MRS. ROBINSON: The driveway's on my side of the house.

BEN: (smiling) We're talking.

MRS. ROBINSON: What?

BEN: We're talking, Mrs. Robinson. We're talking.

MRS. ROBINSON: Calm down, Benjamin.

BEN: Now let's keep going here.

MRS. ROBINSON: Can I undress and talk at the same time?

BEN: Right.

MRS. ROBINSON: Thank you.

BEN: Now. You say the driveway's on your side of the house. So I guess you don't sleep in the same room.

MRS. ROBINSON: We don't.

BEN: So you don't—I mean I don't like to seem like I'm prying, but I guess you don't sleep together or anything.

MRS. ROBINSON: No we don't.

BEN: Well how long has this been going on?

MRS. ROBINSON: (*looking at the ceiling for a moment*) About five years.

BEN: Oh no. Are you kidding me?

MRS. ROBINSON: No. I'm not.

BEN: You have not slept with your husband for five years?

MRS. ROBINSON: Now and then. He gets drunk a few times a year.

BEN: How many times a year.

MRS. ROBINSON: On New Year's Eve. Sometimes on his birthday.

BEN: Man, is this interesting.

MRS. ROBINSON: Is it?

BEN: So you don't love him. You wouldn't say you—

MRS. ROBINSON: We've talked enough, Benjamin.

BEN: Wait a minute. So you wouldn't say you loved him.

MRS. ROBINSON: Not exactly.

BEN: But you don't hate him.

MRS. ROBINSON: No, Benjamin. I don't hate him. Unhook my blouse.

BEN: (*unhooking her blouse*) Well how do you feel about him, then?

MRS. ROBINSON: I don't.

She nods and takes off her blouse.

BEN: Well you loved him once, I assume. When you first knew him.

MRS. ROBINSON: No.

BEN: What?

MRS. ROBINSON: I never did, Benjamin. Now let's—

BEN: Well, wait a minute. You married him.

She nods.

BEN: Why did you do that?

MRS. ROBINSON: (*taking off her stockings*)   See if you can guess.

BEN: Well I can't.

MRS. ROBINSON: Think real hard, Benjamin.

BEN: I can't see why you did, unless . . . you didn't *have* to marry him or anything, did you?

MRS. ROBINSON: Don't tell Elaine.

BEN: Oh no. You had to marry him because you got pregnant?

MRS. ROBINSON: Are you shocked?

BEN: Well I never thought of you and Mr. Robinson as the kind of people who . . .

MRS. ROBINSON: All right. Now let's get to bed.

BEN: Wait a minute. Wait a minute. So how did it happen?

MRS. ROBINSON: What?

BEN: I mean do you feel like telling me what were the circumstances?

MRS. ROBINSON: Not particularly.

BEN: Was he a law student at the time?

She nods.

BEN: And you were a student also.

MRS. ROBINSON: Yes.

BEN: At college.

MRS. ROBINSON: Yes.

BEN: What was your major?

MRS. ROBINSON: Why are you asking me all this?

BEN: Because I'm interested, Mrs. Robinson. Now what was your major subject at college?

MRS. ROBINSON: Art.

BEN: Art?

She nods.

BEN: But I thought you—I guess you kind of lost interest in it over the years then.

MRS. ROBINSON: Kind of.

BEN: Well how did it happen?

MRS. ROBINSON: What?

BEN: You and Mr. Robinson.

MRS. ROBINSON: How do you think?

BEN: I mean did he take you up to his room with him? Did you go to a hotel?

MRS. ROBINSON: Benjamin, what does it possibly matter?

BEN: I'm curious.

MRS. ROBINSON: We'd go to his car.

BEN: Oh no. In the car you did it?

MRS. ROBINSON: I don't think we were the first.

BEN thinks for a moment.

BEN: What kind of car was it?

MRS. ROBINSON: What?

BEN: Do you remember the make of the car?

MRS. ROBINSON: Oh my God.

BEN: Really. I want to know.

MRS. ROBINSON: It was a Ford, Benjamin.

BEN: (*jumping up*) A Ford! A Ford! Goddamnit, a Ford! That's great!

MRS. ROBINSON: That's enough.

BEN: So old Elaine Robinson got started in a Ford.

There is a pause.

MRS. ROBINSON: Don't talk about Elaine.

BEN: Don't talk about Elaine?

MRS. ROBINSON: No.

BEN: Why not?

MRS. ROBINSON: Because I don't want you to.

She walks to the bed.

BEN: Well why don't you?

She pulls the bedspread down. BEN begins to remove his jacket.

BEN: I wish you'd tell me.

MRS. ROBINSON: There's nothing to tell.

BEN: Well why is she a big taboo subject all of a sudden?

MRS. ROBINSON uncovers one of the pillows.

BEN: Well—I guess I'll have to ask her out on a date and find out what's—

MRS. ROBINSON: Benjamin, don't you ever take that girl out.

BEN looks at her.

MRS. ROBINSON: Do you understand that?

BEN: Well look. I have no intention of taking her out.

MRS. ROBINSON: Good.

BEN: I was just kidding around.

MRS. ROBINSON: Good.

BEN: But why shouldn't I?

MRS. ROBINSON: I have my reasons.

BEN: Then let's hear them.

MRS. ROBINSON: No.

BEN: Let's hear your reasons, Mrs. Robinson. Because I think I know what they are.

She pulls the covers down.

BEN: I'm not good enough for her to associate with, am I? I'm not good enough to even talk about her, am I?

MRS. ROBINSON: Let's drop it.

BEN: We're not dropping it. Now that's the reason, isn't it? I'm a dirty degenerate, aren't I? I'm not fit to—

MRS. ROBINSON: Benjamin?

BEN: I'm good enough for you but I'm too slimy to associate with your daughter. That's it, isn't it? ISN'T IT?

MRS. ROBINSON: Yes.

BEN: You go to hell. You go straight to hell, Mrs. Robinson. Do you think I'm proud of myself? Do you think I'm proud of this?

MRS. ROBINSON: I wouldn't know.

BEN: Well, I am not.

MRS. ROBINSON: You're not.

BEN: No sir. I am not proud that I spend my time with a broken-down alcoholic!

MRS. ROBINSON: I see.

BEN: And if you think I come here for any reason besides pure boredom, then you're all wrong.

She nods.

BEN: Because—Mrs. Robinson this is the sickest, most perverted thing that ever happened to me. And you do what you want but I'm getting the hell out.

MRS. ROBINSON: Are you?

BEN: You're goddamn right I am.

He starts putting on his shirt. She sits on the edge of the bed and watches him.

MRS. ROBINSON: That's how you feel about me.

He nods.

MRS. ROBINSON: That I'm a sick and disgusting person.

BEN: Now don't start this.

MRS. ROBINSON: What?

BEN: Don't start acting hurt.

MRS. ROBINSON: Don't you expect me to be a little hurt?

BEN: Mrs. Robinson, you lie there and tell me I'm not good enough for your daughter.

MRS. ROBINSON: Did I say that?

BEN: In so many words.

She shakes her head.

MRS. ROBINSON: Benjamin, I want to apologize to you if that's the impression you got.

BEN: Well two minutes ago you told me I wasn't good enough for your daughter. Now you say you're sorry I got that impression.

MRS. ROBINSON: I didn't mean it. I don't think you'd be right for each other. But I would never say you weren't as good a person as she is.

BEN: You wouldn't.

MRS. ROBINSON: Of course I wouldn't.

MRS. ROBINSON walks to the closet.

BEN: What are you doing?

MRS. ROBINSON: Well it's pretty obvious you don't want me around any more.

BEN: Well look—I was kind of upset there. I'm sorry I said those things.

MRS. ROBINSON: If that's how you feel—

BEN: But it's not.

MRS. ROBINSON: (*smiling at him*) That's all right. I think I can understand why I'm disgusting to you.

BEN: Oh no. Look—I like you. I wouldn't keep coming here if I didn't like you.

MRS. ROBINSON: But if it's sickening for you—

BEN: It's not! I enjoy it! I look forward to it. It's the one thing I have to look forward to.

MRS. ROBINSON: You don't have to say that.

BEN: Well I wouldn't. I would never say it if it wasn't true.

MRS. ROBINSON: May I stay then?

BEN: Yes. Please. I want you to.

MRS. ROBINSON: Thank you.

BEN: Well don't thank me, because I want you to.

There is a long pause.

MRS. ROBINSON: But you won't ever take out Elaine, will you? I want you to promise me that.

There is another pause.

BEN: Look. Why the hell did you bring this up. It never occurred to me to take her out.

MRS. ROBINSON: Then give me your word you won't.

BEN: This is absurd.

MRS. ROBINSON: Promise me, Benjamin.

BEN: All right, for Christ's sake. I promise I will never take out Elaine Robinson.

MRS. ROBINSON: Thank you. (*pause*) Benjamin—

BEN: Let's not talk about it. Let's not talk at all.

At opposite sides of the room, without looking at each other, they begin to take off their clothes.

MIDNIGHT COWBOY

Released through United Artists Corp. Producer, Jerome Hellman. Director, John Schlesinger. Screenplay by Waldo Salt. Based on the novel *Midnight Cowboy* by James Leo Herlihy. Musical Supervision, John Barry. Song "Everybody's Talkin'" by Fred Neil, sung by Nilsson. Director of Photography, Adam Holender. Production Designer, John Robert Lloyd. Film Editor, Hugh A. Robertson. Sound Editors, Jack Fitzstephens, Vincent Connelly. Sound Mixer, Dick Vorisek. Associate Producer, Kenneth Utt. Second unit Director, Burtt Harris. Special Lighting Effects, Joshua Light Show. Color by DeLuxe. Running time, 113 minutes. 1969.

CAST

RATSO	Dustin Hoffman
JOE BUCK	Jon Voight
CASS	Sylvia Miles
MR. O'DANIEL	John McGiver
SHIRLEY	Brenda Vaccaro
TOWNY	Bernard Hughes
SALLY BUCK	Ruth White
ANNIE	Jennifer Salt
GRETEL MCALBERTSON	Viva
HANSEL MCALBERTSON	Gastone Rossilli

Enrico "Ratso" Rizzo lives the life of a rat, scurrying through the gutters of New York City, holing up in an abandoned, condemned tenement without heat or electricity. Beneath the belligerence and prejudice and cunning necessary to his survival is the memory of his father, whose body was broken from a lifetime bent over, shining other men's shoes. Ratso—a name he despises—is a very busy man. There are filthy clothes and rotten food to steal, cigarettes to bum, dumb yokels to hustle. He is always on the run, dragging his crippled leg with grotesque speed. And he is dying, with a cough that cracks him wide open. Out pours the fury at a world that kept his father stooped and keeps him degraded and lame. The shame lies deeply banked; the only time we see him cry for himself is when, finally unable to walk, he wets his pants on a long bus ride to Florida. It is a journey he will not survive. Ratso Rizzo is the epitome of everything magnificent and human in the down-and-out, in the "cheap con artist."

Joe Buck is one of the dumb yokels Ratso hustles. Joe has come from Texas to New York to be "the real thing" in big city male prostitution—a real cowboy, ma'am. In his way, Joe is everything that is magnificent and human in the "dumb blonde stud." His confidence in his own sweet beauty is total, and his faith and joy in life are rooted in his power to love. He is naturally blessed with all the tricks, but he doesn't know the ropes to save his life. When he finally does succeed at getting himself picked up, the woman hustles *him*. Even Ratso tricks him out of his money without a hitch, except that Ratso is so little and weak that Joe can catch him. Unable to pay his bill, Joe has been evicted from his flop-house hotel, and Ratso invites him to share his place.

The two strike up a pathetically unsuccessful client/ manager partnership. Freezing and starving, they're such a peculiar looking pair that they are spotted by two underground filmmakers who are throwing a spectacular party in order to film it. When they arrive, Ratso is miserably out of his element amidst all the psychedelic chic, but Joe is handed his first joint and trips off blissfully into the light show. A woman takes him home; he's scored his first satisfied customer and the beginning of his career. But when he returns with provisions to the flat, he finds Ratso sweating and shivering in fear, no longer able to walk. In Ratso's dreams, he is sprinting along the beach in Florida, chatting amiably with the dowagers in diamonds, being pampered by the beauties in bikinis. Joe buys tickets to Florida and carries Ratso onto the bus.

What chases Joe Buck are his memories. The good ones of

his Grandma Sally's warmth. The confused ones of her many boyfriends. The bad ones of his mother dumping him on Sally, of the gang that grabbed him and raped the girl who loved him, and of the car that carried her away. Joe's past memories, like Ratso's future fantasies, flash through *Midnight Cowboy* as these two characters try to keep their balance in the jerking and shoving of New York's street life realities. Joe's always got a radio at his ear, keeping time to the hits by grinding away at his chewing gum. He believes the parade of promises he's being pitched between songs. When he makes love to what he hopes is his first paying customer, their bodies roll over and over the remote control to a television set that's blasting channel after channel of media hype, as the woman's poodle yaps in its own two cents. All these rhythms of sex and violence and commerce are tangled together inside Joe Buck's head. The music over the film's opening titles sings, "Everybody's talkin' at me/ Can't hear a word they're sayin'/Only the echoes of my mind." With his eyes and ears focused on a make-believe future he has learned over the airwaves, Joe Buck backs into caring about Ratso Rizzo, protesting all the way about what a creepy runt Ratso is. On one of the bus stops, Joe gets out and buys them both warm weather sports clothes. He finally steps out of the sexual parody of his "midnight cowboy" costume, and in carrying off his buddy to save his life, Joe Buck achieves the most archetypal aspects of the cowboy at midnight.

The following two scenes take place in Ratso's freezing rooms. In the first, they have returned from a "shopping" expedition in which Ratso has taught Joe how to steal from the greengrocer. In the second, Joe has just scored and set up another appointment, and he returns filled with excitement that he is finally going to be a real hustler.

SCENE 1

INTERIOR X FLAT—DAY

A few household items have been added—a burnt-out easy chair, a cracked mirror, an improvised kitchen. RATSO stands over the Sterno stove, scraping the bottoms of cans into a simpering fry pan. JOE is stretched on his bed—watching

RATSO cook for him—singing to himself over the machine gun voice of a pro ball announcer.

RATSO: The two basic items necessary to sustain life are sunshine and coconut milk. That's a known fact. In Florida, your only problem is, dietwise, you gotta lift your arm to wipe warm milk off your chin—tough?—and chicks! —statistically speaking Miami has more rich chicks than any resort in the U.S.A. You can't scratch yourself without you brush against a bare belly button.

JOE: You just queer for belly buttons.

RATSO: Okay. C'mon. Eat it while it's hot. Hot it ain't bad.

RATSO shoves the plate on the table, lights a cigarette and pours himself a cup of coffee. JOE rises lazily.

JOE: Smells worse hot 'n it did cold.

RATSO: Starting tomorrow, you cook your own goddam dinner or get one of those rich Park Avenue ladies to cook for you. In her penthouse.

JOE starts shoveling food in his mouth.

JOE: I'm eating it, hell, looka here. Ratso, I'm eating it. Goes down okay. Try some. This shit's okay.

RATSO turns his back, probes the fibre husk of a coconut to find the opening, mumbling to himself . . .

RATSO: I gotta get outa here. Gotta get outa here. Miami Beach—that's where you could score. Anyone could score there. Even you. In New York you need threads and glitter—a front, heh?—no rich chick with any class buys that big dumb cowboy crap anymore. They laugh at you walking down the street . . .

JOE: I never seen anyone laugh . . .

RATSO: . . . behind your back. I seen them.

JOE crosses to scrape the last few bites of food from the fry pan.

RATSO holds the coconut under one arm while he takes JOE'S empty plate to the tub-sink and rinses it.

JOE: What you know about women? When's the last time you scored, boy?

RATSO: That's a matter I only talk about at confession.

JOE: When's the last time you went to confession?

RATSO: That's between me and my confessor. Another thing—frankly—you're beginning too smell. For a stud in New York that's a handicap . . .

JOE: Talk about clean, Ratso—all the time I'm here, I ain't seen you change your underwear once.

RATSO: I just don't do it in public. I don't expose myself.

JOE: I bet you don't. I bet you never been laid, how about that? And you gonna tell me what appeals to women.

RATSO: I know enough to know that big dumb cowboy crap don't appeal to no one except every Jacky on Forty-Second Street. Fag stuff. That's all it is. Fag stuff.

JOE: Shee-it.—John Wayne—you gonna tell me he's a fag?

JOE glances at himself in the mirror, his self-confidence only momentarily shaken.

JOE: I like the way I look. Makes me feel good. And women like me goddamnit. Only damn thing I ever been good for's loving. Women go crazy for me. Fact. Crazy Annie? Had to send her away.

RATSO: So how come you ain't scored once in New York since you been here?

JOE: (*Increasingly violent*)   Cause I need management goddamnit! Cause a twisty little sidewinder that said he was my friend stole twenty dollars from me . . .

RATSO yelps as the icepick slips and stabs his finger. JOE takes the coconut from RATSO, balances it on the window sill and holds it while he raises the X window.

JOE: . . . so you better stop crapping around about Florida and get your skinny butt moving. You gonna fix me up all clean and pretty and start earning that twenty bucks management you owe me! Y'hear!

JOE slams the window. The coconut flies out and down.

[EXTERIOR SIDEWALK—DAY

Street kids gather curiously as the coconut crashes on the pavement below the X flat.]

SCENE 2

INTERIOR MEN'S STORE—DAY

. . . JOE slaps a bill on the counter, admiring a fine new cowboy shirt in the mirror, wriggling new white socks into his boots. Suddenly remembering, he goes to the sock rack and buys two pairs, one large and one small. Gradually dominating, JOE'S love theme recurs, continuing over . . .

INTERIOR CHAIN DRUG STORE—DAY

. . . JOE slaps down money to pay for an assortment of medicine.

INTERIOR CONDEMNED TENEMENT—DAY

JOE takes the stairs two at a time to burst in on]

INTERIOR X FLAT—DAY

. . . RATSO huddled in the overstuffed chair—wearing the stolen sheepskin coat— wrapped in blankets, his teeth chattering, in spite of the sweat on his forehead. JOE stops abruptly, his mood shattered by RATSO'S alarming condition. They simply stare at each other for a moment, then JOE turns away to see soup heating on the Sterno stove. JOE tosses one of his paper bags onto RATSO'S lap . . .

JOE: See what you think of that crap. I'll pour your soup. Got some of that junk you like to swill, too. Mentholatum. Aspirin. All that shee-it . . .

RATSO opens the paper bag, trying to control his shivering, pulling out the socks and a suit of long underwear. He sees JOE watching him for a reaction. The best RATSO can do is a slight shake of his head.

JOE: They wrong?

RATSO: They're okay. Only why buy them? That's dumb. While you got the aspirin, I coulda lifted six pairs of socks.

JOE: We don't have to steal nothing no more, boy. I got nine bucks left and twenty more Thursday and before you know it we gonna be riding on Easy Street.

JOE hands RATSO the soup. RATSO seems momentarily steadied by the warmth in his hands. He grins curiously at JOE.

RATSO: It was okay? I mean, it went okay?

JOE: She went crazy, that's the truth, like a goddam alley cat.

RATSO laughs with JOE, almost spilling the soup. JOE reaches out to steady it. RATSO speaks hesitantly.

RATSO: By the way, thanks for all the crap . . . (*Then*) Hey, Joe, don't get sore about this or anything. You promise?

JOE: Yeah.

RATSO: Well, I don't think I can walk. (*Embarrassed*) I mean, I been falling down a lot and, uh . . .

JOE: And what?

RATSO: I'm scared.

JOE: What of?

RATSO: What'll happen. What they do to—I mean, I don't know—what they do with someone that can't— shit, you know what I mean . . .

JOE: Who?

RATSO: The cops, the medicares, who knows? I gotta lie down.

RATSO is trembling so violently that the soup slops over. JOE takes it, lifts RATSO and carries him to the bed. Scowling, alarmed, JOE places the medicines on the bed beside RATSO and picks up his hat.

JOE: That should hold you till I get back.

RATSO: Where you going?

JOE: Gotta get a doctor.

RATSO: Don't be so dumb. No doctors. No cops. You ain't gonna send me to Bellevue. Once they get their hooks in you you're dead. Don't be so goddam dumb.

JOE: You're sick! What in hell you gonna do?

RATSO: Florida. I just get to Florida I'll be fine.

JOE: I can't go to Florida now!

RATSO: Just get me on the bus.

JOE: Shee-it, you got the fevers. How you think you gonna get to Florida?

RATSO: I'll get there. You just get me on the bus. I'll be okay.

JOE: Just when everything's going my way, you gotta pull a stunt like this.

RATSO: I don't need you. Just get me on the bus. I don't want nothing more from you. I got other plans for my life than dragging around some dumb cowboy who thinks he's God's gift to women. One twenty-buck trick and he's already the biggest stud in New York City. It's laughable.

JOE sets his stetson on his head.

JOE: When I put you on that bus down to Florida tonight, that'll be the happiest day of my life!

THEY SHOOT HORSES, DON'T THEY?

An ABC Pictures Corporation presentation of a Palomar Picture. Distributed by Cinerama Releasing Corporation. Producers, Irwin Winkler & Robert Chartoff. Director, Sydney Pollack. Screenplay by James Poe & Robert E. Thompson. Based on the novel *They Shoot Horses, Don't They?* by Horace McCoy. Executive Producer, Theodore B. Sills. Associate Producer/Music, John Green. Director of Photography, Philip H. Rathrop. Production Designer, Harry Horner. Film Editor, Fredric Steinkamp. Sound, Tom Overton. Assistant Director, Al Jennings. Panavision, color by DeLuxe. Running time, 129 minutes. 1969.

CAST

GLORIA	Jane Fonda
ROBERT	Michael Sarrazin
ALICE	Susannah York
ROCKY	Gig Young
SAILOR	Red Buttons
RUBY	Bonnie Bedelia
ROLLO	Michael Conrad
JAMES	Bruce Dern
TURKEY	Al Lewis
JOEL	Robert Fields
CECIL	Severn Darden
SHIRL	Allyn Ann McLerie
JACKIE	Jacquelyn Hyde
MARIO	Felice Orlandi
MAX	Art Metrano
LILLIAN	Gail Billings

AGNES	Maxine Greene
NURSE	Mary Gregory
COLLEGE BOY	Robert Dunlap
JIGGS	Paul Mantee
DOCTOR	Tim Herbert
SECOND TRAINER	Tom McFadden
FIRST TRAINER	Noble "Kid" Chissell

"They shoot horses, don't they?" This is the question that Robert Syverton asks back to the police when they ask him why he shot and killed Gloria Beatty. She put the gun in his hand and asked him to help her. After having lived through a sixty-two-day ordeal of physical and psychological torture, this was the first time Gloria had asked for help. When Robert speaks, the screenwriter notes that "it is NOT aggressive, NOT pleading, no tough-guy or hero-in-the-movies. Just straightforward."

Robert met Gloria when he was out walking the Santa Monica beach and happened into a giant arena ballroom where a dance marathon was assembling. Outside the ballroom, President Hoover was still sitting in Washington and a lot of Americans were starving to death. Inside, spectators had paid twenty-five cents to watch and cheer a group of couples who were going to keep dancing until all but one couple had collapsed. "One couple, and only one, will waltz out of here over broken bodies and broken dreams carrying the Grand Prize of One Thousand Five Hundred Silver Dollars." They dance all day and they dance all night, with ten minute breaks every two hours. Contestants can go mad or die—and they do—but to remain eligible they have to keep moving. "No excuses, no explanations."

Why do it? You get fed. There is the chance that Hollywood talent scouts will pick you out for a future as a star. Or you're a couple and you don't have any money and you're expecting a baby in a few months. Or, like Robert, you're taking a walk along the Santa Monica beach and you wander in; a girl's partner has just been disqualified, and you find yourself being paired with her because you're an extra warm body in the place. You haven't really got anywhere to go, so you decide to stay on as half of Couple #67 and see what's going on and who she is. . . .

Gloria is "pretty, young, hungry, and essentially an outsider. She seems hard and hostile . . . compulsive. But . . . she is quite unpredictable, complex and strangely vulnerable . . . perhaps frightened." Gloria hasn't got anybody or anything going for her in the outside world, so she fights to stick it out to the end. Robert comes to feel himself her only friend in the world, so he sticks it out with her.

The dance marathon is cruel and violent. The master of ceremonies, Rocky Grazzo, bears the dancers no personal grudge, but he believes in the dance marathon as a show for the audience who come to "feel a little misery out there so they can feel a little better maybe." A sudden and brutal jogging race, eliminating the last three couples from the marathon, is just one of his "wrinkles to hypo up the crowd." Surviving this, as well as Rocky's sexual harassment and hundreds of hours of grueling exhaustion, Gloria discovers that the winners are to be charged all of Rocky's production expenses and will be left with very little of their prize money. She sees that it is all a sick joke, and it doesn't matter how much she endures because life is rigged against her from the start. She walks outside to the ocean, and Robert follows her. From her purse she pulls a gun.

The following two dialogues, which occur between Robert and Gloria during the opening night of the marathon, constitute a "getting-to-know-you-scene," but within some of the most extraordinary physical and psychological circumstances imaginable.

TIGHT ON ROBERT AND GLORIA

dancing. Then, as the tempo of the music slows again, they sag to a sort of two-step shuffle.

ROBERT: *(after beat)* Why California?

GLORIA: *(shrugs)* You don't freeze while you're starving. And there's the movies.

ROBERT: Oh, are you an actress?

GLORIA: I've done four atmosphere bits since I been here. I'd have done more except I can't get into Central Casting. They got it all sewed up.

ROBERT: Have you met anybody who can help you?

GLORIA: In this business how can you tell who'll help you?
One day you're an electrician and the next day you're a
producer. The only way I could ever get close to a big
shot would be to jump on the running board of his car.
Anyway, I don't know whether the men stars can help
me as much as the women stars. From what I've seen
lately I've been letting the wrong sex try and make me.

ROBERT: Oh . . .!?

GLORIA: You in the movies too?

ROBERT: Sort of. I was a dead French villager in "Fallen
Angels."

[SAILOR AND SHIRL
She beams . . . he bows. He takes her hand ceremoniously
and they begin slowly to dance off.]

FULL SHOT to TIGHTEN on GLORIA and ROBERT. They have
been looking off at SAILOR.

GLORIA: I should've learned to tap-dance.

SOUND of a large WAVE against the pilings below the pier.

ROBERT: Can you feel that?

GLORIA: What?

ROBERT: The ocean. (*indicates floor*) The waves . . . you
can feel them right through the floor. (*then*) You know,
even when you're a long ways away from the ocean, you
can still feel it sometimes.

GLORIA: (*looking around at the other couples*) Not where I
come from.

ROBERT: Where's that?

GLORIA: Ohh . . . around. Kansas. Texas mostly. Dallas.

ROBERT: That must've been nice.

GLORIA: (*swinging back to him*) Nice . . .?!

ROBERT: Well, I mean, I never been through there, but
that's the way it always seemed to me . . . like you
could look just about anywhere and see land . . . I mean
without anything set down on it.

GLORIA: Yeah! It's great. I'm a real sucker for dirt and cactus. That's how come I left.

[CECIL AND AGNES dance by, executing a meant-to-be-fancy twirl. GLORIA darts a hard, appraising, sidelong glance at AGNES.]

ROBERT: Why *did* you leave?

GLORIA looks back at him. A beat, then:

GLORIA: You ever sleep with a Syrian who chews tobacco?

ROBERT does a puzzled take.

GLORIA: Well, if anybody ever asks you, you can tell 'em there's no future in it.

ROBERT seems about to protest or change the subject, when AGNES' backside slams into GLORIA during another attempted twirl.

GLORIA: Hey! What d'you want, the whole floor?!

[CECIL: (*as he propels* AGNES *away*) Terribly sorry.]

GLORIA: (*looking after* AGNES) The way she's throwing it around, her feet'll last longer than her rear end. (*turns back*) He was a butcher.

ROBERT: Who?

GLORIA: The Syrian. How's that for the bottom of the barrel?

ROBERT: Hey, listen . . . I didn't mean to be personal. I was just . . . I didn't mean to be personal.

GLORIA: Yeah? Then why'd you ask?

ROBERT: Well . . . just to make conversation. I figure we're going to be stuck together for a long time, so I thought maybe it'd help the time go . . . if I talked some, I mean.

GLORIA: Don't strain anything for me.

ROBERT: (*hurt*) All right.

They continue to dance, but silently now . . . and with a sense of strained distance between them.

[FOLLOWING JAMES AND RUBY. Minimum of movement. RUBY shifts her weight slightly, and JAMES helps her to reposition herself.

JAMES: Okay?

RUBY: (*she smiles*) I hope I don't start lugging on you.

JAMES: You ain't ever lugged yet.

She nods, still smiling, but looks down to her swollen belly.
Then back to JAMES.

JAMES: Just keep thinkin' about those seven meals each day.

STARTING ON SAILOR AND SHIRL

and MOVING PAST MARIO and JACKIE on through CECIL and
AGNES . . . around ALICE and JOEL,] CAMERA comes to rest
on ROBERT and GLORIA. She realizes she has stepped a little
hard on him, but forcing herself to patch it over is something
else again. She cheats a couple of looks at him, then gestures
off toward the bandstand.

GLORIA: Some band, hunh? They probably pay 'em off in
     beer and peanuts.

ROBERT: Probably.

They dance another beat in strained silence.

GLORIA: (*one more try*) I thought maybe *you* came from
     Texas.

ROBERT: (*distant*) No.

CLOSEUP GLORIA

GLORIA: Oh, for crissake, stop sulking!!!

CLOSEUP ROBERT as his face suddenly opens into a wide,
warm grin.

ROBERT: I guess that's what I was doing, all right . . . I'm
     sorry.

GLORIA: Forget it . . . Anyway, you're right, we *are* stuck
     together. (*beat*) Where *are* you from, anyway?

ROBERT: Chicago. That's where I was born. But I lived once
     for a little while in Arkansas. After my father died.

GLORIA: I didn't like it much . . . Chicago. I tried it once,
     but all I could get was a job in a five-and-dime sellin'
     sheet music on commission. So I hitched back to Dallas.
     Boy, was that ever a mistake. At least in Chicago they
     got soup kitchens. In Dallas there's nothing. I mean

nothing! Finally I figured, what the hell, I might as well be in jail . . . let them take care of me . . . so I swiped somethin' from a store and made sure I got caught.

ROBERT: *(surprised at so much)* Jesus . . .

GLORIA: But the cop felt sorry for me and let me go . . . and anyway he didn't press charges . . . the Syrian. That's how I met him, he's the one I shoplifted from. *(beat)* I'll say one thing, I never ate so much in my life. Steak for breakfast.

ROBERT: How'd you stand it?

GLORIA: Steak . . .? Oh, the Syrian. *(beat, then directly to* ROBERT*)* I kept my eyes shut.

FIVE EASY PIECES

A Columbia Pictures presentation of a BBS Production. Producers, Bob Rafelson, Richard Wechsler. Director, Bob Rafelson. Screenplay by Adrien Joyce. Story by Bob Rafelson & Adrien Joyce. Executive Producer, Bert Schneider. Associate Producer, Harold Schneider. Director of Photography, Laszlo Kovacs. Film Editors, Christopher Holmes, Gerald Shepard. Interior Designer, Toby Rafelson. Sound Mixer, Charles Knight. Assistant Director, Sheldon Schrager. Color by MGM Laboratories. Running time, 96 minutes. 1970.

CAST

ROBERT EROICA DUPEA	Jack Nicholson
RAYETTE DIPESTO	Karen Black
CATHERINE VAN OOST	Susan Anspach
PARTITA DUPEA	Lois Smith
CARL FIDELIS DUPEA	Ralph Waite
NICHOLAS DUPEA	William Challee
ELTON	Billy "Green" Bush
STONEY	Fannie Flagg
SPICER	John Ryan
PALM APODACA	Helen Kallianiotes
TERRY GROUSE	Toni Basil
TWINKY	Marlena MacGuire
BETTY	Sally Ann Struthers

Robert Eroica Dupea's middle name comes from the title of a Beethoven symphony. Virtually everything that was valued in his up-bringing centered around classical music. It was expected that he would pursue a career as a concert soloist, as his brothers and his sister had. But Bobby just didn't have the "feeling" for it, and he has never really believed whatever approval he has received for his playing and endless practice. He watched his siblings deform their spirits to fit their father's mold, and he finally took off from the family home (on Roche Island off the coast of the state of Washington) to begin several years of a wandering pilgrimage in search of an authentic self.

When we meet Bobby, he is living in Southern California, working in oil fields and on construction sites. With his buddies, he turns on a roughneck dialect ("Arky talk"), and he outdoes everybody else at the kind of sexual braggadocio and crude flirting of the stereotypic hard-hatted good 'ole boy. Simmering just beneath is an anger at anything that constrains him. There are fairly regular explosions of insolence and rage, so he doesn't get to stay at any one job for too long. Or any one relationship. At the moment he is living with a waitress named Rayette, whose effusive blanketing love for him is suffocating. When he tries to withdraw, Rayette lavishes such emotional blackmail on him, in such huge dollops of corn-pone, that he gives in out of exhaustion. Rayette doesn't try to change him, beyond crooning for more love and attention; she accepts all the unpredictable violence of his personality as part of the package, and this, along with her sexual passion for him, keeps the relationship going. Though Bobby may be quicker than she is, and able to out-dodge her, she's got the staying power. He relies on it, if only to test it and champ against it. (Rayette: "Do you love me Bobby?" Bobby: "Well now, what do you think?")

Bobby's roots start to tug at him. His sister Tita tells him of the strokes that have crippled and silenced his father. He goes home, trying to leave Rayette behind in Los Angeles, but she won't let him go in peace without her. He takes her with him, but he deposits her in a motel on the mainland until he can feel out the situation. The family tensions and pressures have only been aggravated by his father's illness. Bobby is more restless than ever. (He is also faced with the devastating situation of a parent, whom he's always been angry at for not communicating with him, now unable *ever* to communicate with him.) The only person on whom he feels he could have some significant impact is Catherine, an advanced music student of his brother Carl. She is living in the family house. In the long hours while everyone else is either away or practicing, Bobby roams around the grounds and rooms, trying to find Catherine, corner her, seduce her. Although she is cool and subtly superior to him (perhaps *because* of it), he falls in love with her, but he is so invested in his own alienation that he finds it hard to connect with her beyond countering her remarks with suggestive one liners. (Catherine: "I love horses." Bobby: "Ladies usually do." Catherine: "They're quite beautiful." Bobby: "You want to put little boots on them. They want to bite you on the back of the neck.") Bobby and Catherine finally make love and seem to share something lovely, but she is more-or-less engaged to Bobby's brother, and Rayette suddenly shows up. Catherine explains that the real problem for them lies with Bobby himself: "What would it come to? If a person has no respect for themselves, no love of themselves, their work, their friends or family or *something*—why should they *ask* for love in return? How can they expect it?" At the end of *Five Easy Pieces*, Bobby is once again alone and on the move.

In the scene below, Bobby has come to visit Tita, a concert pianist, who is in Los Angeles for a recording date. The sound engineers must repeatedly stop the session to remind Tita that she is audibly singing—painfully off-key—along with her own playing. Bobby enters and stands outside the glass booth with the engineers, looking in at his sister. He is uncomfortable with the impatient contempt they are evidencing toward Tita, but her oppressed, temperamental behavior seems to warrant it. The engineer calls in through the microphone that "Bobby is here," and she puts on her glasses, smiling happily at the sight of him.

(*Note:* Although he has no lines, the errand boy's entrance precipitates some significant "business" and should be included for the fullest playing of the scene.)

SCENE 1

INTERIOR SOUND STUDIO—DAY

BOBBY and TITA embrace.

BOBBY: Hi, Tita . . .

TITA: Oh my goodness . . .

They break from it and regard one another. TITA covers her mouth with her hand, and is certainly about to cry.

TITA: Robert Eroica . . .

BOBBY: Now, Tita . . .

She immediately drops her hand, tries to exercise some control.

TITA: No, I'm not . . . (*She breathes deeply, exhales, then says with assurance*) I'm not.

BOBBY: That's good.

TITA cries. She sits on the piano bench, her face buried in her arms which are resting atop the piano. BOBBY hovers help-lessly behind her, softly patting her on the back, and glancing with some embarrassment toward the booth.

TITA: (*Muffled*) I just can't look at you . . .

BOBBY: Am I that bad?

TITA raises her head up.

TITA: Oh Robert it's not you. It's me . . . You look wonder-ful. Very handsome, as always, and so healthy . . . I'm so . . . (*She starts to break down again*) I just can't seem to look at you right now . . .

BOBBY gently pushes her head back down onto her arms:

BOBBY: Don't then . . .

Behind him, the ERRAND BOY enters the studio with two paper cups and approaches.

TITA: (*Muffled*) You always do this to me.

BOBBY: I don't mean to . . .

The boy hands him the cups and leaves.

BOBBY: (*To him*) Thanks. (*To* TITA) Tita, here's your tea.

TITA: (*Muffled*) Thank you.

BOBBY sets her cup down on the edge of the piano.

TITA'S eyes raise from hiding. She sees the cup and immedi-ately shapes up.

TITA: Oh, don't put it on there . . .

She quickly picks it up, and wipes beneath it with her hand.

BOBBY: Sorry.

Apparently recovered, she begins running one of her hands over the surface of the piano.

TITA: Do you know, this is a very *old* CD 312 . . .

BOBBY: No kidding.

TITA: It has absolutely no objectionable idiosyncrasies . . .

BOBBY reaches down and plays some brief flourish. TITA watches him with devoted fascination. BOBBY stops, shakes his hand out, from its immediate cramping.

BOBBY: Very nice.

TITA: Now Robert . . . I have to talk seriously with you . . .

BOBBY: (*Interrupts*) Everybody's still living up on the island . . .

TITA: Well Herbert is mostly on the mainland because of the orchestra. So at the moment, there's really just Daddy, Carl and myself . . . (*An afterthought*) and Van Oost . . .

BOBBY: Who's Van Oost?

TITA is not that fond of this subject, though the manifestations of that are subtle.

TITA: Catherine . . . She's studying with Carl. Piano.

BOBBY: Carl's a fiddler . . . What's he doing as a piano coach?

TITA: Oh see, Robert, how many things have happened that you don't know anything about. You have to stop disappearing from the face of the earth like this, not getting in touch for months and months.

BOBBY: (*Interrupts*) What about Carl?

TITA: I'm not talking about Carl. Carl's alright. It's just that eleven months ago he got on his bicycle to go down to the Post Office in the village and on the way he crashed straight into a jeep coming up the road and strained his neck . . .

BOBBY laughs.

BOBBY: Strained his *neck*?

TITA laughs.

TITA: It's not funny. He *permanently sprained* his neck, and since then it's been extremely painful for him— (*She demonstrates, turning her neck and lowering her chin on an imaginary violin*) to tuck the violin.

BOBBY: Crashes into a jeep and totals his neck.

TITA: He was despondent. Despondent. Until Daddy persuaded him to coach. I want to talk to you about something, Robert, can't you sit down?

BOBBY: (*Not sitting*) Yeah. What?

TITA: I want you to come up there, come home with me, will you?

BOBBY: What for?

TITA: Because I think you should . . . Because Daddy is very ill . . .

BOBBY: Oh, what's . . . what . . . ?

TITA: He's had two strokes.

For some reason, BOBBY immediately begins looking for a place to set the paper cup down:

BOBBY: (*Over again*) Oh . . .

Instead, he sits down on a chair next to the piano bench.

BOBBY: (*Over above*) Well . . . How is he?

TITA: He's not . . . They feel maybe he might not recover from it . . . They said he'll either fade slowly, or he might have another . . .

BOBBY: (*Interrupting*) Don't tell me about it.

BOBBY drops his head into his hand. She watches him a moment.

TITA: How do you think I feel? It's been very hard on me.

BOBBY says nothing.

TITA: I'm breaking down constantly . . . Carl's really not that helpful.

BOBBY: I wouldn't be either.

TITA: But don't you think it's right that you should see him, at least once . . .

[The 1st ENGINEER breaks in on the microphone.

1ST ENGINEER: (OFFSCREEN) Miss Dupea. We're ready if you are.]

TITA: (*To booth*) Just a minute, please . . .

She looks back to BOBBY, repeats.

TITA: Don't you think it's right that you should see him Robert?

BOBBY: Yeah, I guess I should . . .

TITA: I'm going back up tonight. Will you come with me?

BOBBY stands up.

BOBBY: No. I think I'd like to drive up . . . Maybe take a look through Canada, after . . . (*He emphasizes to her*) I'm not going to stay up there that long, Tita, maybe a week . . .

TITA: I know.

BOBBY glances at booth.

BOBBY: Well . . . ?

TITA: What's wrong with you Robert, I wish I knew.

BOBBY: Nothing's wrong with me.

TITA: Then is it us?

BOBBY: No . . . I'd better let you get on with it.

TITA: I mean, what's wrong that you can't stay any place very long . . .

BOBBY: There's nothing wrong in that, Tita.

TITA: It's unusual, though, isn't it?

BOBBY: Well, in that, I am unusual . . .

He smiles at her, leans down and kisses her cheek.

TITA: Can't I walk you out?

BOBBY: Sure.

TITA grabs her jacket from a chair, and puts it on as she addresses booth.

TITA: I'll be right back, in two minutes . . .

[1ST ENGINEER: (OFFSCREEN) It's been a half hour already, Miss Dupea . . .]

She smiles at BOBBY, adjusting her jacket.

TITA: (*Low*) They hate me, I feel.

BOBBY: I think maybe you better stay, then.

TITA: Oh I want to talk with you about so many things Robert.

BOBBY: Well I'll be seeing you in a couple of days won't I?

TITA: I'm so glad . . .

BOBBY: Me too . . .

They embrace once more, and then BOBBY pulls away.

BOBBY: Bye now . . .

He walks to the studio door and goes out.

SCENE 2

This scene takes place in the family home on Roche Island. Bobby finally makes his mark with Catherine. She has been gone for the day. He has been stuck playing ping-pong with his brother Carl, whom he can outplay and outwit so easily that Bobby is getting mean and dangerously bored. He heads up to Catherine's empty room and is looking idly at her possessions when he hears her car pull in behind the house. He trots downstairs to meet her.

(*Note*: Although the dialogue plays continuously in this second scene, the action moves through several locales in the house, and they will have to be condensed carefully if the flow of activity from kitchen to music room to bedroom is to make sense in a single playing area. The scene can perhaps take place in a large bedroom/study, which contains a piano and which has an adjoining bathroom.)

INTERIOR DUPEA HOUSE—DAY

BOBBY comes downstairs, and moves to kitchen.

INTERIOR KITCHEN—DAY

CATHERINE is putting away the groceries. She also has some fresh flowers. BOBBY enters.

CATHERINE: Hi.

BOBBY: Hello.

CATHERINE: (*nodding towards game*) I've got winners.

BOBBY: They're hard to come by.

CATHERINE: What's the matter?

BOBBY: Nothing.

She exits kitchen with flowers. BOBBY follows her to music room.

INTERIOR MUSIC ROOM—DAY

CATHERINE arranges flowers in vase on piano.

CATHERINE: With the possible exception of fresh orange juice—and music, of course, there's probably nothing in the world I adore more than flowers. Oh, yes, massages. Massages, also. Aren't these marigolds beautiful!

BOBBY: I don't know the names of flowers. Or of anything else, for that matter. Breeds of dogs, cats, wines . . .

CATHERINE: That's a shame, really. Lovely things have lovely names. Robert, would you do something for me . . . so long as you're here.

BOBBY: Massage you? Sure.

CATHERINE: (*laughing*) No. I'm feeling quite relaxed really. No, I'd like you to play something. Now.

BOBBY: How's about instead I squeeze up some juice.

CATHERINE: Please.

[TITA enters hallway.

TITA: (OFFSCREEN) Catherine. Your game.]

CATHERINE: (*softly, to Bobby*) Will you?

[TITA: (OFFSCREEN) Catherine?]

A pause. The door SLAMS OFFSCREEN.] BOBBY moves to the piano. CATHERINE shuts out any sound interference by closing the door. Then she takes a seat. BOBBY plays a scale; shakes his head as if this were a laughable idea. Then, getting no relief from CATHERINE, he plays.

BOBBY concludes the Chopin, with a series of meaningfully

spaced chords. His hands linger on the final one, before he slowly removes them to his lap. He glances over at CATHERINE. Her face is deeply serious.

CATHERINE: That was beautiful, Robert. I'm so surprised.

BOBBY looks away from her.

BOBBY: Thank you.

CATHERINE: I'm really very moved by the way you . . .

BOBBY suddenly drops his head into his hands, covering his face.

CATHERINE: What's wrong?

BOBBY shakes his head in his hands, still hiding his face. CATHERINE rises, sets her package on the piano and moves beside BOBBY, placing a hand on his shoulder.

CATHERINE: What's the matter, Robert?

He lifts his face out of his hands and looks at her. It is apparent that the expression he is restraining is laughter.

BOBBY: Excuse me.

CATHERINE: Oh . . .

BOBBY: I'm sorry.

CATHERINE: What's so amusing?

BOBBY: Nothing . . . nothing. It's just that that's the easiest piece I could remember. I think I first played it when I was about eight years old. In this room. The whole family gathered. Plus their friends. Plus people from town. I was all got up in this suit and bow tie. If I remember correctly . . . that time I let go a resounding fart at the end.

CATHERINE: Can't you understand? . . . It was the feeling I was affected by.

BOBBY: I didn't have any feeling.

CATHERINE: You had no inner feeling while you were playing?

BOBBY: None.

CATHERINE: Oh. I guess I must have been supplying it.

She moves to go. BOBBY rises.

BOBBY: Well, perhaps if you supplied more—it might rub off. Who knows. (*punch drunk*) I might even make a comeback.

CATHERINE: I doubt it, Robert.

BOBBY: Oh, I could get interested.

CATHERINE: Well, I couldn't.

She exits. BOBBY hesitates. He sees CATHERINE head up the stairs. In a moment he turns to the piano, removes a single flower from the vase, then exits.

INTERIOR KITCHEN—DAY

He goes to ice box, gets something out.

INTERIOR STAIRCASE—DAY

He runs up.

INTERIOR OUTSIDE CATHERINE'S ROOM—DAY

He knocks.

CATHERINE: (OFFSCREEN) Who is it?

INTERIOR CATHERINE'S ROOM—DAY.

CATHERINE is in a robe, pinning up her hair, preparing for a bath we can hear running. He enters, an orange in one hand; a flower in the other. Then, like an Italian tenor:

BOBBY: (*singing Mozart*) La che darem La Mano . . .

CATHERINE: Very amusing. Now if you'll excuse me— I'm running a bath.

BOBBY throws flower and orange on bed.

BOBBY: What does it have to be with you—grim and serious?

CATHERINE: Look, you played, I was honestly moved— then you made me feel embarrassed about responding to you. It wasn't necessary.

BOBBY: Yeah, it was. Look what happened. I faked a little Chopin—you faked a big response.

CATHERINE: I don't think that's accurate.

BOBBY: Up 'til now all I've been getting is meaningful looks at the dinner table and tentative suggestions about the day after tomorrow.

CATHERINE: I haven't been conscious of giving you very
        particular "looks". As for the day after tomorrow, it is the
        day after tomorrow and I *am* unfortunately, seeing you
        . . . excuse me.

She goes past him to dresser, searching for oils. He moves
closer, begins aggressively lifting up bottles.

BOBBY: What the hell do you want, anyway?

CATHERINE: Some bath oil.

BOBBY: Oh, how about this one! Avocado. (*and another*) Do
        you want this one? (*and another*) Maybe some jasmine?
        (*another*) What about this one? What about some musk?
        . . .

CATHERINE: What are you doing?

BOBBY: What are *you* doing? Screwing around with this
        crap . . .

CATHERINE: I really don't care for your language, I don't
        find it charming . . .

BOBBY: It's not. It's direct.

CATHERINE: Well then, let me be the same.

She walks away from him, to the night stand beside her bed,
to where some cigarettes lie. She picks them up and takes a
cigarette from the package.

CATHERINE: I'd like you to leave so I can take a bath. Is that
        direct?

BOBBY says nothing. CATHERINE holds the cigarette in her
hand, without a match available to light it, as he moves over
to the door. He does not go out. He closes the door, and
turns to her.

She looks at him a moment, then lays the cigarette back on
the night stand.

CATHERINE: I can't take you seriously, Robert . . . (*pause*)
        The way you live your life, what you say, or coming up
        here like this . . . You're not a serious person, by your
        own admission. That may be interesting, but it doesn't
        interest me.

He starts across to her, very angry.

BOBBY: Oh, "serious" . . . that's what's important, being serious?

CATHERINE: Yes . . .

BOBBY: Okay then, let's be serious.

He pushes her backwards, forcing her to sit on the bed.

BOBBY: (*over above*) Sit down . . .

CATHERINE: (*also angry*) Don't do that Robert.

BOBBY: Shut up! You and I have a different idea about what "serious" is. You think it's making a choice, don't you? *Deciding*. You want to play, going at it eight hours a day and taking hot baths. Let me tell you what serious is . . . when you *inherit* it from a father . . . who only responds to your *musical* accomplishment, and *nothing* else. Then what you get is my sister Tita, who has more ability than anyone in this house, and no assurance—*none*—and as a result, is an incomplete, totally unhappy woman. And you've got Carl who has the conceit of assurance, without any notable ability, so he coaches somebody else to do what he can't. The only serious musician that isn't faking something in the family is Herbert, and you can't talk to the man about anything in life that goes on beyond the top row of the orchestra . . .

CATHERINE: That's not true . . .

BOBBY: (*overlapping her*) And if you want to complete your judgment on me, I came last into this predetermined heritage . . . and I worked at it every day . . . from the age of three to the age of twenty-eight, hating it . . . playing without assurance, without ability, without satisfaction. And their approval, their applause, their enthusiasm—or yours— doesn't mean a crap to me. *I* don't feel it!

CATHERINE says nothing for a moment, then:

CATHERINE: No inner feeling?

BOBBY: Absolutely none.

CATHERINE pauses again.

CATHERINE: About anything?

BOBBY: About anything.

Another long pause, in which she looks intently at him. Then she lies back against the pillows, silently watching his face for any change in the resolute statement. It does not become apparent. It moves her to make a soft challenge:

CATHERINE: I don't believe you . . .

He moves onto the bed beside her, kisses her, begins to make love to her, accompanied by the continuing SOUNDS of TITA and SPICER playing table tennis.

KLUTE

A Warner Bros. presentation. Producer & Director, Alan J. Pakula. Co-Producer, David Lange. Screenplay by Andy Lewis & Dave Lewis. Director of Photography, Gordon Willis. Film Editor, Carl Lerner. Art Director, George Jenkins. Sound, Chris Newman. Executive Associate Producer, C. Kenneth Deland. Music, Michael Small. Assistant Director, William Gerrity. Panavision, Technicolor. Running time, 114 minutes. 1970.

CAST

BREE DANIEL	Jane Fonda
JOHN KLUTE	Donald Sutherland
PETER CABLE	Charles Cioffi
FRANK LIGOURIN	Roy R. Scheider
ARLYN PAGE	Dorothy Tristan
TRINA	Rita Gam
PSYCHIATRIST	Vivian Nathan
TRASK	Nathan George
MR. GOLDFARB	Morris Strassberg
BERGER	Barry Snider
ACTOR'S AGENT	Anthony Holland
SUGARMAN	Richard Shull
HOLLY GRUNEMANN	Betty Murray
GOLDFARB'S SECRETARY	Jean Stapleton
TOM GRUNEMANN	Robert Milli

In the average American town of Tuscarora, family man Tom
Grunemann disappears. A letter is discovered in the paper
shredder of the company that employs him. It is supposedly
signed by him and dated the day before his disappearance. It
is obscene and violent. It is addressed to Bree Daniel, a
high-class call girl who lives in New York City, where Tom
was regularly sent on business. Over a year of investigation
reveals nothing further. A friend of the family, John Klute,
instinctively knows that Tom is dead, and he goes to New
York to find out the truth of how and why.

   Klute moves into the basement apartment of Bree's building so that he can tape her phone conversations and follow
her. She is a bright, bitter, nervous young woman. She tells
him, "Look, I hate everybody; and I'm sorry for everybody;
and I'm scared all the time." A while back, she was set up by
a rival and was almost killed by the client. Since then, except
for some standing appointments, she has been trying to make
it in the straight life as an actress. She has only contempt for
Klute when he comes nosing around into her life. In the
dangerous world of professional crime, sex and drugs, Klute
is a comical figure of plodding integrity. His manner "exhibits
an absolute, untheatrical care and competence." Klute knows
that Tom neither wrote that letter nor was the psychopathic
client. As he closes in on the truth of Grunemann's disappearance, Bree's life is endangered, and she comes to need
Klute to protect her. She cannot tolerate her own vulnerability to Klute. For Bree, being a call girl is a lucrative defense
against being loved by anyone, and she uses sex to humiliate.
In his quiet, methodical way, Klute falls in love with her.

   In the following scene, Klute has not yet fallen in love with
Bree. He has just revealed who he is and what he has been
doing. She is enraged and tries to get the phone tapes from
him. Although he is impervious to her manipulations, he has
an appreciation of what lies beneath them.

   (Note: The following can be played as one continuous scene
in Bree's apartment. Klute's chase happens off stage, leaving
Bree with a "private moment" until his return.)

EXTERIOR BREE'S BROWNSTONE—NIGHT

Near the entrance, outside the door to KLUTE'S apartment below. We open on BREE. She shouts angrily, miserably—

BREE: Whyn't you just cut out?

We WIDEN TO INCLUDE KLUTE. Now she begins to get it. He turns, opens door to his room below. She comes slowly down steps.

INTERIOR KLUTE'S ROOM—NIGHT

She steps in the door, looks slowly around at his various appurtenances—the bed, the necktie over the mirror, etc. —and then, the tape recorder and then the stack of tape boxes.

BREE: (softly, venomously) Oh you bastard.

But then she adjusts—a frightened but matter-of-fact hooker.

BREE: Is it the shakedown hon? You picked a loser, I just don't have it.

KLUTE: No, I'm look—

BREE: (vehemently again) If I was taking calls full time would I be living in this kip? I'd be back on Park Avenue; I could support the whole National Guard!

KLUTE: (gestures upward) Could I ask some questions?

BREE: Or you'll get me shoved back in the brig you mean; another month with the bull-dykes.

She seems to have expressed it; the balance of power. She turns, goes out, heads upstairs. KLUTE unhurriedly takes up his folder of notes, then follows.

INTERIOR BREE'S APARTMENT—NIGHT

BREE disposes her belongings. KLUTE moves to table. There is a group of plants on the table that long since died of neglect. He notices them and the disorganization of the room without comment, opens his folder, rummages for the photographs.

BREE: (exasperatedly) Look, I told the police everything: I don't even remember the schlub!

KLUTE doesn't respond. KLUTE sets out a photograph for her to look at.

INSERT: PHOTOGRAPH, TOM GRUNEMANN

KLUTE, BREE

BREE: They showed me that one. I understand it's Grunemann, but I told them, I just don't remember.

KLUTE tosses down a second photograph.

INSERT: SECOND PHOTOGRAPH, TOM GRUNEMANN, ELAINE
GRUNEMANN, two daughters.

BREE, KLUTE

BREE: (*cool*) A family sort of man.

KLUTE grunts, meaning 'yes'. She echoes his grunt, meaning
we don't know what. He tosses another—

INSERT: WIDE PHOTOGRAPH, COMPANY PICNIC

An everybody-over-here, fellow-employees, sort of picture.
(Including the figures of Streiger and Cable among many
others, male and female.) The usual impedimenta—picnic
baskets, balls, bats, a held sign:'Tole-American'. KLUTE'S finger indicates—

KLUTE: (OFFSCREEN) —Tom again.

KLUTE, BREE—She looks at the picture briefly, at him questioningly.

KLUTE: Company outing or picnic or something like that.

BREE: Isn't that sweet. (*then*) Well it could be any one of
them bubi; I get to see them all.

She separates from KLUTE, around the table (but remains
standing, restless). KLUTE puts photo aside, prepares to take
notes.

BREE: (*pleadingly*) Look—please—will you just try to get it
from my side? A year ago. I was in the life full time. I was
living on Park with leather furniture and a million
dresses. Then they dropped on me, the fuzz, they caged
me—they started asking me about a man, some man, I'm
supposed to have seen a year before *that*. Two years ago,
two. He could be in Yemen!

She waits for KLUTE to respond—he doodles permissively on
his pad of paper—she goes on.

BREE: A name. Grunemann. Nothing. And they showed me

pictures like this and *they* meant nothing. Then they asked me, well had I been getting letters, from someone out there in Cabbageville—

KLUTE: —Tuscarora—

BREE: All right, yes, I had been. Those sick, wild letters— I'm watching you, gonna follow you, gonna punish you, kill you et cetera. Well, they said, all right that's Grunemann. So try to remember when you and he— when—well I don't know, there was that dumper once, he sounded like that dumper— (*explains*) dumpers: they get their kicks beating you up. A man hired me once, then tried to really kill me—*that'd* be about two years ago.

Without warning she wheels to the open window and shouts out full-voiced—both startling and somewhat intriguing KLUTE—

BREE: (*shouts*) OK Tommy-baby, Allie-Allie-in-free kid, I got the gumdrops.

Turns around again, to KLUTE. Cheerfully—

BREE: You remind me of my uncle.

KLUTE: What? (*then*—) What do you remember about that— dumper?

BREE: Nothing. Except he wasn't kidding. Usually it's a fakeout, you probably know. They pretend to tie you up, and you wear a dress with a cloth belt, and they pretend to whip you or you—(*beat*) Hell it's their money. I'll hang from the shower rod and whistle Maytime. Except this guy was really tripped out on it; he—

KLUTE: But you can't say that dumper was Tom Grunemann.

BREE: I can't say he was anybody!

A brief pause. KLUTE sorts his notes. She may take it that he's packing to leave—hopes so anyhow. For an instant we see the undefended girl underneath.

BREE: So—OK—that's all?

Then again she changes manner—remembering a practical problem, approaching it as a matter-of-fact hooker.

BREE: Well could I have them back now hon?—those tape recordings you've got downstairs—OK?—and if you want, you can have a good time and I'll have a good time and—

KLUTE: What about everything since?

She draws back again. Up to now she's been reasonably on top of things. Starting now we see her driven toward the things she'd *really* rather not talk about—and increasingly more shaken.

KLUTE: *(prompts)* Everything that's happened *since* Tom Grunemann disappeared. The phone calls and the—

BREE: Just phone calls, right? They ring, you answer, they don't say anything, just blank. Kids getting kicks. Burglars looking for an empty apartment. I mean there's nothing that proves—

KLUTE: What about the other things you've reported? —*(consulting notes)*—being followed on the—

BREE: *(interrupts—awkwardly—)* Look—I'm sorry—I've led everybody wrong. I mean yes, I get those feelings, but that's just me, that's just feelings. *(beat)* I'm sure this will amuse you; I'm scared of the dark. And sometimes I get shook up, I *hear* people or—well, I'll come out in the morning and think someone's been prying at my mailbox, or there's a little—trash outside my door and I wonder if someone left it there for—do you see?—things other people wouldn't even *notice*. Well that's not real, it's just nerves; it's got nothing to do with—

The PHONE RINGS. She startles. Then approaches with some difficulty—but then answers with complete calm in her Smith-girl voice.

BREE: Bree Daniel. *(listens. Brightly)* Oh yes, Ted Carlin, how *is* Ted? *(listens)* Oh, well, thank you very much but maybe the *next* time you're in town? *(listens)* Well I just love Ted and I'd love to meet you—you have a very nice voice—but I just—*(listens, grows impatient)* Well I'm having a chat with a very nice cop. Actually not a real cop; he's a private inves—

A BUZZING from the phone; the connection abruptly broken. She hangs up.

KLUTE: Is that how you get most of your dates? Someone gives your name to someone else?

BREE: Most of them.

KLUTE: Is that how you met the Dumper?—Someone else gave—

BREE: How would I *remember*?

KLUTE: How else do you meet them? Pimps? (*a beat*)

BREE: (*patient*) You're very square. Pimps don't get you dates, cookie; they just take the money.

KLUTE takes up the slip of paper previously given him by Trask. In the same manner as before—

KLUTE: I have some names the police gave me. Frank Ligourin. Will you tell me what—

BREE: (*trembling*) Look, I'm sure *this'll* amuse you too. I'm trying to get away from all that.

KLUTE: What about the old gentleman the other night, Mr. Faber?

She freezes again, looking at him.

BREE: (*savagely*) You saw that, goddamn you? You *saw* it? He's seventy. His wife's dead. He started cutting garments at fourteen. His whole life, he's maybe had a week's vacation, I'm all he has and he never, never touches me, and what harm in it, what—(*She chokes— then goes on*)—Klute, tell me, what's *your* bag? Are you a talker, or a button man or a doubler, or maybe you like them very young—children—or get your chest walked around with high-heeled shoes, or have us watch you tinkle? Or—

KLUTE: (*under*)—OK—

BREE: —You want to wear women's clothes, or you get off ripping things—

She grabs up the company picture, raging on—

BREE: —you perverted hypocrite square bastards,

KLUTE: OK.

Something in his inflection—very slight—cautions her. She falls silent as suddenly as she began. Then cheerfully—

BREE: Gee I hope this doesn't make my cold any worse.

KLUTE: Tell me about Frank Ligourin.

BREE: (*casual, pleasant*) Mm? Oh, he was my old man. We broke up.

She wanders away toward a bureau. Her shirt seems to itch her; she scratches her ribs. Then opens drawer, takes out a different shirt as—

KLUTE: When? (*beat*) When did you and Ligourin break up?

She pulls off her shirt, unhooks her brassiere and discards it, apparently quite un-self-conscious. KLUTE reacts; then, carefully maintaining his cool—

KLUTE: Mind not doing that?

She turns to him in total innocence, holding the shirt rather carelessly in front of her—a new attack.

BREE: What? This?

KLUTE: —OK?

BREE: (*ingenuously*) I thought you could trick me for those tapes. Don't you get lonely in that little green room? Or let me get you someone; I have terrific friends, wild.

KLUTE: No thanks.

At this point—or about this point—KLUTE takes note of something. A little above her. He grows more watchful, but containing it carefully. We don't understand the change in his manner—or even notice; she doesn't.

BREE: (*in mock dismay*) Gee. I've had men pay two hundred dollars for me—here, you're turning down a freebie. (*pause*) You can get a perfectly good dishwasher for that.

He has risen, is approaching her slowly—carrying his notes as if to check something. She is hopeful again—

BREE: You've changed your mind? You *do* want to play?

KLUTE: (*quietly, steadily*) I don't want you to look up. There's someone on the skylight.

She gasps, terrified—immediately—almost beyond control. He taps the pencil on his notes.

KLUTE: Easy—pretend you're looking here—(*more insistently*)—here.

She manages to take hold of a corner of the notes, trembling. He goes on—

KLUTE: Now I'm going to walk around—you just keep talking, straight through, *straight* through.

He strolls away from her. His destination is the area of the
door—*out* of view from the skylight—from where he can
head for the roof. But he doesn't head that way directly—
first takes a turn in another direction, his bearing casual.

KLUTE: (*prompting*) Tell me about acting—what are you
doing tomorrow—where do you go?

BREE: (*manages, barely*) I go on rounds.

KLUTE: Rounds, what are they?—don't—watch—me, keep
talking.

BREE: You go see agents—or Equity calls, open casting calls.
And ad agencies—commercials—you don't get work, you
just go around.

KLUTE has strolled out of view from above—instantly flattens
himself against the wall, eases the door open, about to slip
and charge. As BREE labors on—

BREE: And they're always polite—show people—they say
thank you very much. You lie there covered with blood,
smiling, they say—

[INTERIOR LANDING AND LADDER TO ROOF—NIGHT

FOOTSTEPS across the roof above, as the watcher discovers
KLUTE'S ruse. KLUTE opens the door—climbs ladder to roof.

EXTERIOR ROOFTOPS—NIGHT

KLUTE out, looking around.

EXTERIOR ROOFTOPS—PAST KLUTE TO FLEEING FIGURE— NIGHT

The FIGURE—the man—scissoring over the low walls where
one brownstone joins another. KLUTE gives chase—over ridg-
es, past water tanks, oddments of roof furniture—

EXTERIOR SEVERAL ROOFTOPS BEYOND—NIGHT

The FIGURE races to a roof door disappearing into abandoned
building.

INTERIOR STAIRWELL ABANDONED BUILDING

CAMERA FOLLOWS KLUTE as he cautiously makes his way down
the stairwell of the boarded up old brownstone. He gets to

the first floor. He can see no exit in the building. He opens door that leads to a narrow staircase into the cellar.

CELLAR ABANDONED BROWNSTONE

It is as black as a dungeon and as low. He lights a match, but sees no one. There is a sound of movement coming from the floor above. He runs up the steps to the floor above and sees a very faint light coming through one of the closed apartment doors. Carefully takes out a gun and then with one quick movement he breaks through the door.

INTERIOR ABANDONED APARTMENT

The walls, ceiling, floors are entirely covered with crudely painted psychedelic signs and sayings. The room is lighted by some candles stuck in bottles. Sitting on a blanket on the floor are several teenaged boys and girls having a pot party. They have obviously made a clubhouse for themselves in the abandoned house. It is a moot point whether they or KLUTE is more stunned at the sight that faces them. He puts his gun away in embarrassment. Again he has been made to feel like an awkward peeping tom in this hidden world of the city.

INTERIOR CELLAR ABANDONED BUILDING

CAMERA wanders restlessly through the blackness and stops at a pinpoint of light coming through a low door. CAMERA goes through opening into long narrow furnace room with the ceiling so low that an ordinary man could not stand up. We hear the sound of breathing. CAMERA follows the sound through the darkness revealing a sweaty man huddled in the corner looking like some strange animal from a painting by Bosch. It is CABLE.]

INTERIOR BREE'S APARTMENT—NIGHT

BREE has wrapped herself in the quilt—standing up against a corner shivering, immobilized. We hear KLUTE'S FOOTSTEPS descending—she flinches—he enters.

KLUTE: I couldn't get him.

He sees her condition.

KLUTE: (gently) It's all right.

He reaches to touch her—she quails away from him.

BREE: Well do you think it was *him*?

KLUTE: What do *you* think?

BREE: Can't you *get* him?

KLUTE: Maybe, if you tell me the things you haven't.

BREE: (*pause*) You asked me where I got that date with the dumper—Frank sent me on it.

KLUTE: Do you know where he got the dumper?

BREE: He never told me.

KLUTE: Well, let's go down and ask him.

CARNAL KNOWLEDGE

A Joseph E. Levine presentation of an Avco Embassy release. Producer & Director, Mike Nichols. Executive Producer, Joseph E. Levine. Associate Producer, Clive Reed. Screenplay by Jules Feiffer. Director of Photography, Giuseppe Rotunno. Film Editor, Sam O'Steen. Production Designer, Richard Sylbert. Art Director, Robert Luthardt. Sound, Lawrence O. Jost. Assistant Director, Tim Zinnemann. Panavision, Technicolor. Running time, 97 minutes. 1971.

CAST

JONATHAN	Jack Nicholson
SANDY	Art Garfunkel
SUSAN	Candice Bergen
BOBBIE	Ann-Margret
LOUISE	Rita Moreno
CINDY	Cynthia O'Neal
JENNIFER	Carol Kane

We first meet Jonathan and Sandy as college roommates at Amherst in the 1940s, when they are both virgins, wondering about the relationship between love and sex. During the course of the film, they stagger through the sexual revolutions, double standards, and chauvinisms of the changing decades. (The film was released in 1971, just prior to the years of great momentum in the women's liberation movement.)

Jonathan's bitter and distorted sexism leads him to loneliness and eventual impotence. Sandy attempts the more con-

ventional forms and phrases of marriage, divorce, and then
living with a "love teacher" half his age; but he seems the
same bewildered, self-conscious guy through it all. The in-
terplay of Jonathan's aggressive cynicism and Sandy's aggressive shlumpiness creates a dynamic that continues to connect
and interest them in each other long after they've come to
disapprove of each other. This dynamic is evident in the
following two dialogues between them during their Amherst
days.

(*Note:* The following two dialogues may be played through
as one scene. The girl they are discussing is Susan, who will
eventually marry and divorce Sandy, all without his ever
knowing that she and Jonathan lost their virginities together.)

SCENE 1

EXTERIOR AMHERST CAMPUS—NIGHT

JONATHAN and SANDY are walking down the street that leads
to their dorm. Fall leaves cover the ground.

JONATHAN: And then what?

SANDY: She told me to take my hand off her breast.

JONATHAN: And then what?

SANDY: I said I didn't want to.

JONATHAN: And then what?

SANDY: She said how could it be fun for me when she didn't
like it.

JONATHAN: (*Disgusted*) Jesus!

SANDY: So I said, I thought you liked me.

JONATHAN: Yeah?

SANDY: And she said, I like you for other reasons.

JONATHAN: Other reasons?!

SANDY: So I told her how I really needed this.

JONATHAN: What did you tell her?

SANDY: You know—that it was my first time.

JONATHAN: Your first time what? What did you say exactly?

SANDY: I don't remember exactly—that she's the first girl I ever tried to feel up.

JONATHAN: You told her that?

SANDY: Was it a mistake?

JONATHAN shrugs.

JONATHAN: I wouldn't.

SANDY: Then she got nicer to me.

JONATHAN: What do you mean, nicer?

SANDY: She put my hand on her breast.

JONATHAN: You mean you put it on and she left it.

SANDY: No, she picked it up and put it on.

JONATHAN: She picked up your hand like this—

Mimes motion with his own hand.

JONATHAN: —and put it on like this?

Puts hand on his own breast.

SANDY: That's right. So I didn't know what to think.

JONATHAN leers.

JONATHAN: You didn't, huh?

SANDY: I mean from just wanting to be friends, she's suddenly getting pretty aggressive.

JONATHAN: And then what?

SANDY: I asked her if she was a virgin.

JONATHAN: (*Laughs*) You're kidding!

SANDY: Was that a mistake?

JONATHAN shrugs.

SANDY: Anyhow, she is.

JONATHAN: *She* says. So now you got what? One hand, or two hands, on her tits?

SANDY: By this time she's put the other hand on her other one.

JONATHAN: She put *both* hands on?

SANDY nods.

JONATHAN: *Two* hands?

SANDY nods.

SANDY: So I said, what are you gonna do with *your* hands?

JONATHAN (*laughs*): You didn't say that.

SANDY (*pleased*): It just came out!

JONATHAN: Then what?

SANDY: She . . . let me see if I got this right—yeah—she unzipped my fly.

JONATHAN: Bullshit artist!

He slaps his hands together.

JONATHAN: And then what?

A spreading grin from SANDY.

JONATHAN: *Then what?!*

SANDY: She did it.

JONATHAN: Did *what?*

SANDY makes a hand motion indicating masturbation.

JONATHAN: Bullshit artist!

SANDY shakes his head, grinning.

JONATHAN: She really did *that?*

SANDY is virtually jumping up and down in excitement. He and JONATHAN begin to giggle. The giggle explodes into a roar.

JONATHAN: She did *that?!*

*   *   *

INTERIOR JONATHAN AND SANDY'S DORMITORY ROOM—MORNING

JONATHAN is asleep. SANDY lies awake in bed, staring at the ceiling.

SANDY: I think I'm in love. (*No response. He tries again*) I think I'm in love.

JONATHAN: (*Slowly wakening*) Bullshit artist.

SANDY: I really think so.

JONATHAN: You get in yet?

SANDY: What's that got to do with it?

JONATHAN: How do you know if you don't know how you are in bed together?

SANDY: That's not everything.

JONATHAN: It's a lot.

SANDY: She tells me thoughts that I didn't even know I had, until she tells them to me. It's unbelievable! I can talk to her!

JONATHAN: You can talk to me too. Are you in love with me?

SANDY: I can say things to her I wouldn't dare say to you.

JONATHAN: What, for instance?

SANDY: Things you'd laugh at.

JONATHAN: Listen, I'm laughing now.

SANDY: She thinks I'm sensitive.

JONATHAN: Sensitive. (*Laughs*) Oh boy! Sensitive! (*Laughs*) What do you talk to her about? Flowers?

SANDY: Books.

JONATHAN: Books? You phony. I read more books than you do.

SANDY: I'm going to start. I'm reading *The Fountainhead*.

JONATHAN: *The Fountainhead?* What's that?

SANDY: It's her favorite book. You ever hear of *Jean Christophe?*

JONATHAN: What's that?

SANDY: It's a classic, you moron. I'm going to read it right after *The Fountainhead*.

JONATHAN: Yeah—you ever read *Guadalcanal Diary* by Richard Tregaskis?

SANDY: No.

JONATHAN: That was a best-seller, and I read it. You ever read *Gentleman's Agreement* by Laura Z. Hobson? You ever read *A Bell for Adano* by John Hersey?

SANDY: I'm going to read everything from now on.

JONATHAN: I read a lot more than you. So who's the one who's sensitive? You or me? Come on! Who's sensitive?!

SANDY stares at him, puzzled by the sudden outburst.

SCENE 2

Jonathan's most involved and committed relationship occurs during the late 1950s and early 1960s with Bobbie, a voluptuously beautiful commercial model. She and Jonathan share a vigorous, almost violent attraction for each other, as well as a similar kind of humor; but Bobbie wants to get married, and when Jonathan refuses, she seems to lose any sense of herself, spending more and more time in bed, watching television and sleeping. (Some time after this scene, Bobbie will attempt suicide.)

INTERIOR JONATHAN'S BATHROOM—EVENING

[JONATHAN stands under the shower. Through the shower door he watches BOBBIE enter the bathroom, naked, and wash her face. The sink water cuts into his shower water and he glowers with suppressed rage. BOBBIE leaves the bathroom, reenters, and proceeds to make up her face.]

JONATHAN enters the bedroom and begins rummaging through the dresser drawers. He picks a bill off the top of the dresser and reads it.

JONATHAN: You and Lord and Taylor's are going to have to work out a trial separation.

BOBBIE: (*Opens the bathroom door*) I had the water running, what did you say?

JONATHAN: You and Lord and Taylor's are going to have to work out a trial separation.

She reaches for the bill.

BOBBIE: Look at the date.

JONATHAN: What do you mean?

BOBBIE: Five months ago.

They continue to dress in silence.

BOBBIE: I'm sorry I cost you so much money.

She sips a drink. The phone rings. Neither answers. The phone stops. BOBBIE stops dressing and just sits. JONATHAN looks over at her, goes to her, fondles and kisses her.

BOBBIE: I want to get married.

He enters the bathroom and loudly slams the door. She sips her drink. After a moment, he exits from the bathroom, then quickly reenters, this time leaving the door open.

BOBBIE: Are you tired of me, Jonathan?

JONATHAN: (*Under his breath*) Am I ever.

BOBBIE: The answer is yes.

JONATHAN: I didn't say yes.

He returns to the bedroom.

BOBBIE: You said, "Am I ever." I need more in life than this.

JONATHAN: Who put you up to this? Your psychiatrist? After a long exhaustive bed-hunt, you've chosen me.

BOBBIE: Cindy's not a virgin either.

JONATHAN: What? Oh, I get it! Is that what brought this on? Your mind is unbelievable! You really have to have a low opinion of me—thinking I'd do that to Sandy.

BOBBIE: No, you wouldn't want to cheat on Sandy.

JONATHAN: Oh-ho—now it's Sandy.

BOBBIE: He spends half his life over here.

JONATHAN: Wait a minute—a second ago you had me screwing Cindy. Who'm I screwing now? Sandy?

BOBBIE: You're going too fast for me.

JONATHAN: I'm going too fast for *you!* That little mind of yours operates like an IBM—like a pinball machine. First Cindy—oh, not Cindy? How about Sandy? How about Cindy *and* Sandy? Talk about the pot calling the kettle. The day I got an earful of your checkered past I felt like a celibate.

BOBBIE: You made me tell you.

JONATHAN: Sure—I twisted your arm.

BOBBIE: It got you hot.

JONATHAN: Well, something has to!

He slams into the bathroom. She slumps onto the bed for a moment. She takes a pill out of a bottle on the bed table and downs it with her drink. He stalks out of the bathroom.

BOBBIE: You have such contempt for me.

JONATHAN: Kid, you worked hard for it, it's yours.

BOBBIE: The way you paw me at parties.

JONATHAN: Now affection is contempt. Upside down. Everything upside down.

BOBBIE: Feeling me up in public is not affection.

JONATHAN: Will you come on!

BOBBIE: I know I sleep all day—I know I'm doing a terrible job—but you're not helping me any.

JONATHAN: And who helps me?

BOBBIE: I help you.

JONATHAN: Your kind of help I can do without.

BOBBIE: Oh, can you? Can you, really?

He charges into and out of the bathroom. He has on a new tie.

JONATHAN: You'll do anything you can to ruin my day, won't you? I got up feeling so good—(*He rips off his tie and starts changing shirts*) You couldn't leave us alone. We were doing so well—

BOBBIE: *What?!*

JONATHAN: At one time! At one time it was great what we had. The kidding around. It can't have a natural time span? Affairs can't dissolve in a good way? There's always got to be poison? I don't see why. I really don't see why.

BOBBIE: Jonathan, you want it to be over between us?

JONATHAN: Why does it have to be one way or the other?

BOBBIE: You don't want me to leave.

JONATHAN: I want you right here, where you belong.

BOBBIE: And what about you?

JONATHAN: When I'm here I'm here, when I'm not here
I'm there.

BOBBIE: Where?

JONATHAN: Wherever.

BOBBIE: No. I'm a man-eater, a ball-buster and a castrater.
I want to get married.

JONATHAN: Where the fuck is my shoehorn?! This place is a
mess. There's never any food in the house, half the time
you look like you fell out of bed—you're in bed more
than any other human being past the age of six months
that I ever heard of—

BOBBIE: The reason I sleep all day is I can't stand my life.

JONATHAN: *What* life?

BOBBIE: Sleeping all day.

She laughs.

JONATHAN: (*Smiles*) You do that sort of thing, I love you all
over again.

BOBBIE: Marry me, Jonathan. Please marry me.

JONATHAN: You're trying to kill me!

BOBBIE: Marriage isn't death.

JONATHAN: Why *now?!*

BOBBIE: Because two years ago I slept eight hours, a year
ago it was twelve, now it's up to fifteen, pretty soon it's
gonna be twenty-four!

JONATHAN: What are you trying to do—scare me?

She takes a pill and downs it with Scotch.

BOBBIE: I need a life.

JONATHAN: Get a job!

BOBBIE: I don't want a job, I want you!

JONATHAN: I'm taken. By *me!* Get out of the house, goddamn it—do something useful.

BOBBIE: You wouldn't let me work when I wanted to.

JONATHAN: That was a year ago.

BOBBIE: You throw a tantrum every time you call and I'm not home.

JONATHAN: Look, sister, I'm out there in the jungle eight hours a day.

BOBBIE: You wouldn't even let me canvass for Kennedy!

JONATHAN: You want a job? I got a job for you—fix up this goddamn pigsty. Listen, you get a pretty goddamn good salary for testing out that bed all day. You want another fifty a week? Try vacuuming. You want an extra hundred? Try making the bed. Try opening some windows! That's why you can hardly stand up. The goddamn place smells like a coffin!

She takes a pill, downs it with Scotch.

JONATHAN: Bobbie, you don't need me. Why do you take this kind of abuse? Walk out! Leave me! Please leave me, Bobbie. I'd almost marry you if you'd leave me.

He goes to her. She takes him in her arms.

BOBBIE: You call that abuse? You don't know what I'm used to. With all your carrying on, to me, Jonathan, you're a gift. (*Pause*) So what's it gonna be?

He pulls abruptly away.

JONATHAN: You really know how to screw things up.

BOBBIE: So where does that leave us?

JONATHAN: You giving me an ultimatum?

She doesn't answer.

JONATHAN: Is this an ultimatum? Answer me, you ball-busting, castrating, son-of-a-cunt bitch! Is this an ultimatum or not? Well, I'll tell you what you can do with your ultimatum! I'll tell you what you can do with it!

He starts ripping the bed apart.

JONATHAN: You can make the goddamn bed! That's what you can do with it! You can change these filthy sheets—

The doorbell rings. He turns panic-stricken toward the sound of the bell.

HAROLD AND MAUDE

A Paramount Pictures presentation. Producers, Colin Higgins
& Charles B. Mulvehill. Executive Producer, Mildred Lewis.
Director, Hal Ashby. Screenplay by Colin Higgins. Director
of Photography, John Alonzo. Film Editors, William A. Saw-
yer, Edward Warsehilka. Music, Cat Stevens. Production
Designer, Michael Haller. Sound, William Randall, Richard
Portman. Assistant Director, Michael Dmytryk. Technicolor.
Running time, 90 minutes. 1971.

CAST

MAUDE	Ruth Gordon
HAROLD CHASEN	Bud Cort
MRS. CHASEN	Vivian Pickles
SCULPTOR	Cyril Cusack
UNCLE VICTOR	Charles Tynor
SUNSHINE	Ellen Geer
PRIEST	Eric Christmas
PSYCHIATRIST	G. Wood
CANDY	Judy Eagles
EDITH	Shari Summers
MOTORCYCLE COP	M. Borman

When asked by his psychiatrist what he does for fun, Harold
says that he attends funerals. He also enjoys construction site
demolitions. Otherwise, Harold is doing his best to contend
with the fact that he is numb. He strives against this most
successfully in the creation and execution of brilliant and

bloody suicide tableaux for the attention of his widowed mother, with whom he lives in a mansion. The major involvement of Harold's mother's life is the making and cancelling of appointments at her hairdresser's. Harold is not yet twenty-one.

At one of the funerals, Harold meets Maude. In a week Maude will be eighty. In addition to attending funerals regularly, Maude poses in the nude for an ice sculptor whose work melts nightly. Maude transplants sick trees to the forest from their smog-soaked plots in the middle of town, *any* town, and borrows whatever wheels she needs. All without bothering to ask. The world is an open gift certificate to Maude, and she takes Harold with her on a buying spree of all earthly delights. She teaches him to sing and to dance. And he falls in love and decides to marry her. Although his mother has been urging him to marry, she is not amused.

The end of the film reveals two of the spurs in Maude's joyful pursuit of youth: a concentration camp number tattoo on her arm, and an appointment to fly this world's coop on her eightieth birthday. When Harold proposes, she explains that she has taken the pills an hour before. From celebration he is plunged back into mourning, but he has learned from Maude and climbs back up.

The following scene is the first time we see Harold opening himself up to anyone since the beginning of the story.

INTERIOR MAUDE'S PLACE—NIGHT

MAUDE and HAROLD are dressed in bright Japanese kimonos. They are relaxing on cushions in the Japanese nook after having just finished supper. MAUDE puffs pleasantly on a hookah.

HAROLD: I like Glaucus.

MAUDE: Yes, so do I. But I think he is a little . . . old-fashioned. Like a puff, Harold?

HAROLD: Well, I really don't smoke.

MAUDE: It's all right. (*she offers him the hose*) It's organic.

HAROLD: (*smokes*) I'm sure picking up on vices.

MAUDE: Vice? Virtue? It's best not to be too moral. You

cheat yourself out of too much life. Aim above morality.
As Confucius says, "Don't simply be good. Make good
things happen."

HAROLD: Did Confucius say that?

MAUDE: Well—(*she smiles*)—they say he was very wise, so
I'm sure he must have.

HAROLD: You are the wisest person I know.

MAUDE: Me! (*she laughs and shakes her head*) When I look
around me, I know I know nothing. I remember though,
once long ago in Persia we met a wise man in the bazaar.
He was a professional and used to sell his wisdom to
anyone willing to pay. His specialty for tourists was a
maxim engraved on the head of a pin—"The wisest," he
said, "the truest, the most instructive words for all men
at all time." Frederick bought one for me and back at the
hotel I peered through a magnifying glass to read the
words—"And this too shall pass away." (*fluttery laugh*)
And the wise man was right—if you remember that, you
can't help but live life fully.

HAROLD: Yes. I haven't lived. (*he suddenly giggles*) I've
died a few times.

MAUDE: What was that?

HAROLD: (*he is getting a little high*) Died! Seventeen times—
not counting maiming. (*he laughs*) Shot myself in the
face once with a pop gun and a pellet of blood.

MAUDE: (*laughing with him*) How ingenious! Tell me about
them.

HAROLD: Well, it's a question of timing, and the right
equipment, and plenty of patience . . . You really want
to hear about this?

MAUDE: Of course.

HAROLD: (*he smiles*) Okay.

Partly because of the pot, but mostly because he has found a
friend, HAROLD opens up for the first time in his life. As he
gets into the story he tells it with such animation and delight
that we are amazed at all the fun and zest he has kept locked
up inside him.

HAROLD: Well, the first time, it wasn't even planned. It was when I was at boarding school and they were getting ready for the school Centennial Celebration and they put all the fireworks and food and stuff in this room in the West Wing. Well, on the floor above they had the Chemistry Lab and I had to stay in and clean it up. So I thought I'd do a little experimenting. I got all this stuff out and began mixing it up. It was very scientific. I was measuring the amounts. Well, suddenly there was this big fizzing sound, and this white kind of porridge stuff began erupting out of the beaker, and moving along the desk and falling onto the floor. It was making an awful mess. So I got the hose to try to spray it into the sink. I turned on the water and—POW! There was this massive explosion. Knocked me down. Blew out the floor. Boards and brick and flames leaping up. Singed my hair. Smoke everywhere. I got up, then this sound like bombs going off. It was the fireworks in the room below. And all this stuff came flying out the hole. PACHAU! Skyrockets and pinwheels. And fire balls all whizzing and bouncing. And I was just standing there stunned—I couldn't believe it—just watching—being pelted by these little pellets— turns out to be the goddamn popcorn spewed up from below. The whole place was a crazy inferno with the rockets and everything, and I couldn't get to the door. But behind me was this old laundry chute, so I hopped in that and slid down to the basement. When I got outside, I saw that the whole top of the building was on fire, and, of course, it was pandemonium with people running around and fire alarms ringing. So I decide to go home. When I get there, my mother is having this big party, so I creep up the back stairs to my room. Then there is this ring on the doorbell. It's the police. I creep over to the banister to see what they say, and they tell my mother that I had been killed in a fire at school. Well, everyone got very quiet.

HAROLD has calmed down and speaks in a matter-of-fact way.

HAROLD: People were whispering and looking at my mother. I tried leaning forward to see her face but I couldn't. (*slowly*) She began to sway. She put one hand to her forehead. With the other she reached out, as if groping for support. Two men rushed to her side, and then—

with a long, low sigh—she collapsed in their arms. (*pause*)
I decided then I enjoyed being dead.

MAUDE doesn't say anything for a moment. Then she speaks
softly.

MAUDE: Yes. I understand. A lot of people enjoy being
dead. But they are not dead really. They're just backing
away from life. (*with a twinkle*) They're players—but
they sit on the bench. The game goes on before them. At
any moment they can join in. (*she jumps up and shouts*)
Reach out! Take a chance! Get hurt maybe. But play as
well as you can. (*she leads a cheer before the stands*) Go
team, go! Give me an "L." Give me an "I." Give me a
"V." Give me an "E." LIVE!!!!! (*she sits down by* HAROLD
quietly composed) Otherwise you'll have nothing to talk
about in the locker room.

HAROLD: (*smiles*) I like you, Maude.

MAUDE: (*smiles*) I like you, Harold. (*pause*) Come, I'll teach
you to waltz.

Music comes in from nowhere. HAROLD joins MAUDE and,
though they both realize how ridiculous they look waltzing in
kimonos, they begin to dance, and thoroughly enjoy it.

We go into a MONTAGE as they dance together similar to the
one MAUDE danced alone. They dance on the beach, the
forest, the fields, the hills and end up back in her apartment
for the courtly finale.

THE LAST PICTURE SHOW

A Columbia Pictures presentation of a BBS Production. Producer, Stephen J. Friedman. Executive Producer, Bert Schneider. Director, Peter Bogdanovich. Screenplay by Larry McMurtry & Peter Bogdanovich. Based on the novel *The Last Picture Show* by Larry McMurtry. Director of Photography, Robert Surtees. Film Editor, Donn Cambern. Associate Producer, Harold Schneider. Design, Polly Platt. Art Director, Walter Scott Herndon. Sound Mixer, Tom Overton. Assistant Directors, Robert Rubin, William Morrison. Running time, 118 minutes. 1971.

CAST

SONNY CRAWFORD	Timothy Bottoms
DUANE JACKSON	Jeff Bridges
JACY FARROW	Cybill Shepherd
SAM THE LION	Ben Johnson
LOIS FARROW	Ellen Burstyn
RUTH POPPER	Cloris Leachman
GENEVIEVE	Eileen Brennan
ABILENE	Clu Gulager
BILLY	Sam Bottoms
CHARLENE DUGGS	Sharon Taggart
LESTER MARLOW	Randy Quaid
SHERIFF	Joe Heathcock
COACH POPPER	Bill Thurman
GENE FARROW	Robert Glenn

One of the hallmarks of a Peter Bogdanovich film is the affectionate warmth with which the characters are presented. It's not that the characters aren't flawed, or that they don't hurt each other, but they are all, for the most part, forgiven. The only truly irredeemable force in the tiny, desolate, west Texas town of Anarene is time.

It is 1951, there is a war in someplace called Korea, and television is just beginning to spread itself over America in a change that will soon close down many movie houses. But for now in Anarene, the Saturday night picture show is still where you go to date and neck and be seen. Jacy, the prettiest girl in town, is for the moment satisfied to be on view there with Duane, a "tall, about seventeen, good-looking jock." In the darkened theater, Sonny, "an appealing teenager, neither handsome nor ugly," stares at Jacy instead of the screen, as his own arm hangs over the shoulder of his pouting girlfriend. Duane and Sonny, both in love with Jacy, are best friends, so Sonny keeps his distance from Jacy out of respect for his buddy.

The picture show, the cafe, and the pool hall are all owned by Sam the Lion, who also provides the moral glue that holds Anarene together. Years before, Sam was the one true love of Jacy's mother, Lois, "a rangy, tall blonde of forty, still most attractive." When Sam suddenly dies, there is for a time nothing to counterbalance the machinations of the supremely selfish and beautiful Jacy. Devious without being imaginative, she's the kind of girl who tells Duane that she does love him or that she doesn't love him depending upon which party she wants to be escorted to and by whom. Jacy dumps Duane for a richer boy, and Duane leaves to find work in the town of Odessa. But when the rich boy drops Jacy, she turns her sights on Sonny, who is just ripe for the picking.

Sonny lives by himself in a boarding house. He has just graduated from high school and upon Sam's death, he inherited the pool hall. Without school or his mentor Sam or his best friend, Sonny spends his days staring out the pool hall window as the "wind blows dust down the empty main street, past the picture show." When Duane returns to Anarene, he and Sonny fight over Jacy (in the first scene below). Sonny almost loses an eye; Duane goes off to join the army, and Jacy is just thrilled by it all. She cons Sonny into eloping, but she is relieved when the police sent by her parents finally catch up to them. The marriage is annulled. Jacy's father takes her home, snarling that as far as he's concerned, Sonny can walk.

Lois gives Sonny a ride back to Anarene (in the second scene below). In addition to the bond of love they shared for Sam the Lion, Lois likes Sonny for having had an affair with her friend Ruth, the badly neglected wife of the high school football coach. (The affair ended abruptly when Jacy took hold of Sonny's life.) Lois' own marriage has not been fulfilling; by her own admission, her husband grew rich because she scared him into it. For years now, Lois has been having an affair with a cold and attractive man who does little beyond distract her from her restlessness. When the man casually seduces Jacy, Lois realizes that it is long past due to make some changes. She has been urging Jacy to go away to college "because everything's flat and empty here—and there's nothing to do." Anarene is the kind of place where the townspeople sneer at the high school football team when they lose a game. Although she loves her daughter, Lois is philosophical and realistic enough to be glad that Sonny is free of Jacy. At the conclusion of *The Last Picture Show*, both Duane and Sonny have escaped Jacy's maneuvers, as life forgives and reclaims them from their infatuations.

SCENE 1

EXTERIOR POOLHALL—DAWN

A bright, second-hand Mercury is parked in front of the poolhall, as a pickup full of ROUGHNECKS pulls up and SONNY jumps out, dirty and greasy. He looks in the car, sees DUANE just sitting up, blinking in the sunlight. SONNY is uneasy.

SONNY: Hey, Duane.

Tanned dark, DUANE gets out, wearing a Levi shirt with the arms cut out; they shake hands.

DUANE: Hi, buddy. Didn't know you'd turned roughneck.

SONNY: Got to make a livin' somehow, so's I can afford to keep the poolhall open. When'd ya get in?

DUANE: 'Bout two. Thought I'd surprise you.

A moment of stiff silence; both grin, but they're not really friendly. SONNY looks at the car.

SONNY: This yours?

DUANE: Yeah, how about that? Thirty-eight thousand miles on her. Runs like new. (*lights a cigarette*) Wanna beer?

SONNY: Not me.

DUANE: (*getting one from front seat*) 'S about all I eat for breakfast anymore.

SONNY: Sure is a nice car.

DUANE: I like to drive it so much I thought I'd run home for the weekend.

DUANE drinks his beer and absently wipes bugs off the grill with a kerchief.

DUANE: Can't take too good care of a car like this. I wash her every week.

SONNY: Looks great. (*pause*) You heard about Joe Bob?

DUANE: Yeah. I always knew he was crazy.

SONNY: Doctor said he didn't really do nothing—just got her to take off her underpants.

DUANE: (*skeptical*) Yeah? Hey, you still screwin' that old lady?

SONNY: No. Yeah. Been kinda busy.

DUANE: Seen old Jerry last week . . . said he thought you and Jacy'd been going together a little.

SONNY: Yeah, we have, a little—she's been kinda bored . . . once and a while we eat Mexican food or something.

DUANE: Way I hear it that ain't all you been eatin'.

SONNY: Whoever told you didn't know what he was talkin' about. Sure, I been *goin'* with her, why not?

DUANE: I never said I blamed you for it. I don't blame you much. I jus' never thought you'd do me that way—I thought we was still best friends.

SONNY: We are. What are you so mad for? I never done nothin' to you.

DUANE: I guess screwin' my girl ain't nothing to you.

SONNY: I ain't screwin' her.

DUANE: The hell you ain't.

SONNY: Well, I ain't—but she's not your girl anymore, anyway.

DUANE: She *is* my girl—I don't care if we did break up.

SONNY: Hell, you don't even live here anymore.

DUANE: Don't make no difference—I'll *always* live here. An' I'm gonna get her back, I'm tellin' you right now. She's gonna marry me one of these days, when I get a little more money.

SONNY: Why, she won't marry you.

DUANE: Sure she will! We always meant to get married.

SONNY: She's goin' off to college. I doubt I'll ever get to go with her again myself, once she gets off. I never saw what it could hurt to go with her this summer, though. She's never gonna marry you.

DUANE: She is, by God! Don't you tell me she won't. She'll never let *you* screw her, that's for sure. Hell, I was just seein' how honest you was—I knew Jacy wouldn't let you screw her . . . You ain't that good a cocksman. You never even screwed Charlene Duggs all the time you went with her.

SONNY: *'Course* I didn't. You know why? 'Cause you had the pickup all the time Saturday nights . . . nobody coulda screwed her in the time I had left.

DUANE: (*smugly*) I coulda screwed her in five minutes—I wouldn't even need no pickup.

SONNY: Yeah!? Well, the only reason Jacy went with you long as she did was 'cause you was in the backfield. I was in the goddamn line!

DUANE: What are you talkin' about . . . me an' her was in love.

SONNY: *You* was! She likes *me* as good as she ever liked you.

DUANE: That's a lie!

SONNY: I'll stay all night with her, too, one of these nights. She's done promised.

DUANE: You won't either!

SONNY: Yes, I will—why shouldn't I? She's done told me you couldn't even do it that time in Wichita Falls—What about that?

Enraged, DUANE hits him with the bottle, catching him on his eye. They slug at one another wildly, close, and struggle. SONNY'S eye bleeds, almost closed. Some men run out of the cafe; Genevieve behind them. SONNY slowly collapses to his knees. DUANE goes to him, scared. SONNY passes out as the others run up.

SCENE 2

(*Note*: Scene two begins outside the police station in Oklahoma and moves through a car ride back to Anarene. In order to play the scene continuously within the limits of the acting studio, the actors must clarify, and perhaps simplify, the changes in location.)

EXTERIOR OKLAHOMA JAIL—NIGHT

[GENE FARROW is coming out with LOIS, SONNY and JACY, whom he grabs by the arm away from SONNY.

GENE: Think I worked like a dog all my life so my daughter could end up in a poolhall?

SONNY: We was gonna get another apartment.

GENE: I bet you was. Where's your car keys, hon?

Sniffing, JACY fishes them out.

GENE: It's a hell of a note, a hell of a note.

LOIS: Oh, shut up and take her home.

GENE: It's just a hell of a note.

LOIS: I'm tired of this.

GENE: You bet I will. You take her car. So far as I'm concerned *he* can walk.

JACY looks back. GENE leads her to the Cadillac, spins off with her. SONNY stands watching her go off.] LOIS comes over, taps his arm.

LOIS: Not much of a wedding night.

SONNY: No, not much of one.

She brings out a little flask.

LOIS: (*drinks*) Here. Have a little bourbon—take the rest of it—might pick you up—I've gotta drive.

SONNY sips from it several times. LOIS grins. They walk back toward the car.

LOIS: You won't believe me, Sonny, but you're lucky we got you clear of her quick as we did . . . you'd've been a lot better off stayin' with Ruth Popper.

SONNY: Does *everybody* know about that?

LOIS: 'Course. Sounded like a good thing to me, Kiddo— you shouldn't've let Jacy turn your head.

SONNY: She's prettier. I guess I shouldn't've though. (*pause*) Guess I treated her terrible.

LOIS: I guess you did.

They get in the car.

[EXTERIOR OKLAHOMA ROAD #3—NIGHT

They drive by. Thunder is heard.

INTERIOR JACY'S CAR (OKLAHOMA ROAD #3)—NIGHT]

LOIS frowns at the sky as SONNY sips; she turns on radio.

LOIS: That'll be a big help if you mean to live your life in Anarene.

SONNY: I don't.

LOIS: (*shakes her head*) Strange to have a daughter who wouldn't go through with her wedding night. When I was her age I'd go through with just 'bout any old night.

SONNY: (*sips bourbon*) I guess I can't get in the Army now—not with this eye.

[EXTERIOR RED RIVER BRIDGE —NIGHT

Moonlight on the water; they drive into Texas again.

EXTERIOR POOLHALL—NIGHT

The car pulls up in front.]

SONNY: Sure wasn't outta Texas very long.

LOIS: Well, Oklahoma's not much of an improvement.

SONNY: (*sips bourbon, pauses*) 'S not the same now. Nothing's really been right since Sam the Lion died.

LOIS: (*starts; sadly*) No, it hasn't. (*eyes water slightly*) I get sad when I think of Sam for long. Did you know he had beautiful hands?

SONNY: I guess you liked him, didn't you? I guess everybody did.

LOIS: No, it was more than that with me, honey—I loved him. He loved me.

Surprised, SONNY looks at her and it dawns on him.

SONNY: Are you the one he used to take swimming? Out to the tank?

LOIS: (*looks at him; smiles*) He told you about that, huh? Oh yeah, I was the one. (*pauses*) If it hadn'ta been for him, you know, I'd have missed it—whatever it is. I'd have been one of those Amity types that think bridge is the best thing life has to offer. He's the only man I ever met who knew wh.at I was worth. Sam the Lion. (*smiles*) Sam the Lion. Nobody knows where he got that name. I gave it to him—one night. Just came to me. He was so pleased. I was twenty-two then—can you imagine?

Looks at SONNY briefly, holding back her tears; a few spill over.

LOIS: You know something, Sonny? It's terrible only to find one man your whole life that knows what you're worth. It's just terrible—I wouldn't be tellin' you if it wasn't. I've looked, too—you wouldn't believe how I've looked. When Sam . . . was sixty-five years old he could jus' walk into a room where I was and do more for me . . . (*pause*) Nobody was like him. (*falls silent*)

SONNY: (*hesitantly*) Now I know why Sam liked you.

LOIS: *Loved me!*

SONNY: Loved you, I mean.

LOIS: Aw, do you? (*looks at him, gently puts hand on his cheek*) I can kinda see what he saw in you too.

She looks forward again, then back at him a moment, with a reckless smile. He looks back, curiously. Finally:

LOIS: Nope. I'll just go on home.

SONNY: Think I could learn to drink?

Throws back his head and swallows, then coughs and sputters. LOIS is amused. He hands her back the flask.

LOIS: You might. Keep practicing.

She drives away. He goes into the poolhall.

LAST TANGO IN PARIS

A United Artists presentation of a co-production of PEA Produzioni Europee Associate S.A.S. & Les Productions Artistes Associes S.A. Producer, Alberto Grimaldi. Director, Bernardo Bertolucci. Screenplay by Bernardo Bertolucci & Franco Arcalli. Director of Photography, Vittorio Storare. Film Editor, Franco Arcalli (in collaboration with Roberto Perpignani). Music, Gato Barbieri. Sound, Michael Billingsley. Assistant Directors, Fernand Moskowicz, Jean David Lefebvre. Color. Running time, 129 minutes. 1972.

CAST

PAUL	Marlon Brando
JEANNE	Maria Schneider
TOM	Jean-Pierre Leaud
MARCEL	Massimo Girotti
ROSA'S MOTHER	Maria Michi
GIOVANNA GALLETTI	Prostitute
CONCIERGE	Darling Legitimus
CATHERINE	Catherine Allegret

Paul is an American in his forties who lives in Paris. He used to work as an actor and then as a journalist, but for many years now he has been sponging off his French wife who owned and ran a cheap hotel. She has just committed suicide.

Jeanne is a French girl of twenty. She lives in ample bourgeois comfort with her widowed mother; her father was a colonel. In a week she's to be married to her fiancé, who loves her and loves making improvisational *verité* films. He combines both of his loves by relentlessly following her around with a movie camera and documenting her real life, all the while directing her to make it more cinematic.

Paul and Jeanne know none of this about each other. They meet while looking at a vacant flat for rent. They are violently attracted to each other; they have sex. Paul rents the apartment, and they meet there for three days. Paul's need to escape from his own life is so overpowering that he demands ground rules of total anonymity: they are not to speak their names; they are not to share their outside lives, either present or past. He insists on an isolation chamber that extracts sex from love or personality or previous experience. They enter a private limbo so hypnotically and erotically compelling that Jeanne, despite her growing confusion, keeps returning for more. He needs to imprison her in the psychological jungle-gym of an American machismo myth, but his brutality is made of grief and self-rage. He finally sits beside his wife's body, feeling and telling the truth of his love and hate for her. This releases him to re-unify his world; he now feels that he and Jeanne are ready to know each other as people, not just as sexual soldiers. When they try to meet in the "real world," she sees him as a middle-aged failure because that is the way he sees himself.

In the following scene, Jeanne has come back to the apartment for the first time since their initial meeting.

SCENE 1

INTERIOR APARTMENT—DAY

JEANNE sees PAUL enter. His back is to her while he double-locks the door. There is just enough time for her to retreat to the living room without being seen. We follow PAUL into the living room. JEANNE is seated in the armchair, still and falsely composed. PAUL looks at her without surprise, as if her being there is absolutely normal.

PAUL: That chair goes in front . . .

He heads for the armchair in which she is sitting, frightened, hugging her knees.

PAUL: In front of the window.

PAUL pulls the armchair over to the window, with her in it.

He arranges it in front of the window, then takes off his jacket and hangs it on the window. His gestures are precise, irreversible.

JEANNE: I came to return the key. To return it to *you*.

PAUL: What do I care? Take off your coat. Come help me. Take these chairs . . . and put them here . . . Put them on the other side.

She obeys; his tone leaves no other choice. Together they begin to move the table. In the center of it, perfectly in view, is the key that JEANNE brought back. She indicates it with her chin.

JEANNE: There it is.

PAUL retreats several steps to survey the new position of the table. Then he takes the chairs and passes them to her, one by one.

PAUL: Around the table.

She does it, and, looking at the furniture, she speaks.

JEANNE: You didn't waste any time.

She puts the last chair in place. When she turns around, the man is no longer there. She goes to the door. She wants to call him, but doesn't know his name.

JEANNE: Listen . . . Mister . . . I have to go now.

She advances cautiously toward the spare room with the bed protruding from the doorway. PAUL is there, comically passive before the crushing reality—the room is smaller than the bed.

PAUL: The bed is too big for the room.

JEANNE: I don't know what to call you.

PAUL: I don't have a name.

JEANNE: You want to know mine?

She can't finish her phrase. PAUL'S slap is not very violent. . .

PAUL: No! No, I don't—I don't want to know your name. You don't have a name, and I don't have a name either. No names here. Not one name.

. . . but it is completely unexpected. JEANNE doesn't even have time to dodge it. She moves a hand to her cheek.

JEANNE: You're crazy!

Tears of rage well up in her eyes. He presses his point.

PAUL: You don't have a name. Neither do I. No names.

JEANNE: Yes, yes . . . no names. Why?

PAUL: Maybe I am. But I don't want to know anything about you. I don't want to know where you live or where you come from. I want to know . . . nothing, nothing! You understand?

JEANNE: You scared me.

PAUL: Nothing. You and I are going to meet here without knowing anything that goes on outside here.

She has backed up into a corner. He lifts her chin. Then he slides a hand behind her neck.

JEANNE: But why?

PAUL: Because . . . because we don't need names here. Don't you see. We're going to forget everything we knew—every—all the people, all that we do, all that we—wherever we live. We are going to forget that, everything—everything.

JEANNE: But I can't, can you?

PAUL: I don't know. Are you scared?

JEANNE takes his hand and carries it up to her eyes. She discovers his wrist, caresses it, studies it.

JEANNE: No, not anymore. Not now . . . let me go. I'll come back.

She speaks with her eyes lowered, suddenly timid.

JEANNE: Tomorrow . . .

Her lips caress his hand.

JEANNE: Please. I'll want it more tomorrow. I want you too much now.

PAUL: Yes. That's good. That way it won't become a habit. It's a way of making love.

PAUL kisses her, touches her. She loses herself in his shoulder.

JEANNE: Don't kiss me. If you kiss me, I won't be able to leave.

PAUL: I'll walk you to the door.

They walk with their arms around each other. But, instead of the front door, they are in front of the spare room. PAUL sits down on the end of the bed jutting into the hallway. JEANNE disappears into the room. We follow her movements in his expression.

SCENE 2

In this scene, Paul has gone to the room in the hotel occupied by Marcel, his wife's lover. We know almost nothing about Marcel: this is the only time that he appears in the film.

INTERIOR: MARCEL'S ROOM, HOTEL—NIGHT

The red shadow of PAUL'S robe. A newspaper page. Long scissors cut out a photograph with its caption. Someone knocks at the door.

MARCEL: Come in.

PAUL comes in. Marcel, sitting, with the scissors, barely looks at him.

PAUL: You wanted to talk to me? Go ahead, but I didn't come here to cry with you.

MARCEL: I hope it won't bother you if I keep working. It helps me a great deal.

Only now does PAUL notice that MARCEL is wearing an identical robe. He is about to mention it, but changes his mind. The other man, with spectacles balanced on the end of his nose, continues.

MARCEL: It helps me a great deal, after what happened.

While he is saying this, with a side glance over his spectacles he has observed PAUL'S curiosity about the robe.

MARCEL: The same color. The same pattern. If you only knew how many things we have in common.

More annoyed than embarrassed, PAUL goes over to MARCEL'S table and picks up one of the clippings, if only to have something to do.

PAUL: You can't tell me anything that I don't know already.

I've always wondered, Marcel, you keep these press clippings . . . Is it your work or is it a hobby?

MARCEL: Hobby? I don't care for that word. Let's say, it helps me out at the end of the month. I do it for an agency. It's a job that makes you read. Very instructive. Be sincere. Didn't you know we had identical bathrobes? We have lots of things in common. And I like it. I wanted to tell you before that perhaps you didn't know about the robe. And maybe you don't know so many little things more.

PAUL: I know everything. Rosa told me everything. If you only know how many times we talked about you. I don't think there are many marriages like that . . . I'm thirsty.

He goes toward the door.

PAUL: You want a little bourbon?

MARCEL: Wait!

He leans over and takes a bottle of bourbon and two glasses out of the night table.

MARCEL: Here you are.

This time PAUL is sincerely surprised, and doesn't attempt to hide it.

PAUL: Is that a present from Rosa too?

He sits on the bed.

MARCEL: Personally, I don't like bourbon. But Rosa always wanted me to have a bottle in the night table. That's the question I've been asking myself. If . . . with these details . . . unimportant things . . . we could think back, understand together . . . It's been almost a year that Rosa and I . . . not passionately but regularly . . . I thought I knew her as is possible one can know . . .

PAUL: One's mistress.

MARCEL: For example, some time ago something happened which I haven't been able to explain . . . You see the wall over there?

He indicates a corner near the ceiling, where the wallpaper has obviously been torn.

MARCEL: She climbed on the chair and tried to tear the

paper with her bare hands. I stopped her because she was breaking all her nails.

He looks at PAUL, waiting for an explanation. None comes.

MARCEL: She was so violent about it, so strange. I'd never seen her like that.

PAUL rises and looks around him, as if searching for other signs. He also opens the bathroom door.

PAUL: Our room is painted white. Rosa wanted it to be different from the other rooms. To have the feeling of a normal home. Here . . . it had to change too . . . She started with the wallpaper.

There's a note of bitterness in MARCEL'S voice now.

MARCEL: Maybe I was never anything more than a replacement.

MARCEL stands up suddenly, letting his clippings and his scissors fall. He presses the thumb of his left hand in the right hand.

MARCEL: Shit! That's the first time in ten years . . .

A rivulet of red blood trickles out of his cut hand and quickly spreads over the back of it. PAUL takes him over to the sink and puts his hand under running water. A lot of blood but not a serious cut, only a scratch.

MARCEL: She bathed and dressed, fixed her hair and climbed the stairs. She came here as if she were going downtown . . . I can't stand physical pain.

PAUL goes back into the room to pick up the bourbon bottle. With one hand he takes MARCEL'S wrist and with the other pours the alcohol over the cut, after taking the cork out with his teeth. MARCEL looks away.

PAUL: We always told each other everything. From the beginning . . . No secrets, no lies . . . even adultery . . . adultery became part . . . part of our marriage.

MARCEL: It burns!

PAUL continues to pour out the bourbon without stopping.

PAUL: But this was not my agreement with Rosa. Here Rosa constructs a second husband . . . dresses him like the first . . .

MARCEL: Makes him drink the same rotgut . . .

PAUL: You were lucky enough . . . You must have been a good-looking man twenty years ago.

MARCEL: Not as much as you.

PAUL: You have all your hair.

MARCEL: I have to cut it often. And wash it.

PAUL: Do you have massages?

MARCEL: Yes. Massages also.

PAUL: You're in good shape. What do you do for—for the belly?

MARCEL: The belly?

PAUL: That's my problem.

MARCEL: Here . . . I have a secret.

PAUL: What?

MARCEL: Thinking of leaving? I saw your suitcase . . . eh . . . America . . . Why did she betray you with me?

PAUL: You don't think Rosa killed herself? It's difficult for me too, to believe it.

MARCEL: Here's my secret. Thirty times, every morning.

MARCEL chins himself.

PAUL: I was looking for a letter from Rosa. But the letter is you . . .

The bottle is now empty. PAUL doesn't seem to have noticed it. He continues to hold MARCEL'S wrist in his hand, tighter and tighter. MARCEL is not afraid or worried any more.

MARCEL: Paul, let go of my wrist, you're hurting me. Let go, Paul!

PAUL lets go. On the white porcelain, in a glass is MARCEL'S razor. That one is also a straight razor.

PAUL goes quickly toward the door.

PAUL: Really, Marcel, I wonder what she ever saw in you.

SUNDAY BLOODY SUNDAY

Released through United Artists Corporation. Producer, Joseph Janni. Director, John Schlesinger. Screenplay by Penelope Gilliatt. Associate Producer, Teddy Joseph. Director of Photography, Billy Williams. Film Editor, Richard Marden. Production Designer, Luciana Arrighi. Art Director, Norman Dorme. Sound Mixer, Simon Kaye. Assistant Director, Simon Relph. Color. Running time, 110 minutes. 1972.

CAST

ALEX GREVILLE	Glenda Jackson
DR. DANIEL HIRSH	Peter Finch
BOB ELKIN	Murray Head
MRS. GREVILLE	Peggy Ashcroft
MR. GREVILLE	Maurice Denham
ALVA HODSON	Vivian Pickles
BILL HODSON	Frank Windsor
LUCY HODSON	Kimi Tallmadge
PROFESSOR JOHNS	Thomas Baptiste
MR. HARDING (BUSINESSMAN)	Tony Britton
DANIEL'S FATHER	Harold Goldblatt
DANIEL'S MOTHER	Hannah Norbert
ANSWERING SERVICE LADY	Bessie Love
SCOTSMAN	Jon Finch

Daniel, Alex and Bob are all English and all three live in London. Daniel is a warm and cultured Jewish physician who is in love with Bob. Alex, the daughter of a moneyed, "incon-

spicuously upper class" family, is unhappily working in executive placement; she says she's "fed up with grooming people
to be thrusters." She also is in love with Bob. In addition to
Bob, Alex and Daniel also share a few overly sympathetic
friends, as well as the same incompetent answering service,
which insists upon confusing their respective messages to and
from Bob. What is even more awkward is that they share a
civilized respect for each other's right to exist and to love
Bob, so they are ashamed at their own desperation not to lose
someone whom they already know they cannot finally have.
In his way, Bob loves them both, but his choice is not
between two lovers—it's between anybody and his ambition.
He will eventually leave for America where he will sell his
beautiful kinetic glass and light sculptures. Only after he is
gone, at the end of the film, do Daniel and Alex allow
themselves a brief meeting.

Alex has just been through an emotionally exhausting weekend. It was to have been spent with Bob, but he kept
disappearing, either to work or to be with Daniel. Her mind
understands that the relationship with Bob is untenable, but
her heart is refusing to get the message. The weekend over,
Alex is having dinner with her parents at the long walnut
table in their quiet, large dining room. In what is almost an
echo of Bob and his distractions, a business call from New
York comes in for her father and he immediately takes it,
thereby abruptly ending the meal and leaving the two women
sitting alone.

(*Note*: The preliminary scene of Alex's father in his study is
provided here as Alex's prior moment.)

[MR. GREVILLE'S STUDY—MONDAY NIGHT.

Telephone ringing.

MR. GREVILLE is on the telephone to New York. On his right
is a tickertape machine carrying share and commodity prices:
tin, gold, lead, copper, sugar, pepper from all over the world.
On his left is a comptometer for working out yields.

ALEX comes in with coffee and sugar on a silver tray. She
tries to attract his attention.

MR. GREVILLE shoos her away, continuing his conversation.]

GREVILLE DINING ROOM—MONDAY NIGHT.

MRS. GREVILLE is at the far end of the dining room.

A maid takes away the pudding plates.

ALEX comes in.

ALEX: What's all the stuff to Wall Street about?

MRS. GREVILLE: Bank rate.

ALEX makes a tired sound.

MRS. GREVILLE: No, he's in fine form. (*grinning to herself*) I haven't seen him so spry since the General Strike.

ALEX: When he was a smart undergraduate, strike-breaking.

MRS. GREVILLE: Before you were born. Should you talk about what you don't know about?

ALEX: O.K. But you agreed with him, yes?

MRS. GREVILLE: I didn't, as it happened. But we were very young. I didn't think it would matter.

ALEX: Well, it hasn't mattered, has it? (*sharp*) The marriage has lasted. (*long silence*)

[SERVANT comes in with a silver tray of coffee and a science-fiction book on the tray. She puts it in front of MRS. GREVILLE.]

ALEX: I wish you didn't have David to dine here.

MRS. GREVILLE: He wants you back, you know.

ALEX: (*shakes head*) *Please*.

MRS. GREVILLE: Daddy and I are fond of him.

ALEX: Look, I don't want to talk about it.

MRS. GREVILLE: He feels very bitterly about your having taken the books.

ALEX: They were mine. They were all I took.

MRS. GREVILLE: They leave gaps, he says.

ALEX: Oh Jesus. Does being married ever come down to anything but property, ever?

MRS. GREVILLE: Sometimes. (*she looks at the book she would like to be reading*)

ALEX looks at her. Sympathy. That sounded sad.

ALEX: What's the book tonight? (*friendly. Quite tender*) Town Planning in 1580?

MRS. GREVILLE holds up a pulp science-fiction book.

ALEX: Good lord.

MRS. GREVILLE: I know it looks lurid, but it's rather interesting.

ALEX: No, I didn't mean that. (*pause*) You see too little of people.

MRS. GREVILLE: Enough.

ALEX: I mean too little of Daddy.

MRS. GREVILLE makes a movement brushing the idea away.

MRS. GREVILLE: Well, it's not much use to start wanting things of him. (*pause*) Though I'm not always very good at stopping myself.

ALEX: (*looking at her carefully*) What? *You?*

MRS. GREVILLE looks away. The telephone outside goes again.
MRS. GREVILLE pours herself more coffee.

ALEX: Well, I wish you didn't have to put up with it. But why do you?

A telephone rings again.

ALEX: The other line, naturally.

MRS. GREVILLE: He's busy. It's a heavy week.

ALEX: Oh, stop protecting him. It's *always* a heavy week.

MRS. GREVILLE: You complain about your father. Perhaps you're complaining about whoever it is you see.

ALEX plays with the RETRIEVER under the table with her feet.

MRS. GREVILLE: Are you in trouble?

ALEX shrugs.

MRS. GREVILLE: Who *are* you seeing now?

ALEX: (*gets up*) Same person. On and off.

MRS. GREVILLE: On and off. You're not giving it a chance.

ALEX: I can't see why having an affair with someone on and off is any worse than being married for a course or two at mealtimes. (*pause*)

MRS. GREVILLE gets up and goes to the sideboard. She finds some dinner mints.

MRS. GREVILLE: What sort of man is he?

ALEX: I don't think you'd like his haircut.

MRS. GREVILLE: Is he a hippie? But I *like* hippies. (*to herself*) They hate business and competitiveness. I think that's what's always attracted me to them.

ALEX: (*rudely*) What, you? (*pause*) I'm sorry. I'm sorry. I'm sorry.

MRS. GREVILLE stands near her daughter and hands her a mint.

MRS. GREVILLE: Darling, you keep throwing in your hand because you haven't got the whole thing. (*pause*) There *is* no whole thing. One has to make it work.

Close-up on ALEX'S face. Startled and moved. Waiting to hear the rest. MRS. GREVILLE hesitates and then goes on. An offering.

MRS. GREVILLE: What you don't know is that there was a time when I left him. We had different opinions about everything. *Everything* seemed impossible.

ALEX: When?

MRS. GREVILLE: You were three. He left me alone. It was good of him. (*pause*) But I was mad not to know how much I was going to miss him.

MRS. GREVILLE moves to the door. The RETRIEVER gets up and follows her and then pads out, preceding her. She pauses with her hand on the handle and then looks back at ALEX.

MRS. GREVILLE: You think it's nothing, but it's not nothing.

ALEX watches her mother leave. Shot shows MRS. GREVILLE wavering at her husband's door and then leaving it, hearing him on the telephone. She is used to that particular disappointment by now. She goes down a long corridor. Sound of adding machine over.

MINNIE AND MOSKOWITZ

Released through Universal Pictures. Producer, Al Ruban. Director, John Cassavetes. Screenplay by John Cassavetes. Associate Producer, Paul Donnelly. Directors of Photography, Alric Edens, Arthur J. Ornitz, Michael Margulies. Film Editor, Robert Heffernan. Sound, Melvin M. Metcalfe, Sr. Musical Supervisor, Bo Harwood. Assistant Directors, Kevin Donnelly, Lou Stroller. Technicolor. Running time, 114 minutes. 1973.

CAST

MINNIE MOORE	Gena Rowlands
SEYMOUR MOSKOWITZ	Seymour Cassel
ZELMO SWIFT	Val Avery
JIM	John Cassavetes
HOBO	Tim Carey
MRS. MOSKOWITZ	Katherine Cassavetes
GIRL	Elizabeth Deering
FLORENCE	Elsie Ames
GEORGIA MOORE	Lady Rowlands
KELLY	Holly Near
WIFE	Judith Roberts
DICK	Jack Danskin
MRS. GRASS	Eleanor Zee
NED	Sean Joyce
MINISTER	David Rowlands

The characters of the title are two people of extremely high behavior, none of which is calculated or affected. Their need for the "real feeling" in life is what drives them forward, so that even when they are stammering, it is not in vagueness, but in active search. Their search leads them to each other; they fall in love, and they get married. A logical enough progression of events—except to them and to their respective families.

Because of the way John Cassavetes writes and directs a film, these respective families are played by the relatives of the actors, more or less. And there are distinct differences of text between what has been written in the original screenplay and what is improvised in front of the camera and then edited into the film. But the boisterous intimacy and the exhilarating fluidities of emotional transition, the particular romance of realism in Cassavetes' filmmaking, is there in the writing:

MINNIE AND MOSKOWITZ was written for the screen . . . It was written for some friends to perform. The basic story came out of certain remembrances of loneliness. The need for family and love, friendship, and an understanding between certain people that you like and love.

A Minnie Moore with all the values in the world, but no place to put them. An empty bed, a fixed-up apartment, a job, a boyfriend who is married and who comes once in a while. Minnie, in my mind, searching her mirror, continually looking at the past so much so that there can be no future.

Her affair with Seymour Moskowitz, a feet-on-the-ground, nine-to-five worker, who loves his mother, wears long hair, parks cars for a living with the cool of a Bogart, seeks out adventure in lonely Times Square movie houses and all-night eateries and with girls who mean something to him. To me Moskowitz is the new symbol of hope in America. His symbols are not success, sipping wine, television, *Playboy, Screw,* or the *Village Voice*. He's not interested in puffing smoke or getting caught up on a street corner standing around talking and all. When life achieves sameness he gets bored and moves on. He's a footloose, practical, uncomplicated American dreamer who sees romance in a cup of coffee and pretty eyes. A Seymour Moskowitz has his own style. He's been tugged at and pushed like the rest of us and has emerged like we all wish to be—a guy that knows romance is better than loneliness. . . .

The screenplay calls all these problems lies—makes the past the past and the present now. It evades the insanity that life subjects us all to—places two people in a position to need each other. And in my mind, like life, gives them another chance.

—John Cassavetes
August 1972

Fed up with the dead-end affair she is having, Minnie has made a blind date to have lunch with one Zelmo Swift, who turns out to be everything wrong. She tells him she's not interested in him personally, she just wanted lunch. He refuses to drive her back to her job, at the Los Angeles Museum of Art. When Zelmo drives back, yelling obscenities at Minnie, Seymour, the restaurant parking lot attendant, gets into a fistfight with him and then drives Minnie back to work in his truck. On their first date (chili dogs and malteds), Minnie tells him, "You know before I met you I thought I was in trouble." Seymour asks her, "What is with you? You have a way of depressing me . . . you got a way of looking down on people . . . it's so goddamn boring to sit with someone who takes himself so seriously." After he takes Minnie home, he picks up a pretty young girl and spends the night with her, but it's not what he's looking for. The following scene takes place the next morning after Seymour has dropped off the girl at her car and has then headed over to Minnie's apartment with a bunch of balloons.

SCENE 1

[We see SEYMOUR much closer now. We see the white Ford in the background pull out of the garage. SEYMOUR turns on the truck radio automatically. We hear a voice—it's the farm news program. He changes the dial. He gets a lot of static and turns off the radio.

He gets out of the truck, takes ten or twelve deep breaths. He bends over and touches the ground five or six times. He reaches into his pocket, pulls out his Luckys, goes over to the truck, gets in, presses his lighter. He starts up his truck.

We see the truck swing out into the Santa Monica traffic going back in a western direction toward the area of his house. The truck screeches to a halt, veers around in a U-turn, and streaks past us.

CUT TO:

EXTERIOR ELAINE APARTMENTS—VINE.

SEYMOUR'S truck pulls up. He gets out and stomps on his cigarette.

EXTERIOR COURTYARD ELAINE APARTMENTS.

Door to MINNIE'S apartment.

SEYMOUR knocks on the door. There's no answer. He rings the doorbell.

CUT TO:

INTERIOR MINNIE'S APARTMENT.

The bed is made, not slept in. The camera swings to the bathroom and we see MINNIE sitting on the toilet, fully clothed, with the seat down. She smokes. She's drawn and tired but still nervous from the night before. She's done a lot of thinking but she can't calm her hysteria. She holds an ashtray in her left hand and flicks ashes in it. There is a pack on her lap crumpled and there are matches in the sink. The doorbell rings again.]

CUT TO:

EXTERIOR MINNIE'S APARTMENT.

SEYMOUR pounds on the door. The door opens and SEYMOUR goes in.

CUT TO:

INTERIOR MINNIE'S APARTMENT.

MINNIE goes to the little wrought iron table and sits down. SEYMOUR flicks ashes in the ashtray.

MINNIE: I've been thinking about what you said. I've been thinking about what you said. I do look down on people. What's your name? Tell me your name, will you, for God's sake.

SEYMOUR: Seymour. Moskowitz.

MINNIE: Oh, God.

SEYMOUR: That's right. Laugh. Go ahead, laugh. It's good for you. People only laugh at people they like.

MINNIE: Give me one of your cigarettes.

SEYMOUR throws his package of Lucky's on the table.

MINNIE: Where were you last night?

SEYMOUR: *(with some difficulty)* Why?

MINNIE: Your clothes . . . they're the same. What did you do—pick someone up? What did you do—pick some little ten cent barfly up? One of those hitch-hiking infants? Don't tell me about it . . . and come back here at seven in the morning with a bunch of balloons . . . I know about guys. What a way to end it—sitting in a room with Seymour Moskowitz. I'm sorry, it's not your fault . . . you see, I have such a good sense of humor that I have trouble feeling. You have to forgive me, I'm very depressed. I'm not feeling anything, but I'm depressed. I would feel something, but I don't know what to feel. Is there anything interesting going on?

SEYMOUR: No, not really.

MINNIE: Well, Seymour, I guess I owe you an apology. You came back. I felt you would . . . but, that's funny too, isn't it? I mean, we have nothing in common. Did you ever get so that whatever you say . . . sounds like you hear it the minute you say it . . . like a hollow room . . . or a headache . . . a bad stomach or something . . . Anyway, I'm not myself . . . whoever that is. But, I'm a little out of control. Can't seem to work it out alone . . . so, I'm glad you're here. But I didn't ask you in . . . you came . . .

SEYMOUR starts diddling with a balloon . . . keeps tapping it with his finger as MINNIE talks. He pops it up in the air. He gets up and follows it. He pops it over to the table. It bounces on the table and SEYMOUR lets it roll there.

MINNIE: I don't know what it is, except that I don't feel as much as I used to. I have trouble crying . . . you know? And I never had that trouble before. You probably don't understand what I'm talking about . . .

SEYMOUR takes MINNIE by the head and holds her head near his hip.

MINNIE: Thanks, buddy, you're a nice boy.

SEYMOUR: You're a nice girl.

MINNIE: No, you're a nice boy.

SEYMOUR: No, you're really a nice girl.

MINNIE: All right, all right.

He sits down with her and he keeps diddling with the balloon. Her head comes up and she looks at him and the balloon begins to annoy her and she goes after it with her cigarette. He pulls the balloon away, takes the cigarette from her hand, and puts it in the ashtray. He flips the balloon over her head. She flicks it away from her. He pops it to her. She pops it back. He won't let it touch the table. He hits it twice and the balloon curves—he can hardly control it—he pops it back to her. She pops it back to him. He pops it back to her. And this continues.

DIRECTOR'S SEQUENCE. BALLOON SCENE.

MINNIE: I think with me it's a question of feeling. I think it's happening to everyone. I just don't smile as much as I used to. It's . . . mainly being tired . . . just tired and I don't like men. They smile too much—you see a lot of teeth. Oh, it's not just men . . . I think it's the waste of everything . . . the waste of not being able to give what you're capable of giving. And then it's too late . . . it's too late and you get old.

SEYMOUR: If I had my way, I'd kill anyone over thirty.

MINNIE: It's not age . . . it's oh, you see, thinking this way is coarse. It's not healthy . . . I know that. God, I was raised in a small town . . . I know church hymns and I'm not afraid of God or little people . . . I just can't find anyone. So, maybe you're right. I do look down. Also, I'm envious of people who have real problems. Like your mother.

SEYMOUR: My mother's fine.

MINNIE: What did the baby die of?

SEYMOUR: The baby didn't die, my sister died.

MINNIE: Oh, was her baby a girl?

Dishes go over, chairs go over, but they can't let the balloon touch the ground.

SEYMOUR: No, my sister was a girl, the baby was a boy. But don't worry about it. She lived in Toledo . . . I didn't know her very well . . .

MINNIE: Well, you see, there it is, it's hopeless. That's what I do, I forget about it when it's hopeless.

The end of the balloon playing.

SEYMOUR touches her face. She looks at him.

SEYMOUR gets to his knees, and holds her face with both hands now and looks at her.

MINNIE: I used to feel all the time . . . used to feel every-thing . . . by God, I'd cry at the drop of a hat. They used to get ahold of me for laughs . . . roommates in college . . . They'd say, Minnie, cry for us . . . and then I'd start laughing. I'm having trouble being myself. I'm having trouble figuring out . . . what it is . . . that is right. What it is to do . . . I mean, like being alone . . . should you go out or relax to it . . .

SEYMOUR very gently picks MINNIE up, and takes her to bed. He lies down next to her and holds her very closely in his arms . . . MINNIE talks during the time SEYMOUR carries her and as she lies on the bed . . . she never stops talking.

MINNIE: . . . everything used to make me feel like smiling . . . but I notice that I don't smile as much, any more . . . did you ever notice that? And it's an effort to breathe sometimes because the air isn't light enough . . . you see, my friend . . .

MINNIE: Seymour, I don't have any real problem of any size . . . it's being alone mainly that is irritating . . . I hear room tone . . . frequency when I'm alone . . . noises like the bathtub running, or the sink, or the stove, or the distant traffic . . . that irritates me . . . God knows why . . . when I'm with someone, I want to get away. Someone I could love makes me run, someone I hate makes me retreat . . . someone light bores me, and someone heavy depresses me . . . and makes me want to be alone . . . so now, you know . . . I do look down on people. I see you and I think what can this poor sucker know of my hidden irritations . . . I'm very uncomfortable. It's hot, isn't it?

Would you like a cup of tea, a drink?

Some eggs?

What a lovely night it was . . . did you feel that night . . . I talked to a cab driver . . . I didn't look down on him . . . I admire people that are straight . . . people that work and can really feel.

Seymour, I'm very lonely . . . I'm not with anyone, you know? . . . nothing really to hide,

SEYMOUR: Minnie, I see you. I see you crumbling inside. Your whole insides, all your guts are just crumbling . . . Minnie, you're a beautiful woman . . .

No . . .

No . . .
No . . .

You're gonna be all right,

nothing to fear, nothing to be ashamed of . . . my mind is so practical, my imagination has forbidden any strange fantasy . . . any thought of legs and body intertwined in a fantasy . . . it makes me laugh . . . I was born seeing things clearly. I was taught to laugh at fate. . . .

. . . I look at myself like people do when they knock their heads with gooney smiles . . . and say—what an idiot I am. I come home . . . you see, and look at what this sum total is and it's quite a disappointment . . . oh, I suppose I've had my just share of childhood flings and phoney love affairs . . . my share of son-of-a-bitches, and mistakes . . . but never do I fall . . . never is my heart crushed or sudden memory flashing back . . . nor do I dream . . . nor am I compassionate or kind . . . or raging at some small injustice . . .

Minnie. You're gonna sleep . . . I'm gonna lie here with you and watch you until I get tired. Then I'm gonna sleep next to you . . .

. . . I'm thinking about you Minnie . . . I'm thinking about how nice you're sleeping . . . boy, do you sleep nice . . . what a great sleeper you are, Minnie . . . you're breathing nice and easy, Minnie . . . and dreaming of pretty things . . . Minnie, everything's fine . . . .

SCENE 2

Minnie and Seymour go out to the Palamino dance bar. Seymour coaxes Minnie out of her self-consciousness about dancing, but not about him and what he looks like. When she runs into well-intentioned friends who want to take her home, it leads to another fistfight. They return to Minnie's apartment bloody and bruised. Right in the middle of Minnie's insistance that the relationship just isn't going anywhere, Seymour shaves off his moustache. The next thing they do is to take a midnight splash in the pool.

INTERIOR MINNIE'S APARTMENT—NIGHT.

MINNIE and SEYMOUR come in soaking wet, carrying clothes. They drop the things in the bathroom. Put on a bathrobe and a coat and bobby socks. There is silence.

MINNIE: You want some hot chocolate?

SEYMOUR: I don't want a cook.

MINNIE: A cook? Oh, you're so funny.

SEYMOUR: Sure, a cook. That's what people get married for . . . do my laundry, do my socks, cook my meals, rub my back, fix me drinks . . . (*makes a sound with his mouth*)

MINNIE: I can't cook.

SEYMOUR: It's like trying to get closer to someone, you know. You can't do it by making provisions . . . I, I, I . . . I can't make any promises. I'm not gonna make any promises to you. There's no promises I can make. I've seen too many guys make promises.

MINNIE: Really.

SEYMOUR: Sure. Nobody keeps promises. I mean, how can you keep a promise? I mean, a promise is a chore—it's what . . . I mean, if it's there, it's there. And that's what I mean—straight—no delusions.

MINNIE: All I asked you was if you want hot chocolate and you said to me, I don't care, or something, or cooking, or something . . . or something.

SEYMOUR: Well, that's, oh, because I never felt . . . I never felt anything. One minute you're just soaring through life and the next minute you're down on your ass, and uh . . .

MINNIE: You're hurting . . .

SEYMOUR: Yeah, yeah.

MINNIE: Yeah, I know, I know.

SEYMOUR: I mean just it's stupid, you know? Just, I mean, you just, you know, you don't, I mean, after all this time you don't . . . I mean, you just don't . . . I mean . . . (*laughs*) I don't know . . . just it's stupid, I mean . . .

MINNIE: I get the feeling you're trying to tell me something.

SEYMOUR: Oh, no. I'm not. It's just that you, you're everything I ever wanted. So, I'm not trying to tell you
anything . . . I just . . .

MINNIE: You have too many theories . . . it's just confusing
me. It makes me tired. It makes me sleepy. I don't want that.

SEYMOUR: No, no, no, no, no . . . no, no. I don't know. Just,
you know, I was gonna in the pool, you know? Just do it.
You know, just kind of stupid, and childish, you know, I
wanted to be . . . to be . . . Jesus, I can't talk to you!

MINNIE: Mmmm, hmmmm. You can't talk to me.

SEYMOUR: Well, what is it? I mean, what is it?

MINNIE: I can't talk to you. Because you see, my whole
thing, my whole thing, my whole life is uh, geared, just
geared to be that way. And I'm, I'm . . . very, very
intelligent—that I know. And, uh, and, uh . . . what,
what was it? . . . what did you say?

SEYMOUR: Where do I stand? What am I to you? Big, beautiful blonde, and uh, crazy looking and nutty looking and
I don't know anything about you and you've lived and
probably had a lot of guys and what the hell . . . I'm just
a car parker . . . oh shit!!

MINNIE: I can't tell you how if anyone were listening to this
conversation there would be no one in the world who
would understand what you're saying. You're the most
ignorant man . . . you don't say what you want to say.
You go round and round with uhs and ooohs . . . now
say what you want to say!

SEYMOUR: So, it's on the brink. It's on the brink. I mean it
could go that way or it could go that way depending on
. . . boy, it's tough . . . it's tough to say what you want
. . . I keep getting the feeling who gives me the right to
say what I want to say?

SEYMOUR: I love you.

MINNIE: Oh, please.

SEYMOUR: Oh, for God's sake, please don't laugh . . . don't
laugh . . . that's all I ask, give me a break. I'll go away
. . . jeez, don't laugh—it would be terrible, it would be
awful.

MINNIE: "I love you"—is that what you said?

SEYMOUR: Mmmm, hmmmm.

MINNIE: Oh. A lot of lonely nights . . . I just, it seemed like I was two steps away from the grave, like I would never find anyone, like it was all over and my heart was pounding and it was all confusion . . .

SEYMOUR: Well, I know that. I got that feeling that you were . . . the thing that confused me was that you worked in a museum. I mean, that confused me—that part confused me.

MINNIE: Yeah, when you followed me in the truck that cemented it, that was the coup d'etat.

SEYMOUR: . . . that was lousy. That was awful.

MINNIE: Oh, no. That wasn't awful. I mean the way it turned out and everything.

SEYMOUR: I got to stop this—this is silly.

MINNIE: Okay. Then ask me what you want to ask me and we'll settle it; cement it.

SEYMOUR wraps his arms around MINNIE.

SEYMOUR: I want to ask you about those guys.

MINNIE: Well, just, just . . . I was in love just a couple of times with nice guys . . . they were nice, nice guys, and . . . oh God, I wish I'd never seen them. I'd like to be everything that you want me to be.

SEYMOUR: But?

MINNIE: Well, I've, I've, I've been there with men . . .

SEYMOUR: But?

MINNIE: . . . Oh, God, what's the use of making excuses. I don't give a damn. I don't care!

She turns and pushes her hair back.

SEYMOUR: Hey, man, you know what it means to me to see a girl like you and you respond, to be responsive, to respond to me . . . I think to myself— whooooo, that's a fantastic lovely long-legged blonde. I got to confess this to you, hey bullshit, I mean—I love you. That's it. Plain and simple.

MINNIE: Okay. Good.

SEYMOUR: Bullshit, man. I mean I just got the whole feeling that this whole thing went up in smoke and now you're going back the other way over the other side of the mountain. Relax!

MINNIE: Seymour.

SEYMOUR: I said relax—goddamn it! Or I'll knock you right on your ass. Just say I love you, goddamn it, that's what I want you to say.

MINNIE: No.

SEYMOUR: Say it!

MINNIE: No!

SEYMOUR: Say it, goddamn it. Say it. Say it.

MINNIE doesn't answer. SEYMOUR slaps her across the face.

SEYMOUR: Say it, goddamn it.

MINNIE: No!

SEYMOUR: Okay. Forget about it. It's just bullshit!

MINNIE looks at him and squints her eyes.

MINNIE: Okay, Seymour, you want to be crude? You want to be the big man? You want to be the tough guy?

SEYMOUR: I don't want to be a tough guy.

MINNIE: You want to marry me?

SEYMOUR: (shrugs) Yeah . . . I'll marry you.

MINNIE: Don't tell me that unless you mean it . . . (SEYMOUR doesn't reply—just looks at her) . . . 'cause I'm gonna call my Mother and I don't want to call my Mother and tell her I'm getting married unless you mean it.

SEYMOUR: Call her.

MINNIE goes to SEYMOUR, throws her arms around him.

SEYMOUR: Hey!

MINNIE pulls him over to the bed, throws him down, wrestles around with him.

SEYMOUR: Hey, what are you doing? You crazy or something?

MINNIE: I got to warn you, buddy. I have a Mother complex. I love my Mother and I can't have anyone say anything about her and she always has to be welcome in the house . . . okay?

SEYMOUR: Sure.

MINNIE gets up on the bed and jumps up and down.

SEYMOUR: *(looking at her)* Are you crazy or what?

MINNIE jumps off the bed and goes to the phone. She's breathing very heavily. She dials the operator, she calls Long Distance.

MINNIE: *(standing with the phone in her hand)* Hello, Long Distance? I'd like to place a call to Mrs. Georgia Moore in Vancouver. The number is 643-2130. Well, thank you. Thank you. *(to SEYMOUR)* She said I sounded out of breath. She doesn't know. (MINNIE *now lies down on the bed—her back against it.* SEYMOUR *comes over and strokes her hair. She puts one forefinger up to fend* SEYMOUR *away and speaks into the phone)* Hello, Vancouver? Mother? Minnie. Guess what? No. Nothing bad. I have a friend. Yes, he's handsome. (SEYMOUR *covers his face)* He's about six something and blonde and nice and unchicken and intelligent and strong and really perfect . . . and we're gonna be married. Can you come? Mother? Mother? Can you come? Right away. I'll get you a reservation right away or you could stay here . . . okay? You want to say hello to him? He's right here right now. *(to SEYMOUR)* She wants to say hello to you.

SEYMOUR grabs the phone.

SEYMOUR: Hello, Mom. Ahhhh. Seymour Moskowitz. Right. Jewish. Right. No, not terribly religious. Hey, Minnie tells me she has a Mother complex—is that right? *(he laughs)* Okay, hold on—I'll put her on.

He hands MINNIE the phone.

MINNIE: Mama, I'll call you later as soon as he goes. I love you too. Bye-bye.

SEYMOUR looks at her and she goes to him.

SEYMOUR: Wait a minute. I got to call my Mother.

MINNIE starts laughing. It's uncontrollable wrinkled nose time. SEYMOUR enjoying it.

SEYMOUR: *(picking up phone and dialing Long Distance)* Hello, operator. Placing a call to area code 212-TR6-3441. Very good. Very good. Person to person. Mrs. Seymour Moskowitz, Sr. Right. Right. Thank you.

SAVE THE TIGER

A Paramount Pictures presentation of a Filmways (Martin Ransohoff)—Jalem (Jack Lemmon)—Cirandinha Production. Producer, Steve Shagan. Executive Producer, Edward S. Feldman. Director, John G. Avildsen. Screenplay by Steve Shagan. Photography, Jim Crabe. Film Editor, David Bretherton. Music, Marvin Hamlisch. Art Director, Jack Collis. Sound, Bud Alper & Robert I. Knudson. Assistant Directors, Christopher Seiter, Ron Schwary. Color by Movielab. Running time, 100 minutes. 1973.

CAST

HARRY STONER	Jack Lemmon
PHIL GREENE	Jack Gilford
MYRA	Laurie Heineman
FRED MIRRELL	Norman Burton
JANET STONER	Patricia Smith
CHARLIE ROBBINS	Thayer David
MEYER	William Hansen
RICO	Harvey Jason
ULA	Liv Von Linden
MARGO	Lara Parker
JACKIE	Eloise Hardt
DUSTY	Janina
SID FIVUSH	Ned Glass
CASHIER	Pearl Shear
TIGER MAN	Biff Elliott
TAXI DRIVER	Ben Freedman
RECEPTIONIST	Madeline Lee

Harry Stoner—co-owner of Capri Casuals, a Los Angeles garment manufacturing firm—is a man not only in love with the past, but in love with the loss of it. He drifts off into reveries of his youth and the heroes of his idealism— the baseball players and the jazz and swing musicians. He tries to remember all the names and dates of celebrated starting line-ups and dance bands. Harry is "comfortable" with Jan, his wife of many years ("a very attractive woman in her late 30's"), but he is possessed of a wild longing for what he recalls as that "fleeting moment when one is very young, very free and all the dreams are attainable."

Harry's most treacherously transporting memories are of his time in Italy during World War II. He carries three gruesomely painful scars on his back from the battle at Anzio. He remembers the beach at Capri splattered with blood, but his business visit there last year found the sands littered with bikinis. His company is throwing a fashion show/party to sell its new collection, and while addressing the audience of buyers, Harry hallucinates, seeing the faces of the long-ago wounded among them. The collection is a success, but the company is going under because it hasn't got the money to buy the cloth to fill the orders. Harry grieves that "Fifteen years we met our obligations—same mills, same unions, same bank—but no more—all they respect is money. History doesn't count anymore." All around him Harry Stoner sees the society he has believed in and fought for disintegrating, and he knows he is disintegrating along with it. "I'm floating, I'm— going on nerve."

Save the Tiger covers one day in the life of Harry Stoner—a day which begins in his Beverly Hills house as he wakes up screaming from a nightmare. Over the intercom, he tells the Spanish-speaking housekeeper Carmela to bring in the morning coffee. Jan's first groggy words, from under the covers, are "Tell her to put some goddamn cream in it." Harry listens briefly to the morning news about wars, pollution levels and earthquakes. After Carmela has arrived and departed, the couple lies in bed sipping coffee as Harry reads the newspaper and chats with Jan about her departure for New York to attend her uncle's funeral.

SCENE 1

TWO SHOT—NEW ANGLE

JAN: He was a louse. A real thoroughbred.

HARRY nods, still looking at paper.

HARRY: When's the funeral?

JAN: Thursday.

HARRY: Sorry about the airport thing.

JAN: It's all right, Harry. Hard to believe Uncle Bernie's dead. God, what a bastard.

HARRY: (*nods*) Screwed everybody. How long will you be away?

JAN: A week, ten days.

HARRY flicks a button at the side of his bed, activating a tape machine off screen. We HEAR an old Benny Goodman tune, something like "Stompin' At The Savoy." A beat.

HARRY: (*softly*) Christ . . .

TWO SHOT

JAN: You screamed in your sleep. That's the second time this week.

HARRY: (*nods*) Same nightmare. I'm sitting in this tribal council in the jungle. And there's Billy Graham, wearing a $400 tie. And he's showing us the road to God. And I jump up and I yell something . . . and I don't know what it is I say . . . But he points at me and screams "There's Cuban Pete, King of the Rhumba Beat—get him!" Then all these naked tribesmen start chasing me through the jungle. Then I'm in this path, and in front of me . . . this black cobra, its head is fanned out . . . it rises up about eight feet high, weaving back and forth, measuring me. And I can't move.

JAN: See Dr. Frankfurter.

HARRY: He'll tell me it's repressed sex.

JAN: Maybe it is.

HARRY: No. It's Willie.

JAN: Who?

HARRY: The guy that parks my car downtown—at the factory—
it's Willie.

There's a pause. HARRY listens to Benny Goodman.

ANOTHER ANGLE—After a pause:

HARRY: (*indicating newspaper*) Kamu died.

JAN: He died a long time ago.

HARRY: Not him, Kamu, the Whale. For three years he's
been swimming against the current.

JAN: What current?

HARRY: The current in the tank at Pacific World. The fric-
tion damaged his dorsal fin—that beautiful animal, Jan—
dead. I took Audrey to see him once—years ago.

JAN: Harry, you insulted Dr. Sorell last night.

HARRY: Insulted? What insult? He's drinking my booze and
climbing all over my wife.

JAN: Insecurity. He's insecure.

HARRY: Insecurity? . . . For Christsake, he's got everything
up front except trumpets.

JAN: He happens to be a fine doctor. Everyone's using him.

HARRY: You swung me over to him, Jan. But I still like Doc
Fisher.

JAN: (*smiling*) Fisher still uses leeches. He's an old man.

HARRY: Yeah, old and smart. He can diagnose hemmorrhoids
through a suit of armor.

NEW ANGLE—Holding him from JAN's point of view.

HARRY wearily swings his legs over the side of the bed. He
removes his pajama top and stares down at the rug. We
clearly see three jagged, vicious-looking scars; they are closely
spaced near the top of his spinal column—and bluish in color.

JAN: Those scars are positively hideous.

HARRY: So's the pain—the thousand year Reich . . . they
still may make it.

JAN: Wouldn't hurt to have them checked again.

HARRY: (*turns; indicates newspaper; brightens*) Saw an item

in the sports section—that nine-year-old—Judy Miller—
they're gonna let her play ball with the boys—her father
had to go to court—but they're gonna let her play.

He rises, goes to the console and shuts Goodman off. Turns
to JAN and smiles.

HARRY: I think that's terrific. Kid's a good ballplayer, what's
the difference if she's a girl—I mean at that age who
notices? Her father must be a hell of a guy—took it all
the way to court.

JAN: You used to love baseball . . . Why don't you go to a
game once in a while?

He comes around to the front of the bed.

HARRY: They still play, but they don't play on dirt any more.
They play on plastic. The ballplayers are antiseptic kids,
they don't chew tobacco, they don't use spikes, and the
pitchers don't wind up—they used to wind up.

JAN: Wind up?

HARRY: Yes, wind up. Remember Johnny Vandermeer?

He proceeds to do a very professional full wind-up, double
pump, with a high kick and complete follow-through.

HARRY: That was pitching. What about Hugh Casey. Lumbering out of the bullpen—in the clutch, the pressure
on—his sinker would fall off a cliff—and if he ran out of
stuff, he'd throw his balls up at the plate. Goddammit,
they were something!

JAN: Harry, Dr. Frankfurter. Hypnosis. Hypnosis is the thing.

HARRY: Frankfurter didn't help me. "Bring me dreams . . .
Bring me dreams."

JAN: They can tell a lot from dreams.

HARRY: Frankfurter said I murdered myself.

JAN: You're worried.

He turns to her.

HARRY: Cuban Pete never worries.

JAN: You're worried.

HARRY: I don't know why. It only costs me two hundred
dollars a day to get out of bed.

JAN: Two hundred a day?

HARRY: That's what the accountant tells me. With everything—three hundred a day. Taxes, insurance, the cars,
the tree surgeon, the poolman, the gardener, Carmela,
the house, the Swiss school, and downtown, that's something else. I've got to finance the new line. Money's
tight, payroll to meet, textile mills to pay—and we may
be audited . . .

JAN: Audited for what?

HARRY: Last year. We did a little ballet with the books.

JAN: What does Phil say?

HARRY: He's worried.

NEW ANGLE—as HARRY comes around to her side of the bed,
sits down.

HARRY: When you get back, let's go to Zurich and see the
kid.

JAN: She's better off in Switzerland. Europe is civilized.
Things are too crazy in this country. A man came out of
Marioni's restaurant, someone walked up and shot him
to death. They didn't even know each other. That's only
a few blocks away.

HARRY: Well, maybe we can get a brigade of Cambodians to
patrol Beverly Hills. The Mexican maids can cook their
rice.

JAN: She's better off in Switzerland—

JAN rises, goes to the bathroom. CAMERA HOLDS on HARRY.
He gets up and goes to the open luggage, picks up a dress,
fondles it, then lets it drop back into the suitcase.

NEW ANGLE—HARRY looks toward the bathroom and raises his
voice.

HARRY: I miss her. I miss the kid. I keep hearing that song
from Babar; the elephant's song—crumda, crumda, ripalo
. . .

REFLECTION SHOT—JAN creaming her face.

JAN: (shouts) Harry, they're . . . they're shooting horse in
the toilets at the high school.

BACK TO HARRY

HARRY: (*shouts*) Cuban Pete's daughter doesn't shoot horse.

He starts for the bathroom.

INTERIOR BATHROOM—NEW ANGLE

HARRY comes into the bathroom, sits on the toilet seat watching JAN toweling off the white cream and beginning to apply a colorless oil.

HARRY: Every time one of us leaves, I wish we had made it.

She turns to him.

JAN: I'm not going to Mars.

He rises, goes to her, puts his hands on her shoulders.

HARRY: I know . . . but these hijackings and these monster jets. I don't know how they get up and down . . . the old propellers you could see them spinning. You knew why the goddamn things were in the air.

JAN: Well, that's a happy thought. I really need that before a flight.

HARRY: I just wish we had made it last night.

JAN: You left me with the company. By the time I got to bed you were out cold.

HARRY: Still, we . . . we should have—You could have woke me up, what would I have missed—a nightmare—

TWO SHOT

They look at one another. There's love, or need, or whatever that thing is, but time has eroded the heart of it all.

JAN: Promise me you'll see Dr. Frankfurter—

She goes past him, but his voice stops her as she reaches the door.

HARRY: You taking the 747?

JAN: I don't know. It's the one o'clock American.

HARRY: (*not really hearing*) Jan, I should have been a ballplayer. With my arm, I could have made Brooklyn— (*a beat*) . . . At least Philadelphia.

She studies him for a beat, then walks out of the SHOT into the bedroom. CAMERA HOLDS on HARRY. He goes to the medicine chest, takes out some shaving cream and starts to lather his face. He rubs slower and slower as the faint SOUNDS of a baseball crowd are up, and Red Barber describing some action at Ebbetts Field. CAMERA GOES IN TIGHT on his reflected image and with the tone of one calling up some ancient deity he whispers:

HARRY: First base . . . Dolph Camilli . . . Dolph Camilli . . . Second base . . . Second base . . . Pete Coscarot . . . Sonofabitch . . .

SCENE 2

En route to work, Harry drives down Sunset Boulevard and picks up a hitchhiker about the same age as his daughter. She casually suggests to him that they sleep together; he's bewildered and flattered, concerned for her and envious of her carefree youth. He drops her off, but he will meet her again later that night on the way home and spend the night with her. Harry stops in for a visit with his masseuse/mistress Ula, and leaves after having called his partner Phil to say he's been delayed with car trouble. Immediately upon arriving at the office/factory, Harry must completely shift gears as he is drawn in to the on-going feud between the temperamental Eastern European cutter and the temperamental Mediterranean designer. When Harry asks the cutter what he is trying to do to him, the cutter responds, "To you? Who can do anything to you? You're a playback." With a morning of jarring, disconcerting exchanges and lies not yet behind him, Harry goes into his partner's office to discuss the financial crisis threatening their livelihood.

INTERIOR PHIL GREENE'S OFFICE

The only decoration on the wall is a picture of an old office building. No other decorations. PHIL is older than HARRY, wears glasses, graying at the temples, smokes a cigar. He is on the phone. During the conversation, HARRY walks in, goes to the coffee pot and pours himself a cup of coffee.

PHIL: (after a pause) Yes, Mr. Norris. I appreciate your problems—I told you, I can't meet a thirty-day note. We've been doing business with you for fifteen years.

Maybe that's been a mistake. What do you want? You
want to foreclose? Okay. I'll see you in court in five years
. . . Okay, Sam.

NEW ANGLE—PHIL hangs up.

PHIL: Good afternoon. Where the hell've you been?

HARRY: It was just a clogged plug.

PHIL: Thank God for that. At least you got your plug fixed.

HARRY: Never mind my plug. What happened at the
bank?

PHIL: What do you think happened? No dice—no dice. The
best is a fifty percent discount on every dollar.

HARRY goes to the bathroom to take off his jacket.

HARRY: (*sighs*) Not enough.

PHIL: What?

HARRY: I said, not enough.

PHIL rises and goes to water cooler.

PHIL: Goddamn shame. We have a helluva line. Rico did a
brilliant job. I've been over all the patterns with Meyer.
Everything figures—everything. Materials, labor, fittings,
accessories, packaging, shipping, sales commissions—
everything.

PHIL tosses the paper cup on the floor and goes and sits
behind the desk.

PHIL: If the country doesn't go in the crapper. We'll have a
great season.

HARRY is leaning on the work table near the window.

HARRY: How many dollars do we need?

PHIL: Dollars, if you can write three hundred thousand
dollars this afternoon . . .

HARRY: I'll write three hundred thousand dollars.

PHIL: Alright. If you write three hundred thousand dollars
discounted at the bank, we get one hundred fifty thousand. We'll need another one hundred forty-two thousand in less than sixty days. The mills are on my back,
we owe 'em a bundle from last year. Harry, I've only got
two thousand yards of jersey left.

WIDE ANGLE—HARRY has walked across the room and is looking out the factory door window near the photograph of the
Long Beach factory. PHIL watches him.

HARRY: (*indicates photo*) What about the factory in Long
    Beach?

PHIL: What about it?

HARRY: Well, what are we using it for?

PHIL: I don't know. We're turning out three numbers down
    there—pants suits.

CLOSE SHOT—HARRY

HARRY: Are our policies all paid up?

PHIL: Of course they are . . .

HARRY walks to PHIL'S desk, reaches into his wallet and pulls
out a slip of paper. He tosses it on the desk and crosses to the
work table.

PHIL: What the hell is that?

HARRY: Charlie Robbins. Get him.

CLOSE SHOT—PHIL does not pick it up.

PHIL: Charlie Robbins . . .

TWO SHOT—HARRY opens the window near the work table.

HARRY: What's the policy worth?

PHIL: Forget it, Harry. We'll ask the unions, the mills to
    carry us. After all these years, those bastards owe us
    something.

HARRY: We tried that last year and they told us to take a
    walk. What's the floater worth?

PHIL: (*shakes his head*) I won't get involved with Robbins.
    There's a line, a line I won't cross.

HARRY: (*angry*) Goddamn it, Phil—I asked you a question.
    What's the floater worth?

PHIL: Forget the fucking floater.

HARRY: Listen, do I have to go out and ask Marvin?

PHIL: A hundred thousand.

HARRY: Enough to squeeze through.

PHIL: We've cut a lot of sharp corners together, but this is insanity.

HARRY shuts the door between the two offices.

HARRY: Look. If we were falling on our ass and making missiles, Congress would send us a certified check. We're making dresses.

PHIL: That's bullshit. You can't rationalize a thing like this. I won't permit, Harry.

HARRY: Robbins is the best. There'll never be any questions.

PHIL: Will you wake up. There are always questions.

HARRY: Charlie is a pro. How do you think Beckman pulled out? You think his fire was spontaneous combustion?

PHIL: I don't give a good goddamn about Beckman.

HARRY: We got killed last year. This is our only chance to pull out—

PHIL: We'll file for bankruptcy.

HARRY: We can't go bankrupt. We'll be audited. You want Linda to visit you in Chino?

PHIL: Arson, Harry. Arson . . . that's a major felony. You're talking about twenty years.

HARRY indicates the slip of paper with Robbins' number on it.

HARRY: Fraud or arson, the accommodations are the same. Come on, call him.

PHIL swivels chair away from HARRY, turning his back on him.

PHIL: I won't do it. It's out of the question. I am not going to get involved with Robbins.

HARRY grabs the slip of paper with ROBBINS' telephone number off of PHIL'S desk and storms out of PHIL'S office. Slamming the door behind him. PHIL sits for a beat, then notices the light going on on the push-button telephone, indicating that HARRY has picked up the phone in his office. He gets up and crosses to the connecting door and opens it.

INTERIOR HARRY'S OFFICE

PHIL is standing in doorway. HARRY is seated behind desk with phone in hand in the midst of dialing. He looks up at PHIL and slams the phone down.

HARRY: (*angry*) Sonofabitch! You think I enjoy doing this? What are we going to do? Come on, you tell me. We invented some new arithmetic last year.

PHIL crosses to HARRY'S desk.

PHIL: But we survived, kept our people working. Seventy-one women—fourteen salesmen—secretaries— all making a living.

HARRY: The government has a different word for survival . . . it's called "fraud." Fraud.

PHIL turns from HARRY trying to find the words.

PHIL: What the hell have I got left?

He turns to HARRY.

PHIL: Harry, I'm fifty-seven years old. All I want to do is get out in a boat and smell the sea. Thirty-eight years in this business. All I want to do is catch a fish. Am I being unreasonable? Is that too much to ask?

HARRY: Why ask me? I don't make the rules. You haven't been out in those streets for thirty-eight years. You want to start looking for a job? (*pause*) Well, neither do I.

PHIL stands looking at HARRY, HARRY begins to dial.

HARRY: (*on phone*) Hello . . . Charlie Robbins, please . . . Harry Stoner calling.

PHIL turns and looks to the doorway between the two offices.

HARRY: Hello, Charlie? Harry Stoner.

HARRY'S really doing it. PHIL leaves, closing the door sharply behind him.

INTERIOR PHIL'S OFFICE

PHIL paces by his work table.

INTERIOR HARRY'S OFFICE

HARRY on phone.

HARRY: Sorry to wake you. Good, thanks. Charlie, listen, I mentioned it to you last week. We have a plumbing problem in one of the factories . . . Yeah, goddamn water's all over the place—needs fixing right away. (*pause*) No, that's too early. Can you make it four-thirty? . . . Right . . . Thank you, Charlie . . .

HARRY hangs up and looks towards PHIL'S office. Gets up and goes to the door between their offices.

INTERIOR PHIL'S OFFICE

The door opens. HARRY walks in. PHIL turns from him looking out the window.

HARRY: We meet him at the Mayan Theatre on Hill Street at four-thirty, right side of the balcony. He gets a twenty-five hundred dollar retainer, and fifteen percent of the final settlement. Draw the cash, put it in an envelope with a key to the Long Beach factory.

HARRY walks into the bathroom to wash his hands. We hear the SOUND of the intercom.

ANOTHER ANGLE as PHIL goes to his desk, presses the speaker button.

PHIL: What do you want? [RECEPTIONIST'S VOICE: (filtered) Fred Mirrell is here.]

PHIL: Fred Mirrell?

HARRY: Christ. Tell Gloria to take him to my office.

[PHIL: What's he doing here?

RECEPTIONIST'S VOICE: Gloria's out sick.

HARRY: Well, leave the switchboard and take him into my office.]

NEW ANGLE—PHIL flicks off the button, turns to HARRY.

PHIL: What's Freddie doing here? He knows the show is at three, at the hotel.

HARRY: He wants to get laid.

PHIL: Here?

HARRY: Yeah, on your desk.

PHIL: I wonder what would happen if once you asked that sonofabitch to buy the line on its merits.

HARRY comes out of the bathroom putting on his jacket and walks to PHIL'S desk.

HARRY: We would lose the account. Get Margo on the phone. We have the same suite at the Belgrave.

PHIL: Yes. The show . . . the broads . . . all under the

same roof. The show, the screwing. The whole goddamn mess.

HARRY: (*with hand outstretched*) It's business. Give me the key.

PHIL: Business?

HARRY: Give me the key!

PHIL reaches into desk drawer, pulls out key and slams it on the desk.

PHIL: Business for what?

HARRY picks up the key and turns to the door.

PHIL: To become a pimp? To commit a major felony. For what?

HARRY: So you can fish. Call Margo—set it up for one-thirty.

NEW ANGLE—HARRY opens the door. [We see Fred Mirrell in HARRY'S office.]

HARRY: Hello, Freddy. How was the trip?

The door shuts behind him.

THE WAY WE WERE

A Columbia-Rastar Productions presentation. Released through Columbia Pictures. Producer, Ray Stark. Director, Sydney Pollack. Screenplay by Arthur Laurents. Based on the novel *The Way We Were* by Arthur Laurents. Photography, Harry Stradling. Music, Marvin Hamlisch. Production Designer, Stephen Grimes. Film Editor, Margaret Booth. Assistant Director, Howard Koch, Jr. Sound, Jack Solomon. Eastman Color. Running time, 118 minutes. 1973.

CAST

KATIE	Barbra Streisand
HUBBELL	Robert Redford
J.J.	Bradford Dillman
GEORGE BISSINGER	Patrick O'Neal
PAULA RESINER	Viveca Lindfors
CAROL ANN	Lois Chiles

Katie Morosky and Hubbell Gardiner first meet at university in 1937. She has frizzy hair, wears lumpy skirts, and lives in a boarding house. He wears cashmere sweaters and lives in a fraternity house. She's a Young Communist activist who wants the campus to join her in a Strike for Peace. He helps her out by calling it a Rally for Peace, which the apathetic student body will be more willing to attend. She is movingly successful at quieting the catcalls of "Komrade Katy!" and unifying her audience behind the dignity of her cause, but she loses their attention when she cannot laugh along with them at what is legitimately funny. Above all, Katie wants to be a writer, and no one is more stunned than she when the highest mark in her short story class goes to Hubbell. Except maybe Hubbell himself. With "fierce eyes glittering in a pale face," she stares at this "handsome, blond, suntanned" varsity god whom she'd dismissed as a smoothly beautiful but shallow jock. Hubbell's short story is about a young man of his own blessings for whom, like the country he lives in, it all comes too easy. Nothing comes easy to Katy, and Hubbell admires the commitment and tenacity of the girl.

By World War II, the focus of Katie's political allegiances have shifted from Loyalist Spain to F.D.R. She is working for the radio division of the Office of War Information. Though it is still a daily struggle to maintain ceaseless vigilance in defense of her every belief, Katie has begun to smooth out some of the rougher edges. Her clothes are getting better, but her oversized beads and earrings are still all wrong. She is learning how to "pass" in the beige-and-blonde world typified by Hubbell. It will be another twenty years, after the McCarthy blacklisting nightmare and after years in Holly-wood married to Hubbell, before Katie learns that she doesn't *want* to pass in that world, that she doesn't have to apologize, and that she doesn't need to iron out her frizzy hair.

Working late one night on an O.W.I. broadcast, Katie is taken by her boss to the swank Stork Club. There, asleep in his seat, is Hubbell on leave, in a white uniform. She is as dazzled by him as ever. He's so drunk that she takes on the thrilling job of putting him up at her apartment for the night. He passes out in her bed. Although he makes love to her before finally losing consciousness, the following morning he apparently remembers nothing. The next time he is in town on leave he calls her again, and she is delighted for him to stay at her apartment, as the hotels are filled. This time, though, Katie is prepared: she's spent all her food rations on steaks and baked potatoes. Hubbell casually announces that he's going to dinner with friends and doesn't know what time he'll be back. She tells him that he can't, he just can't . . . so he doesn't.

INTERIOR KATIE'S LIVING ROOM—NIGHT

Gentle rain on the windows, music on the radio. They are finishing dinner at the candle-lit gate-leg table. She cuts him a big piece of pie.

HUBBELL: I also remember your hero didn't lift a finger for Spain.

KATIE: Well, Congress was isolationist and F.D.R. had to—

HUBBELL: I'll bet you can justify the Nazi-Soviet Pact!

KATIE: Easier than you can justify the Allies sitting on their behinds—

HUBBELL: Why don't you say "asses"?

KATIE: Because I can't.

HUBBELL smiles. She shrugs. He stares at her.

HUBBELL: You know it's all politics but you hold on. To Roosevelt, to Stalin, to the Soviet Union. (*shakes head*) I don't know how you do it.

KATIE: I don't know how you can't.

HUBBELL: Maybe you were born committed. (*pushes his chair back*) Anyway, you're a great cook and no real Navy gentleman would have spoiled your dinner by being so deep shit serious.

He gets up. She quickly pours the last of the wine for both of them.

KATIE: What's wrong with being deeply serious?

HUBBELL picks up the wine, but remains standing.

HUBBELL: You die of frustration.

KATIE: Then why are you jealous? (*He laughs*) You are!

HUBBELL: I'll live. (*finishes wine*) Maybe longer.

He starts for his hat.

KATIE: You won't write another novel.

HUBBELL stops, turns and looks at her. She goes to her desk and opens a drawer.

INSERT—DRAWER. Her hands come into frame with a novel— still in its shiny yellow dust jacket—titled: "A Country Made of Ice Cream" by HUBBELL GARDINER.

FULL SHOT—LIVING ROOM—HUBBELL AND KATIE

KATIE: How about an autograph? With a personal inscription. Like "To my Sis-Grad-U-Ate".

HUBBELL, moved, takes the novel and slowly sits.

HUBBELL: You must've gotten one of the two copies sold.

KATIE: It came in a cracker jack box.

He laughs, yawns, looks at the ceiling.

HUBBELL: Did you get through it?

KATIE: I managed. Three times. It's very good, Hubbell.

He crosses his legs and brushes something off the tip of a spotless white shoe.

KATIE: If it weren't for Pearl Harbor, I'm sure it would've done very well. The reviews I read—

HUBBELL: Ohhhhh—

KATIE: O.K. It stinks.

HUBBELL: (opening the book, pretending to read) . . . I'm glad you liked it, Katie.

KATIE: So was I.

HUBBELL: (looking up) What didn't you like?

KATIE: . . . Do you really want to know?

HUBBELL: Yes. No! (He laughs and loosens his tunic) Yes! But wait. Fortification! Any more wine?

KATIE: Oh, Jesus. I'm sorry. Oh! Hey! There's a bottle of brandy Bill Verso gave me when I moved in a hundred years ago! You think it's still good?

HUBBELL laughs and puts his arm around her.

HUBBELL: Oh, Katie!

KATIE: What?

HUBBELL: It's still good.

INTERIOR KATIE'S LIVING ROOM—NIGHT

CAMERA HOLDS the table and the remains of dinner. Two candles are almost burned down.

KATIE'S VOICE: . . . Your style is gorgeous, really.

PAN to HUBBELL stretched out on the floor in white pants and T-shirt, a brandy glass on his chest. KATIE sits in a chair, the brandy bottle and her glass on an end table.

KATIE: But you're too much the observer. Finally you have to declare yourself.

HUBBELL: Well, you know there *were* one and a half nibbles from Hollywood—but the war ended that.

As she talks, she brings her glass and the brandy to him; sits by him, fills his glass; finds moments to touch him, supposedly for emphasis.

KATIE: Oh, they never would've bought it anyway.

HUBBELL: (*deadpan*) No, I know. It's too good.

KATIE: It is!

HUBBELL: (*laughs*) Oh, Katie! And you're sure I'll write another that'll be even better!

KATIE: Absolutely.

He rolls over on his stomach and looks at her.

HUBBELL: Are you really so sure of everything you're so sure of?

KATIE: Sure. Aren't you? . . . Winners and losers?

HUBBELL: . . . Not *as* sure.

He rolls again, so that now his head is in her lap. She touches his hair tentatively. Then:

KATIE: "In a way, he was like the country he lived in: everything came too easily to him."

HUBBELL: (*softly*) What in hell made you remember that?

KATIE: I always wondered if it would stay true.

He turns his cheek to her thigh, half-kissing it.

HUBBELL: . . . Not altogether.

KATIE: What doesn't come easy now?

HUBBELL: (*grins*) Hotel rooms.

KATIE: No, be serious.

HUBBELL: . . . Your kind of commitment . . . But then I find myself thinking: what difference does it make?

KATIE: What difference??

HUBBELL: All the hollering on the barricades, and it ends where it began.

KATIE: But it *can* change. And even if it doesn't, you *have* to care!

HUBBELL: Why?

KATIE: Because that's what keeps you alive!

HUBBELL: Keeps *you* alive.

KATIE: O.K. And you?

HUBBELL: (*shrugs*) Hope for a surprise . . . From myself, maybe. Or from other people. (*He looks up at her*) You're a surprise, Katie.

She remains very still. He pulls her head down and kisses her.

HUBBELL: (*softly*) But you mustn't be too serious.

KATIE: Oh, I won't be.

In the candlelight, he undresses her. She watches as he looks at her body, shaking his head.

HUBBELL: Oh, Katie. Katie, you don't dress right. Don't you know you're beautiful?

KATIE: You are.

She reaches up to pull him down and stop his looking.

HUBBELL: It'll be better this time.

ALICE DOESN'T LIVE HERE ANYMORE

A Warner Bros. presentation of a David Susskind Production. Producers, David Susskind & Audrey Maas. Director, Martin Scorsese. Screenplay by Robert Getchell. Associate Producer, Sandra Weintraub. Director of Photography, Kent L. Wakeford. Film Editor, Marcia Lucas. Production Designer, Toby Carr Rafelson. Sound Mixer, Don Parker. Assistant Directors, Mike Moder, Mike Kusley. Technicolor. Running time, 112 minutes. 1974.

CAST

ALICE	Ellen Burstyn
DAVID	Kris Kristofferson
DONALD	Billy Green Bush
FLO	Diane Ladd
BEA	Lelia Goldoni
RITA	Lane Bradbury
MEL	Vic Tayback
AUDREY	Jodie Foster
BEN	Harvey Keitell
VERA	Valerie Curtin
JACOBS	Murray Moston
JOE & JIM'S BARTENDER	Harry Northup
TOMMY	Alfred Lutter
ALICE (AGE 8)	Mia Bendixsen
OLD WOMAN	Ola Moore
LENNY	Martin Brinton
CHICKEN	Dean Casper

When Alice Graham was ten years old and living in Monterey, California, she could do a passable imitation of Alice Faye singing, "You'll Never Know." Alice wanted to grow up to be a singer. Twenty-two years later, she finds herself the mother/maid of a one-child family in Ponca City, New Mexico. Her husband is a lout who grabs both his food and his wife with the same grunts. His idea of dinner table conversation is to growl, "It's too hot to breathe." When their eleven-year-old loveable loudmouthed son Tommy adds, "It's too hot to live," his father's response is "Shut up." Alice has two safety valves for her own enormous humor in life—her habit of making ironic asides to some invisible listener, and her warmly open relationship with her best friend and neighbor Bea. Suddenly, when Alice's husband is killed in an accident, her old dream of returning to Monterey and becoming a singer is revived. She decides to "go for it."

In Albequerque, Alice gets a job as a singer in a bar. She and Tommy manage on fast food and cheap motels as Alice saves every cent she can to keep her promise to get Tommy to Monterey by his twelfth birthday. When she becomes involved with a man who turns out to be both married and excessively violent, Alice and Tommy flee to Tucson. There are no jobs for singers in Tucson. With her heart in her mouth, Alice begins working in Mel's Diner as a waitress, something she vowed she'd never do. Mel's place is fast and boisterous. The other waitresses are Vera, who can cope with nothing, and Florence, who can cope with anything and who gives the diner its rowdy bustle. Uncertain of herself and her new role, Alice finds Flo's colloquial vulgarities extremely unnerving, and she responds with a withdrawn prissiness that is not characteristic of her. Finally, the sheer outrageousness of Flo's ribaldry breaks through Alice's reserve, and the two women become friends.

At first, Alice also keeps a hands-off distance from David, a "slow, easy, charming" rancher who decides to break down her resistance by winning over Tommy. He succeeds. Although it's Tucson and not Monterey, Tommy's twelfth birthday party happens with streamers and presents and a loving father figure. Alice has begun to relax with David on the rolling, easy spread of his farmland. But David has an authoritarian streak that collides with Tommy's snottiness, and the birthday party explodes. In his humiliation, Tommy gets so abusive to Alice that she makes him walk the last mile home. He stays out all night and gets sick-drunk on cheap wine. After a terrified, endless night, Alice receives a phone call from Juvenile Court.

Alice brings Tommy home, puts him to bed, and goes in to work. When Flo asks her if she wants to talk about what is troubling her, Alice says no, and then bursts into tears. Flo escorts Alice through the café, right past the staring customers, into the Ladies Room.

(*Note:* It's important that scene be interrupted, but the intruders may remain offstage while Flo plays to them through the bathroom door.)

INTERIOR LADIES ROOM—DAY

The bathroom is small and empty. FLORENCE stands guard by the door, while ALICE leans against a sink.

FLORENCE: Okay, okay Alice. Now let me have it.

ALICE says something unintelligible, through sobbing; what she says is muffled as she cries.

FLORENCE: What? Alice, what's the matter?

ALICE: Everything!

FLORENCE: Is it David?

ALICE: (*through tears, angry*) To hell with David!

FLORENCE: (*understanding*) Uh-huh. Okay, sugar. What then, the kid?

ALICE: No, I don't know. It's everything, I mean. Everything's just so screwed up. (*a beat*) This morning I woke up, and I just didn't want to get up. I never felt so rotten in my whole life. (*a beat*) I planned on being in Monterey over a week ago. (*a beat*) Monterey, hell—I didn't even make it to California.

FLORENCE: So what's holding you here?

ALICE: I don't know. When I left home, I said okay: I want to go to Monterey and I want to be a singer. And *that's* what I'm gonna do. And I started out, and somehow I just thought I'd do it.

FLORENCE: (*trying again to make sense*) So how come you're here?

ALICE: Well, 'cuz it didn't work. I don't know, life is really hard. (*a beat*) I mean it's harder than I thought.

FLORENCE: Well, life's hard for everybody walkin' on this earth. But that don't mean you can't smile. Just 'cuz you know there ain't no Santa Claus, don't mean you can't enjoy Christmas better than anybody else.

[CUT TO:

INTERIOR CAFE—DAY—PARALLEL TIME

VERA, who realizes something is wrong, and is trying to help out, is rushing around like a mad woman, covering the entire café by herself.

CUT TO:]

INTERIOR LADIES ROOM

ALICE: It's really disgusting, you know, I was bragging to Bea one time, and I said I didn't need men, and now this is the first time in my life that I've been without a man, and I'm falling apart. I was so sacred of . . . of Donald, you know, and I was always trying to please him, and—

FLORENCE: You were scared of him?

ALICE: Yeah, and now I'm without him and I'm more scared than I ever was before. It's like I always felt he was taking care of me, you know, and now I don't know what to do.

FLORENCE: Well, that's real nice that you had someone to take care of you.

ALICE: But he didn't! I just felt like he did, just 'cuz he was there, I mean. I don't know how to be without a man.

A WOMAN enters the door and steps in, wanting to use the bathroom.

FLORENCE: Sorry, it's full up.

WOMAN: What?

FLORENCE: It's busy in here.

WOMAN: But I just want to use the—

FLORENCE: (*snappish*) Didn't you hear me?

WOMAN: *(bristling a bit)* It's not in use.

FLORENCE: *(low, dangerous; her old self)* You want a crack across the mouth, lady?

The woman scurries out, frightened.

FLORENCE: Listen, Alice, I want to tell you something. Now you know, I got problems, too; I didn't exactly have my heart set on this job, either. I mean, I got a daughter, and she needs about four thousand dollars worth of dental work, and honey, I haven't got the money. I got a man, and my old man, he hasn't talked to me since the day Kennedy got shot.

ALICE: Why, did he think you had something to do with it?

FLORENCE: *(laughs; then)* I don't know what he thought. I wish I could get into that man's head. *(a beat)* Alice, honey, I think you're going shock you know? I mean even if a man's bad, honey—my old booger is not too good, but he's there. And you just went through a death and all, and that's not easy.

ALICE: I just don't know what to do.

FLORENCE: Sugar, I want to see you smile; you got a thing going for you, why my golly—look at that face, look at that body! Why, honey, you can sing!

ALICE: Well, I don't know about that, you never heard me sing.

ALICE and FLORENCE both laugh.

FLORENCE: Honey, if you know what it is in life that you want, you just jump in there and let the devil take the hindmost.

ALICE: But that's what I was trying to do! I know you're right, I just get so . . . I mean Tommy's not happy, I promised him I'd get him to Monterey, I promised him all these things, and David, I'm so mad, I tell you, I could just kill him, I really could!

FLORENCE: Sounds to me like you love him.

ALICE: Oh. *(sobs)* I do!

At this point MEL appears at the doorway.

MEL: Flo? Alice? What's going on?

FLORENCE: Beat it, Mel, we'll be back.

MEL: Vera's going crazy out here.

FLORENCE: Give us a minute. (*as* MEL *starts to come through door*) Mel, you come through that door and there's going to be a three-legged race to the undertaker. (*beat*) You wanna' get through the day with just Vera?

MEL goes away, muttering.

ALICE: (*crying, furious*) But I don't want to love him. I don't ever want to love a man again, I really don't. I think they all stink.

FLORENCE: Oh, honey, don't say that. There's only two people on this earth, a man and a woman.

ALICE giggles.

ALICE: But I mean it's *my* life, it's *my* life, you know? It's not some man's life that I help him out with, you know—

FLORENCE: No, ma'am, you gotta live for yourself.

ALICE: I want it all. (*a beat*) I'd just like to run down the street yelling "the hell with everybody"! (*she shakes her head*) That sounds awful.

FLORENCE: (*nodding*) Sure does.

ALICE: But I don't give a damn.

FLORENCE: So what do you want most?

ALICE: If I knew that, I wouldn't be back here crying in the toilet, now, would I?

FLORENCE: You know something? It's going to work out. I know what you need; you need a "Rattlesnake Cocktail".

ALICE: What's a "Rattlesnake Cocktail"?

FLORENCE: Well, honey, that's just like a "Harvey Wallbanger"! That's going to put the old bite right back in you! What do you say?

ALICE nods, and rises, smiling.

CHINATOWN

A Paramount Pictures presentation. Producer, Robert Evans. Director, Roman Polanski. Screenplay by Robert Towne. Associate Producer, C.O. Erickson. Director of Photography, John A. Alonzo. Film Editor, Sam O'Steen. Music, Jerry Goldsmith. Production Designer, Richard Sylbert. Art Director, W. Steward Campbell. Set Designers, Gabe Resh, Robert Resh. Sound Mixer, Larry Jost. Assistant Directors, Howard W. Koch, Jr., Michele Ader. Panavision, Technicolor. Running time, 130 minutes. 1974.

CAST

J. J. GITTES	Jack Nicholson
EVELYN MULWRAY	Faye Dunaway
NOAH CROSS	John Huston
ESCOBAR	Perry Lopez
YELBURTON	John Hillerman
HOLLIS MULWRAY	Darrell Zwerling
IDA SESSIONS	Diane Ladd
MULVIHILL	Roy Jenson
MAN WITH KNIFE	Roman Polanski
LOACH	Dick Bakalyan
WALSH	Joe Mantell
DUFFY	Bruce Glover
SOPHIE	Nandu Hinds
LAWYER	James O'Reare
EVELYN'S BUTLER	James Hong
MAID	Beaulah Quo
GARDENER	Jerry Fujikawa
KATHERINE	Belinda Palmer
CURLY	Burt Young
CURLY'S WIFE	Elizabeth Harding

Cynical, dapper, vain, honest and not always as bright as he thinks he is—J. J. Gittes is certainly an intriguing personality. He is a private eye in Los Angeles in the 1930s, whose office door reads, "Discreet Investigations." One day the wife of Hollis Mulwray, Chief Engineer of the Department of Water and Power, hires Gittes to investigate her husband for adultery. But Mrs. Mulwray turns out to be an imposter, and within a few days both the imposter and Hollis Mulwray are dead.

The key to the interwoven mysteries that thread through *Chinatown* lies in the real Mrs. Evelyn Mulwray, who is the extremely beautiful daughter of Noah Cross. Cross is immeasurably wealthy, powerful, charming, and evil. He had originally owned the Department of Water and Power in partnership with Mulwray, but it was Mulwray's belief that the water should belong to the people of the city. The real break between the two men was occasioned by the loss of five hundred lives in the collapse of a dam that Cross had insisted on building over Mulwray's objections.

Before Mulwray's death, Gittes observes him discovering tons of water being inexplicably dumped into various run-offs right in the middle of a serious drought. Later it will come out that this water is being stolen from the Valley by Noah Cross in order to force out the farmers, buy up their land cheap, and then incorporate the Valley into the City of Los Angeles once a new dam has provided abundant irrigation. Mulwray at first refuses to build this new dam on the grounds that the intended site is as unsafe as the previous one that had collapsed. As soon as Mulwray discovers the run-offs and the real purpose of the new dam, Cross kills him.

At the time of the first of the following scenes, neither the audience nor Gittes has fit together any of these intricate pieces. Gittes has photos of Cross and Mulwray arguing in front of a restaurant, but he does not know about what. All Gittes knows for certain is that he has been set up by an imposter to discredit Mulwray (which he does with photos of Mulwray and a slender blonde girl at the El Macando Apartments), that Mulwray has subsequently been killed, and that now Mulwray's widow Evelyn has hired him to investigate her husband's murder. Gittes' investigations have thus far brought him a slashed nose and the certainty that Evelyn is hiding something. He does not know what.

In the following scene Noah Cross has invited Gittes to have breakfast out at Cross' compound on Catalina Island.

SCENE 1

[EXTERIOR WINDING ROAD—RANCHO DEL CRUCE

GITTES, driven in a station wagon, passes under the sign with a cross painted below the name.

The ranch itself is only partially in a valley on the island— as the wagon continues one can SEE that it is actually a miniature California, encompassing desert, mountains and canyon that tumble down palisades to the windward side of the sea.

The wagon comes to a halt where a group of hands are clustered around a corral. The circle of men drift apart, leaving JUSTÍN CROSS* standing, using a cane for support, reedy but handsome in a rough linen shirt and jeans. When he talks, his strong face is lively; in repose it looks ravaged.]

EXTERIOR BRIDLE PATH—GITTES & CROSS

walking toward the main house—a classic Monterey. A horse led on a halter by another ranch hand slows down and defecates in the center of the path they are taking. GITTES doesn't notice.

CROSS: Horseshit.

GITTES pauses, not certain he has heard correctly.

GITTES: Sir?

CROSS: I said horseshit. (*pointing*) Horseshit.

GITTES: Yes, sir, that's what it looks like—I'll give you that.

CROSS pauses when they reach the dung pile. He removes his hat and waves it, inhales deeply.

CROSS: Love the smell of it. A lot of people do, but of course they won't admit it. Look at the shape.

GITTES glances down out of politeness.

CROSS: (*smiling, almost enthusiastic*) Always the same.

*The character Justin Cross in the script is called Noah Cross in the film.

CROSS walks on. GITTES follows.

GITTES: (*not one to let it go*) Always?

CROSS: What? Oh, damn near—yes. Unless the animal's sick or something. (*stops and glances back*)—and the steam rising off it like that in the morning—that's life, Mr. Gittes. Life.

They move on.

CROSS: Perhaps this preoccupation with horseshit may seem a little perverse, but I ask you to remember this—one way or another, it's what I've dealt in all my life. Let's have breakfast.

EXTERIOR COURTYARD VERANDA—GITTES & CROSS AT BREAKFAST

Below them is a corral where hands take Arabians, one by one, and work them out, letting them run and literally kick up their heels. CROSS' attention is diverted by the animals from time to time. An impeccable Mexican butler serves them their main course, broiled fish.

CROSS: You know, you've got a nasty reputation, Mr. Gittes. I like that.

GITTES: (*dubious*) Thanks.

CROSS: —if you were a bank president that would be one thing—but in your business it's admirable. And it's good advertising.

GITTES: It doesn't hurt.

CROSS It's why you attract a client like my daughter.

GITTES: Probably.

CROSS: But I'm surprised you're still working for her— unless she's suddenly come up with another husband.

GITTES: No—she happens to think the last one was murdered.

CROSS is visibly surprised.

CROSS: How did she get that idea?

GITTES: I think I gave it to her.

CROSS nods.

CROSS: Uhh-huh—oh I hope you don't mind. I believe they should be served with the head.

GITTES glances down at the fish whose isinglass eye is glazed over with the heat of cooking.

GITTES: —Fine, as long as you don't serve chicken that way.

CROSS: (laughs) Tell me—what do the police say?

GITTES: They're calling it an accident.

CROSS: Who's the investigating officer?

GITTES: Lou Escobar—he's a lieutenant.

CROSS: Do you know him?

GITTES: Oh yes.

CROSS: Where from?

GITTES: —We worked Chinatown together.

CROSS: Would you call him a capable man?

GITTES: Very.

CROSS: Honest?

GITTES: —Far as it goes—of course he has to swim in the same water we all do.

CROSS: Of course—but you've got no reason to think he's bungled the case?

GITTES: None.

CROSS: That's too bad.

GITTES: Too bad?

CROSS: It disturbs me, Mr. Gittes. It makes me think you're taking my daughter for a ride—financially speaking, of course. How much are you charging her?

GITTES: (carefully) My usual fee—plus a bonus if I come up with any results.

CROSS: Are you sleeping with her? Come, come, Mr. Gittes— you don't have to think about that to remember, do you?

GITTES laughs.

GITTES: If you want an answer to that question I can always put one of my men on the job. Good afternoon, Mr. Cross.

CROSS: Mr. Gittes! You're dealing with a disturbed woman who's lost her husband. I don't want her taken advantage of. Sit down.

GITTES: What for?

CROSS: —You may think you know what you're dealing with— but believe me, you don't.

This stops GITTES. He seems faintly amused by it.

CROSS: Why is that funny?

GITTES: It's what the D.A. used to tell me about Chinatown.

CROSS: Was he right?

GITTES shrugs.

CROSS: . . . Exactly what do you know about me, Mr. Gittes?

GITTES: Mainly that you're rich and too respectable to want your name in the papers.

CROSS: (*grunts then*) 'Course I'm respectable. I'm old. Politicians, ugly buildings and whores all get respectable if they last long enough. I'll double whatever your fees are—and I'll pay you ten thousand dollars if you can find Hollis' girlfriend.

GITTES: His girlfriend?

CROSS: Yes, his girlfriend.

GITTES: You mean the little chippie he was with at the El Macando?

CROSS: Yes. She's disappeared, hasn't she?

CROSS: —Yeah.

CROSS: Doesn't that strike you as odd?

GITTES: No. She's probably scared to death.

CROSS: Wouldn't it be useful to talk to her?

GITTES: Maybe.

CROSS: If Mulwray was murdered, she was probably one of the last people to see him.

GITTES: You didn't see Mulwray much, did you?

CROSS: —No—

GITTES: —When was the last time?

CROSS starts to reply, then there's the SOUND of a MARIACHI BAND and some men in formation clear a bluff about a hundred yards off. They are dressed like Spanish dons on horseback. For the most part they are fat in the saddle and pass along in disordered review to the music.

CROSS: Sheriff's gold posse . . . bunch of damn fools who pay $5,000 apiece to the sheriff's re-election. I let 'em practice up out here.

GITTES: —Yeah. Do you remember the last time you talked to Mulwray?

CROSS shakes his head.

CROSS: —At my age, you tend to lose track . . .

GITTES: Well, it was about five days ago. You were outside the Pig 'n Whistle—and you had one hell of an argument.

CROSS looks to GITTES in some real surprise.

GITTES: I've got the photographs in my office—if they'll help you remember. What was the argument about?

CROSS: (a long pause, then) My daughter.

GITTES: What about her?

CROSS: —Just find the girl, Mr. Gittes. I think she is frightened, and I happen to know Hollis was fond of her. I'd like to help her if I can.

GITTES: I didn't realize you and Hollis were so fond of each other.

CROSS looks hatefully at GITTES.

CROSS: Hollis Mulwray made this city—and he made me a fortune . . . We were a lot closer than Evelyn realized.

GITTES: —If you want to hire me, I still have to know what you and Mulwray were arguing about.

CROSS: (painfully) Well . . . she's an extremely jealous person. I didn't want her to find out about the girl.

GITTES: How did you find out?

CROSS: I've still got a few teeth in my head, Mr. Gittes— and a few friends in town.

GITTES: Okay—my secretary'll send you a letter of agree-

ment. Tell me—are you worried about that girl, or what
Evelyn might do to her?

CROSS: Just find the girl.

GITTES: —I'll look into it—as soon as I check out some
avocado groves.

CROSS: Avocado groves?

GITTES: We'll be in touch, Mr. Cross.

SCENE 2

When Gittes first discusses the compromising photographs
with Evelyn, she seems particularly unperturbed, intimating
that this is not an abnormal reaction for a wife who may be
having affairs of her own. She denies knowledge of or interest
in the slender blonde girl. But later, Gittes secretly observes
Evelyn visiting the girlfriend (who has supposedly disappeared)
and sedating her. When confronted, Evelyn explains that the
girl is her sister, who has been devastated and hysterical over
the news of Hollis' death. A police lieutenant informs Gittes
that Mulwray died with salt water in his lungs; so when
Gittes discovers what he believes are Mulwray's broken bifocals lying at the bottom of a salt water pond on Mulwray's
property, he is convinced that Evelyn, with whom he has
begun an affair, murdered her husband and is keeping the
girl quiet because she knows. He telephones Noah Cross to
inform him of the girl's whereabouts. He drives to the house
where he suspects Evelyn is hiding the girl against her will,
only to find them both about to leave for Mexico. In this
scene, the mysterious Evelyn reveals one of the last secrets of
Chinatown. Once again Gittes is forced to face something he
had learned years before while working in Chinatown: that
protecting someone and hurting someone may be inextricably
bound together.

[EXTERIOR BUNGALOW–HOUSE, ADELAIDE DRIVE

GITTES pulls up in MULWRAY'S Buick. He hurries to the front
door, pounds on it.

The CHINESE SERVANT answers the door.

CHINESE SERVANT: You wait.

GITTES: (*short sentence in Chinese*) You wait.]

GITTES pushes past him. EVELYN, looking a little worn but glad to see him hurries to the door. She takes GITTES' arm.

EVELYN: How are you? I was calling you.

She looks at him, searching his face.

GITTES: —Yeah?

They move into the living room. GITTES is looking around it.

EVELYN: Did you get some sleep?

GITTES: Sure.

EVELYN: Did you have lunch? Kyo will fix you something—

GITTES: (abruptly) —where's the girl?

EVELYN: Upstairs. Why?

GITTES: I want to see her.

EVELYN: . . . she's having a bath now . . . why do you want to see her?

GITTES continues to look around. He sees clothes laid out for packing in a bedroom off the living room.

GITTES: Going somewhere?

EVELYN: Yes, we've got a 4:30 train to catch. Why?

GITTES doesn't answer. He goes to the phone and dials.

GITTES: —J. J. Gittes for Lieutenant Escobar . . .

EVELYN: What are you doing? What's wrong? I told you we've got a 4:30—

GITTES: (cutting her off) You're going to miss your train! (then, into phone) . . . Lou, meet me at 1412 Adelaide Drive—it's above Santa Monica Canyon . . . yeah, soon as you can.

EVELYN: What did you do that for?

GITTES: (a moment, then) You know any good criminal lawyers?

EVELYN: (puzzled)—no . . .

GITTES: Don't worry—I can recommend a couple. They're expensive but you can afford it.

EVELYN: (evenly but with great anger) What the hell is this all about?

GITTES looks at her—then takes the handkerchief out of his breast pocket—unfolds it on a coffee table, revealing the bifocal glasses, one lens still intact. EVELYN stares dumbly at them.

GITTES: I found these in your backyard—in your fish pond. They belonged to your husband, didn't they?. . . didn't they?

EVELYN: I don't know. I mean yes, probably.

GITTES: —yes positively. That's where he was drowned . . .

EVELYN: What are you saying?

GITTES: There's no time for you to be shocked by the truth, Mrs. Mulwray. The coroner's report proves he was killed in salt water, just take my word for it. Now I want to know how it happened and why. I want to know before Escobar gets here because I want to hang onto my license.

EVELYN: —I don't know what you're talking about. This is the most insane . . . the craziest thing I ever . . .

GITTES has been in a state of near frenzy himself. He gets up, shakes her.

GITTES: Stop it!—I'll make it easy.—You were jealous, you fought, he fell, hit his head—it was an accident— but his girl is a witness. You've had to pay her off. You don't have the stomach to harm her, but you've got the money to shut her up. Yes or no?

EVELYN: . . . no . . .

GITTES: Who is she? and don't give me that crap about it being your sister. You don't have a sister.

EVELYN is trembling.

EVELYN: I'll tell you the truth . . .

GITTES smiles.

GITTES: That's good. Now what's her name?

EVELYN: —Katherine.

GITTES: Katherine? . . . Katherine who?

EVELYN: —she's my daughter.

GITTES stares at her. He's been charged with anger and when EVELYN says this it explodes. He hits her full in the face. EVELYN stares back at him. The blow has forced tears from her eyes, but she makes no move, not even to defend herself.

GITTES: I said the truth!

EVELYN: —she's my sister—

GITTES slaps her again.

EVELYN: —she's my daughter.

GITTES slaps her again.

EVELYN: —my sister.

He hits her again.

EVELYN: My daughter, my sister—

He belts her finally, knocking her into a cheap Chinese vase which shatters and she collapses on the sofa, sobbing.

GITTES: I said I want the truth.

EVELYN: (almost screaming) She's my sister and my daughter!

[KYO comes running down the stairs.

EVELYN: (in Chinese) For God's sake, Kyo, keep her upstairs, go back!

KYO turns after staring at GITTES for a moment then goes back upstairs.]

EVELYN: —my father and I, understand, or is it too tough for you?

GITTES doesn't answer.

EVELYN: . . . he had a breakdown . . . the dam broke . . . my mother died . . . he became a little boy . . . I was fifteen . . . he'd ask me what to eat for breakfast, what clothes to wear! . . . it happened . . . then I ran away . . .

GITTES: . . . to Mexico . . .

She nods.

EVELYN: . . . Hollis came and took . . . care of me . . . after she was born . . . he said . . . he took care of her . . . I couldn't see her . . . I wanted to but I couldn't

. . . I just want to see once in a while . . . take care of
her . . . that's all . . . but I don't want her to know . . .
I don't want her to know . . .

GITTES: . . . so that's why you hate him . . .

EVELYN looks slowly up at GITTES.

EVELYN: —no . . . for turning his back on me after it happened! He couldn't face it . . . (*weeping*) I hate him.

GITTES suddenly feels the need to loosen his tie.

GITTES: —yeah . . . where are you taking her now?

EVELYN: Back to Mexico.

GITTES: You can't go by train. Escobar'll be looking for you
everywhere.

EVELYN: How about a plane?

GITTES: That's worse . . . just get out of here—walk out,
leave everything.

EVELYN: I have to go home and get my things—

GITTES: —I'll take care of it.

EVELYN: Where can we go?

GITTES: . . . where does Kyo live?

EVELYN: —with us.

GITTES: On his day off. Get the exact address.

EVELYN: —okay . . .

She stops suddenly.

EVELYN: Those didn't belong to Hollis.

For a moment GITTES doesn't know what she's talking about.
Then he follows her gaze to the glasses lying on his handkerchief.

GITTES: How do you know?

EVELYN: He didn't wear bifocals.

GITTES picks up the glasses, stares at the lens, is momentarily
lost in them.

[EVELYN from the stairs. She has her arm around KATHERINE.

EVELYN: Say hello to Mr. Gittes, sweetheart.

KATHERINE: *(from the stairs)* Hello.

GITTES rises a little shakily from the arm of the sofa.

GITTES: Hello.

With her arm around the girl, talking in spanish, EVELYN hurries her toward the bedroom.] In a moment she re-emerges.

EVELYN: *(calling down)*—he lives at 1712 Alameda . . . do you know where that is?

REACTION—GITTES. He nods slowly.

GITTES: —sure. It's in Chinatown.

DOG DAY AFTERNOON

A Warner Bros. presentation of An Artists Entertainment Complex Production. Producers, Martin Bregman & Martin Elfand. Director, Sidney Lumet. Screenplay by Frank Pierson. Based on a magazine article by P.F. Kluge & Thomas Moore. Associate Producer, Robert Greenhut. Director of Photography, Victor J. Kemper. Film Editor, Dede Allen. Production Designer, Charles Bailey. Art Director, Doug Higgins. Sound Mixer, James Sabat. Assistant Directors, Burtt Harris, Alan Hopkins. Technicolor. Running time, 130 minutes. 1975.

CAST

SONNY	Al Pacino
SAL	John Cazale
MULVANEY	Sully Boyer
SYLVIA	Penny Allen
MARGARET	Beulah Garrick
JENNY	Carol Kane
DEBORAH	Sandra Kazan
MIRIAM	Marcia Jean Kurtz
MARIA	Amy Levitt
HOWARD	John Marriott
EDNA	Estelle Omens
BOBBY	Gary Springer
SHELDON	James Broderick
MORETTI	Charles Durning
VI	Judith Malina
VI'S HUSBAND	Dominic Chianese
ANGIE	Susan Peretz
LEON	Chris Sarandon

The first look we get of Sonny Abramowicz is at 2:51 P.M. on August 22, 1972, the day on which almost all of the events depicted in *Dog Day Afternoon* actually took place. He is described as "in his mid-twenties, dark, with a mobile face, merry eyes, a mouth with a tough defiant twist. Right now he's looking at himself in the mirror, and with a little spit on his finger adjusts his already tidily combed hair, pasting a lock back in place." It is 94°F outside in Flatbush, Brooklyn, and Sonny's wife Heidi and two little kids, to whom he is a wonderful father, are lying out on the beach. A baseball game is in progress at Shea Stadium. The Americans have just unleashed the heaviest bombing of the war in Indochina. This can all be seen on the television that Sonny's parents watch in their apartment, which he provides for them. Sonny has to get downstairs, and over to the bank before it closes at three. He is going to rob the bank. His parents will be able to see all this on television as well.

As a bank robber, Sonny knows all of his lines, but his timing is totally off. He delivers his opening "this-is-a-stickup" speech long after everyone already knows. Having worked in a bank, Sonny has been able to plan carefully, right down to the spray paint he brings to black out the lenses of the surveillance cameras. But when he burns the registers in a wastebasket, so that there will be no record of the bills' serial numbers, the smoke is sucked up through the air-conditioner and is visible outside the "slightly seedy little branch bank." Soon a call comes in for Sonny. It's Moretti from the police.

The police are jammed into the barbershop directly across the street where they've set up a direct phone line into the bank. During the next several hours, huge crowds of spectators and vendors will mass into the street for a live game of Pass the Hostage, a thrilling entertainment for those stuck in the city on a miserable summer day. Others will prefer to watch on television, and another ring is added to the circus with the television lights, camera crews, and helicopters. A newscaster calls for a live interview but refuses to answer Sonny's questions, at which point Sonny demands that if he is going to be used as entertainment, then the television station will have to pay him. What started out as a little heist has mushroomed totally out of control.

On one level, *Dog Day Afternoon* is the story of a bank

robbery that goes haywire. A terrifying standoff ensues between those trapped inside the bank and the police and FBI on the outside. Sonny and his partner Sal get as far as the airport, but they don't make it onto the plane that they've been promised will fly them to freedom in return for all the employees they've been holding hostage. The driver of their car is a plainclothesman with a gun. Sal is shot dead, and Sonny's last lines are screamed to the police, begging them to kill him, too. On another level, however, the story is a chaotic farce about a couple of nice, over-strung guys who try to pull off a simple, friendly holdup and get involved way over their heads in the colliding incongruities that characterize American life on one sweltering August day in 1972. While Sonny may be roaring, "We're Vietnam veterans so killing don't mean nothing to us," he is also horrified by a crank call urging him to kill all the hostages. He's the one who's been helping them on and off with their jackets, holding doors open for them, patiently calming away their terror. When the police cut the air-conditioner and Mulvaney the manager collapses, it's Sonny who insists that a doctor be admitted. Neither the doctor nor a pizza delivery boy will accept Sonny's payment, so he tosses the money to the crowd outside, and he and Moretti share a moment of contemptuous disbelief as the police join in the diving for dollars. The crowds cheer Sonny as he plays directly to them, screaming about police brutality and stupidity. He ignites into a sudden media hero/punk—a brilliant, tragic, armed hostage of society.

The ultimate symbol of all these incongruities is Leon, Sonny's male lover, who suffers from suicidal depression stemming from his belief that he is a woman trapped inside a man's body. Sonny has married Leon in a church service because that is what Leon thought would make him happy. The only thing that will really help Leon is a sex-change operation, and it is in order to pay this bill that Sonny has decided to rob the bank. In a long telephone conversation with Leon, Sonny comes to understand that Leon neither wants him nor his help. The hostages feel real sympathy for Sonny. They've all laughed together until the tears have run down their faces, until they've looked at each other in embarrassed bewilderment at how inappropriate their behavior is in their given roles and circumstances. They wish Sonny luck. He dictates his will to one of them: "Life and love are not easy and we have to bend a lot. I hope you find the places and the people to make you all happy as I could not. God bless you and watch over you as I shall, until we are joined in the great hereafter."

The scene below is between Sonny and his mother Vi, who first learns of what her son is doing by seeing it on the television. Soon after this meeting, Sonny will leave for the airport. Vi is described as "a small woman in her fifties with a perpetual smile . . . dumpy and gray, tentatively waving, a figure that bends over baby carriages in the park, picks beans one by one out of the supermarket bins, lip reads get-well cards in pharmacies." (The meeting between Sonny and his mother, interestingly enough, is a meeting which never actually occurred according to the man who really did rob that bank that day.)

EXTERIOR BANK—NIGHT

as SONNY walks to his MOTHER. Baker tactfully moves away, leaving the two of them in the center of the floodlighted street. Again the crowd can be HEARD but not seen; armed police fringe the lights and shadows, in background.

SONNY: What do you want here, Ma? You could of watched it on TV.

VI: My God, Sonny—you oughtta see—Alla Brooklyn is here! On all three networks!

SONNY: Mom—I got it all worked out; it's over. The best thing is you go home. Watch it on TV.

VI: I talked to the FBI, I told them about you, they said if you just come outta the bank it's gonna be okay.

SONNY: You did what? Who did you talk to? What for?

VI: Well, I'm only trying to get you outta this. I told them you were in Vietnam, you always had good jobs, you were with Goldwater at the '64 convention, but you had marital problems . . .

SONNY: Oh my God, mother!

VI: I said you were never a faggot.

SONNY: Don't talk to them anymore. Sal and me are getting a jet, we're going to Algeria—I'll write you from there.

VI: He was very understanding—you ought to talk to him . . . Algeria?

SONNY: We can't stay here.

VI: Oh my God! I don't understand. If you needed money, why couldn't you come to me? Everything I got is yours. I got two hundred and maybe twenty-five in the savings. It's yours. You know it.

SONNY abruptly realizes he is getting sidetracked by MOM—like always. Tries to get it back again.

SONNY: Mom—they're sending a bus to take us to the airport. You understand? If you're here—they're not gonna send it. They'll think I'm gonna come out with you.

VI: What's wrong with that? The FBI was very understanding when I explained it to him. Everybody knows it isn't you . . . It's the pressures from your home life.

SONNY: For God's sake don't start in on Heidi again . . .

VI: Did I say a thing against her? God forbid I should say anything against that fat cunt.

SONNY: Mom. Mom. There are some things a mother shouldn't say in front of her son.

VI: If she comes down here, so help me I'm gonna mash her brains in. Everything in your life was sunlight and roses until you met her. Since then, forget it.

SONNY: She doesn't have anything to do with it! You understand that? Mother? This is *me!*

VI: I know you wouldn't need Leon if Heidi was treating you right. The thing I don't understand is why you come out and sleep with Heidi anyway? You got two kids on welfare now. What're you goin' to bed with her, you don't have enough with one wife and two kids on welfare, you want a wife and three kids on welfare?

SONNY: (*this is old stuff*) Not now, Mom, please.

VI: What'll you do? Come out.

SONNY: (*patient—I told you a hundred times*) I can't, Mom. If I come out Sal will kill them.

VI: Oh. (*she thinks for a moment*) Run.

SONNY: What the hell for? Twenty-five years in the pen?

VI: Maybe . . .

SONNY: *Maybe!* Aw Christ, what dreams you live on! Maybe *what?*

She stares at him. He talks slowly and carefully to her.

SONNY: I'm a fuckup and an outcast. There isn't one single person in my life I haven't hurt through my love. You understand that? I'm the most dangerous person in the world, because if I love you, watch out, you're gonna get fucked, fucked over and fucked out!

VI: No!

SONNY: Did Pop come down?

VI: No. This really pissed him off, Sonny. He says you're dead. He says he doesn't have a son.

SONNY: He's right. You shoulda done what he did. Go home. (*embraces her*) Don't talk to the FBI anymore.

He walks away and moves toward the bank door.

ON VI

Her desperate smile, apologetic and false at the same time, glistens with a mother's tears. After a long beat:

VI: I remember how beautiful you were. As a baby you were so beautiful. We had such hopes.

[INTERIOR BANK—CLOSE ON DOOR—NIGHT

as SONNY enters and stops, controlling his emotions]

SHAMPOO

A Columbia presentation of a Rubeeker Production. Producer, Warren Beatty. Director, Hal Ashby. Screenplay by Robert Towne & Warren Beatty. Associate Producer, Charles Maguire. Director of Photography, Laszlo Kovacs. Film Editor, Robert Jones. Production Designer, Richard Sylbert. Art Director, Stu Campbell. Music, Paul Simon. Sound, Tom Overton. Assistant Directors, Art Levinson, Ron Wright. Technicolor. Running time, 110 minutes. 1975.

CAST

GEORGE ROUNDY	Warren Beatty
JACKIE SHAWN	Julie Christie
JILL HAYNES	Goldie Hawn
FELICIA KARPF	Lee Grant
LESTER KARPF	Jack Warden
LORNA KARPF	Carrie Fisher
JOHNNY POPE	Tony Bill
NORMAN	Jay Robinson
MR. PETTIS	George Furth
TINA	Jaye P. Morgan
MARY	Ann Weldon
DENNIS	Randy Scheer

Shampoo is set in Beverly Hills during the day and the night of November 4, 1968, when Richard Nixon was elected President of the United States. The story whirls around like a French bedroom farce set in a high school, the characters obsessed with the choice of their dates and how they're going to look when they're with them. Rolls Royces, Mercedes-Benzes, and motorcycles race past each other, speeding their single-minded riders to the next urgent romantic assignation.

At the hub of all this spinning is George Roundy. He's a very popular, virile hairdresser who's more talented than his boss; he wants to open his own shop, but he hasn't got the capital to do so. George makes love more times per day than most of us check our watches. When he's not in bed with someone, he's cutting hair with a precision and skill that is in direct contradiction to the slapdash mess he makes of his inarticulate conversations, his house, and his personal life.

Felicia, one of George's most ardent customer/lovers, has suggested to her husband Lester that to set George up in his own shop would be a wise investment. While George is at Lester's office, in walks Jackie, Lester's very beautiful mistress. If Lester were not oblivious to anything beyond his immediate business affairs, he would sense that George and Jackie had been lovers and that a very strong connection still crackles between them. Instead, he asks George to escort Jackie to his Republican victory party at the swank Bistro Restaurant; she is desperate to go and Lester must obviously escort his wife Felicia. Jackie feels guilty about causing George to break his evening date with Jill, his steady girlfriend, so she arranges for Jill to attend the Bistro party as well—after all, Jill is Jackie's best friend.

At the party, Jackie gets drunk and spectacularly vulgar. Felicia realizes Jackie's relationship to Lester and tells him she is divorcing him. The Bistro party is terminated suddenly by a bomb threat, and all of the characters—except Felicia—eventually find themselves at another party, which is everything the Bistro party wasn't. In place of alcohol and politicians are joints and jacuzzis; in place of tuxedos and propriety are caftans and skinny-dipping. In the pool house, George and Jackie find themselves, much against their wills, admitting that out of all the alliances and motives in which they are embroiled, theirs is the only one that comes from the heart. They make passionate love, only to discover, as things come hurtling in through the windows, that both Lester and Jill have been watching.

Jackie doesn't know what to do. On the one hand, she wants, as does George, the security and sensibleness that Lester embodies. On the other hand, she wants, as does Lester, the romantic passion that George embodies. Jill knows exactly what she wants, which is never to see George again. She has been neglecting her career as a model because long location shoots at the Pyramids would mean separation from George. He used to be the man she would call when a noise frightened her in the middle of the night. Now, she sees him as the man who has done nothing but lie to her.

The following two scenes occur in sequence immediately after the party, when George must first reconcile with Jill, then with an outraged Lester.

SCENE 1

INTERIOR. JILL'S HOUSE. EARLY MORNING.

GEORGE opens his eyes. Above him is the carport and JILL'S yellow Mustang has just pulled in. GEORGE rises. He walks into the living room as JILL comes down the steps to the kitchen, carrying the paper. The kitchen clock reads 4:44.

GEORGE glances at it. Then back at JILL. She looks at him, frightened but not moving. Her hair is stringy, and she's got no makeup on. There's a bruise on the inside of her upper arm, a small one on her neck, and one on her left thigh—all of which GEORGE will note in the course of the scene.

GEORGE looks her up and down.

JILL: I don't want to fight, George.

GEORGE: I don't want to fight either. Look . . . uh—I love you.

JILL: Bullshit.

GEORGE: (moving to her, taking her arm) I do, Jill.

At this point he notes the arm bruise. JILL stares back at him unflinching. GEORGE smiles.

GEORGE: How come you took your own car?

JILL: (getting a cigarette) I didn't want him meeting me here.

GEORGE: Well that's something.

JILL: What is.

GEORGE: You didn't *plan* on fucking him tonight.

JILL doesn't answer.

She walks into the bedroom, kicks off her shoes, starts to take off her dress, then changes her mind and puts on a robe over it.

GEORGE: You did fuck him, didn't you?

JILL: I'm very tired, George.

JILL goes into the living room. GEORGE grabs her arm again.

GEORGE: Didn't you, baby?

JILL: Let go of me.

GEORGE doesn't.

JILL: Let go of me or I'll scream, I'll call the police.

GEORGE: Oh, Christ.

He lets go of her. The PHONE RINGS. JILL answers it. Her tone alters appreciably.

JILL: Oh, hi . . . listen, can I call you back? . . . Yes . . . no, everything's fine, really . . . bye.

She hangs up.

GEORGE: That was him.

JILL: Yes.

GEORGE: You told him I was here and he wanted to know if I was beating you up.

JILL smiles thinly.

JILL: Yes.

GEORGE: Well, did you get a job out of it at least?

JILL: I'd like you to leave now.

GEORGE doesn't move. JILL goes over and fishes into a tote bag by the wall. She returns with FELICIA'S missing earring.

JILL: —and take this with you.

GEORGE: Where did this come from?

JILL: Who knows, I'm sure you don't—but if it'll help any, I found it in your bed.

GEORGE nods. JILL'S anger is growing and her hurt is beginning to surface now. Tears start welling in her eyes.

JILL: *(unsteadily)* So who else was there besides Jackie? Huh? . . . huh?

GEORGE: Baby, don't do this. I do love you.

JILL: Obviously there were others, weren't there?

GEORGE stares at JILL. Then:

GEORGE: Obviously.

JILL: How many?

GEORGE: What do you wanna know for?

JILL: I just want to know, that's all.

GEORGE: What difference does it make?

JILL: I just want to know while we were seeing each other . . . I just don't want girls looking at me and knowing and me not knowing . . .

JILL is crying a little now and looks very vulnerable. GEORGE moves to her and tries to put his arms around her.

GEORGE: Baby, please don't . . . I love you.

JILL: *(breaking away)* I don't want to be a fool! . . . I want to look them in the eye and say, I know!

GEORGE: *(she's backing up, he's trying to touch her)* Baby, don't do this—

JILL: *(fighting for control)* —it'll help me if you'll tell me.

GEORGE: —please, baby—

JILL: —no, it'll help me, really—

GEORGE: How?

JILL: I'll know you've lied to me . . . all along. I'll know you're incapable of . . . love . . . that'll help me . . . not now, but eventually.

It's been rising in him the last few exchanges. Now all GEORGE'S restraints seem to leave him. He stops trying to touch her and stands his ground, exploding:

GEORGE: You dumb cunt, everybody fucks everybody, grow up, for Christ's sakes. You're an antique, you know that? Look around you—all of 'em, all these chicks, they're all fucking, they're getting their hair done so they can go and *fuck;* that's what it's all about. Come into the shop tomorrow and I'll show you—'I fucked her, and her and her, and her, and her—I fucked 'em all! . . . That's what I do, I fuck. That's why I went to beauty school, to fuck. I can't help that, they're there and I do their hair and sometimes I fuck 'em. I stick it in and I pull it out and that's a fuck; it's not a crime.

GEORGE leans on a glass-topped coffee table for support, not even bothering to look at JILL. JILL has been pulled together a little more by the speech.

JILL: . . . well I'm glad you told me.

GEORGE: (*his eyes closed*) Jesus.

His tone has indicated disbelief and disgust.

JILL: I am . . . I mean, you know, that's . . .

She can't finish it.

GEORGE: What? What? What? What? What?

JILL: . . . honest. At least you're honest with me.

GEORGE: Does it make you happy?

JILL doesn't answer.

JILL: I wish you'd go now.

GEORGE: That's all you've got to say?

JILL: —yes.

GEORGE: —tell me something—did you talk about me?

JILL: George . . .

GEORGE: Did you?

JILL: Please! . . . that's not like you.

GEORGE: Yeah, I know. Did you?

JILL: George, now cut this out.

GEORGE: Did you?

JILL: Stop it.

GEORGE: Did you?

JILL: Yes, yes, I did.

GEORGE: What did you say?

JILL: George, if you keep this up I'm going to scream.

GEORGE: What did you say?

JILL: George . . .

GEORGE: What did you say?

JILL: I said you were a loser!

She starts to cry again. GEORGE smiles.

GEORGE: No, I'm not a loser, baby, I just sort of break even.

GEORGE turns and walks up the stairs and out the door.

SCENE 2

[EXTERIOR GEORGE'S HOUSE

GEORGE shuffles up the steps to his front porch and into the living room.]

INTERIOR GEORGE'S LIVING ROOM

[GEORGE finds himself facing LESTER and two other MEN who look like hoods. LESTER sits in the chair GEORGE sat in the other night. Before him is a bottle of J & B, a paper bucket filled with melting ice. The other men rise when] GEORGE walks into the room.

LESTER, glass in hand, stares silently at GEORGE.

[LESTER: (to the other two) Wait outside, would you?

The two MEN walk toward GEORGE and pass him on either side, coming very close. Both of them are much bigger than GEORGE. They stare through GEORGE as they pass him.

GEORGE continues to stand there. LESTER, drinking, continues to stare.] LESTER glances idly around the living room. Then back to GEORGE.

LESTER: You live like a pig.

GEORGE: Yeah. (LESTER doesn't answer) How long have you been here?

LESTER: (looking it) All night.

GEORGE: Well . . . who are those guys?

LESTER: What do they look like? . . .

GEORGE: Look, Lester . . . are you unhappy with me about something?

LESTER: Yeah, I'm unhappy with you about something.

GEORGE: Well, what?

LESTER: Godammit, George . . .

GEORGE: Now wait a minute . . .

LESTER: Sit down.

GEORGE: But . . .

LESTER: I said sit down!

[One of the MEN opens the door and peers through the screen.

MAN: Everything all right?

LESTER: I'll call you, it's okay.]

GEORGE sits down. LESTER has risen to his feet, a little unsteadily.

LESTER: Now, George, I want to hear it from you. Either you admit it, man to man, to my face or I'll have him pound it out of you, and he does a hell of a job, believe me.

GEORGE nods.

GEORGE: I believe you . . .

LESTER waits, standing over GEORGE.

LESTER: I wanna hear about it.

GEORGE: Oh Jesus Christ.

LESTER slaps him.

LESTER: I wanna hear about it, George.

GEORGE: Hey, have 'em put me away, or whatever you're gonna do, okay? . . . I'm too tired to lie, I'm too tired to tell the truth . . . I'm too tired for anything.

LESTER: I wanna hear about it.

GEORGE: What can I say!

LESTER: I wanna know your thinking, I wanna know how someone like you thinks. Did you think you could get away with it, did you think you could put something over on me? Does a guy like you get his kicks sneaking around behind people's backs and taking advantage of them? Maybe that's your idea of being anti-Establishment!

GEORGE: . . . I'm not anti-Establishment.

LESTER: That's got nothing to do with it . . . You're so beyond my comprehension I can't even discuss it with you.

GEORGE: Then don't . . . just have 'em beat me up or whatever you're gonna do.

LESTER: No, not yet, not yet. You worry about it for a while, I've been worrying all night, now you can worry.

A pause. LESTER freshens his drink.

LESTER: Was it me, did you have something against me?

GEORGE: What, do you think I planned it?

LESTER: Did they have something against me?

GEORGE: Didn't they tell you?

LESTER: I wanna *hear* it from you!

GEORGE: (*agonized*) . . . how am I gonna tell you what they have against you? I mean Jesus fucking Christ, they're women, aren't they? Have you ever listened to women talk, man? Have you? Well I do, I do 'til it's fucking coming out of my ears. I'm on my feet all day, every fucking day, listening to women talk and you know what they talk about, don't you? Being fucked up by some guy. That's all that's on their minds. I'm sure you've done something they could get pissed off about, what's that got to do with it? All women are pissed off, man, all of 'em. They fucking hate us! Don't you know that?

LESTER has listened to this with some alteration of his intensity.

LESTER: . . . yes, I follow your thinking on that.

GEORGE: We're always trying to fuck them . . . they know it and they like it and they don't like it . . . that's just how it is . . . look, it's got nothing to do with you, man. It just happened. Felicia's got nothing to do but shop and get her hair done and she knows she's getting older . . . her daughter hates her, what's she going to do, go to PTA meetings?

LESTER: Do you think Lorna hates her? I don't think she hates her. I mean she may resent her a little . . .

GEORGE: Oh, are you kidding, man? She *hates* her.

LESTER: Why, why do you think that is?

GEORGE: Oh, fuck, Lester, how should I know?

LESTER: Well, I don't know.

A pause. LESTER goes to pour himself another drink.

LESTER: (*to* GEORGE) Want a drink?

GEORGE: No thanks.

LESTER: Have a drink.

GEORGE: Okay, thanks.

LESTER gets up and goes to the kitchen.

LESTER: You don't have a clean glass in the house.

GEORGE: I know.

LESTER: (*talking to himself*) I'll have to wash one out.

He turns on the faucet in the kitchen. He brings the glass.

LESTER: Jesus, what a way to live. I never lived like this, not even when I was your age, not even when I never had a dime.

GEORGE takes the drink. LESTER just shakes his head.

LESTER: Hell of a way to treat a business partner, that's all I can say.

GEORGE: Who?

LESTER: Me!

GEORGE: Hey, you were never going to give me the money.

LESTER: (*after a moment*) I was gonna give you the money. Probably I was. Shit, I don't know, I don't know anything anymore.

LESTER sits and stares into his drink.

LESTER: I tell you, you never know . . . you just never know . . . one minute you're here and the next . . . I mean a man at my age, how long have I got—ten years? Five years? I wish I knew . . . what I was living for.

GEORGE looks at him.

LESTER: . . . You can lose it all, you can lose it all no matter who you are . . . I don't know, what's the point of having it all. Look at me. I don't have a goddam thing . . . the market's terrible right now, went down ten points last week, goddam Lyndon Johnson!

GEORGE: Oh yeah . . .

LESTER: Yeah, it goes up a little and then it goes down, maybe Nixon will do something. What's the difference, they're all a bunch of jerks. I wouldn't let 'em run my business, I can tell you that much. Not if I had any choice in the matter. (*after a moment*) I don't know what to do with you. I don't know, I don't know what's right or wrong anymore.

GEORGE: I don't either, Lester, I swear to you I don't.

LESTER: (*suddenly*) What about Jackie?

GEORGE: What about her?

LESTER: I mean, how did that happen?

GEORGE: Lester, it just happened.

LESTER: She's nothing but a whore.

GEORGE: No—

LESTER: Just a whore, I go over there, have a few drinks and get my gun off. I'm through with her, she's nothing but a whore.

GEORGE: No, man, no. You can say everybody's a whore. She's okay. I mean Jackie'll fuck around but not that much. Somewhere she really likes you, Lester, and it's not just the bread. She's okay.

LESTER sits and thinks about that.

LESTER: You really think so?

GEORGE: Yes I do.

LESTER: I'm finished with her.

LESTER goes to the door. He turns as if he'd just thought of something.

LESTER: Oh, by the way, I think you oughta know—Lorna
     thinks she's got the clap.

GEORGE: What?

LESTER: Yeah, the clap. That's what she thinks. But who
     knows—I don't know.

GEORGE nods. LESTER shakes his head.

LESTER: I don't know anything anymore.

He opens the door and goes out. [The two hoods are standing
there. They look to LESTER.]

LESTER: (to hoods) Go easy on him, he's a nice boy.

GEORGE looks shocked. LESTER laughs, gives GEORGE a play-
ful punch.

LESTER: Just having a little fun, George . . . (to hoods) Go
     on home. (to GEORGE) I'll call you later about the shop.
     God, I'm beat.

With that, LESTER is off.

NETWORK

A Metro-Goldwyn-Mayer presentation released through United Artists Corporation. Producer, Howard Gottfried. Director, Sidney Lumet. Screenplay by Paddy Chayefsky. Photography, Owen Roizman. Film Editor, Alan Heim. Music, Elliot Lawrence. Production Designer, Philip Rosenberg. Sound, Richard Varisek, James Sabat. Assistant Director, Jay Allan Hopkins. Panavision, Metrocolor. Running time, 120 minutes. 1976.

CAST

DIANA CHRISTENSON	Faye Dunaway
MAX SCHUMACHER	William Holden
HOWARD BEALE	Peter Finch
FRANK HACKETT	Robert Duvall
NELSON CHANEY	Wesley Addy
ARTHUR JENSEN	Ned Beatty
EDWARD GEORGE RUDDY	William Prince
LOUISE SCHUMACHER	Beatrice Straight
LAUREEN HOBBS	Marlene Warfield
GREAT AHMED KAHN	Arthur Burghardt
T.V. DIRECTOR	Bill Burrows
MARY ANN GIFFORD	Kathy Cronkite
BILL HERRON	Darryl Hickman
SAM HAYWOOD	Roy Poole
NARRATOR	Lee Richardson

"In his time, Howard Beale had been a mandarin of television, the grand old man of news, with a HUT (Homes Using Television) rating of 16 and a 28 audience share. In 1969, however, he fell to a 22 share, and by 1972, he was down to a 15 share. In 1973, his wife died, and he was left a childless widower with an 8 rating and a 12 share."

U.B.S. network decides to fire Howard, and the man who must tell him is "craggy, lumbering, rough-hewn" Max Schumacher, U.B.S. News Division president and one of Howard's oldest friends and admirers. Howard announces on the evening news that as his work was really the only thing going for him, he will blow his brains out on the air in a week. On the following night's broadcast, Howard begins ranting about the meaninglessness of life.

The reaction of the network hierarchy is one of outrage at this violation of "every canon of respectable broadcasting." But the young, hard vice president of programming, Diana Christenson, notes the rise in ratings for Howard's sound-offs, and she knows that if properly developed, a news show that "articulates the popular rage" could be so successful as to pull U.B.S. out of its deep financial hole, something which "respectable broadcasting" has failed to do. Furthermore, when terrorist groups are negotiating with the network's news division over home movies of their own bank robberies, the definition of what is "respectable broadcasting" seems rather murky.

Diana is a very beautiful machine, on a single track for success, and it is a track condoned by the megaconglomerate C.C. and A., which has recently acquired control of U.B.S. The corporate take-over is emblematic to Max of the collapse of a world of values in which his identity as a newsman is rooted.

(*Note:* The following two dialogues may be worked on as one scene in Max's office.)

INTERIOR MAX'S OFFICE—7:00 P.M.

On the office console, the Network News Show has come to an end; the CLOSING THEME MUSIC emerges into SOUND, and the show's CREDITS begin to roll. MAX clicks off the set, folds his hands on the desk and sits glumly regarding his folded hands. After a moment, he becomes aware of another presence in the room and looks to the doorway where DIANA CHRISTENSON is standing, wearing a white blouse and dark slacks and carrying her jacket and purse. If we haven't already noticed how attractive she is, we do now—standing as she is, framed in the doorway, backlit by the lights of the deserted common room, suddenly sensuous, even voluptuous.

DIANA: (*entering the office*) Did you know there are a number of psychics working as licensed brokers on Wall Street? (*she sits across from* MAX, *fishes a cigarette out of her purse*) Some of them counsel their clients by use of Tarot cards. They're all pretty successful, even in a bear market and selling short. I met one of them a couple of weeks ago and thought of doing a show around her—The Wayward Witch of Wall Street, something like that. But, of course, if her tips were any good, she could wreck the market. So I called her this morning and asked her how she was on predicting the future. She said she was occasionally prescient. "For example," she said, "I just had a fleeting vision of you sitting in an office with a craggy middle-aged man with whom you are or will be emotionally involved." And here I am.

MAX: She does all this with Tarot cards?

DIANA: No, this one operates on parapsychology. She has trancelike episodes and feels things in her energy field. I think this lady can be very useful to you, Max.

MAX: In what way?

DIANA: Well, you put on news shows, and here's someone who can predict tomorrow's news for you. Her name, aptly enough, is Sybil. Sybil the Soothsayer. You could give her two minutes of trance at the end of a Howard Beale show, say once a week, Friday, which is suggestively occult, and she could oraculate. Then next week, everyone tunes in to see how good her predictions were.

MAX: Maybe she could do the weather.

DIANA: *(smiles)* Your Network news show is going to need some help, Max, if it's going to hold. Beale doesn't do the angry man thing well at all. He's too kvetchy. He's being irascible. We want a prophet, not a curmudgeon. He should do more apocalyptic doom. I think you should take on a couple of writers to write some jeremiads for him. I see you don't fancy my suggestions.

MAX: Hell, you're not being serious, are you?

DIANA: Oh, I'm serious. The fact is, I could make your Beale show the highest-rated news show in television, if you'd let me have a crack at it.

MAX: What do you mean, have a crack at it?

DIANA: I'd like to program it for you, develop it. I wouldn't interfere with the actual news. But teevee is show biz, Max, and even the News has to have a little showmanship.

MAX: My God, you are serious.

DIANA: I watched your six o'clock news today—it's straight tabloid. You had a minute and a half on that lady riding a bike naked in Central Park. On the other hand, you had less than a minute of hard national and international news. It was all sex, scandal, brutal crimes, sports, children with incurable diseases and lost puppies. So I don't think I'll listen to any protestations of high standards of journalism. You're right down in the street soliciting audiences like the rest of us. All I'm saying is, if you're going to hustle, at least do it right. I'm going to bring this up at tomorrow's network meeting, but I don't like network hassles, and I was hoping you and I could work this out between us. That's why I'm here right now.

MAX: *(sighs)* And I was hoping you were looking for an emotional involvement with a craggy middle-aged man.

DIANA: I wouldn't rule that out entirely.

They appraise each other for a moment; clearly, there are the possibilities of something more than a professional relationship here.

MAX: Well, Diana, you bring all your ideas up at the meeting tomorrow. Because, if you don't, I will. I think Howard is making a goddam fool of himself, and so does everybody Howard and I know in this industry. It was a fluke. It didn't work. Tomorrow, Howard goes back to the old format and this gutter depravity comes to an end.

DIANA: (*smiles, stands*) Okay.

She leans forward to flick her ash into MAX'S desk ash tray. Half-shaded as she is by the cone of light issuing from the desk lamp, it is nipple-clear she is bra-less, and MAX cannot help but note the assertive swells of her body. DIANA moves languidly to the door and would leave, but MAX suddenly says:

MAX: I don't get it, Diana. You hung around till half-past seven and came all the way down here just to pitch a couple of looney show biz ideas when you knew goddam well I'd laugh you out of this office. I don't get it. What's your scam in this anyway?

DIANA moves back to the desk and crushes her cigarette out in the desk tray.

DIANA: Max, my little visit here tonight was just a courtesy made out of respect for your stature in the industry and because I've personally admired you ever since I was a kid majoring in speech at the University of Missouri. But sooner or later, with or without you, I'm going to take over your network news show, and I figured I might as well start tonight.

MAX: I think I once gave a lecture at the University of Missouri.

DIANA: I was in the audience. I had a terrible schoolgirl crush on you for a couple of months.

She smiles, glides to the doorway again.

MAX: Listen, if we can get back for a moment to that gypsy who predicted all that about emotional involvements and middle-aged men—what're you doing for dinner tonight?

DIANA pauses in the doorway, and then moves back briskly to the desk, picks up the telephone receiver, taps out a telephone number, waits for a moment—

DIANA: (*on phone*) I can't make it tonight, luv, call me tomorrow.

She returns the receiver to its cradle, looks at MAX; their eyes lock.

MAX: Do you have any favorite restaurant?

DIANA: I eat anything.

MAX: Son of a bitch, I get the feeling I'm being made.

DIANA: You sure are.

MAX: I better warn you I don't do anything on the first date.

DIANA: We'll see.

She moves for the door. MAX stares down at his desk.

MAX: (mutters) Schmuck.

He sighs, stands, flicks off his desk lamp.

INTERIOR: A RESTAURANT

MAX and DIANA at the end of their dinner. In fact, MAX is flagging a WAITER for two coffees, black—

DIANA: (plying away at her ice cream) You're married, surely.

MAX: Twenty-six years. I have a married daughter in Seattle who's six months pregnant, and a younger girl who starts at Northwestern in January.

DIANA: —Well, Max, here we are—middle-aged man reaffirming his middle-aged manhood and a terrified young woman with a father complex. What sort of script do you think we can make out of this?

MAX: Terrified, are you?

DIANA: (pushes her ice cream away, regards him affably) Terrified out of my skull, man. I'm the hip generation, man, right on, cool, groovy, the greening of America, man, remember all that? God, what humbugs we were. In my first year at college, I lived in a commune, dropped acid daily, joined four radical groups, and fucked myself silly on a bare wooden floor while somebody chanted Sufi suras. I lost six weeks of my sophomore year because they put me away for trying to jump off the top floor of the Administration Building. I've been on the top floor ever since. Don't open any windows around me because I just might jump out. Am I scaring you off?

MAX: No.

DIANA: I was married for four years and pretended to be happy and had six years of analysis and pretended to be sane. My husband ran off with his boyfriend, and I had an affair with my analyst. He told me I was the worst lay he had ever had. I can't tell you how many men have told me what a lousy lay I am. I apparently have a masculine temperament. I arouse quickly, consummate prematurely, and can't wait to get my clothes back on and get out of that bedroom. I seem to be inept at everything except my work. I'm goddam good at my work, and so I confine myself to that. All I want out of life is a 30 share and a 20 rating.

[The WAITER brings the coffee.]

MAX: (*sipping coffee*) The corridor gossip says you're Frank Hackett's backstage girl.

DIANA: (*sipping coffee, smiles*) I'm not. Frank's a corporation man, body and soul. He has no loves, lusts or allegiances that are not consummately directed towards becoming a C. C. and A. board member. So why should he bother with me? I'm not even a stockholder.

MAX: How about your loves, lusts and allegiances?

They smile at each other.

DIANA: Is your wife in town?

MAX: Yes.

DIANA: Well, then, we better go to my place.

ROCKY

A United Artists Corporation presentation. Producers, Irwin Winkler & Robert Chartoff. Director, John G. Alvidsen. Executive Producer, Gene Kirkwood. Screenplay by Sylvester Stallone. Director of Photography, James Crabe. Film Editors, Richard Halsey, Scott Conrad. Art Director, James H. Spencer. Production Designer, Bill Cassidy. Special Camera Effects, Garrett Brown. Assistant Directors, Fred Gallo, Steve Perry. Color by DeLuxe. Running time, 119 minutes. 1976.

CAST

ROCKY	Sylvester Stallone
ADRIAN	Talia Shire
PAULIE	Burt Young
APOLLO	Carl Weathers
MICKEY	Burgess Meredith
JERGENS	Thayer David
GAZZO	Joe Spinell
MIKE	Jimmy Gambina
FIGHT ANNOUNCER	Bill Baldwin
CUT MAN	Al Salvani
ICE RINK ATTENDANT	George Memmoli
MARIE	Jodi Letizia
CHAMPIONSHIP FIGHT	
ANNOUNCER	Lou Fillipo
OWNER OF PET SHOP	Jane Marla Robbins
DIPPER	Stan Shaw

Rocky Balboa lives in South Philadelphia, and he is a very sweet guy. He doesn't approve of the casual racism and sexism in the banter of his buddies. As a collection man for a loan shark, he takes verbal I.O.U.'s from the people he is supposed to injure. (He reasons that with broken thumbs, how can a man work to pay off his debts?) He lives alone with his two turtles, Cuff and Link. He's the kind of fellow who pulls passed-out drunks into the shelter of open doorways, and who escorts home a neighbor's kid sister whom he spots hanging around with the wrong crowd too late one night in front of the drugstore. He's got charm and easy wit. Unfortunately, Rocky once wanted to be a prizefighter; being a sweet guy hasn't helped much in the fulfillment of his dreams.

He doesn't really seem to mind. He doesn't even mind too much the battering his body takes in the low-paying bouts for which he qualifies and sometimes wins. He now looks on boxing as a hobby and figures he never had the chance to prove himself a pro because he's left-handed "an' most pugs won't fight a southpaw 'cause we mess up their timin' an' look awkward, nobody wants to look awkward." What Rocky *does* mind is anybody thinking he is a bum. Mickey Goldmill, the owner of the gym where Rocky works out, thinks he is a bum. Mickey explains why he gave away Rocky's locker to another rising young boxer:

> "Ya want the truth—ya got heart, but ya fight like an ape—The only thing special about you is ya never got ya nose broke—keep ya nose pretty—what's left of ya brain an' retire."

The American Bicentennial Heavyweight Championship of the World is to be held in Philadelphia. Apollo Creed returns home to defend his title. When the contender has to withdraw because of a broken hand, none of the other ranking fighters are able to fill in. Creed gets the idea of opening the bout up to "a local poor underdog. . . . a snow-white underdog." He conceives the event as a solidification of his media image as "Afro-American Folk Hero." Believing America to have been discovered by an Italian, Creed stops pursuing the list of possible names when he comes to Rocky Balboa, "The Italian Stallion"—it's the perfect Bicentennial match.

After staying up all night scrutinizing films of Creed in

action, Rocky comes to believe he cannot win. But Rocky's goals, as he explains them to his girlfriend Adrian, have never changed: "I just wanna prove somethin'—I ain't no bum . . . It don't matter if I lose . . . Don't matter if he opens my head . . . The only thing I wanna do is go the distance— That's all." In an extended fight sequence, which is as excruciatingly vivid to read off the pages of the script as it is to see on the screen, Balboa and Creed enter "a dimension far beyond blood and pain" and Rocky goes the distance.

The following scene is the second half of Rocky's first real date with Adrian Klein. "She's not very attractive, but pleasant-looking. Thirty years old. Brown hair pulled back. Light-skinned. She wears glasses." Rocky has been a regular visitor at the Animal Town Pet Shop where Adrian works, but she's too shy to go out with him. She's too shy to go out with *anyone*. Her boorish brother Paulie, for whom she cooks and keeps house, is afraid she is going to be on his hands forever. Paulie invites Rocky over for Thanksgiving—without telling Adrian. When she protests that she is unprepared for guests, Paulie flings the turkey out the window. Mortified, Adrian locks herself in the bedroom, but Rocky is able to coax her out. Learning that Adrian likes to ice-skate, Rocky chivalrously bribes the cleaning man at the closed rink to give them ten minutes on the ice. He finally gets her to laugh when he tells her that his "ol' man who was never the sharpest told me—I weren't born with much brain so I better use my body." She confesses that she is laughing because her mother always told her just the reverse.

(*Note:* This scene picks them up out on the street just after their ten minutes have expired in the rink and the cleaning man has kicked them out. The scene can be played entirely in Rocky's apartment. Rocky is as yet unaware of Creed's choice of him as opponent and won't find out about it until the following day.)

SCENE 1

EXTERIOR STREET—NIGHT

ROCKY: Some people are very shy by nature.

ADRIAN: . . . I suppose.

ROCKY: I would say you're very shy by nature.

ADRIAN: . . . I suppose.

ROCKY: Some people think bein' shy is a disease, but it don't bother me.

ADRIAN: It doesn't bother me either.

ROCKY: Then why did I bother bringin' it up? 'Cause I'm dumb, that's why . . . Y'know, I think we make a real sharp coupla coconuts—I'm dumb an' you're shy.

ADRIAN: . . . It is just hard for me to understand why anybody wants to be a fighter.

ROCKY: Ya gotta be a little soft to wanna be a pug . . . It's a racket where ya' almost guaranteed to end up a bum.

ADRIAN: I don't think you're a bum.

ROCKY: . . . I'm at least half a bum. Yeah, fightin' is a crazy racket. The roughest part is the mornin' after.

ADRIAN: Morning after?

ROCKY: After a rough fight, ya' nothin' but a large wound. Sometimes I feel like callin' a taxi to drive me from my bed to the bathroom . . . Ya' eyes hurt, ya' ears hurt, ya' hair even hurts . . . But the thing I'm proud of is I been in over sixty fights an' never had a busted nose—Bent an' twisted an' bitten but never broke . . . That's rare.

ADRIAN: Why do you do it if it hurts so bad?

ROCKY: . . . Guess.

ADRIAN: (*pause*) 'Cause you can't sing or dance?

ROCKY smiles.

INTERIOR ROCKY'S APARTMENT—NIGHT

ROCKY and ADRIAN enter his one-room apartment. She is nervous and taken aback by the bleakness of the room. ROCKY goes to the icebox.

ROCKY: Would ya like a glass of water?

ADRIAN: . . . No thanks.

ADRIAN looks at the mirror above ROCKY'S dresser. She sees a high school photo of ROCKY. He once was handsome and smooth-faced. ROCKY steps up behind her, and his face is reflected in the mirror.

He turns on his cheap RECORD PLAYER. He reaches into the turtle bowl.

ROCKY: Here's the guys I was tellin' ya about—This is Cuff an' Link.

ADRIAN: I sold them to you.

ROCKY: (*very embarrassed*) . . . Oh, yeah, I bought the whole kit—Yeah, ya sold me the turtles, the bowl, an' the mountain—I had to get rid of the mountain 'cause they kept fallin' off.

ADRIAN: Do you have a phone?

ROCKY: I had it pulled. People callin' all the time. Who needs it—Who'd you wanna call?

ADRIAN: I wanna let my brother know where I am.

ROCKY: D'you really wanna call?

ADRIAN: Yes, I do.

ROCKY: You sure?

ADRIAN: Yes.

ROCKY: Why?

ADRIAN: I think he might be worried.

ROCKY: I'll call your brother.

ROCKY flings open the window and bellows like a foghorn.

ROCKY: !!Yo, Paulie—Ya sister's with me! I'll call ya later.

ROCKY closes the window and faces the woman. She is not smiling. She looks frightened.

ROCKY: What's the matter? Ya don't like the room?

ADRIAN: It's fine.

ROCKY: It's only temporary.

ADRIAN: It's not that—

ROCKY: What's the problem? You don't like me—Don't like the turtles—What is it?

ADRIAN: I don't think I belong here.

ROCKY: It's okay.

ADRIAN: No, I don't belong here.

ROCKY: It's all right—You're my guest.

ADRIAN: . . . I've never been in a man's apartment before.

ROCKY: (*gesturing*) They're all the same.

ADRIAN: I'm not sure I know you well enough—I don't think I'm comfortable.

ROCKY: Yo, I'm not comfortable either.

ADRIAN: (*standing*) I should leave.

ROCKY: But I'm willin' to make the best of this uncomfortable situation.

ADRIAN moves to the door. ROCKY intercepts her.

ROCKY: (*softly*) Would ya take off your glasses?

ADRIAN: (*dumbstruck*) What?

ROCKY: The glasses . . . Please.

ROCKY removes her glasses and looks deeply into her eyes.

ADRIAN: (*timidly*) . . . T-thank you.

ROCKY: Do me another favor?

ADRIAN: . . . What?

ROCKY: Could ya take off that hat.

After a moment, ADRIAN removes the hat . . . She is becoming rather pretty.

ROCKY: I always knew you was pretty.

ADRIAN: Don't tease me.

The woman melts into the corner and begins lightly sobbing. ROCKY steps forward and fences her with his arms and body.

ROCKY: I wanna kiss ya—Ya don't have to kiss me back if ya don't feel like it.

ROCKY softly kisses the woman. Her arms hang limp. He puts more passion into the kiss and she starts to respond. Her hand glides like smoke up his back. She embraces his neck. The dam of passion erupts. She gives herself freely for the first time in thirty years.

SCENE 2

Rocky has just quit his job as collection man, with the loan shark's blessings, to devote himself full-time to preparing for the fight with Apollo Creed. Mickey Goldmill, the gym owner, pays an unexpected visit to Rocky's apartment.

INTERIOR ROCKY'S APARTMENT—NIGHT

ROCKY returns home and enters his apartment. After turning on the light, he flips on his RECORD PLAYER. He now feeds the turtles.

ROCKY: Look who's home!

ROCKY notices two telegrams laying inside the threshold. He approaches them with a sense of awe. He opens and reads one. Settling on the bed, he reads the other.

A KNOCK is HEARD. ROCKY opens the door. MICKEY GOLD-MILL, the gym owner, stands framed in the doorway.

MICKEY: (stiffly) I seen the light. I figure somebody was home.

ROCKY: Hey, Mickey—Whatta ya doin' here? Here, sit down.

ROCKY tosses soiled clothing off a mangled armchair.

ROCKY: Best seat in the house—Hey, Mick, this is too much.

MICKEY: How do you mean?

ROCKY: I'm usta seein' ya at the gym, but seein' ya here, in my house, it's kinda outta joint.

By the manner in which GOLDMILL listens, it is obvious something important is preying on his mind.

ROCKY is slightly uncomfortable, almost embarrassed at having outsiders see how he lives.

MICKEY: Listen, Rock, you're a very lucky guy.

ROCKY: Yeah.

MICKEY: What's happened is freak luck.

ROCKY: Freak luck for sure.

MICKEY: Look at all them other fighters. Real good boys. Good records. Colorful. Fight their hearts out for peanuts— But who cared? Nobody. They got it shoved in their back door. Nobody ever give them a shot at the title . . .

ROCKY: (*uneasy*) Freak luck is a strange thing.

MICKEY does not hear. His attention is drawn to the turtles.

MICKEY: Whatta' those?

ROCKY: Turtles—domestic turtles.

MICKEY: (*businesslike*) I'm here tellin' ya to be very smart with this shot. Like the Bible sez, ya don't get no second chance.

MICKEY looks hard into ROCKY'S eyes.

MICKEY: Ya need a manager. An advisor. I been in the racket fifty years. I done it all, there ain't nothin' about the world of pugilism that ain't livin' up here.

He lights a half-smoked cigar.

ROCKY: (*at a loss*) Fifty years, huh.

MICKEY: (*stronger*) Fifty years. The rep is known around Philly, an' a good rep can't be bought, but I don't have to tell you that.

ROCKY: How 'bout a glass of water?

MICKEY: Rocky, d'ya know what I done?

ROCKY: (*uneasy*) . . . What?

MICKEY: (*driving each word hard*) *I done it all*. I've done an' seen everythin'. Believe what I'm tellin' ya—Ya shoulda seen the night in Brooklyn, I smacked the "Ginny" Russo outta the ring, September 14, 1923—same night Firpo knocked Dempsey outta the ring. But who got the Press? He did. He had a manager—September 14, 1923.

ROCKY: (*softly*) Ya got a good mind for dates.

MICKEY deafly continues, becoming more engrossed every second.

MICKEY: Look at this face—twenty-one stitches over the left eye, thirty-four over the right—my nose was busted seventeen times, the last being the Sailor Mike fight New Year's Eve, 1940, in Camden, New Jersey—What a professional pastin' I give him. Here, read about it. (*shows a tiny press clipping; points to cauliflower ear*) An'

he give me the vegetable on the ear. I got pain an'
experience . . . an' you got heart—kinda remind me of
Marciano, ya do.

ROCKY points to his most prized possession.

ROCKY: Nobody ever said that—There's his picture.

MICKEY: Yeah, ya kinda remind me of the Rock. Ya move
like 'im.

MICKEY has rung the bell. Nothing could please ROCKY more
than being compared to his idol.

ROCKY: Really think so?

MICKEY: Ya got heart.

ROCKY: Heart, but I ain't got no locker.

ROCKY shifts against the wall and lowers himself into a crouch.

MICKEY: Christ, I know this business. Rocky, when I was
fightin' it was the dirtiest racket goin', see. Pugs like me
was treated like fightin' dogs—throw ya in the pit an' for
ten bucks ya try to kill each other. We had no management . . . fought in boxcars, in whorehouse basements,
any joint with a floor—October 1931, I fought a bum
who put a tack in the thumb of his glove an' punched so
many holes in my face I had spit shootin' outta my
cheeks—I never had no manager watchin' out for me—
See that picture outside the gym— "Mighty Mick," that's
me in my prime. I had all the tools. I coulda starched
any lightweight husky on the East Coast— But I had no
management. Nobody ever got to know how slick I was,
but I had a head for business an' stashed a few bucks an'
opened the gym—It's a dirt hole, I know it, but that an'
a lotta scars is what I got to show for fifty years in the
business, kid—now you come along with this shot, an' I
feel like it's me gettin' the shot I never got . . . Yeah,
we was treated like dogs—like them Dagos, no offense,
in the Colosseum in Rome there—An' now I got all this
knowledge, I wanna give it to ya so I can protect ya an'
make sure ya get the best deal ya can!

ROCKY rises and opens a window.

MICKEY: Respect, I always dished ya respect.

ROCKY: . . . Ya give Dipper my locker.

MICKEY: *(almost begging)* I'm sorry, I—I made a mistake. Kid, I'm askin' man to man. I wanna be ya manager.

ROCKY: The fight's set—I don't need a manager.

MICKEY: Look, you can't buy what I know. Ya can't. I've seen it all! I got pain an' I got experience.

ROCKY: I got pain an' experience too.

MICKEY: Please, kid.

ROCKY: *(tightly)* Whatever I got, I always got on the slide. This shot's no different. I didn't earn nothin' —I got it on the slide . . . I needed ya help about ten years ago when I was startin', but ya never helped me none.

MICKEY drops the ashtray and kneels to pick it up. He remains on one knee.

MICKEY: If ya was wantin' my help, why didn't ya ask? Just ask.

ROCKY: I asked, but ya never heard nothin'!—Like the Bible sez, ya don't get no second chance.

MICKEY: *(yells)* Rocky, I'm seventy-six years old. Maybe you can be the winner I never was—your shot is my last shot!

ROCKY is choked and goes into the bathroom and closes the door.

MICKEY struggles to his feet and, like a beaten man, leaves.

Several moments later ROCKY steps out and lowers himself into bed. Springing up a second later, he runs outside.

[EXTERIOR STREET OF ROCKY'S APARTMENT—NIGHT

ROCKY races up the block toward the shadowy and hunched form of MICKEY. Way in the distance, we SEE ROCKY stop the old man beneath a street lamp. He places an arm around his shoulder.]

THE SEVEN PER-CENT SOLUTION

A Universal Pictures release. Producer & Director, Herb Ross. Executive Producers, Arlene Sellers, Alex Winitsky. Screenplay by Nicholas Meyer. Based on the novel *The Seven Per-Cent Solution* by Nicholas Meyer. Photography, Oswald Morris. Film Editors, William Reynolds, Chris Barnes. Second unit Photography, Alex Thomson. Music, John Addison. Song, Stephen Sondheim. Production Designer, Ken Adam. Art Director, Peter Lamont. Sound, Gordon McCallum, Cyril Swern. Second unit Director, Howard Jeffrey. Assistant Director, Scott Wodehouse. Technicolor. Running time, 113 minutes. 1976.

CAST

SHERLOCK HOLMES	Nicol Williamson
DR. WATSON	Robert Duvall
SIGMUND FREUD	Alan Arkin
LOLA DEVEREAUX	Vanessa Redgrave
PROFESSOR MORIARTY	Laurence Olivier
LOWENSTEIN	Joel Grey
MRS. WATSON	Samantha Eggar
MRS. FREUD	Georgia Brown
MYCROFT HOLMES	Charles Gray
BARON VON SEINSDORF	Jeremy Kemp
MADAME	Regine

The opening title of *The Seven Per-Cent Solution* reads: "In 1891 Sherlock Holmes was missing and presumed dead for three years. This is the true story of that disappearance. Only the facts have been made up."

The story, which spins and chases to Vienna and Istanbul, begins in London where an unraveling Sherlock Holmes is suffering from advanced cocaine addiction; he administers the dope to himself in injections of a seven per-cent solution. Holmes is tricked into a journey to Vienna, believing he is in pursuit of his nemesis, Professor Moriarty, whom he calls "the Napoleon of Crime." It is the faithful Dr. Watson who has gone to Sherlock's brother Mycroft, as the only mind capable of outwitting Sherlock's, to devise this scheme to bring Sherlock to No. 19 Bergasse Strasse in Vienna. This is the address of the revolutionary doctor who is doing work with addiction as well as something he calls the "unconscious." The doctor is Sigmund Freud.

(*Note:* Although Dr. Watson is bracketed out of the scene, and Holmes' lines to him could be addressed rhetorically, the fullest playing of the scene requires the presence of Dr. Watson.)

INTERIOR FREUD'S STUDY—DAY

THE DOOR to the study is opened, and into it steps a MAN who looks older than his thirty-five years, with a beard and the saddest, wisest eyes imaginable. He stoops slightly.

ANGLE on HOLMES reacting—DAY

MAN: (*in slightly accented English*) Good morning, Herr Holmes. [And you, Doctor Watson.] I am glad to see you [gentlemen] in my house.

[WATSON is unable to shake the MAN'S hand; he cannot take his eyes from HOLMES' livid face.]

HOLMES: (*his voice shrill and raving again*) You may remove that ludicrous beard! And kindly refrain from employing that ridiculous comic operetta accent! I warn you, you'd best confess or it will go hard with you, *Professor Moriarty*!

ANGLE on the MAN watching HOLMES carefully—DAY

FREUD: (*slowly; distinct*) My name is Sigmund Freud.

[TITLE CARD: A HOLIDAY IN HELL]

Dead silence. HOLMES walks right up to him and inspects him very closely.

HOLMES: You are not Professor Moriarty. But Moriarty was here. Where is he now?

FREUD: At an hotel, I believe.

HOLMES: (*brisk*) I see.

[He regards WATSON, who flinches before the gaze.]

HOLMES: You knew of this deception from the first, Watson. You were the last individual I would have suspected capable of betraying me to my enemies—

He starts coldly out, throwing open the door to the consulting room [as WATSON starts after him in protest.

WATSON: Holmes—!]

FREUD: (*overlapping*) You do your friend an injustice, Herr Holmes. He and your brother paid Professor Moriarty to journey here in the hope that you would follow him to my door.

HOLMES hesitates, standing by himself in the consulting room. He doesn't even turn around.

HOLMES: And why did they do that?

FREUD: Because they were sure it was the only way they could induce you to see me.

HOLMES: (*turning to face them*) And why were they so eager for that particular event?

FREUD: (*smiling suddenly*) What reason occurs to you? Who am I that your friends should wish us to meet?

HOLMES: (*coldly*) Beyond the fact that you are a brilliant Jewish physician who was born in Hungary and studied for a time in Paris, and that some radical theories of yours have alienated the respectable medical community so that you have severed your connections with various hospitals and branches of the medical fraternity—beyond this I can deduce little. You are married, with a child of five; you enjoy Shakespeare and possess a sense of honor.

As he speaks, FREUD'S expression changes from confidence, to bewilderment, wonder, and, finally, almost to laughing, gleeful amazement as he sinks into the chair behind his desk.

FREUD: But this is wonderful!

He lights one of his ever-present cigars.

HOLMES: (*not moving*) Commonplace. I am still awaiting an explanation.

FREUD: But you must tell me how you guessed the details of my life with such an uncanny accuracy.

HOLMES: (*smooth*) I never guess. It is an appalling habit—destructive to the logical faculty.

He wanders back into the study as Freud [and WATSON] watch, looking like an anatomy lecturer before a class. His vanity, too, has warmed to the task.

HOLMES: A private study is an ideal place for observing facets of a man's character. That the study belongs to you exclusively is evident from the dust. Not even the maid is permitted here—else she would scarcely have ventured to let matters come to this pass.

He runs a finger over some book bindings and holds it up towards the camera—it is covered with soot.

ANGLE on delighted FREUD—DAY

FREUD: Go on!

HOLMES: Very well. Now when a man collects books on a subject they are usually grouped together—but notice that your King James Bible, Book of Mormon, and Koran are separate, across the room in fact, from your Hebrew Bible and Talmud, which sit on your desk. These books have a special importance for you, not connected with a general study of religion, obviously. The nine-branched candelabra on top of your desk confirms my suspicion that you are of the Jewish faith. It is called a menorah, is it not?

FREUD smiles, nods. HOLMES ignores the smile, crosses to the French medical texts.

HOLMES: That you studied medicine in Paris is to be inferred from the great number of medical texts in that language. Where else should a German use French textbooks but in France, and who but a *brilliant* German could study the complexities of medicine in a foreign tongue? That you are fond of Shakespeare is to be deduced by the book being upside down—

ANGLE on upside down SHAKESPEARE—DAY

HOLMES: The fact that you have not adjusted the volume suggests to my mind that you no doubt intended referring to it again in the near future. The absence of dust on the book would tend to confirm this hypothesis.

He strolls back to the consulting room, standing near FREUD'S medical plaque on the wall, which is surrounded by some rectangular blank spaces, where pictures used to be.

HOLMES: That you are a physician is evident when I observe that you maintain a consulting room. Your separation from various societies is indicated by these blank spaces surrounding your diploma, clearly used at one time to display additional certificates. Now what can it be that forces a man to remove such testimonials to his success? Why, only that he has ceased to affiliate himself with those various societies, hospitals and so forth. And why do this, having once troubled to join them all?

His attitude becomes more hostile.

HOLMES: It *is* possible that he became disenchanted with one or two of them, but not likely that his disillusion extended to *all*.

He returns to the study.

HOLMES: (*aggressive*) Rather I postulate that it is they who became disenchanted with *you*, Doctor, and asked you to resign—from all of them. Why? I have no idea, but some position you have taken—evidently a professional one—has discredited you in their eyes. I take the liberty of inferring a theory of some sort—too radical or shocking to gain ready acceptance in current medical thinking. The wedding ring you wear tells me of your marriage; your Balkanized accent hints Hungary or Moravia. The toy soldier there on the floor ought, I think, to belong to a little boy of five. Have I omitted anything of importance?

FREUD: (*he can't stop smiling*) My sense of honor.

HOLMES: It is implied by the fact that you have removed the plaques from societies to which you no longer belong. In the privacy of your study only you would know the difference. And now I think it is for you to do some explaining. In candor I ask you again why I have been brought here.

FREUD: You cannot guess?

HOLMES: I never guess. I cannot think.

FREUD: Then it is you, not I who is being less than candid, Herr Holmes. For you are suffering an abominable addiction, and you choose to wrong your brother and your friend who have combined to help you throw off its yoke rather than admit your own culpability. You disappoint me, sir. Can you be the man I have come to admire, not merely for his brain, but for his passion for justice? In your heart of hearts you must acknowledge your illness and your hypocrisy in condemning your staunch friends.

As FREUD speaks, HOLMES hangs his head lower and lower.

HOLMES: (*he does not raise his head; his voice is painfully soft*) I have been guilty of these things—I make no excuse. But as for help, you must put it from your minds, all of you. I have summoned all my will to the task but it is no use—my feet are on the inexorable path to destruction.

FREUD: (*softly*) A man may sometimes retrace his steps.

HOLMES: (*a despairing groan*) Not from the fiendish coils of drug addiction! No man can do it!

FREUD: I have.

ANGLE on HOLMES looking up sharply, questioningly—DAY

FREUD: I have taken cocaine and am free of its power. It is now my intention to help others. If you will allow me, I will help you.

CLOSEUP—DAY—HOLMES, sweat covering his face.

HOLMES: You cannot do this.

FREUD: I can—but it will take time—and it will not be pleasant. (*he stands*) For the duration I have arranged for both of you to remain here as my guests. Will that be agreeable to you?

HOLMES rises to accept, then suddenly swerves away with a cry, clapping a hand to his face.

HOLMES: No use! Even now I am overcome by this hideous compulsion!

[WATSON half rises from his chair, but] FREUD [waves him back,] comes around his desk and places a hand on HOLMES' shoulder, gently forcing him back into his chair.

FREUD: I will reduce this compulsion—for a time.

He pulls up a chair in front of HOLMES.

FREUD: Do you know anything of the practice of hypnotism?

HOLMES: (dully) Do you propose to make me bark like a dog and crawl about the floor?

FREUD: Through hypnosis I will banish your craving when it exerts itself. In this way we shall artificially reduce your addiction until the chemistry of your body completes the process.

He takes a watch on a fob from his waistcoat.

FREUD: Now, I want you to keep your eyes fastened upon this as it swings. I want you to think of nothing else.

He begins to swing the watch like a pendulum back and forth. HOLMES forces himself to concentrate on it—for dear life.

ANNIE HALL

A United Artists Corporation presentation of a Jack Rollins–Charles H. Joffe production. Producer, Charles H. Joffe. Director, Woody Allen. Screenplay by Woody Allen & Marshall Brickman. Executive Producer, Robert Greenhut. Associate Producer, Fred T. Gallo. Director of Photography, Gordon Willis. Film Editors, Ralph Rosenblum, Wendy Green Bricmont. Art Director, Mel Bourne. Sound Mixer, James Sabat. Assistant Directors, Fred T. Gallo, Fred Blankfein. Panavision. Color by DeLuxe. Running time, 94 minutes. 1977.

CAST

ALVY SINGER	Woody Allen
ANNIE HALL	Diane Keaton
ROB	Tony Roberts
ALLISON	Carol Kane
TONY LACEY	Paul Simon
MRS. HALL	Colleen Dewhurst
ROBIN	Janet Margolin
PAM	Shelley Duvall
DUANE HALL	Christopher Walken
MR. HALL	Donald Symington
GRAMMY HALL	Helen Ludlam
MRS. SINGER	Joan Newman
MR. SINGER	Mordecai Lawner
ALVY (AGE 9)	Jonathan Munk
AUNT TESSIE	Rashel Novikoff
ACTOR BOYFRIEND	John Glover

COMIC	Johnny Haymer
MAN IN THEATRE LINE	Russell Horton
HIMSELF	Marshall McLuhan

Annie Hall is described by Woody Allen as "a romantic comedy about a contemporary urban neurotic" named Alvy Singer, a man who is funny about how miserable he is. Just turned forty, he has achieved a certain kind of New York City success, which, in the kingdom of entertainment, is like living at court. He's watched and listened to. He is a writer and performer who has crafted himself into a relentlessly vigilant walking satire of all the rationales of fear. Life has rewarded him richly for paying comic attention to what is fearful, so he gives scrupulous chase to every real or imagined windmill of bigotry and pretension, hoisting his ever-present lance of mocking disbelief. The lance is bigger than he is. In a physical boxing match, Alvy would be the one wearing the miniature purple satin robe with "M-O-U-S-E" stitched on the back. Alvy feels responsible for safeguarding the traditions of all that's decent and valuable in Western thought and culture; given the history and state of the world, this is a never-ending job requiring brilliance and paranoia. Which brings us right up to Dostoevsky, who wrote that the opposite of love is not hatred, but the persistant use of rational mind. No wonder both of Alvy's marriages have failed.

When Alvy falls in love with Annie Hall, he offers up all the tools of his trade in service to his love for her. He delights her with mockeries of himself in love, as well as mockeries of any love she may have misguidedly attempted before she met him. He perceives himself as such a cultural freak in the world of Annie's Chippewa Falls, Wisconsin, upbringing that it is mandatory he make chopped liver out of every detail of it, from the quirks of her speech ("neat" and "Well, la-dee-da!") to her palate (pastrami and mayonnaise). They sit together in the park, and he sketches quick comic stereotypes of every passing stranger; he fills Annie with joy—not so much with the accuracy of any description, but with his lightning dexterity at playing this game.

Of course, when Annie starts to play with some of Alvy's toys, she arranges them somewhat differently. She takes courses in the subject areas of his concerns, but she becomes friends with the teacher, and Alvy gets jealous. She goes to see a psychiatrist and cries during her first session, when Alvy hasn't been able to weep once in all of his fifteen years of Freudian whining. She's begun singing in nightclubs, and he guides her beyond her initial stage fright; then she is picked up by the sort of Hollywood music business people whose California style sends Alvy up the wall. When he'd first met her, Alvy admired Annie's photographs and began to discuss aesthetic criteria. "Aesthetic criteria?" she asked. "You mean, whether it's, uh, a good photo or not?" Not only is Annie not constrained by a critical vocabulary, but her photographs are wonderful without it, and her singing voice is affectingly sweet and true. Annie wants to try things, and Alvy adores the lovely and direct contact she makes with whatever she tries. But it starts to feel to him as if these contacts on Annie's horizon, which he has helped to expand, are excluding him. The shakier he feels his footing, the harder he seeks out foibles to tilt at, and his scraping mockeries are now being shot *at* Annie, not *for* her.

Alvy Singer's consuming anxiety stems from his understanding that he is going to die at some point in his own lifetime. No matter how high he climbs as a comic writer and playwright, his soul quakes in the knowledge that Death is the top banana. At age five, trembling in his family's house under a roller coaster at Brooklyn's Coney Island, (where he worked out his aggressions in his father's bumper car concession), Alvy was plunged into a deep depression by the news that the Universe was expanding and would one day fly apart. At age forty, being a minute late for the movies is a crisis. ("I've gotta see a picture exactly from the start to the finish, 'cause, 'cause I'm anal.") He knows he's strident, but his conflicts are too central to his sense of his own purpose in life to simply dismantle them. ("Right, I'm a bigot, you know, but for the left.")

Annie Hall suffers from an extreme lack of self-confidence as well, except that it's not cosmic or mortal, it's localized into her daily gestures. She expresses herself in little halting monologues of self-consciousness and self-effacement that are charming because they are invitations for clarification from her listener. If she is mocking anybody, it is herself. There is a scene in *Annie Hall* where she and Alvy try to get a lobster into a pot of boiling water. Annie gets to try; Alvy gets to mock. They both get to laugh with each other over their fear of the snapping lobster, over their own fumbling attempts at the task, and because they finally *do* get the lobster into the pot, the scene is a celebration of their mutual delight at getting to be exactly who they are in the approving presence of each other. Later in the film, after they have broken up, the scene is replayed by Alvy with another young woman, but she doesn't respond to his jokes or improvise with him, and since she's not offering any vulnerability herself, the scene reprises with a rueful sadness.

The following scene occurs after Annie and Alvy have broken up for the first time. He has been to a concert with a rock journalist, and went to bed with her, but as far as he could see, she is a total air-head. When he gets an urgent telephone call from Annie, he rushes right over to her apartment.

CAMERA OPENS ON THE DOOR*

ALVY: (OFFSCREEN) What's . . . It's me, open up.

Door opens.

ANNIE: Oh.

ALVY: (OFFSCREEN) Are you okay?

MEDIUM CLOSE TWO SHOT (MC2S). ALVY moves into House and ANNIE moves side angle Left as they look at one another.

ALVY: What's the matter?

ANNIE: (*sighing*)

ALVY: Are you all right? What . . .

ANNIE: There's a spider in the bathroom.

ALVY: (*reacting*) What?

ANNIE: There's a big, black spider in the bathroom.

Note: This scene is excerpted from the continuity script, not from the shooting script. (Please see the source appendix at the end of this volume for an explanation of these terms.) The actor must view the action—which has not been written by the screenwriter—only as a guideline, and not as the screenwriter's stage directions.

ALVY: That's what you got me here for at three o'clock in the morning, 'cause there's a spider in the bathroom?

ANNIE: *(overlapping above speech)* My God, I mean, you know how I am about insects.

ALVY: *(overlapping, sighing)* Oooh.

ANNIE: *(overlapping)* . . . I can't sleep with a live thing crawling around in the bathroom.

ALVY: *(overlapping)* Kill it! For Go- . . . What's wrong with you? Don't you have a can of Raid in the house?

ANNIE: *(shakes head)* No.

CAMERA PULLS BACK as ALVY disgusted, waving hand, moves Right as CAMERA PANS with him.

ALVY: *(sighing)* I told you a thousand times you should always keep, uh, a lotta insect spray. You never know who's gonna crawl over.

CAMERA PULLS BACK as ALVY, followed by ANNIE, moving thru the Hallway.

ANNIE: I know, I know and a first aid kit and a fire extinguisher.

They stop in Living Room Center, ALVY Left with ANNIE Right.

ALVY: *(overlapping)* Jesus. All right, gimme a magazine. I—'cause I'm a little tired.

ANNIE moves passing ALVY and OFFSCREEN Left.

ALVY: You know, you, you joke with—about me, you make fun of me, but I'm prepared for anything.

He looks over on Bookcase and picks up pamphlet.

ALVY: An emergency, a tidal wave, an earthquake. Hey, what is this? What? Did you go to a Rock Concert?

ANNIE: (OFFSCREEN) Yeah.

ALVY: Oh, yeah, really? Really? How, how'd you like it? Was it, was it, I mean did it . . . was it heavy? Did it achieve total heavy-ocity? Or was it, uh, . . .

ANNIE moves in Left, FOREGROUND (FG) and OFFSCREEN Right.

ANNIE: It was just great!

ALVY thumbs thru book.

ALVY: Oh, humdinger. When . . . Well, I got a wonderful idea. Why don'tcha get the guy who took you to the Rock Concert, we'll call him and he can come over and kill the spider. (*tosses pamphlet down* OFFSCREEN *Left and looks* OFFSCREEN *Right*) You know, it's a . . .

ANNIE: (OFFSCREEN) I called you, you wanna help me . . .

ANNIE moves in Right to ALVY Center for CLOSE TWO SHOT (C2S).

ANNIE: . . . or not? H'h? Here.

ALVY: (*he looks down at magazine and takes it from* ANNIE) What is this? What are you . . . Since when do you read the National Review? What are you turning into?

CAMERA PANS Right with moving ANNIE.

ANNIE: Well, I like to try to get all points of view.

ALVY: (OFFSCREEN) (He reaches into her bag on the chair.) It's wonderful. Then why don'tcha get William F. Buckley to kill the spider?

She spins around looks OFFSCREEN Left.

ANNIE: Alvy, you're a little hostile, you know that? Not only that, you look thin and tired.

ALVY moves in Left for MC2S to ANNIE who puts piece of gum in her mouth.

ALVY: Well, I was in be- . . . It's three o'clock in the morning. You, uh, you got me outta bed, I ran over here, I couldn't get a taxi cab. You said it was an emergency, and I didn't ge- . . . I ran up the stairs. Bel- . . . I was a lot more attractive when the evening began. Look, uh, tell . . . whatta you . . . are you going with a right wing rock and roll star? Is that possible?

ANNIE sits down on Chair looking up at ALVY.

ANNIE: (*overlapping above speech*) Would you like a glass of chocolate milk?

ALVY: Hey, what am I, your son? Whatta you mean? . . . I, I came over t' . . .

ANNIE touches chest and holds up hand to ALVY.

ANNIE: I got the good chocolate, Alvy.

ALVY: *(overlapping)* Yeah, where is the spider?

ANNIE: *(overlapping)* It really is lovely. It's in the bathroom.

ALVY: *(overlapping)* Is he in the bathroom?

ALVY turns moves Left as CAMERA PANS up with rising ANNIE and CAMERA PANS slightly Left with moving ALVY.

ANNIE: Hey, don't squish it and after it's dead flush it down the toilet, okay?

ALVY moves back into Center with ANNIE.

ANNIE: And flush it a couple o' times.

ALVY: *(overlapping)* Darling, darling, I've been killing spiders since I was thirty, okay?

He turns moves OFFSCREEN down Hallway leaving ANNIE upset, putting hands on her neck.

ANNIE: Oh.

ALVY moves back into view with ANNIE as she reacts.

ANNIE: What?

ALVY: Very big spider.

ANNIE: Yeah?

ALVY moves Left followed by ANNIE.

ALVY: Too . . . Yeah. Lotta, lotta trouble. There's two of 'em.

ANNIE: Two?

He opens closet door.

ALVY: Yep. I didn't think it was that big, but it's a major spider. You got a broom or something with a . . .

ANNIE: *(overlapping above speech)* Oh, I, left it at your house.

ALVY: *(overlapping)* . . . snow shovel or anything or something.

ANNIE: *(overlapping)* I think I left it there, I'm sorry.

Reaching into Closet ALVY takes out Tennis Racket covered

and moves Right as CAMERA PANS with him and ANNIE beside him moving Right.

ALVY: (*overlapping*) Okay, let me have this.

ANNIE: (*overlapping*) Well, what are you doing, what are you doing with . . .

ALVY: (*overlapping*) Honey, there's a spider in your bathroom the size of a Buick.

ALVY moves down Hallway as ANNIE moves to Right Center and looks toward Center BACKGROUND (BG) after ALVY.

ANNIE: Well, okay. Oooh.

FULL SHOT thru opened Bathroom Door—ALVY Center with Racket in one hand and rolled Magazine in other looks at the Shelf reacting and picks up small container and looks OFFSCREEN Right holding up for OFFSCREEN ANNIE to see.

ALVY: Hey, what is this? You got black soap?

ANNIE: (OFFSCREEN) It's for my complexion.

ALVY: Whatta . . . whatta yuh joining a minstrel show? Geez.

ALVY turns and swats with racket OFFSCREEN Left. Turning in small bathroom, racket hits Shelf knocking articles from it. SLAM OF RACKET, CRASHING GLASS.

ANNIE: (OFFSCREEN) What are you doing?

ALVY: Don't worry.

ALVY continues swatting with the racket. ALVY moves out of door with hands up close to his body. He moves down steps and OFFSCREEN Right FG.

ALVY: I did it! I killed them both.

High Down FULL SHOT. ANNIE sits on her bed in corner leaning against wall with hand over her face.

ALVY: What, what's the matter? Whatta you . . .

ANNIE: (*sobbing overlapping*)

ALVY: . . . whatta you sad about? You . . . What'd you want me to do? Capture 'em and rehabilitate 'em?

ANNIE takes arm of ALVY and he sits down beside her.

ANNIE: (*sobbing*) Oh, don't go, okay? Please.

ALVY: Whatta you mean, "don't go?" Whatta, whatta, what's the matter? Whatta you expecting termites? What's the matter?

ANNIE: (*sobbing*) Oh, uh, I don't know. I miss you. Tsch.

She beats fist on bed and reacting ALVY puts arm around her shoulder as he leans against wall.

ALVY: Oh, Jesus, really?

ANNIE: Oh, yeah. Oh.

She leans on his shoulder and they kiss.

ANNIE: Oh! Alvy?

ALVY: What?

He touches her face gently as she wipes tears from her face.

ANNIE: Was there somebody in your room when I called you?

ALVY: W-W-Whatta you mean?

ANNIE: I mean was there another . . . I thought I heard a voice.

ALVY: Oh, I had the radio on.

ANNIE: Yeah?

ALVY: I'm sorry. I had the television set—I had the television—

ALVY pulls her to him and they kiss again.

ANNIE: Yeah.

ALVY: (*indistinct*)

Low Angle Up MC2S—over prone side angle ALVY lying in bed with ANNIE leaning on elbow beside him looking down at ALVY. He rubs her arm and she smiles.

ANNIE: Alvy, let's never break up again. I don't wanna be apart.

ALVY: Oh, no, no, I think we're both much too mature for something like that.

ANNIE: Living together hasn't been so bad, has it?

ALVY: It's all right for me, it's been terrific, you know? Better than either one of my marriages. See, 'cause,

'cause there's something different about you. I don't
know what it is, but it's great.

ANNIE: (*snickering overlapping above speech*) You know I
think that if you let me, maybe I could help you have
more fun, you know? I mean, I know it's hard and (not
distinct) . . . Yeah.

ALVY: (*overlapping*) I don't know.

ANNIE: Alvy, what about . . . what if we go away this weekend, and we could . . .

ALVY: (*overlapping*) Tsch, why don't we get, why don't we
get Rob and the three of us'll drive into Brooklyn, you
know, and we show you the old neighborhood.

ANNIE: (*overlapping*) Okay, okay. Okay.

ALVY: (*overlapping*) That'd be fun for yuh. Don't you think
. . .

ANNIE: (*overlapping*) Yeah.

ALVY raises his head and they kiss.

JULIA

A Twentieth Century-Fox Film presentation. Producer, Richard Roth. Director, Fred Zinneman. Screenplay by Alvin Sargent. Based on the story "Julia" from the book *Pentimento* by Lillian Hellman. Executive Producer, Julien Derode. Associate Producer, Tom Pevsner. Director of Photography, Douglas Slocombe. Film Editors, Walter Murch, Marcel Durham. Production Designers, Gene Callahan, Willy Holt, Carmen Dillon. Music, Georges Delerue. Sound Mixer, Derek Ball. Second Unit Photography, Paddy Carey, Guy Delattre. Assistant Directors, Alain Bonnot, Anthony Wayne. Color by DeLuxe. Running time, 118 minutes. 1977.

CAST

LILLIAN	Jane Fonda
JULIA	Vanessa Redgrave
HAMMETT	Jason Robards
JOHANN	Maximilian Schell
ALAN	Hal Holbrook
DOTTIE	Rosemary Murphy
ANNE MARIE	Meryl Streep
WOMAN PASSENGER	Dora Doll
GIRL PASSENGER	Elisabeth Mortensen
SAMMY	John Glover
GRANDMOTHER	Cathleen Nesbitt
BUTLER	Anthony Carrick
YOUNG JULIA	Lisa Pelikan
YOUNG LILLIAN	Susan Jones

Julia is based on Lillian Hellman's memoir of a childhood friend who once saved her life when she was too paralyzed with panic to move out of danger. For the next few decades Julia provided the kind of figure by which a life may measure its own learnings and responsibilities. Hellman writes, "I think I have always known about my memory. I know when the truth is distorted by some drama or fantasy. But I trust absolutely what I remember about Julia."

Born very beautiful and brilliant and courageous, Julia leaves the frigid New York wealth of her upbringing and by the 1930s is in Vienna, fighting in the anti-Nazi underground, where she is eventually, and brutally, killed. Lillian is a playwright, often in struggle with herself and her work. She is possessed, as is Julia, by the need to know right from wrong, to fight what is evil. But Lillian is not fearless, and her inability to always act with the immediate grace and decisive courage epitomized for her in Julia can lead to an anger that has always been both Lillian's gift and her trouble. And it is this anger that Julia prizes so highly in her friend.

In 1934, having a hard time with her first play, Lillian goes briefly to write in Paris and to visit Julia in Vienna. She is stunned by the rise of Fascism and finds Julia badly smashed up in a hospital. Three years later, this first play a success and her second one a failure, Lillian is again in Paris en route to a theatre festival in Moscow, where she is intercepted by a messenger from Julia. Can Lillian, despite the danger of her Jewish name, smuggle $50,000 into Berlin to buy freedom for prisoners of the Nazi horror? Julia warns Lillian through the messenger not to attempt it merely because she is "afraid of being afraid." Cryptic instructions lead Lillian through a sweltering, panic-gripped train ride during which she is to wear a large fur hat that conceals the money. She passes through border patrols, customs, and finally through more cryptic instructions which bring her to Albert's Café.

(*Note:* For the fullest playing of the scene in class, the interventions of Albert and the waiter are helpful, but the same actor can play both moments.)

[LILLIAN'S POINT OF VIEW ACROSS THE STREET— DUSK

We can see an electric sign reading "ALBERT'S."

BACK TO LILLIAN—DUSK

She moves slowly, anxiously across the street. Finally, at the other side, in front of Albert's, she looks into the window, but it is not possible to see anyone inside. She moves to a revolving door. A GROUP OF PEOPLE are coming out. She has to wait to catch a slot in the door. She does and she pushes the door in. It is difficult with the hatbox and her small suitcase.]

INTERIOR ALBERT'S RESTAURANT—NIGHT

LILLIAN appearing out of the revolving door. She stops. She looks around. Suddenly, she reacts to something OFFSCREEN.

HER POINT OF VIEW—JULIA—NIGHT

sitting at a table at the rear of the restaurant. She is looking at LILLIAN. Leaning against the wall behind her chair are two crutches. A drink is on the table. Cigarettes.

ANGLE FAVORING LILLIAN—NIGHT

Frozen. She only looks.

ANGLE FAVORING JULIA—NIGHT

She smiles. She raises one hand. LILLIAN slowly moves toward JULIA.

CLOSER ANGLE—LILLIAN AND JULIA—NIGHT

LILLIAN closer to her now. For the first time she sees the crutches. JULIA takes her hand. LILLIAN'S eyes begin to tear. They do not speak. LILLIAN looks again at the crutches, then she sits next to JULIA. JULIA continues to hold her hand. LILLIAN can't speak. Then finally:

JULIA: Fine, fine.

LILLIAN studies her, looks at the crutches.

JULIA: I've ordered caviar. We'll celebrate. Albert had to send for it, it won't be long. Look at you. Oh, just look at you!

LILLIAN: (whispers) Tell me what to say to you.

JULIA: It's all right. Nothing will happen now, everything's fine now.

LILLIAN: I want to say something.

JULIA: I know.

LILLIAN: How long do we have?

JULIA: Not long.

LILLIAN: You still look like nobody else. (*pause*) Why do you have the crutches?

Pause.

JULIA: (*quickly*) I have a false leg!

LILLIAN: What?

JULIA: I have a false leg!

LILLIAN: No! I don't want to hear that. Don't tell me that!

JULIA: (*sharp*) No tears, Lilly.

LILLIAN: I'm sorry.

JULIA: It's done. It's what it is.

LILLIAN: When?

JULIA: You know when. You were there. In Vienna.

LILLIAN: I don't want to hear about it, please, just let me look at you.

JULIA: You have to hear about it, you have to hear about everything. (*taking LILLIAN'S hand*) Your fingers are cold, here . . .

She begins to rub LILLIAN'S hands.

LILLIAN: They took the candy box. A man and a woman.

JULIA: That's right. Everything's fine and what I want you to do now is take off your hat, the way you would if it— Lilly, listen to me, you aren't listening.

LILLIAN: I'm listening, I am.

JULIA: Take off your hat, as if it were too hot in here. Comb your hair. Put your hat on the seat between us. Do as I tell you . . . Make conversation . . . It has to be this way.

LILLIAN looks around the room. Then she looks at JULIA. She takes off the hat.

JULIA: (*calmly*) Who were you with in Paris? Good friends?

LILLIAN: Yes. Good friends. But they don't know anything about this.

She puts the hat on the seat between them.

JULIA: Get your comb.

LILLIAN: Comb . . .

She reaches for her purse. Opens it. Looks for the comb. The purse is full.

LILLIAN: I still carry too much.

JULIA: *(looking in purse)* There it is, take it out and use it.

LILLIAN takes out the comb. Starts to comb her hair back.

JULIA: Keep talking to me. I read your play. Don't look down. Look at me. Be natural. You look so very well.

During this JULIA has pulled the hat into her open coat. Then she'll proceed to pin it deep inside the lining.

LILLIAN: Did you like it? My play?

JULIA: I'm proud of you. It was wonderful.

LILLIAN: But my second play failed.

JULIA: I know. I heard. Are you writing your third?

LILLIAN: I'm writing it.

JULIA: Now, I'm going to the toilet. You come with me. If the waiter tries to help me up, wave him away.

JULIA reaches for her crutches. LILLIAN goes to help her.

JULIA: I'm all right, I can do it. If I had more time to practice, I wouldn't need the crutches. But this leg doesn't fit properly. Come along. Act gay. Can you act gay?

LILLIAN tries to laugh.

LILLIAN: No, I can't act gay.

They start on, toward the washroom. We can see a man, ALBERT, bringing caviar, wine to their table.

JULIA: What's your new play about?

LILLIAN: I don't know. I'm not sure yet. Shall I come with you?

JULIA: *(In German re caviar—to ALBERT)* Thank you very much, Albert.

They reach the washroom door.

LILLIAN: Shall I come in with you?

JULIA: No, the toilet door will lock. If anybody tries to open it, then knock very hard and call to me. But I don't think that will happen.

JULIA opens the toilet door. Moves in. As the door closes, her crutch is at a wrong angle. It gets caught. She pulls irritably at the crutch. There's some humiliation in the gesture. The door closes. LILLIAN waits outside the door. [Some PEOPLE are moving in to be seated. One of them is the FAT MAN we saw on the train. He is alone. He moves to a small table against the wall and takes a newspaper from his side pocket.]

LILLIAN looks toward their table. The wine and caviar have been placed on it. [She looks back toward the FAT MAN at his table.] She looks at other faces. They all "seem" to be looking at her.

The door to the toilet opens. JULIA moves out. She smiles at LILLIAN. She starts slowly back toward their table. As they go:

JULIA: The German public toilets are always clean. Much cleaner than ours. Particularly under the new regime. (*under her breath*) The bastards. The murderers.

NEW SHOT as they sit. JULIA nearly losing her balance. But managing. LILLIAN next to her. The WAITER comes to pour the wine. JULIA smiles, acts "gay."

JULIA: (*in German—to* WAITER) Aren't we fancy people. Maybe you'll start stocking caviar from here on.

WAITER: (*in German*) We don't want to serve caviar, we'll all have to be too polite.

They laugh and the WAITER moves away.] JULIA slips the hat from under her coat, back onto the seat.

JULIA: Nothing will happen now. We're all right now. I want you to know this. You've been better than a good friend to me. You've done something important . . . It's my money you brought in. We can save five hundred people, maybe. If we bargain right, maybe a thousand.

LILLIAN: Jews?

JULIA: About half are Jews. Political people. Socialists, Communists, plain old Catholic dissenters. Jews aren't the only people who suffer here. But that's enough of that. We can only do today what we can do today. And today you did it for us.

She drinks some wine. LILLIAN drinks too.

JULIA: Do you need something stronger?

LILLIAN: No.

JULIA: We have to talk fast now. There isn't much time.

LILLIAN: How much?

Some people move by.

JULIA: A few minutes. (*louder, to be heard*) You must have some pictures for me. Do you have a picture of Hammett?

LILLIAN: Yes, yes, I do. (*opens her purse, wallet*) One. I have one picture.

JULIA: Show me!

LILLIAN: I wrote you about him. Did you get that letter? Do you get my letters?

JULIA: Some. (*looks at snapshot—speaks loud*) Ahh, this is Hammett! Is he the one we dreamed of? I like the face. Tell me what he is?

LILLIAN: He's remarkable, and difficult, and it isn't simple together. I can't describe him. He's an extraordinary kind of American man, I want you to meet him.

JULIA: I want to.

LILLIAN: When?

JULIA: Soon.

LILLIAN: How soon?

JULIA: I'll be coming to New York.

LILLIAN: When?

JULIA: A few months. My leg is clumsy. I need a better one. (*laughs*) My God, Lilly, are we having this conversation?

LILLIAN: Just come back, I don't care about the conversation.

JULIA: There's something else. I'll need you to do something else for me.

LILLIAN: You know I will . . . What?

JULIA waits. Then, quickly:

JULIA: I have a baby.

Pause. LILLIAN is stunned. JULIA doesn't speak. She smiles, touches LILLIAN's face. LILLIAN trying not to cry, lighting a cigarette, fumbling with it. Finally:

JULIA: She's fat and she's handsome and she's very healthy. She's not even one yet. Can you imagine not even being one yet?

LILLIAN: Yes . . .

JULIA: And I don't even mind that she looks like my mother.

LILLIAN: Where is she?

JULIA: She's across the border in Alsace in a town near Strasbourg. She lives with good people. The man is a baker. Remember we used to want to live in a bakery? I can see her whenever I can cross over. But she shouldn't be in Europe. It ain't for babies these days.

LILLIAN: When can I see her? What's her name?

JULIA: (pause) Lilly.

LILLIAN is obviously very moved, she does not speak. Close to tears.

JULIA: When I come to New York for my leg, I'll bring her with me. I want to leave her with you. You're the only one there I can trust.

LILLIAN: I'll take care of her. You know that.

JULIA: I won't stay away long. I can't last much longer in Europe. The crutches make me too noticeable. There'll be plenty of money. You won't have to worry about anything.

LILLIAN: I don't care about that. You know that doesn't matter.

JULIA: And you don't have to worry about her father, he doesn't want anything to do with her. Or with me. A medical student I knew. I don't know why I did it. But I know I wanted to. Maybe a person finally needs their own blood to be more courageous. And, oh God, but we need such courage now. All of us.

They are quiet another moment. Then:

LILLIAN: *(quiet rage)* What is it? Why is it like this?

JULIA: *(studies* LILLIAN *a moment)* Are you as angry a woman
as you were a child?

LILLIAN: I try not to be. It isn't easy.

JULIA: I like your anger. Don't let people talk you out of it.

JULIA reacts to something OFFSCREEN.

JULIA: The man who will take care of you has just come into
the street.

LILLIAN: But we haven't talked. We've had no time. I need
more time.

JULIA: Now I want you to stand up. Take the hat . . .
Listen to me. Put the hat back on, and then say goodbye
to me and then go. Walk across the street.

LILLIAN has become visibly upset.

JULIA: The man will see that you get on the train safely.
Someone else will stay with you 'til Warsaw tomorrow
morning. He's in Car A, Second Class, compartment
thirteen. Zweite Klasse. Say it!

LILLIAN: Zweite Klasse.

JULIA: Compartment 13. Abteilung Dreizehn. Say it!

LILLIAN: Abteilung Dreizehn. I don't want to leave you. I
want to stay with you longer.

JULIA: No. Something could still go wrong. We aren't sure
who anyone is anymore.

LILLIAN: I'll have room for Lilly. I'll try to make it wonderful.

JULIA: I know you will. Put the hat on . . . Lillian, put the
hat on!

LILLIAN waits for a beat, then puts on the hat. As she does:

JULIA: Write to me from Moscow to American Express in
Paris. Someone picks up for me every few weeks. *(takes*
LILLIAN'S *hand and raises it to her lips)* Oh, yes . . . Oh,
yes, my beloved friend.

She kisses LILLIAN's hand. Another pause. Then JULIA brings
her hands down.

JULIA: Leave! . . . (*sharp*) LEAVE!

LILLIAN gets up quickly as if powered by something outside of herself.

WIDER ANGLE—NIGHT

LILLIAN turns and moves to door. When she gets there she stops, turns, looks back at JULIA, who is holding her glass of wine. LILLIAN seems to take a small step toward her, JULIA quickly shakes her head, looks at another part of the room. LILLIAN turns and moves out through the revolving door.

[EXTERIOR THE STREET OUTSIDE ALBERT'S—NIGHT

LILLIAN alone. Her purse, the hatbox, her small bag. She looks up and down the street. Then she looks across the street at the station entrance. She crosses. Much traffic. In her confusion she has to dodge a few cars. Is stranded a moment in the middle. Suddenly a MAN is at her side. He takes her arm. She looks at him and they continue to the station.]

SATURDAY NIGHT FEVER

A Paramount Pictures Corporation presentation. Producer, Robert Stigwood. Director, John Badham. Screenplay by Norman Wexler. Based on a script from an article "Tribal Rites of the New Saturday Night" by Nik Cohn. Executive Producer, Kevin McCormick. Director of Photography, Ralph D. Bode. Film Editor, David Rawlins. Production Designer, Charles Bailey. Music, Barry Gibb, Robin Gibb, Maurice Gibb. Additional Music & Adaptation, David Shire. Choreography, Lester Wilson. Color by Movielab. Running time, 119 minutes. 1977.

CAST

TONY	John Travolta
STEPHANIE	Karen Lynn Gorney
BOBBY C.	Barry Miller
JOEY	Joseph Cali
DOUBLE J	Paul Pape
ANNETTE	Donna Pescow
GUS	Bruce Ornstein
FLO	Julie Bovasso
FRANK, JR.	Martin Shakar
FRANK, SR.	Val Bisoglio
FUSCO	Sam J. Coppola
GRANDMOTHER	Nina Hansen
LINDA	Lisa Peluso

Norman Wexler writes that for Tony Manero,

"walking down the street is a performance. . . . Tony is eighteen, a few months short of nineteen, tall, well-built, carries himself with studied cockiness, a bit of a swagger. His face is handsome and, in repose, has a sweet likability, even loveability. His personality is colored by environments, more than most people—tough-cool with friends, macho-masterful with girls—sullen and obstinate at home where he is respectful of his parents but suspicious of them, always anticipating their demands and criticism. He often appears preoccupied, but if he were asked what he is thinking, he wouldn't know. He lives in the immediate present, the future means no more than the next weekend at the disco—although there are some rare private moments, quickly repressed, when he experiences some tremors about the rest of his life . . . He eats . . . with remarkable speed but with indifference, mechanically, not sensually, giving the impression not of gluttony, but insatiable hunger that goes beyond food."

Tony is at his best in the disco. When he steps out on the floor, he is "a superb dancer, graceful and strong, his movements quick, smooth and precise, his body and carriage emitting a presence and pride." Everyone stops to watch him, and he's the undisputed king of his collection of buddies. Whatever bluster Tony may hide behind, when he encounters a dancer as fine as he is, he freely offers his respect and admiration. Such a dancer is Stephanie Mangano.

"Stephanie, twenty, about five-seven, willowy, with an intense, attractive face, long black hair parted in the center, is in the painful process of re-creating herself, eradicating the traces of her Bay Ridge origins and refashioning herself into a sophisticated, knowledgeable woman of the world, or what she considers such to be, hip, tuned-in. Presently she is a loveable fake, caught between identities, full of airs and pretensions, seeking to impress who and where she can, pushing her limits, a name-dropper—but somehow redeemed by an ironic, giggling sense of what she's doing and the fact that her act is still rather naive, transparent and clumsy. But most important, her endearing qualities—a certain sweetness and courage—save her and keep her sympathetic even when her words or actions are outrageous."

Tony and Stephanie first see each other at the Disco 2001. Later they meet at the dance rehearsal studio where each works out. Tony works in a paint store in Bay Ridge; Stephanie is trying to work her way up in a show business agency in Manhattan. Although Stephanie keeps him at arm's length, she accepts Tony's proposal that they partner to compete for the 2001 Sweepstakes. He invites her for coffee.

(*Note:* Although the waitress has no lines, her presence is vital to the fullest possible playing of the scene, which can occur entirely in the restaurant.)

SCENE 1

EXTERIOR BAY RIDGE STREET—DUSK

TONY and STEPHANIE walking.

STEPHANIE: Where I work, the people are very remarkable— so . . . different . . . from Bay Ridge people.

TONY: The snobs insteada the slobs.

STEPHANIE: What?

TONY: Bay Ridge ain't the worst part of Brooklyn, you know. It ain't like a hellhole.

STEPHANIE: It ain't, isn't Manhattan. You have no idea how different, how it changes over there, just across the river. The people are beautiful, the offices are beautiful, the secretaries, they all shop at Bonwit Taylor. Even the lunch hours are beautiful. They let you take two hours if you do something related. We seen, saw Zefferelli's *Romeo and Juliet*.

TONY: Shakespeare wrote that. Read it in high school.

STEPHANIE: (*showing off her knowledge*) Zefferelli was the director. It was the movie. I mean, film.

TONY: Romeo, he coulda waited a minute. He didn't have to take that poison so fast.

STEPHANIE: *(feeling attacked)* That's how they took poison in those days.

They reach the Venus II Coffee Shop, start to go in.

INTERIOR VENUS II COFFEE SHOP—NIGHT

TONY and STEPHANIE are seated in a booth. The WAITRESS comes by, drops two menus on the table. TONY picks up one.

TONY: You eating?

STEPHANIE: Just tea. With lemon. I started drinking tea recently. It's really more refined. The women executives at my office, they all drink tea. I . . . I've only been with the Agency a while but I'm already operating in a public relations capacity as well as filling in for some of the agents. This week I had business lunches with Eric Clapton at Le Madrigal and at Cote Basque with Cat Stevens.

TONY: Far out!

STEPHANIE: You heard of them . . . those restaurants?

TONY: No.

STEPHANIE: You know who those artists are?

TONY: No. Well, maybe sort of.

STEPHANIE: So why did you say "far out?"

TONY: It sounded like "far out." It was "far out," wasn't it?

The WAITRESS comes over, pad in hand.

TONY: Tea with lemon, three hamburgers and a coffee.

The WAITRESS nods, goes off, scribbling down the order. STEPHANIE continues to lay on the glitz—and as she delivers her rap—TONY'S face fills with a certain awe, though he manages to retain some skepticism. From time to time his expression shows he thinks she's full of bull—but he is nonetheless intrigued and fascinated. She knows something he doesn't—possesses a key to something and somewhere else.

STEPHANIE: Laurence Olivier was in the office the other day and he said . . .

TONY: *(cutting in)* Who's that?

STEPHANIE: You don't know who Laurence Olivier is?

TONY: No.

STEPHANIE: (*strained patience*) He's only one of the most famous actors in the . . . oh, you know, the English actor did the Polaroid commercials.

TONY: Oh, yeah.

STEPHANIE: Well, he was in the office and I did a couple errands for him and he told everybody I was really the brightest, most viv . . . viv . . . vivacious thing in the office in years.

TONY: Could he get you one of them cameras, like at a discount, you know what I mean?

STEPHANIE: (*huffily*) I didn't ask.

TONY: You already got one?

ANOTHER ANGLE

The WAITRESS brings the order, puts it on the table, leaves. STEPHANIE and TONY proceed to eat and drink.

STEPHANIE: Are you enjoying what I'm telling you?

TONY: Sure.

STEPHANIE: Because maybe you can't handle hearing about a life so different than yours. (*pause*) You gotta unner . . . understand . . . I'm getting an apartment in Manhattan. You have no idea how much I'm growing.

TONY: Go on a diet.

STEPHANIE: (*scowls*) That's why we can only dance together—but nothing more, nothing personal, no coming on to me.

TONY: Why not?

STEPHANIE: 'Cause I don't dig guys like you no more. You're too young, you haven't any class. I'm tired of jerk-off guys who haven't got their shit together.

TONY: I got my shit together. It's easy—all you need is a salad bowl and a potato masher.

STEPHANIE: Very funny.

TONY: So why don't you laugh?

STEPHANIE: (*pleased with herself*) I'm one of those people who say "very funny" instead of laughing.

TONY: You want to know what I do?

STEPHANIE: It's not necessary.

TONY: I work in a paint store. Got a raise this week.

STEPHANIE: Right, you work in a paint store, you probably, probably live with your family, you hang out with your buddies and blow it all off Saturday night at 2001.

TONY: (*pleased, a "Hey, that's me!" response*) Right.

STEPHANIE: You're a cliché—nowhere . . . on your way to no place.

TONY: Whaddya you got—a stairway to the stars!

STEPHANIE: Maybe. You didn't get any college, did you?

TONY: No.

STEPHANIE: I'm taking a course nights at NYU, two next semester. You ever think about going to college.

TONY: (*angry*) No.

STEPHANIE: Not ever?

TONY: No! What the fuck you bugging me about it!

STEPHANIE: Didn't you want to?

TONY: Fuck off, willya! No! I didn't!

STEPHANIE: Why not?

TONY: SHIT, COME OFF IT! COME OFF IT, WILL YA?!

STEPHANIE, taken aback by TONY's burst of anger, looks at him warily, says nothing. TONY devours his hamburger moodily, sullen, while she sips her tea.

EXTERIOR STREET—NIGHT

TONY and STEPHANIE walk toward the corner. TONY is trying to impress her, but what he says is heartfelt, and perhaps voiced for the first time.

TONY: The high I get at 2001, just dancing, not just being the best . . . I wanta get, have, that high someplace else in my life, ya know what I mean?

STEPHANIE: Where?

TONY: I don't know. Somewhere. (*pause*) I mean it can't last forever . . . it's a short-time thing . . . you get older

. . . so what does that mean . . . like I ain't never gonna feel like that again about anything ever?

She looks at him sympathetically. They reach the corner.

STEPHANIE: We gotta split here.

TONY: I'll walk you home.

STEPHANIE: No. I'll see you at the studio. And nothing personal, right.

She turns and goes. TONY watches her walk away. Then he turns, walks off, silent and dejected. A half-block down, he savagely kicks over a wire mesh trash basket, kicks it again so it rolls into the street spewing refuse.

He stands immobile for several beats, his gaze remote. Then he takes a step or two—and begins to run.

SCENE 2

Tony and Stephanie become wary, casual, Platonic friends, but Tony doesn't trust it. First, because he's never thought of being a friend with a female before. And second, because he knows that the clear, exhilarating sensation that passes between them when they are dancing is not Platonic. When Tony helps Stephanie move into her new Manhattan apartment, which is being vacated by one of her former lovers, that sensation erupts in him, and he expresses his jealousy.

INTERIOR BOBBY C.'S CAR—MOVING SHOT—DAY

TONY, driving, shoots furious glances at STEPHANIE. She, observing this, sits quietly, anticipating some kind of explosion.

TONY: (finally) What's he to ya?

STEPHANIE: He's an arranger, record producer, wants to do films. I met him at the Agency. He's moving into a better apartment, more expensive, now that his divorce is final. Didn't want his wife to know how much money he had. (after a hesitation) I lived with him for awhile.

TONY: Shit.

STEPHANIE: He taught me things. I learned a lot from him.

TONY: (seething) He sure knows how to put you down fast. He your first guy?

STEPHANIE: No.

TONY: No?

STEPHANIE: No.

TONY: He your last guy?

STEPHANIE: No.

TONY: NO!?

STEPHANIE: No.

TONY: Shit. Who else?

STEPHANIE: You want a list?

TONY: (*pause*) What happened—you and him?

STEPHANIE: He got bored with me I guess. Shit! But he's
    still fond of me, he still likes me.

She looks ready to cry.

TONY: (*savagely*) Likes to have you around for a quick piece
    now and then when he feels like it, right?

STEPHANIE bursts into tears. TONY, torn between sympathy
and outrage, glances harshly at her.

STEPHANIE: (*finally—amid sobs*) He helped me.

TONY: Helped you in and out of the sack . . . the old
    fucking fart.

STEPHANIE: You don't know what working in a place like
    that is, the Agency. It's scary. There's so much you don't
    know. He built up my confidence, told me I could do it.
    People there, they all went to college, and they got
    style, like the kind you don't just pick up overnight.
    They talk about things I never heard of—theater, poli-
    tics, history. I feel so out of it, so dumb sometimes. If I
    said "I don't know" every time I didn't know something,
    when I get asked to do something, I'd be saying "I don't
    know" 10 times a minute, so I just smile and fake some-
    thing. I hope I learn how to do it. Figure it out later. It
    kills you, you feel scared and stupid.

STEPHANIE looks small and vulnerable, her eyes almost im-
ploring as she looks at TONY—who appears astonished.

EXTERIOR SHORT ROAD—BAY RIDGE—DAY

TONY parks the car. He and STEPHANIE get out. She is still crying.

STEPHANIE: I haven't cried with anyone for two months.

TONY: Where you been doing your crying?

They walk down into the park, proceed in the direction of the bridge.

TONY: (*bitter*) How come he couldn't help you move?

STEPHANIE: He doesn't have a car.

TONY: He coulda rented one. Shit, could you win a dance contest with that old fuck?

STEPHANIE: Please, Tony.

They walk awhile.

TONY: You know how tall that bridge is?

STEPHANIE shakes her head.

TONY: The towers go up six hundred ninety feet. Center span is two hundred twenty-eight feet. They got forty million cars going across it a year. They got one hundred twenty-seven thousand tons of steel, almost three quarter million cubic yards of concrete. Center span is four thousand two hundred and sixty feet—total length including approach ramps—over two and a half miles.

STEPHANIE: (*impressed*) You know all that!

TONY looks pleased.

TONY: Know everything about it. They even got a guy buried in the concrete, fell into it—they was building the bridge. I come down here a lot, I get ideas.

STEPHANIE: What kind of ideas?

TONY: You know . . . ideas. Daydreams like . . . ideas.

She looks at him curiously, perceiving another dimension in TONY.

EXTERIOR STEPHANIE'S FAMILY'S HOUSE—DAY

BOBBY C.'S car pulls up in front.

INTERIOR BOBBY C.'S CAR—DAY

STEPHANIE starts to get out of the car, opens the door, then turns and kisses TONY quickly on the cheek—a peck.

STEPHANIE: Thanks.

TONY seizes this as an opening and grabs her, putting his arms around her. She twists away.

TONY: *(furiously)* Goddamit! How come you won't make it with me?

STEPHANIE: I told you once. For me to go to bed with you would be a step backward.

TONY: So take a step backward. Then take a step forward. Ain't that what they call progress.

STEPHANIE: I'm also into being, imitating a nice girl these days.

TONY: What the fuck are you? You ain't a nice girl—and you ain't a cunt exactly.

STEPHANIE: How about, maybe . . . a person, a friend?

She smiles, blows him a kiss and leaves.

TONY: *(calling after her)* The way we feel when we dance— that ain't friends.

He starts the car and drives off.

SCENE 3

When Tony and Stephanie dance in the competition at 2001, they win first prize. But Tony is enraged because it is obvious that a Puerto Rican couple were the better dancers. He gives them his trophy. He's incensed at the narrowness of his world, but he knows how to express his anger only through the codes of that world, and he attempts—unsuccessfully—to rape Stephanie. That same night, one of his buddies, to prove false a dare against his manhood, goes too far, falls off a bridge, and is killed. The following day, Tony goes into Manhattan to Stephanie's apartment. He wants to apologize, and to try a new kind of relationship.

(*Note:* In order to allow the scene to be played continuously in an acting studio, the action in the vestibule can be brought to Stephanie's door.)

EXTERIOR STEPHANIE'S BROWNSTONE—WEST 74TH STREET—DAY

TONY comes down the block, looks back and forth, unsure of which building Stephanie lives in. Then he walks into Stephanie's brownstone.

INTERIOR VESTIBULE—STEPHANIE'S BROWNSTONE—DAY

TONY enters, looks at the names, presses STEPHANIE's buzzer, waits. STEPHANIE is heard on the intercom.

STEPHANIE: (OFFSCREEN) Who's there?

TONY: Stephanie, it's Tony.

STEPHANIE: (OFFSCREEN) Go away!

TONY: Please, I gotta talk to you.

STEPHANIE: (OFFSCREEN) You kidding?

TONY: I mean it, please, Stephanie.

STEPHANIE: (OFFSCREEN) Tony, I'll call the cops.

A click can be heard—switching off the intercom.

TONY: Stephanie . . . Stephanie!

He presses the buzzer again.

STEPHANIE: (OFFSCREEN) Get the hell out, Tony.

The switch-off click is heard. TONY presses the buzzer again, then again—with no response. A YOUNG MAN, early twenties, comes through the inner door. TONY grabs it before it closes, enters.

INTERIOR STAIRWAY—STEPHANIE'S BROWNSTONE—DAY

TONY races up the stairs.

INTERIOR THIRD FLOOR HALLWAY—STEPHANIE'S BROWNSTONE—DAY

TONY walks to STEPHANIE'S door, knocks on it softly.

TONY: Stephanie, please. Let me talk to you. There won't be any of that shit like last night, I promise. I'm sorry about that, Stephanie.

STEPHANIE: (OFFSCREEN) You're sorry?

TONY: Yes. Stephanie, please, I gotta talk to you. I need to talk to you. Please.

STEPHANIE: (OFFSCREEN) You need . . . you need to talk to me?

TONY: That's what I been saying. Please.

STEPHANIE: (OFFSCREEN) What you been saying is you gotta talk to me.

TONY: Same thing.

STEPHANIE: (OFFSCREEN) No, it isn't.

The door opens slowly. STEPHANIE eyes him warily.

STEPHANIE: No funny stuff?

TONY: No.

STEPHANIE: Come on in.

TONY enters.

INTERIOR STEPHANIE'S APARTMENT—DAY

TONY comes into the room, stands unmoving at the door. STEPHANIE closes the door and backs away cautiously.

STEPHANIE: First time I ever let a known rapist in.

TONY: I'll just stand right here so you won't have to worry about me jumping you.

STEPHANIE: (scrutinizing him) What's wrong?

TONY: Nothing. I'll tell you later.

STEPHANIE: You don't have to stand there.

TONY nods gratefully, wanders about the apartment, looking at the books, the pictures. He turns to her.

TONY: I been up all night. Riding the subways, walking around. Looking.

STEPHANIE: At what?

TONY: Looking, just looking. Stephanie, could I stay here tonight?

STEPHANIE: (admonitory) Tony.

TONY: I'll sleep on the floor. Tomorrow—I got some money saved up the bank—I'll get a room. I don't wanna go back there, I wanna get outa there, Stephanie.

He shakes his head, puzzled, wonderingly.

STEPHANIE: Whaddya gonna do?

TONY: Get a job.

STEPHANIE: What?

TONY: I don't know. Something. I'll look. I'll look.

STEPHANIE: What can you do?

TONY: Nothing. Just like you when you started.

STEPHANIE: (*piqued*) I could type!

TONY: You mind . . . I sit down?

She nods and he sits, his expression inward and sad.

STEPHANIE: Tony . . . I'm sorry too, what I said . . . using you, practicing my act on you. There're lots of reasons, other reasons.

TONY: Like what?

STEPHANIE: Well, like I always felt better when I seen, saw you. I got sort of like admiration, respect from you . . . support like.

TONY rises, moves aimlessly about the room, speaks without facing her.

TONY: Stephanie, maybe, me being around, in town, we could see each other.

STEPHANIE: (*nettled*) Tony, we had that out a long time ago, Tony!

TONY: I don't mean that. I ain't like promoting your pussy. I mean . . . I mean like . . . friends . . . like you said once. We could . . . help each other.

STEPHANIE: (*scoffing*) Help each other!

TONY: Sure. You ain't so solid what you're doing, where you're at. And I sorta think I ain't gonna be for a while.

STEPHANIE stares at him, incredulous.

STEPHANIE: You want to be . . . friends?!

She begins to laugh wildly. TONY stares at her, begins to smile.

STEPHANIE: (*subsiding*) You think you know how? With a girl? Could you stand it?

TONY shrugs "I don't know," a silly grin on his face.

STEPHANIE: Awright, awright.

She is suddenly in some private area, solemn, thoughtful.

STEPHANIE: (*fervently*) Okay, okay, we'll help each other. We'll be friends.

She smiles, TONY, exuberant, rushes toward her, abruptly stops a couple of steps from her.

STEPHANIE: *(almost a whisper)* Okay?

TONY: Okay.

She holds out her hand to him. TONY starts to take it, hesitates, then grasps her hand. They look at each other, smile grave smiles. He puts his other hand over their joined hands. They look down at their clasped hands, then at each other—their gaze warm and searching.

THE TURNING POINT

A Twentieth Century-Fox Film presentation. Producers, Herbert Ross & Arthur Laurents. Director, Herbert Ross. Screenplay by Arthur Laurents. Executive Producer, Nora Kaye. Associate Producer, Roger M. Rothstein. Artistic Adviser for American Ballet Theatre, Oliver Smith. Photography, Robert Surtees. Film Editor, William Reynolds. Production Designer, Albert Brenner. Sound, Harry Jost. Music Adapter, John Lanchbery. Assistant Directors, Jack Roe, Tony Bishop. Color by DeLuxe. Running time, 119 minutes. 1977.

CAST

EMMA	Anne Bancroft
DEEDEE	Shirley MacLaine
YURI	Mikhail Baryshnikov
EMILIA	Leslie Browne
WAYNE	Tom Skerritt
ADELAIDE	Martha Scott
SEVILLA	Antoinette Sibley
DAHKAROVA	Alexandra Danilova
CAROLYN	Starr Danias
CARTER	Marshall Thompson
MICHAEL	James Mitchell
ETHAN	Phillip Saunders
JANINA	Lisa Lucas
ROSIE	Anthony Zerbe
FREDDIE	Scott Douglas
PETER	Jurgen Schneider
ARNOLD	Daniel Levans
BARNEY	Donald Petrie

Emma and Deedee were best friends and two of the brightest
lights of the American Ballet Company. Both were up for the
title role of a newly choreographed production of *Anna
Karenina*. Deedee married Wayne, one of the company's
most attractive dancers, and became pregnant. Emma, who
had urged the marriage, won the role—as well she might
have, even if Deedee hadn't become pregnant. But no one
knows for sure. What is certain is that it was Emma, and not
Deedee, who achieved the special and grueling life of the
ballet star.

Seventeen years have passed. Emma comes on tour with
the Company to the Oklahoma town where Deedee and Wayne
run a ballet school. Emma meets again her goddaughter
Emilia, who is now an aspiring ballerina, and Emma is in-
strumental in having the brilliantly talented girl invited into
the company. Deedee accompanies her daughter for the summer to New York. She begins to feel that Emma is stealing
her child's affections from her, just as she had stolen the role
of Anna Karenina seventeen years before. Both mother and
daughter experience brief, unsatisfying affairs, but Emilia has
the triumph of her dancing, while Deedee is left even more
alienated from a world to which she had once struggled so
hard to belong.

After a spectacular gala performance, Emma makes a public bow of homage—and is it abdication, as well?—to Emilia
as she enters the glittering post-performance party in the
Rainbow Room. Her grand gesture turns sour on her, though,
as Adelaide, the pragmatic director of the Company, suggests
to Emma that the following season she do *Sleeping Beauty*—
not dance it, but stage it. Behind her cool, gracious facade,
Emma is stunned and frightened at what looks like the end
of her life: her career as a soloist.

Emma goes to the bar, where Deedee is sitting alone. These
two women, who love and envy each other, order a drink and
tell the truth.

(*Note:* Because the scene should be played continuously,
the actresses must take cognizance of the fact that if they try
to remain indoors the whole scene, particularly during the
physical fight, people could notice them and it would inhibit
their behavior as it is written in the script. It may be useful,

then, to dispense with the bartender, and/or to move off to another section of the room, or to carry the scene out onto a "terrace" in order to take it out-of-doors.)

INTERIOR BAR—RAINBOW ROOM

DEEDEE is alone at the bar, drinking champagne. As EMMA, on her way to the Ladies' Room, comes toward her, DEEDEE smiles and does a half-curtsey. EMMA stops and smiles back. Then she tosses her evening bag onto the bar.

EMMA: *(to the bartender)* Champagne, please.

Declaration of war accepted. During the following, they both get refills, but they do not guzzle; there is no need for them to get drunk. Emotionally, each is ready to burst anyway. They (and we) are unaware of the bartender and he is unaware of them. For despite the lines, despite what each feels underneath, they are totally charming: two smiling, lovely, delightful friends having a chat.

DEEDEE: Remember the fairy tales we used to take turns reading to Emilia? Like the one about the two princesses? Every time one opened her mouth, out came diamonds and rubies. Every time the other opened her mouth, out came newts and hoptoads. Newts and hoptoads— *(taps her chest)*—coming out.

EMMA: One of those little toads has already made an appearance.

DEEDEE: Really! When?

EMMA: In my dressing room. When you said I shouldn't have bought Emilia that dress. Twice, you said it. Just before a performance . . . I danced better tonight than I have in years.

DEEDEE: So I heard.

EMMA: Oh, another little toad! You've kept quite a few bottled up all these years, haven't you?

DEEDEE: Ohhh—embalmed, really.

EMMA: I think not. Why don't you let them out? I don't have a performance tomorrow.

DEEDEE looks at her, then accepts the challenge. She puts her glass down on the bar and holds out her hands with her fists clenched.

DEEDEE: Okay. Pick.

EMMA puts her glass down and points to a fist. DEEDEE opens it.

DEEDEE: Ah, a tiny one. I'd practically forgotten him. (*looks up now*) Why'd you make your best pal doubt herself and her hubby, Emma? Why'd you take the chance of lousing up her marriage? Why'd you say: "You better have that baby. It's the only way you can hold on to Wayne." I'm just curious now.

EMMA: You have a curious memory. But don't we all? As I remember, I said if you had an abortion, you might lose Wayne.

DEEDEE: Sweet, but inaccurate. I've remembered your exact words for lo, these too many moons. I eventually figured out why you said 'em. Because you also said: "Forget Michael's ballet, there'll be others." You clever little twinkletoes! You knew a ballet like that comes once in a career. You wanted it real bad, so you lied to make sure you got what you wanted.

EMMA: I've never had to lie to get what I wanted, Deedee. I'm too good.

DEEDEE: Really?

EMMA: Oh, yes.

DEEDEE: Well, I suppose if you said "bullshit," you'd say it in French.

CLOSE SHOT

EMMA: If that word came as naturally to me as it does to you, I'd have used it several times by now. In English. I think it's more appropriate that you say it—to yourself. For trying to blame me for what you did, for example. The choice was yours. It's much too late to regret it now, Deedee.

DEEDEE: And the same to you, Emma me darlin'.

EMMA: I certainly don't regret mine.

DEEDEE: Then why are you trying to become a mother at your age?

EMMA: Ooh, that's not a little toad. That's a rather large bullfrog. I don't want to be anybody's mother. I think of Emilia as a friend. And one reason I tried to help—stupid me!—I thought it would make you happy if your daughter became what you wanted to be and couldn't be.

DEEDEE: Meaning you. It's so lovely to be you.

EMMA: Obviously, you think so.

DEEDEE: Oh, no no no no no no!

EMMA: No no no no?

DEEDEE: No; alas. And I doubt if Emilia could become you. Oh, she's as talented. She works as hard. But there's one thing, dearest friend, that you are that she, poor darling, is not.

EMMA: And what, pray tell, is that?

DEEDEE: A killer. You'll walk over anybody and still get a good night's sleep. That's what got you where you are, Emma.

She is smiling adorably. EMMA smiles back, finishes her drink, pushes the glass to the bartender, keeps smiling until it is refilled, then picks it up. They are both smiling, almost laughing as EMMA looks at her drink, looks at DEEDEE, then throws the champagne in DEEDEE'S face. A moment. Then DEEDEE sets down her glass.

DEEDEE: Good girl.

She picks up her evening bag and starts out of the bar toward the exit and the elevators. The cool reaction infuriates EMMA. She puts down her glass and starts after DEEDEE.

INTERIOR CORRIDOR OUTSIDE RAINBOW ROOM

EMMA comes through the entrance to the Rainbow Room just as DEEDEE steps into an elevator.

EMMA: Deedee!

She runs for the elevator and just gets in as the doors are closing.

INTERIOR ELEVATOR—ROCKEFELLER CENTER

EMMA: I'm sick to death of your jealousy and resentment!

DEEDEE: So am I.

EMMA: Then stop blaming your goddamn life on me! You picked it!

DEEDEE: You did. You took away the choice, you didn't give me the chance to find out if I was good enough.

EMMA: I can tell you now: you weren't.

The elevator doors open and DEEDEE strides out, EMMA after her.

EXTERIOR ROCKEFELLER PLAZA—NIGHT

EMMA is fast after DEEDEE, their heels clicking on the stone.

EMMA: You knew it yourself. That's why you married Wayne!

DEEDEE: (*whirls around*) I loved him!

EMMA: So much that you said to hell with your career!

DEEDEE: Yes!

EMMA: And got pregnant to prove you meant it!

DEEDEE: Yes!

EMMA: Lie to yourself, not to me. You got married because you knew 'you were second-rate; you got pregnant because Wayne was a ballet dancer, and that meant queer!

DEEDEE: *He wasn't!*

EMMA: Still afraid someone will think he is? You were terrified then! You had to *prove* he was a man! *That's* why you had a baby!

DEEDEE: That's a goddamn lie!

EMMA: It's the goddamn truth! You saddled him with a baby and blew his career! And now she's grown up and better than you ever were and you're jealous!

DEEDEE: You're certifiable! You'll use anything for an excuse.

EMMA: What's that an excuse for?

DEEDEE: Trying to take away my child!

EMMA: I return the compliment: you're a liar!

DEEDEE: And you're a user. You have been your whole life!

Me, Michael—pretending to love him!—Adelaide and now Emilia!

EMMA: How Emilia?!

DEEDEE: "How Emilia." That display five minutes ago: curtsey! Applause! Embrace! For *you*, not her! You were using her so everyone'd say: "Emma's so gracious, Emma's so wonderful!"

EMMA: Untrue!

DEEDEE: You *are* wonderful! You're amazing! It's incredible how you keep going on. You're over the hill; you know it and *you're* terrified. All you've got are your scrapbooks and your old toe shoes and those stupid, ridiculous dogs! What are you going to fill in with, Emma? Not my daughter. You keep your goddamn hands off!

EMMA: I'm better for her than you are.

DEEDEE: Like hell!

EMMA: She came to me because her mother wasn't there. Her mother was too busy screwing her head off!

DEEDEE: You bitch!

She whacks EMMA with her evening bag. For a moment, EMMA is too startled to move. But as DEEDEE lifts her bag again, EMMA blocks it with one hand and with the other whacks DEEDEE with her evening bag. They both go at it: rarely hitting, ducking blows, slamming out blindly with their evening bags.

EXTERIOR ROCKEFELLER CENTER—NIGHT

There they are, these two ladies in their evening gowns, each making a last pass, a last weak attempt to hit the other, and missing. They are panting, exhausted; and at last, they stop and just stand there, breathing hard.

CLOSE SHOT—Their breath is coming back. DEEDEE smiles.

DEEDEE: If there'd been a photographer handy, you'd have a whole new career.

EMMA: I must look awful.

She opens her bag.

DEEDEE: No: beautiful. I don't know how you do it.

EMMA has taken out a mirror and is looking in it.

EMMA: If I can borrow your comb, I'll show you. Oh, I lost an earring.

DEEDEE: (*handing her a comb*) I'm sorry.

EMMA: I'm not.

DEEDEE: Really?

EMMA: Yes.

She returns the comb, and they start walking, looking for the lost earring. The following is very quiet:

DEEDEE: Jealousy is poison. Makes you a monster.

EMMA: Well, it does make one unfair. (*smiles*) Two.

DEEDEE: Two?

EMMA: Me, too.

DEEDEE: (*a second, then laughs*) Oh, Emma, you made a good joke!

EMMA: Yes, I did . . . I'm really not so humorless.

DEEDEE: Listen, you got off some really good ones before. Oh, look!

She picks up the earring and gives it to EMMA.

EMMA: How did it get over here? Thank you.

DEEDEE: You also hit a couple of bull's-eyes before.

EMMA: So did you.

DEEDEE: Sit?

EMMA: Oh, please.

They sit on the rim of the fountain.

EMMA: I don't really remember what I said about having the baby. But I do know I would have said anything to make sure I got that ballet . . . I had to have it, Deedee. I just had to.

DEEDEE: My God. Oh Emma. Emma, I didn't know how much all I wanted was for you to say just that . . . Let's have a drink!

EMMA: Absolutely!

They get up. EMMA links her arm through DEEDEE'S as they start walking.

EMMA: It's good.

DEEDEE: You bet.

EMMA: I'm glad Wayne's coming.

DEEDEE: Me, too . . . How's with Carter?

EMMA: Ca va . . . *That's* bullshit in French.

DEEDEE laughs and walks toward the street, to a taxi. But EMMA has stopped, turned toward the entrance to the party.

DEEDEE: Not back to the party?

EMMA: I have to.

DEEDEE: (*nods, understands*) Call me when you wake up.

EMMA: If not before.

They smile—and walk in opposite directions.

AN UNMARRIED WOMAN

A Twentieth Century-Fox Film presentation. Producer (with Tony Ray) & Director, Paul Mazursky. Screenplay by Paul Mazursky. Photography, Arthur Ornitz. Film Editor, Stuart H. Pappe. Music, Bill Conti. Production Designer, Pato Guzman. Sound, Arthur Piantadosi, Dennis Maitland. Assistant Director, Terry Donnelly. Color by Movielab. Running time, 124 minutes. 1978.

CAST

ERICA	Jill Clayburgh
SAUL	Alan Bates
MARTIN	Michael Murphy
CHARLIE	Cliff Gorman
SUE	Pat Quinn
ELAINE	Kelly Bishop
PATTI	Lisa Lucas
JEANETTE	Linda Miller
BOB	Andrew Duncan
DR. JACOBS	Daniel Seltzer
PHIL	Matthew Arkin
TANYA	Penelope Russianoff
JEAN	Novelle Nelson
EDWARD	Raymond J. Barry
HAL	Paul Mazursky
LADY MACBETH	Ultra Violet

By the middle of the 1970s, Erica's life is right on schedule. After attending Vassar, she married Martin (good-looking and on Wall Street); she had a daughter Patti (now fifteen and Erica's best friend); she works in a fashionably avant-garde New York City art gallery. Erica and her women friends meet once a week to raise both their consciousnesses and their blood alcohol content. She and Martin jog and make love together almost daily. She appears to be living out the upper middle-class dream of the modern woman's life: she has health, family, friends, and fulfilling work.

When one day Martin meets someone in Bloomingdale's department store and leaves Erica for her, Erica wakes up from the dream. If she is not the sum of all these enviable social roles, who is she? Erica suddenly discovers that this time it is she—*Erica*—and not someone else, who is getting divorced, who is "an unmarried woman." For the first time in Erica's life, society's label for her is out of sync with the way she wants to view herself. She embarks on the uncharted journey of living not as someone's wife or lover or employee, but as Erica.

The following scene occurs before the separation, before Erica is even aware that there is any problem in her marriage.

SCENE 1

[INTERIOR APARTMENT—NIGHT

As ERICA lets herself in . . . She looks towards PATTI'S room, then crosses to her bedroom.]

BEDROOM

MARTIN is in bed, watching the news on television, sipping a martini . . .

MARTIN: Hi . . . You had a long meeting tonight.

ERICA: They're not meetings. What's on the news?

MARTIN: (*as she sits next to him*) Looks like war in Rhodesia. The market's up. There may be a garbageman's strike. The usual.

ERICA: Jeannette is going out with a nineteen-year-old boy.

MARTIN: She's flipped.

ERICA: Men go out with younger women all the time.

MARTIN: Nineteen is four years older than Patti.

ERICA: Where is Patti?

MARTIN: She went to the movies with Phil.

ERICA is undressing by now . . .

ERICA: I like Phil.

MARTIN: Maybe Phil should meet Jeannette.

ERICA: Don't be hostile.

MARTIN: How are Elaine and Sue?

ERICA: They're fine.

MARTIN: Elaine makes me very nervous.

ERICA: She likes you.

MARTIN: I like her. But she comes on too strong.

ERICA: So do you, sometimes.

MARTIN: Sometimes I get the feeling that you prefer Elaine
and Sue and Jeannette to me.

ERICA: That's silly.

MARTIN: Do you?

ERICA: Sometimes.

MARTIN kisses ERICA.

MARTIN: I feel sexy.

ERICA: Patti's coming home and I have to get up early
tomorrow.

MARTIN kisses her again. She returns the kiss. He is very
passionate. ERICA breaks the moment.

ERICA: I really am not in the mood.

MARTIN: (*suddenly angry*) You give me a headache.

ERICA: Take an aspirin.

                                                    CUT TO:

[LIVING ROOM as PATTI lets herself in.

PATTI: (*calls out*) Anybody home?

ERICA: (OFFSCREEN *from bedroom*) We're in here, honey.

PATTI: What's going on in there? Should I go out and come in again?

MARTIN comes into the room. He pads his way to the kitchen and makes himself another drink.

MARTIN: Hi.

PATTI: Hi, Dad.

ERICA comes in. She's wearing a bathrobe.

ERICA: How was the movie?

PATTI: We saw the new Lina Wertmuller film. I loved it, but Phil thought it was flawed.

MARTIN: How old is Phil again?

PATTI: You know how old he is. Eighteen.

MARTIN: Your mother's friend Jeannette is having an affair with a nineteen-year-old guy.

PATTI: Good for her.

MARTIN: Would Phil go out with Jeannette?

PATTI: You'd have to ask Phil.

MARTIN goes back to the bedroom.

ERICA: (*to* PATTI) Don't tell anyone about Jeannette.

PATTI: . . . Are you and Daddy fighting?

ERICA: No. Why?

PATTI: He doesn't look too happy.

ERICA: See you in the morning . . . (*kisses her*) Goodnight.

PATTI: Goodnight.]

BEDROOM—MARTIN in bed, drinking. ERICA comes to bed.

ERICA: You're acting like a five-year-old kid, Martin.

MARTIN: Maybe.

ERICA: Can't you understand my feelings? I can't turn sex on and off. When I'm in the mood and you're in the mood, it's wonderful . . . But it's not much fun when you make me feel like it's an obligation.

MARTIN: Maybe you're right.

ERICA: *(smiles)* Besides, we had sex this morning.

MARTIN: I'm not much fun to live with, am I?

ERICA: Are you okay?

MARTIN: I don't know.

ERICA: What's the matter?

MARTIN: . . . I feel anxious lately.

ERICA: Is it me? Is it us?

MARTIN: Could be. I don't know . . . I feel old . . . I find myself fantasizing a lot . . .

ERICA: *(takes a sip of his martini)* About women?

MARTIN: About taking off. Changing my life for something else. Give up Wall Street and become a disc jockey or something.

ERICA: Are you tired of your job?

MARTIN: I'll tell you something. I've been a take-over type for twenty years. In school, in the army, at work, and probably in our marriage.

ERICA: Is there something wrong with being a strong man?

MARTIN: That's the point. I don't feel very strong . . . I'm tired.

ERICA: Maybe you should see an analyst.

MARTIN: Maybe . . . I don't think so.

ERICA: It sounds like you're tired of me.

MARTIN: I love you.

ERICA: I hope so . . . I'd hate to join the crowd.

MARTIN: What do you mean?

ERICA: Elaine is boozing a lot. Jeannette is totally confused. . . . Thank God for Sue. She's a strong woman.

MARTIN: So are you.

ERICA: I'm beginning to wonder about me.

MARTIN looks at her. He takes her in his arms. He holds her. They hold each other . . . they kiss . . . very tenderly . . .

ERICA: It's nice to have a man to come home to. Is that just luck?

MARTIN: Luck and a fabulous body.

They kiss again . . . they begin to get passionate. Soon ERICA begins to abandon herself.

SCENE 2

These two dialogues occur between Erica and her therapist after she and Martin have separated.

INTERIOR PSYCHIATRIST'S OFFICE—DAY

The analyst is a woman in her late forties. Her name is TANYA BERKEL. Tall, dark, very dynamic. She is listening to ERICA.

ERICA: . . . I had a date with a guy and he made some comment and I said to him, it's an unfair universe. . . . That's how I feel about what's happened to me. It's unfair. Why me?—And I'm afraid. I have never been afraid of anything in my life. Oh, some things. You know . . . when Patti was a baby and she had a hundred and five fever . . . I was afraid she'd die . . . I was afraid . . . I was afraid of the usual things when I was a little girl. . . . But I've never really been afraid. . . . Do you understand?

TANYA: Afraid of what things?

ERICA: Oh . . . I don't know. . . . Afraid of my report card. Afraid I'd get my white pinafore dirty . . . Afraid when I got my period the first time . . . (smiles) . . . I got my period when I was thirteen. Some of my friends . . . well, not really some . . . My best friend was Karen Finestein, and she got her period when she was twelve. So I figured there was something wrong with me. I had a terrible year from twelve to thirteen. Whenever I went to the bathroom I looked to see if I was getting my period yet. That's all Karen and I talked about. "Did you get it yet?" "No." Jesus . . . Then I got it. I was wearing white lace panties that my grandmother gave me for my birthday and I was sitting in my Spanish class and I suddenly felt this strange warm wetness in my crotch.

And I had this weird, crazy feeling of elation. Then suddenly I was afraid. . . . I was afraid of getting blood all over my white panties. . . . Then the bell rang and all the kids got up and I saw Karen and I caught her eyes with mine and I smiled and she came over and she said what are you smiling about and I said I got my period and she said "Thank God". . . .

ERICA laughs . . . TANYA doesn't.

ERICA: . . . But what does all this have to do with anything? I don't really see how you can help me. What can you do? You can't live my life for me. Can you?

TANYA: Hell, no.

ERICA: So what's the point?

TANYA: If you're looking for a miracle, you've come to the wrong place. If you're looking for help, you might find it here. I don't know. Nothing's certain except death. That's the only guarantee. But you're very confused and some of that confusion might just clear up.

* * *

INTERIOR ANALYST'S OFFICE—CLOSE-UP ERICA—DAY

ERICA: . . . Everywhere I go I see couples. Holding hands, arms around waists, cheek-to-cheekers . . . I'm jealous . . .

TANYA (THE ANALYST) listening, watching.

ERICA: (OFFSCREEN) My bed feels cold . . . There are so many things I want to share at the end of the day . . . I tell Patti everything. . . .

ERICA AND TANYA

ERICA: I think you helped her. She's very strong. Very. Martin called her yesterday and he's going to see her . . . She's happy . . . I'm glad . . . I think about her leaving home . . . Going to college. It's a couple of years away, but I think about it as if it's going to happen tomorrow. . . .

TANYA: It's not abnormal to think about it.

ERICA: I guess I'm lonely.

TANYA: I was lonely too when I got divorced.

ERICA: I didn't know you were divorced.

TANYA: Now you know. There's nothing wrong with feeling lonely. Or depressed. Or angry. Or anything. They're feelings. Sometimes I feel good, sometimes I feel lousy. But I'm not ashamed of how I feel.

ERICA: I feel guilty about it.

TANYA: You're entitled to your feelings. They're *yours*. Enjoy them.

ERICA: When were you divorced?

TANYA: Three years ago . . . Did you ever feel lonely when you were married?

ERICA: Not much. I don't think so.

TANYA: Never???

ERICA: It was a different kind of loneliness. It was . . . This is different. I wasn't scared then. This scares me.

TANYA: Didn't you ever want to be alone?

ERICA: Yes, but I knew it wasn't forever.

TANYA: You think you're going to be alone forever?

ERICA: . . . I haven't had sex in seven weeks. It's been seven weeks since Martin left me. I always took sex for granted.

ERICA stops talking. TANYA says nothing . . .

ERICA: Oh, boy, this isn't fun . . . Where was I?

TANYA: Sex.

ERICA: (*smiles*) I was hoping you'd forgotten . . . You know, I've always thought of myself as being well adjusted sexually.

TANYA: I don't know what that means.

ERICA: I had a good sex life. I wasn't embarrassed about sex. I took it for granted. It was fun. We were pretty wild, Martin and I . . .

TANYA: I don't know what that means either.

ERICA: (*almost shouts*) It means we fucked and we sucked. Now do you know what it means?

TANYA: Why are you angry?

ERICA: *(angry)* If I knew why I wouldn't be here. . . . I'm
        sorry, Tanya . . . I guess I'm thinking about seeing
        other men and it's scary and I'm sort of asking you what
        to do.

TANYA: I can't tell you what to do.

ERICA: I know.

TANYA: I know what I would do.

ERICA: *(afraid)* What?

TANYA: I would go out and get laid.

SCENE 3

Erica is just beginning to know and like Saul Kaplan, a
painter of large abstract canvases being shown at the gallery.
The irony of the times is that immediately upon meeting each
other, Saul and Erica go to bed together because Erica wants
to "see how it feels to make love with a man I'm not in love
with." She finds it "sort of empty" and leaves his loft. Now
the two of them have bumped into each other at a party. Also
at the party are Erica's therapist (with her female lover) and
Charlie, Erica's first "experiment" after her separation from
Martin. Charlie is drunk and making crass remarks about his
night with Erica. Saul grabs him, ready to punch him out,
but the other guests intervene. The following scene takes
place outside the party, immediately afterwards.

EXTERIOR SOHO STREETS—NIGHT

CAMERA PANS DOWN THE EXTERIOR OF THE LOFT BUILDING as
ERICA and SAUL come out. They walk down the steps and
start down the darkish, empty street.

ERICA: I thought you were going to kill him. . . .

SAUL: I wouldn't give the bastard the satisfaction. It would
        make the front page of the *Daily News* and make him
        famous.

ERICA: Actually, his work is good. I was surprised.

SAUL: Oh, you can be a bastard and have talent. As a matter of fact, some of my best friends . . . Where did you see his work?

ERICA: At his place . . . Are you disappointed in me?

SAUL: I don't know you well enough to be disappointed in you . . . (*puts his arm through hers*) But if you ever do it again, I'll kill you.

ERICA: I can't figure out who you really are.

SAUL: I have very simple tastes. I like Rembrandt, Botticelli, Titian, Kojak, Camembert cheese, expensive shoes—I have bad feet . . . Paris, Vermont, New York about half the time, and being madly in love . . . I've been without the latter for too long now.

ERICA starts to laugh. She can't stop. Almost out of control.

SAUL: What the hell is so funny? A man bares his soul and a woman laughs at him.

ERICA: You stepped in dog shit.

SAUL examines his shoe and sure enough he did. He begins to walk around, wiping his shoe on the ground in a comical way as he walks.

SAUL: This is the only city in the world where there is dog shit piled on top of other dog shit . . . Future archaeologists will learn about our civilization by examining layers of dog do . . . (*drags his foot*) I'd say this was poodle shit . . . Oh, yes, after a while you can tell one kind from another . . . I can even tell if it's an uptown dog or a Village dog or an East Side dog . . . East Side dogs shit only the best . . . Village dogs shit art . . . in London, the dogs don't shit at all . . . they're not permitted to, you know . . . I've always had the theory that there's a hidden underground passage in London where all the dogs crap . . .

SAUL wipes his foot and finally his shoe is clean.

SAUL: I was born in London, you know . . . My father owned a delicatessen in Stepney Green . . . That's the Lower East Side of London . . . One day when I was six, my parents had an argument . . . My mother threw a pickled herring at Dad . . . It missed him, but splattered against the wall . . . I took one look at the herring on the wall and that's when I decided to become an abstract expressionist . . .

ERICA: Come to think of it, your work does remind me of pickled herring.

CORNER—SAUL puts his arm around ERICA as they stroll. The city lights are beautiful . . . streets are wet . . . a few people walking.

SAUL: I'm curious about the kind of man you lived with . . . Were you passionate with each other?

ERICA: You mean sexually?

SAUL: In every way.

ERICA: Sometimes . . . We were married a long time . . .

SAUL: I was married for nine years. The first eight were very passionate. Passion is probably too mild a word. It was more like war . . . About once a month, regularly, she would toss all my paintings out on the street and I would come running out and pick them up . . . Then we'd make up . . . passionately.

ERICA: I don't think I could take that.

SAUL: Oh, it'll be different with us.

ERICA: How did the marriage end?

SAUL: Not with a whimper, but a bang . . . Matilda . . . her name is Matilda . . . She wrote poetry for her soul and swam a hundred laps a day for her body . . . This was after we had the two kids.

ERICA: Boys?

SAUL: My son is twelve and my daughter is nine. Well, one day I came home and found Matilda in bed with the high diver from the pool. I wanted to kill the poor sap, but something kept me from it.

ERICA: What?

SAUL: He was about seven feet tall . . .

They laugh.

SAUL: . . . The strange thing really was that instead of anger, I felt relief . . . I knew it was truly over and I was glad. For both of us . . . I don't think I was a very good husband. My work is everything to me . . .

ERICA: I don't think I believe you.

SAUL kisses her. They hold each other.

ERICA: Don't you miss your children?

SAUL: I love them. Sometimes I miss them. But we see each other every summer. I have a place in Vermont. You'll like it . . .

ERICA: You seem to have my life worked out for me.

SAUL: For us . . . I want to see you. You know that.

ERICA: I'm getting the message.

SAUL: Do you want to see me?

ERICA: My head tells me to slow down, but I don't think my pulse is normal.

They kiss again.

SAUL: There are three things we can do . . . You can take a taxi home . . . We can walk some more while I lecture you on the real dilemma of Modern Art, or we can go to my place and thoroughly enjoy each other . . .

ERICA puts two fingers in her mouth and whistles super-loud.

ERICA: Taxi!!!

They both enjoy the moment. Then a taxi pulls up.

ERICA: I'll call you tomorrow.

SAUL: Call me tonight.

ERICA: Okay . . .

She gets into the cab.

WHO'LL STOP THE RAIN?

A United Artists Corporation presentation. Producers, Herb Jaffe & Gabriel Katzka. Screenplay by Judith Rascoe & Robert Stone. Based on the novel *Dog Soldiers* by Robert Stone. Associate Producers, Roger Spottiswoode, Sheldon Schrager. Director of Photography, Richard H. Kline. Film Editor, John Bloom. Production Designer, Dale Hennesy. Special Effects, Paul Stewart. Music, Laurence Rosenthal. Sound, Don Sharpe, Chris Newman. Assistant Director, Arne Schmidt. Color. Running time, 126 minutes. 1978.

CAST

RAY HICKS	Nick Nolte
MARGE BENDER CONVERSE	Tuesday Weld
JOHN CONVERSE	Michael Moriarty
ANTHEIL	Anthony Zerbe
DANSKIN	Richard Masur
SMITTY	Ray Sharkey
CHARMIAN	Gail Strickland
EDDIE PEACE	Charles Haid
BENDER	David Opatoshu
ANGEL	Joaquin Martinez
GERALD	James Cranna
JODY	Timothy Blake
JANEY CONVERSE	Shelby Balik
EDNA	Jean Howell
GALINDEZ	Jose Carlos Ruiz
ALEX	John Durren

When John Converse went to Vietnam as a journalist, his wife warned him that it was the wrong thing for him to do. In a few days he'll be leaving Vietnam to go back home to Marge and his daughter Janey. He has a fever, and outside his Saigon hotel window, it's pouring fire and rain. "I can't go on drawing cheap morals from all this death. I can't go on being afraid all the time. . . . I know that I've got to have something real out of this place." The reality that Converse takes out is his own corruption in the form of two to three kilograms of pure heroin.

Converse doesn't think very far or very straight. As a pawn in the network of drug traffic, he's a marked man from the beginning. His simple-minded plan for disposing of the heroin is to have his friend Ray Hicks, who is returning briefly to the States, drop it off with Marge at her Berkeley flat. At the helm of the people who are monitoring Converse and his package is federal narcotics agent Antheil, who is so deeply enmeshed in the world he's policing that he is indistinguishable in purpose from the hoodlums he employs. Hicks and the package are followed by Antheil's giddily vicious henchmen Smitty and Danskin straight to the flat. At the appropriate moment they smash in. Hicks overpowers them and escapes with Marge, Janey, and the heroin. The thugs are fizzing with cruelty as they torture John to find out where the drugs are, but he has just returned to the States and doesn't know where anybody or anything is.

Hicks is skilled in warfare, and his body is supremely trained for survival. His mind replays scenes of violent combat in his nightmares, but in the daytime he is powerfully alert. After dropping Janey off with trusted friends, Marge flees with him to Los Angeles. When his car is sighted by one of Antheil's helicopters, the chase continues to New Mexico, where it ends in an apocalyptic blaze-out in the natural amphitheater of a Jesuit retreat owned by Dieter Bechstein, Hicks' former Zen Master. Hicks fights on, sending Marge and Converse ahead to a safe place where he promises to meet them—it's where the tracks cross the highway in the desert beneath the mountains. He dies while crawling to it.

While Marge is frightened at the turning of these events, she is not really surprised. Her father, who employs her in his Berkeley bookstore, has to be reminded not to launch into lectures to her about John's unreliability. Her father loves her and he loves Janey, so he also bites his tongue about the morphine-based Dilaudid painkillers which Marge is swallowing far too regularly. She may be his baby, but she's all grown up into "a young woman in her late twenties, intelligent, attractive, but . . . a little tired, physically and emotionally . . . [with] a kind of sad cynicism." When Hicks contacts her at the bookstore, all she knows is that John owes this friend some money. Over the telephone, Hicks keeps asking her if she's "ready," but it doesn't really register. Not too much does; she's constantly on the verge of jumpy withdrawal. When they meet, Marge finds Hicks frightening, but she's drawn to him as someone very definite and powerful in a life that has become numb and vague. On the run, Marge uses up all her Dilaudid. Hicks tries to ease her through with some help from the heroin. It blasts her right out of her "sad cynicism" and she keeps taking it, getting ever more strung out in the heightening danger. At the end of *Who'll Stop the Rain?* John and Marge sit together in a downpour, knowing that what they must do first is dry themselves out.

The first scene takes place in Vietnam, when Converse reveals his plan to Hicks.

(*Note:* This scene is written across three locations which cannot be reproduced in the acting studio. Although the dialogue does run continuously, the actors must be aware that without the exterior location shift in the last third of the scene, their characters must make some adjustment to the fact that the package of heroin is still with them. Similarly, if the activity of the opening football game is dropped, the actors must replace it with some given circumstance appropriate to Hicks' "up" spirits.)

SCENE 1

EXTERIOR MUDDY FIELD—MY LAT HARBOR BASE—DAY

[A military base in a small harbor of the delta. A few temporary huts. Army vehicles. Supplies being moved by trucks. Near the water, there is a muddy field in which an improvised game of football is being played by SOME TWENTY PLAYERS. WE HEAR the CALLS of the mud-splattered players.

It is just a pick-up game, all mud and confusion. BLACK SEA MEN, MARINES, and MERCHANT SEAMEN.

WE PICK OUT the figure of RAY HICKS, a tall fierce-looking muscular man in his early 30's, playing very much in earnest.

HICKS receives the ball, runs with it, breaking some tackles. TEAMMATES call to him to pass, but he keeps going. He stumbles, almost falling forward, manages to keep upright, and charges past the end of the improvised field. He drops the ball.

By the edge of the field, CONVERSE is approaching, briefcase in hand. He sits on some oil drums, places the briefcase between his knees, and pulls out a sodden handkerchief to wipe his face. He watches the game.

On the field, HICKS, as quarterback, pauses calmly waiting for protection, then throws the ball high to a RECEIVER. The ball is caught near CONVERSE by a BLACK SEAMAN.]

HICKS notices CONVERSE and is genuinely happy at seeing an old friend.

HICKS: You made it! Holy Christ! You know when you called, I thought you were drunk.

CONVERSE: I was. But I'm a man of my word.

HICKS: Well, it's good to see you, pal. (*watches other players*) How'd you get on the base?

CONVERSE: I'm doing a story on merchant seamen,—guys like yourself, at work and at play. If anybody wants to know.

HICKS: You're mad, doctor. A great mind—but warped! Twisted!

CONVERSE: Can we get out of here? I feel like I've been carrying this forever.

HICKS: Sure. In a minute. We'll go get a beer.

HICKS moves to rejoin the game. CONVERSE calls after him.

CONVERSE: Hey! I've got something for you.

HICKS: No shit!

HICKS returns to the game.

EXTERIOR DECK—THE KORA SEA—DAY

HICKS, carrying his muddy boots, and CONVERSE, still carrying the briefcase, make their way on deck of HICKS' ship. Behind them equipment is being loaded on deck. . . . A BURST OF AUTOMATIC WEAPONS FIRE, CONVERSE looks around.

CONVERSE: (*to* HICKS) Sappers?

HICKS: There ain't no sappers. It's all a beautiful hoax.

INTERIOR HICKS' CABIN AND SHOWER—THE KORA SEA—DAY

[HICKS is in the shower, vigorously washing the mud off.] CONVERSE waits for him, uneasily, sitting in a chair, looking around at HICKS' spare and tidy quarters.

HICKS: Remember Macklin? From Pendleton?

CONVERSE: The C.O.? Yeah?

HICKS: I saw him in Oakland last month. I told him you were a big time reporter now.

CONVERSE: How do you get along with Marines down here?

HICKS: You playing reporter?

CONVERSE: I mean, don't they want you to re-up?

HICKS: Not these guys. Not for this one.

CONVERSE picks up a book lying on the table: *The Viking Portable Nietzche*. He's looking at it when HICKS comes out of the shower.

HICKS: Okay, let's get that beer.

CONVERSE: (*about book*) You still into this? (HICKS *nods*) Jesus. That's really fucking piquant.

HICKS: I don't know what that means. You turned me on to that book.

CONVERSE: Yeah. I used to do stuff like that, didn't I. It's a good book.

HICKS: You look like hell. You're shaking like a cooze.

CONVERSE shrugs. HICKS looks at the briefcase.

HICKS: Is that for me? (CONVERSE *nods*) That's about the sorriest piece of packaging I've ever seen. What you got?

CONVERSE: It's two keys. Of scag.

HICKS: Do you know what you're saying?

CONVERSE nods. HICKS' manner has changed.

HICKS: I didn't know we were that way.

CONVERSE: We're that way.

HICKS: Jesus. You should have been taken off fifty times, by rights.

CONVERSE: Well, I wasn't.

HICKS: Get rid of it. Get it off the base—

CONVERSE: (*overlap*) Ray, there's no place—

HICKS: Go to the Oscar Hotel in town. Ask for Billy. Give him five bucks, tell him I told you you could leave your cameras with him—you're going for a steam and cream. He's got a safe. (HICKS *continues to dress*) Then you find me. We got to talk about this one.

EXTERIOR MY LAT—DOCKSIDE—NIGHT

HICKS' ship in harbor. [VIETNAMESE DOCKWORKERS are carrying cargo. New trucks and jeeps are being off-loaded. Old broken equipment stands on the dockside ready for shipping. We are among a profusion of crates and supplies. ARMY PERSONNEL are supervising the loading.] HICKS and CONVERSE walk near the water, which is floodlit. We see the activity of cranes loading military equipment.

CONVERSE: Ray, you sound like we never talked about this.

HICKS: I thought you'd have something else for me.

CONVERSE: You said you wanted to carry weight. I got you weight.

HICKS: I carry grass, man. Not that shit.

CONVERSE: If your stash is as good as you say, it'll be easier than carrying grass. I'll give you a thousand now, and my wife has another thousand for you in Berkeley. You deliver and you split. It's that simple.

HICKS: It's bad Karma.

CONVERSE: I have reason to believe that this operation concerns Washington—well, I don't mean Washington, I mean . . . certain individuals. They know about you. They checked you out.

HICKS: What are you doing to me?

CONVERSE: Look, they absolutely won't bother you. You're not supposed to know about them, and they won't fuck with you if you deliver.

HICKS: If I deliver, right? But if I don't—if I take you off because I happen to know you're an asshole—then the roof falls in? Washington time?

CONVERSE: Ray, we both go—

HICKS: If I wanted to keep a mule honest, I might make up a bullshit story about Washington. But I wouldn't try and lay it on a friend.

CONVERSE: For God's sake, Ray, what would I be doing in a score like this on my own—

HICKS: This sucks. I may just have to say no, old buddy.

CONVERSE: You can't say no, Ray.

HICKS takes in CONVERSE'S fear—he's looking at a man way out of his depth and drowning.

HICKS: You are really scared, aren't you. I'm impressed.

CONVERSE: I'm a very timid person. I'm a virtual paranoid. If this weren't stone cool, I wouldn't go near it. You can carry it, Ray. You know I can't.

HICKS moves away, thinking it over. He makes a violent gesture, as if throwing off some poison. And then:

HICKS: Okay. I'll carry your scag, John—

CONVERSE: (*interrupting*) Thanks—

HICKS: Hell. Why not. Maybe I need to change levels. A little adrenalin cleans the blood. (*tone changes*) But you'd better see I get treated right. Self-defense is an art I cultivate.

They move on. CONVERSE savors his relief.

HICKS: Why are you doing this?

CONVERSE: I'm tired of being bothered. I feel this is the first real thing I ever did in my life. I don't know what the other stuff was about. (*ironic*) They say that this is where everybody finds out who they are.

HICKS: Yeah? What a bummer for the gooks.

EXTERIOR THE DECK OF THE KORA SEA—NIGHT

HICKS and CONVERSE are sitting on the deck. [In the background, loading continues—either new equipment being off-loaded, or old equipment being on-loaded.] But HICKS and CONVERSE are apart from this. CONVERSE is writing MARGE'S telephone numbers on the page of a notebook. He tears off the page and gives it to HICKS.

HICKS: What's your old lady gonna think is in the package? Your fucking memoirs?

CONVERSE: She thinks I owe you. (*pause*) She'll think it's grass.

HICKS: The two of you must be a scene.

CONVERSE: We're just folks.

HICKS: Go back to the hotel, [tell 'em you need your cameras.] Anything else you want in that case? (CONVERSE *shakes his head*) Leave it [just where it is.]

CONVERSE: Just like that?

HICKS: Like it is.

CONVERSE realizes that it's time to go. He's trying to find a word of farewell.

HICKS: You better be careful, John. It's gone funny in the States.

CONVERSE: It can't be funnier than here.

HICKS: Here it's simple. It's funnier there.

CONVERSE makes a gesture of good-bye/so long. And walks off into the darkness. HICKS watches him disappear.

SCENE 2

This second scene is the first meeting of Hicks and Marge.

[EXTERIOR OUTSIDE CONVERSE HOUSE—BERKELEY—NIGHT

HICKS' Chevy slowly crests a hill and comes to rest within sight of the CONVERSE house. He surveys the scene. Two or three cars are parked within view: all seemingly empty. He picks up a JAL flight bag and makes for the door.

CAMERA HOLDS on the street. After a moment, we see a

movement in a Dodge van with plaid curtains, parked half a block away.

Two men, SMITTY and DANSKIN, sit silently in the front seat.

SMITTY (seen in the Gateway Bar) is the driver. DANSKIN (who was in the Ford) is a big man with a thick beard. DANSKIN checks his watch. He winks approvingly at SMITTY.

EXTERIOR CONVERSE HOUSE—FRONT DOOR—NIGHT

as from DANSKIN'S POINT OF VIEW, HICKS is checking out the windows, surveying the terrain.

He moves up the front steps, glances in the windows, then rings the doorbell. Without pausing, he quickly moves down the steps again and round to the back of the house into darkness.

After a moment, MARGE appears at the door. She's surprised to find no one there.

EXTERIOR THE DODGE VAN—NIGHT

DANSKIN and SMITTY are watching.

DANSKIN: Very cute. He's gonna deliver.

SMITTY: Man, I wouldn't've.

DANSKIN: Way to go, Raymond.]

INTERIOR CONVERSE APARTMENT—NIGHT

MARGE is re-entering the apartment. The room is in semi-darkness, but there is a light on in the kitchen. After a moment she stops. Frozen.

HICKS stands in the door between the kitchen and living room watching her.

MARGE: Who the . . .

HICKS: (*kind but firm*) Don't be scared. I'm Ray Hicks. I'm the guy who phoned you.

He moves into the room. MARGE is about to switch on the light, but he stops her.

HICKS: It's okay—

HICKS starts drawing the curtains. His manner is urgent and practical, but he is trying hard not to frighten her.

HICKS: Somebody's been on my ass all day, and I don't

know if I lost him or not. You understand? (*he switches the light on*)

MARGE: *You're* the guy who phoned . . . John's friend? (HICKS *nods, a pause*) Look, would you like a cup of coffee . . .

HICKS: I better take my money and run.

MARGE: Oh . . . listen. I don't have it.

HICKS: Why not?

MARGE: I mean I don't have it here. Today's been kind of difficult.

HICKS: You said you'd be ready.

MARGE: I had to take my little girl to the aquarium . . . and I missed the bank . . .

HICKS: (*goes still*) Why you dumb cooze. What is this shit?

HICKS goes to the front door and snaps the bolt. Then he moves quickly toward the kitchen.

MARGE: John's coming home tomorrow—I know he'll want to see you.

HICKS: You said you'd be ready.

In the kitchen HICKS has left the flight bag near the back door. He looks out the window.

HICKS: You're not trying to fuck me over, are you, Marge? You and some people?

MARGE won't cross the kitchen—she smells his fear.

MARGE: What's the matter with you?

HICKS picks up a pill bottle from the windowsill.

HICKS: What's this?

MARGE: Dilaudid.

HICKS looks straight at her.

HICKS: Are you a junkie, Marge?

MARGE: Jesus. Do I look like a junkie?

HICKS: That's not always a factor. I called you, right? You didn't tell me John was coming home early.

MARGE: I didn't know.

MARGE goes to the mail corner near the phone, gets the telegram, hands it to him.

HICKS: This sucks.

HICKS looms close to her.

HICKS: If I beat up on you and took off with your smack, I'd be within my rights. You can't deal with people in this outrageous fucking manner.

MARGE: Look. I don't have any *smack*. I don't even know who you are. (*she grabs her purse*) If you want money you can have any cash I've got . . .

HICKS' look stops her.

HICKS: You know something. Your old man's got shit for brains.

He turns to walk out of the kitchen—but stops long enough to slam the refrigerator with his hand.

MARGE comes cautiously into the living room—and freezes. HICKS has opened the JAL flight bag and is taking something out. He puts it on the coffee table; a wrapped bundle (the heroin).

HICKS: You got some place to stash this?

MARGE: What is it?

HICKS: It's smack, Marge. Three keys and never been cut. (*pause*) I'm carrying for your old man.

MARGE sits down heavily in a chair facing the coffee table.

MARGE: You're *what*? . . .

HICKS: That's why you owe me money, stuff.

MARGE: For John? *John sent that?* What am I supposed to do with it? I work in a bookstore, for God's sake.

HICKS: You better hold onto it. (HICKS *strides past her toward the kitchen*) John's made some new friends.

MARGE sways forward as if feeling faint.

MARGE: Oh, boy . . .

HICKS: (*from the kitchen*) You wouldn't have any bourbon around, would you?

MARGE: No. I'm sorry . . . oh, boy.

HICKS appears in the doorway behind her, watching.

HICKS: What did you think you were paying for?

MARGE: I didn't think I was paying for anything. I thought he owed you money. (*suddenly angry*) What the hell does it matter *what* I thought?

HICKS: (*shakes his head in wonder*) You're a couple of marks, Marge. You and John. The people he's dealing with are going to see that right away. Unless they're as unconscious as you are.

MARGE: What people? I don't know any people. You tell me what to do.

HICKS: You and John give me the money. I give you the smack.

MARGE: You already said that. (*pause*) OK. Why don't you join us for breakfast? You two guys can talk about old times and finish what you started.

She gets up, her resolve rising. She picks up the coffee cups and tries to walk past him into the kitchen He puts out his hand to stop her. He holds her.

HICKS: You're all right, Marge.

MARGE: Thanks.

HICKS: We'll work something out.

MARGE: I'm for that.

She starts to break away, but HICKS stops her. She is afraid of him, and he knows it. After a moment, he smiles and let's her break loose. She moves into the kitchen. HICKS just stands there, watching her. Aware of the tension between them, she turns and looks straight at him.

HICKS: So you're what Converse is married to. Far fucking out.

HICKS moves back into the living room. He looks through the curtain to make sure no one is outside.

HICKS: I got a bottle in the car. What do you say, Marge? A few drinks, a few laughs?

MARGE: Sure. Why not? We can listen to records.

[EXTERIOR NIGHT—CONVERSE HOUSE—THE DODGE VAN

SMITTY: How long d'you think he's gonna be in there?

DANSKIN: I think he's dickin' her, that's what I think.

SMITTY: Pain in the ass, man. I wish he'd take off.

DANSKIN: (*soft*) Oooooh, look, look, look.

FROM THEIR POINT OF VIEW—HICKS comes out into the street, unlocks his car door, takes out a bottle of bourbon, and locks the car again. As he moves to the house, he pauses momentarily, looking in the direction of the van. He turns immediately and disappears into the house.

SMITTY: What's he goin' back inside for? What's he doin'?

DANSKIN: I don't know, but I think he made us. Come on, let's move. Get those back stairs.

SMITTY: Aw, shit.]

INTERIOR CONVERSE APARTMENT—NIGHT

HICKS runs in and looks out of the window.

[EXTERIOR STREET—HICKS'S POINT OF VIEW—NIGHT

SMITTY is making for the back of the house; DANSKIN to the front.]

MARGE: What's going on?

INTERIOR CONVERSE APARTMENT—NIGHT

HICKS: We've got company. Go in there with the kid.

He puts the flight bag in a drawer. He bolts the front door.

MARGE: Why? What are you doing?

HICKS: (*very firm*) *Do what I say.*

HICKS props a chair against the front door, then moves towards the back porch. The front doorbell rings.

HICKS: Don't open it.

MARGE moves towards JANEY's room, stands at the door watching. From the back porch comes the sound of a splintering crash. [SMITTY comes crashing from the back porch into the kitchen. His face is bloody. HICKS pounces on him, bends back his arm and forces him to drop a small pistol. He chops him on the back of his neck, pulls up his shirt tails. There is a length of chain taped around his waist. HICKS pulls it off.

The sound of JANEY calling is heard: MARGE goes into her room.]

ORDINARY PEOPLE

A Paramount Pictures Corporation presentation of a Wildwood Enterprises production. Producer, Ronald L. Schwary. Director, Robert Redford. Screenplay by Alvin Sargent. Based on the novel *Ordinary People* by Judith Guest. Photography, John Bailey. Film Editor, Jeff Kanew. Music Adaptation, Marvin Hamlisch. Art Directors, Phillip Bennett, J. Michael Riva. Sound, Charles Wilborn. Assistant Director, Steven H. Perry. Technicolor. Running time, 123 minutes. 1980.

CAST

CALVIN	Donald Sutherland
BETH	Mary Tyler Moore
DR. BERGER	Judd Hirsch
CONRAD	Timothy Hutton
SWIM COACH	M. Emmet Walsh
JEANNINE	Elizabeth McGovern
KAREN	Dinah Manoff
LAZENBY	Fredric Lehne
RAY	James B. Sikking
SLOAN	Basil Hoffman
WARD	Quinn Redeker
AUDREY	Mariclare Costello
GRANDMOTHER	Meg Mundy
GRANDFATHER	Richard Whiting
RUTH	Elizabeth Hubbard
STILLMAN	Adam Baldwin
BUCK	Scott Doebler

Conrad Jarret, aged seventeen, may be having his second nervous breakdown. His first occurred after he and his brother Buck, the star of the family, were out boating and got caught in a sudden storm. Buck drowned, and Conrad has never been able to forgive himself. Much of Conrad's present problem is that his mother Beth has never been able to forgive him either.

Conrad used up the sympathy quotient from Beth when he attempted suicide in the bathroom of her immaculate upper-strata suburban Illinois house. The mess of blood was so enormous that even the tiles had to be regrouted. When confronted by mess, Beth tightens her tennis grip and her social mask and makes more lists. Her studied loveliness says something for this approach. Except that it isn't working. Beneath the oddly chopped hair of the recent mental patient, Conrad's face is growing daily more frozen in anxiety as the memory of Buck and the accident make school and home into unmanageable nightmares. His guilt at surviving is killing him, and his mother's vision of their family life cannot tolerate this kind of behavior. On the gentle proddings of his father, Conrad begins treatment with a psychiatrist. The doctor is an odd one—sympathetic but tough and seemingly careless about all the physical details about which Beth is so rigid. But Conrad knows this time *he's* the one who is drowning, so he gives the doctor a try.

The only thing in school of any interest to Conrad is a lovely girl who sings with him in chorus. It will be a while before he is able to call her for a date, but as a kind of trial run at normal socializing, he calls Karen, who was his friend in the hospital, and meets her in a restaurant in the scene below.

(*Note:* In this scene Conrad is still unaware of the deep fury he feels toward Buck for having died. He is so desperate to "function normally" that he cannot see Karen's optimism as the mask which hides her own desperation. Later in the story, she commits suicide, and this triggers an emotional explosion in him through which that fury is finally released.)

INTERIOR SODA FOUNTAIN—CONRAD and KAREN

in a small booth. She is bright and warm. She smiles at him,
but it is apparent she is nervous. There is an awkward silence.

KAREN: When did you come home?

CONRAD: End of August. (*pause*) It's great to see you.

KAREN: You too. (*looks at watch*) I'm sorry I can't stay long.
I've got a meeting at school. Our drama club is doing *A
Thousand Clowns*—do you know it? We're going wild
trying to get it together. I'm secretary this year, that's
probably why we're so disorganized . . .

CONRAD: Don't let me hold you up, then.

KAREN: No, it's okay. I really want to see you. Although I
was sort of afraid. You seemed so down, over the phone.

CONRAD: (*quickly*) Yeah, well, that was just a gray day.
Actually, everything's going great. I'm back in school,
and I'm swimming—

KAREN: Oh, really? I'm glad.

CONRAD: Well, we haven't had any meets yet. I could end
up on the bench all year.

KAREN: Oh, no, you'll do fine. I'm sure. And your folks'll be
proud, too.

The counterman appears with their drinks. He puts the Cokes
down, walks away. CONRAD watches him, then leans in to
KAREN.

CONRAD: (*re: counterman*) Definitely a low self-image day.

KAREN giggles. CONRAD smiles at her. Then he drinks his
drink. Studies her.

CONRAD: You look beautiful.

KAREN: You do, too.

CONRAD: You miss it?

KAREN: Miss what?

CONRAD: The hospital?

KAREN: No.

CONRAD: Not even Mr. Minnow's goldfish trick?

KAREN: *(laughs)* Oh, God!

CONRAD: You were brilliant that day. You told everybody off. Even the judge.

KAREN: I can't believe I ever did that.

CONRAD: You did it, all right. I'll never forget it. And then we sneaked into the kitchen and talked all night, remember?

KAREN: Yeah . . . Wow . . .

CONRAD: Yeah . . .

KAREN: So what's going on? Are you seeing a doctor?

CONRAD: Yeah. I see a real cracker. How about you?

KAREN: Dr. Crawford gave me a name, and I went for a while, but then, I don't know. Finally I decided it wasn't doing me any good. He wasn't telling me anything I couldn't figure out for myself. Anyway, that's what Dad says, and Dad has confidence in me and I know he's right. The only one who can really help us is ourselves, and this guy was over in Elk Grove Village and expensive as hell. I don't mean there isn't any value in it, if you need it. I mean, for some people it could be just the right thing. If it's working for you, Conrad, that's what counts.

CONRAD: Well, actually, I don't know how long I'll keep it up. I got shoved into it, sort of . . . My father . . .

Silence. Finally:

KAREN: Your hair grew in.

CONRAD: You still painting?

KAREN: No, I quit that. They were so weird, those paintings.

CONRAD: You can't give that up. You taught me everything I know. You got me to stop drawing straight lines. You taught me to draw with ketchup.

She laughs.

CONRAD: Remember? If we can't sell 'em we'll eat 'em.

More laughter. Then silence.

KAREN: How's your mother?

CONRAD: My mother? Good. Real good.

KAREN: That's good.

CONRAD: Yeah. (*pause*) So you don't draw with ketchup anymore, huh?

KAREN: No, but I'm in the church choir.

CONRAD: Hey! Me, too, at school. It's great, isn't it?

KAREN: Yeah. It's great.

CONRAD: (*sings*) "I've got a mule and his name is Sal. Fifteen miles on the Erie Canal." I'm a tenor.

KAREN: Sounds good.

Pause. She reaches into her glass to pick up some ice. CONRAD watches her. She starts to chew on the ice.

KAREN: They're right, you know?

CONRAD: Who?

KAREN: Our parents. They know something we don't know.

CONRAD: What?

KAREN: Oh . . . how to meet obstacles and how to be popular, I guess.

CONRAD: Like *The Waltons*, huh?

She chews the ice.

CONRAD: You still like ice.

KAREN: Oh, God, I'm sorry, it's a terrible habit.

CONRAD: Hey, it's okay. I don't mind. I like it. It reminds me of you.

Pause. She chews very hard; the ice makes a lot of noise, and they both laugh again.

CONRAD: I don't know. I miss it sometimes. The hospital.

KAREN: I know, Connie, but things have to change.

CONRAD: But in the hospital, that's where we had the laughs.

KAREN: But we aren't there now. It has to be different now. That wasn't real life back there.

CONRAD: Yeah . . . I guess you're right.

She looks at her watch.

KAREN: I've really gotta go. I've got a meeting at school. Our drama club is doing *A Thousand Clowns*.

CONRAD: I know. You told me.

KAREN: Oh. Did I . . . Well, I'd better hurry.

CONRAD: Yeah, well, thanks for seeing me, Karen.

KAREN: Connie . . . let's have the most wonderful Christmas of our lives. We can, you know. We can have a wonderful year. It can be the best year ever.

CONRAD: Yeah, okay.

KAREN: (*getting up*) And will you call me again? I'd like to see you. Really, I mean it. Will you?

CONRAD: Sure I will.

KAREN gathers her coat about her shoulders. She's awkward.

KAREN: I wish I could stay longer. It's really good to see you, Con, it really is.

CONRAD: You, too.

KAREN: 'Bye.

CONRAD: 'Bye.

KAREN turns, leaves without a backward glance. CONRAD sits there, palming the empty Coke glass back and forth between his hands; he looks disappointed.

Sample Scripts

Most of the scenes in this anthology are excerpted from the unpublished "shooting scripts" of the screenplays. The scenes from *Annie Hall* and *Dr. Strangelove*, however, are excerpted from the unpublished "release continuity" or "cutting continuity" scripts. The rest of the scenes are reprinted from published sources.

A shooting script comes before a film is shot; a continuity script comes after. The shooting script is a story written by one or more writers, and it is organized into location, action, dialogue. The continuity is a stenographic transcription of what is actually seen and heard on the screen after the "cutting," after the film is "released." Whereas the continuity may say, "EXT. CU: KONG HOLDING GIRL," the shooting script may say, "The CAMERA moves in for a CLOSE UP of KONG'S glittering eyes as his massive hand slowly, lovingly brings her up to his face. He can feel her breath. His eyes roll back into his head." For the actor working on these scenes, the continuity is a better source of dialogue accurate to what is heard in the movie. The dialogue and the sound effects are recorded in the continuity from the soundtrack. But the shooting script— which may vary greatly in its forms—usually indicates the intensions, feelings and moods of the characters, providing the actor with the *hows* and *whys* of what the characters do or say. That it's *done* and that it's *said* are what the continuity documents. In the few instances where both a continuity and a shooting script were available to me for the same film, the two have been combined so that the dialogue is accurate to the movie and the description, direction, and action are accurate to the writer's (or writers') vision.

Much of the dialogue and action may be cut or rewritten from a shooting script as it undergoes several drafts and revisions on its way to the filming. Any one of several writers' drafts, none of them final, may be the copy of the script donated to the film library in which the scripts are available for reading. (Because of copyright restrictions, they may not be circulated or photocopied.) Whenever more than one version of a shooting script was available, the latest draft was used for the excerpted scene. However, even "Final Draft" is no guarantee of absolute accuracy between what you read on the page and what you hear and see in the film itself. Even after shooting is underway, there are location exigencies and rewrites and editing and over-run budgets and studio approval and preview audience responses still to affect what finally reaches the screen in the movie theatre. This is further complicated if more than one cut of a film gets released.

Down the side of each page of a shooting script one or more numbers appear. Theoretically, each shot number signifies a new camera position, so the column provides a consecutive numbering of each time something different is seen or something is seen differently by the camera. But in practice, the shot numbers often actually indicate a new location for the action, a new "scene." The section of dialogue and action between each pair of numbers has come to be called a "scene" and this does not mean an "acting scene." A shooting script may have hundreds of scenes. Only rarely, as in the second scene excerpted from *The Graduate*, does a single acting scene perfectly coincide with a single film scene.

A continuity script has a few columns of numbers down the side of each page. The scenes are numbered, not consecutively from the beginning of the script to the end, but within each reel. There is also a column counting the number of feet of film (and the number of frames within each foot) which have passed. Often there is another column noting how much running time has elapsed.

The scenes from *Annie Hall* and *Dr. Strangelove* are excerpted from continuity scripts because no shooting scripts were available. The data of time and footage and camera shots have not been duplicated in the scenes themselves, but samples of these two forms—shooting script and continuity—appear on the following pages.

The Shooting Script: A Sample from *Chinatown*

74.
Rev. 10/24/73

139   CONTINUED:

> PILOT
>
> She ran off to Mexico—rumor was she was
> knocked up and didn't even know who the
> father was—went there to get rid of it.
>
> GITTES
>
> You don't say?
>
> PILOT
>
> Cross was looking for her all over the
> country—offered rewards, everything. Felt
> real sorry for him, with all his money.

140   ALBACORE CLUB—DAY

A pleasant but unobtrusive clapboard blue and white
building on the bay overlooking the harbor. The sea-
plane lands. A motor launch with a burgee of fish flying
from it turns and heads in the direction of the plane.

141   EXT. WINDING ROAD—RANCHO DEL CRUCE

Gittes, driven in a station wagon, passes under the sign
with a cross painted below the name.

The ranch itself is only partially in a valley on the
island—as the wagon continues one can SEE that it is
actually a miniature California, encompassing desert,
mountains and canyon that tumble down palisades to
the windward side of the sea.

The wagon comes to a halt where a group of hands are
clustered around a corral. The circle of men drift apart,
leaving JUSTIN CROSS standing, using a cane for support, reedy but handsome in a rough linen shirt and
jeans. When he talks his strong face is lively, in repose
it looks ravaged.

The Continuity Script: A Sample from *Dr. Strangelove*

REEL SEVEN

Sc.	Tot.	Length		
6.	cont...			MANDRAKE (cont...): Now, now, supposing I play a little guessing game with you, Jack boy. I'll try and guess—I'll try and guess what the code is...
			Ripper closes door.	
			Gun shot from inside Bathroom as RIPPER commits suicide.	GUN SHOT
			MANDRAKE struggles to open door.	
7.	162.6	17.13	EXT. DAY, SKY LS B-52 flying, PAN R. Mountains BG.	MUSIC IN
8.	171.14	9.8	INT. B-52, MSC High Angle ACE in position. Mountains through window BG.	ACE: Co-pilot to Navigator. I'm ready with the fuel figures now. We have 109,000...
9.	190.12	18.14	MS ZOGG in position. TRACK IN PANNING R. across Instrument panel & bench to MS. KIVEL.	ACE (OFF): ...total, 79,000 in the mains and 30,000 in the auxiliaries. ER. that works out to roughly seven hours fifteen minutes endurance for this time.

10.	194.9	3.13	CU DIETRICH.	DIETRICH D.S.O. to Captain. . .
11.	219.2	24.9	CU RADAR SCREEN.	DIETRICH (OFF): . . . I have an unidentified radar blip. Distance 60 miles. Approximate speed Mach. 3. Looks like a missile tracking us. Confirmed. . .
12.	222.5	3.3	CU DIETRICH.	DIETRICH: . . .definite missile track, commence. . .
13.	225.9	3.4	CS KONG switching controls.	DIETRICH (OFF): . . .evasive action right.
14.	233.2	7.9	<u>EXT DAY, SKY</u> B-52 flying. It banks & climbs steeply.	DRUMS & ROAR OF ENGINES
15.	236.11	3.9	INT. B-52, CS Low Angle KONG at controls.	DIETRICH (OFF): Missile still closing. . .

Sources

The scene from Frank Capra's *It Happened One Night* is reprinted from the published script in *Twenty Best Filmplays* Vol. I, Crown Publishers, edited by John Gassner and Dudley Nichols, New York, 1943.

The scenes from Frank Capra's *Mr. Smith Goes To Washington* are reprinted from the published script in *Twenty Best Filmplays*, Vol. I, Crown Publishers, edited by John Gassner and Dudley Nichols, New York, 1943.

The scene from *Rebecca* is reprinted from the published script in *Twenty Best Filmplays*, Vol. I, Crown Publishers, edited by John Gassner and Dudley Nichols, New York, 1943.

The scenes from *Citizen Kane* are reprinted from scenes 60-62 and scene 71 of the shooting script, dated July 16, 1940, as published in *The Citizen Kane Book*, in the hardcover Atlantic Monthly Book edition by Little, Brown, 1971; and the softcover Bantam Books edition, 1974.

The scenes from *The Maltese Falcon* as presented are a collation of the dialogue from the soundtrack and the action in scenes 17, 18, and 122 from the unpublished shooting script, Final 5/26/41, housed in the Louis B. Mayer Library of the American Film Institute in Los Angeles. The dialogue may be read as captions beneath stills from the film in *The Maltese Falcon*, a Universe Book, © 1974 by Darien House, Inc.

The scene from *Casablanca* as presented is a collation of the dialogue from the soundtrack and the action from the script as published in *Best Filmplays of 1943-1944* by Crown Publishers. The dialogue may be read as captions beneath stills from the film in *Casablanca*, a Universe Book, © 1974 by Darien House, Inc.

The scene from *Adam's Rib* is reprinted from scenes 70–75 in the published script in *Adam's Rib*, a Viking Film Book from MGM Library of Film Scripts, The Viking Press, 1972.

The scene from *Sunset Boulevard* is reprinted from scenes A31–A35 in the unpublished final shooting script March 21, 1949, housed in the Special Collections of the Doheney Library of the University of Southern California.

The scenes from *All About Eve* are reprinted from the published script, which may be found in hardcover in *All About Eve*, Random House, 1951, and *More About All About Eve*, Random House, 1972, as well as in softcover in *More About All About Eve*, Bantam Books, 1974.

The scenes from *The African Queen* are reprinted from the published script in *Agee on Film*, Volume II, Beacon Press, 1960.

The scene from *On The Waterfront* is reprinted from the unpublished original screenplay housed at the Margaret Herrick Library of the Academy of Motion Picture Arts and Sciences, Beverly Hills, California. An edited version of the script is available in *On The Waterfront*, Southern Illinois University Press, copyright 1980.

The scene from *The Goddess* is reprinted from the published script in *The Goddess*, Simon & Schuster, 1958.

The scenes from *Some Like It Hot* are reprinted from scenes 24, 37, 56, 59, and 60 of the unpublished shooting script housed in the Louis B. Mayer Library of the American Film Institute in Los Angeles.

The scenes from *The Misfits* are reprinted from the unpublished script, revised September, 1959, in *Film Scripts Three*, Appleton Century Crofts (reprinted by permission of the Viking Press).

The scenes from *Lawrence of Arabia* are reprinted from scenes 612-627 of Vol. I and scenes 4 and 203-212 of Vol. II of the unpublished shooting script, Version B, housed at the Margaret Herrick Library of the Academy of Motion Picture Arts and Sciences, Beverly Hills, California.

The scenes from *Dr. Strangelove or How I Learned to Stop Worrying and Love the Bomb* are reprinted from the unpublished release continuity script housed in the Special Collections of the Doheney Library of the University of Southern California. The *Dr. Strangelove* continuity has no overall pagination; the pages are numbered only within each designated reel. The scenes used are reprinted from Reel 3, scenes 1-10; Reel 4, scenes 82-84; Reel 5, scenes 33-43; Reel 6, scenes 34-57; Reel 7, scenes 1-6, 63-82, 103-106; Reel 8, scenes 1-20.

The scene from *The Producers* is reprinted from scenes 8B–9N of the unpublished shooting script housed at the Margaret Herrick Library of the Academy of Motion Picture Arts and Sciences, Beverly Hills, California.

The scenes from *The Graduate* are reprinted from scenes 35-38 and 91 of the unpublished shooting script, Final Draft, March 29, 1967, housed at the Margaret Herrick Library of the Academy of Motion Picture Arts and Sciences, Beverly Hills, California.

The scenes from *Midnight Cowboy* are reprinted from the Writers Guild of America copy of the unpublished screenplay housed at the Margaret Herrick Library of the Academy of Motion Picture Arts and Sciences, Beverly Hills, California.

The scene from *They Shoot Horses, Don't They?* is reprinted from scenes 89 and 104-109 in the published script in the softcover *They Shoot Horses, Don't They?*, Avon Books.

The scenes from *Five Easy Pieces* are reprinted from scenes 63, 121-125 in the unpublished shooting script Final Draft, October 20, 1969, housed in the Louis B. Mayer Library of the American Film Institute in Los Angeles.

The scene from *Klute* is reprinted from scenes 64–73 and 81 of the unpublished shooting script, June 26, 1970, housed in the Special Collections of the Doheney Library of the University of Southern California.

The scenes from *Carnal Knowledge* are reprinted from the published script *Carnal Knowledge* in hardcover by Farrar, Straus & Giroux, Inc.; and in softcover by Avon Books.

The scene from *Harold and Maude* is reprinted from scene 110 of the unpublished original screenplay, housed in the Margaret Herrick Library of the Academy of Motion Picture Arts and Sciences, Beverly Hills, California.

The scenes from *The Last Picture Show* are reprinted from scenes 135, 136, and 149–155 in the unpublished shooting script, housed in the Louis B. Mayer Library of the American Film Institute in Los Angeles.

The scenes from *Last Tango in Paris* are reprinted from scenes 8 and 19 of the published script in *Last Tango in Paris*, Delacorte Press in association with Quicksilver Books.

The scene from *Sunday, Bloody Sunday* is reprinted from the published script, in softcover by Bantam Books, 1972.

The scenes from *Minnie and Moskowitz* are reprinted from scenes 374-394 and 521-543 of the published script, Black Sparrow Press, 1973.

The scenes from *Save The Tiger* are reprinted from scenes 14–27 and 74–90 of the unpublished shooting script Final Draft, January 26, 1972, housed in the Margaret Herrick Library of the Academy of Motion Picture Arts and Sciences, Beverly Hills, California.

The scene from *The Way We Were* is reprinted from scenes 136-139 of the unpublished shooting script, May 15, 1972, housed in the Louis B. Mayer Library of the American Film Institute in Los Angeles.

The scene from *Alice Doesn't Live Here Anymore* is reprinted from scenes 132–135 of the unpublished original screenplay Final, February 4, 1974, housed in the Margaret Herrick Library of the Academy of Motion Picture Arts and Sciences, Beverly Hills, California.

The scenes from *Chinatown* are reprinted from scenes 142–148 (revised 10/24/73) and 223–224 of the unpublished shooting script, Third Draft, October 9, 1973, housed in the Margaret Herrick Library of the Academy of Motion Picture Arts and Sciences, Beverly Hills, California.

The scene from *Dog Day Afternoon* is reprinted from scene 127 of the unpublished shooting script, housed in the Margaret Herrick Library of the Academy of Motion Picture Arts and Sciences, Beverly Hills, California.

The scenes from *Shampoo* are reprinted from scenes 207-212 and 213-224 of the unpublished shooting script, 1975, housed in the Margaret Herrick Library of the Academy of Motion Picture Arts and Sciences, Beverly Hills, California.

The scene from *Network* is reprinted from scenes 73 and 74 of the unpublished original screenplay, adjusted as of 2/27/76, housed in the Margaret Herrick Library of the Academy of Motion Picture Arts and Sciences, Beverly Hills, California.

The scenes from *Rocky* are reprinted from scenes 36A–40 and 53 of the unpublished shooting script housed in the Margaret Herrick Library of the Academy of Motion Picture Arts and Sciences, Beverly Hills, California.

The scene from *The Seven Per-Cent Solution* is reprinted from scenes 88-94 of the unpublished shooting script, March 17, 1976, housed in the Margaret Herrick Library of the Academy of Motion Picture Arts and Sciences, Beverly Hills, California.

The scene from *Annie Hall* is reprinted from Reel 4 of the unpublished release continuity script housed at the Margaret Herrick Library of the Academy of Motion Picture Arts and Sciences, Beverly Hills, California. An edited version of this script is available in the paperback *Four Films of Woody Allen*, published by Random House.

The scene from *Julia* is reprinted from scenes 281–287 in the unpublished shooting script, Revised Final Draft, September 20, 1976, incorporating revisions dated June 24th, July 7th, 21st, and 29th, August 11th and 25th, and September 1st, 1976; housed at the Margaret Herrick Library of the Academy of Motion Picture Arts and Sciences, Beverly Hills, California.

The scenes from *Saturday Night Fever* are reprinted from scenes 98A–105 (revised 3/8/77); 183–187 (revised 3/10/77); and 255–272 of the unpublished shooting script *Saturday Night Fever*, formerly *Tribal Rites of Saturday Night*, Final Version, February 26, 1977, housed in the Louis B. Mayer Library of the American Film Institute in Los Angeles.

The scene from *The Turning Point* is reprinted from scenes 134-139 in the unpublished shooting script, Final Draft, July 2, 1976, housed in the Margaret Herrick Library of the Academy of Motion Picture Arts and Sciences, Beverly Hills, California.

The scenes from *An Unmarried Woman* are reprinted from scenes 6A-C, 25, 29, and 39 of the unpublished shooting script Final Draft, November, 1976, housed in the Margaret Herrick Library of the Academy of Motion Picture Arts and Sciences, Beverly Hills, California.

The scenes from *Who'll Stop the Rain* are reprinted from scenes 24-27 (revised 4/6/77) and 128-132 of the unpublished shooting script entitled *Dog Soldiers*, March 14, 1977, housed at the Louis B. Mayer Library of the American Film Institute in Los Angeles.

The scene from *Ordinary People* is reprinted from scene 121 of the unpublished screenplay Second Draft, September 21, 1979, including revisions from October 8, 1979, housed in the Margaret Herrick Library of the Academy of Motion Picture Arts and Sciences, Beverly Hills, California.

Acknowledgments

Courtesy of Columbia Pictures Corporation and with the permission of Stanley Kubrick and Terry Southern.

The Producers screenplay by Mel Brooks. Copyright 1966 Mel Brooks. Copyright 1968 Embassy Pictures Corporation. By permission of Avco Embassy Pictures Corporation and Mel Brooks.

Adam's Rib screenplay by Ruth Gordon and Garson Kanin. Copyright 1949 Loew's Inc. Renewed 1976 Metro-Goldwyn-Mayer, Inc. By permission of Metro-Goldwyn-Mayer, Inc.

Sunset Boulevard screenplay by Billy Wilder and D.M. Marshman, Jr. and Charles Brackett. Copyright 1950 Paramount Pictures Corporation. Courtesy of Paramount Pictures Corporation and with the permission of Billy Wilder.

All About Eve screenplay by Joseph L. Mankiewicz. (Based on the story *The Wisdom of Eve* by Mary Orr.) Copyright 1951 Twentieth Century-Fox Film Corporation. Courtesy of Twentieth Century-Fox Film Corporation and with the permission of Joseph L. Mankiewicz.

The African Queen screenplay by James Agee with John Huston. (Based on the novel *The African Queen* by C.S. Forester.) Acknowledgment is made to Sam Spiegel of Horizon Pictures for permission to include the excerpts from *The African Queen* in this volume.

On the Waterfront screenplay by Budd Schulberg. Based on a story by Budd Schulberg. (Suggested by articles, "Crime on the Waterfront" by Malcolm Johnson.) Copyright 1954 Columbia Pictures Corporation. Courtesy of Columbia Pictures Corporation and by permission of The Dorese Agency on behalf of Budd Schulberg.

The Goddess screenplay by Paddy Chayefsky. Copyright 1957 Carnegie Productions, Inc. Copyright 1957 Susan Chayefsky. Courtesy of Columbia Pictures Corporation and by permission of Susan Chayefsky.

The Graduate screenplay by Buck Henry and Calder Willingham. (Based on the novel *The Graduate* by Charles Webb.) Copyright 1967 Embassy Pictures Corporation and Lawrence Turman, Inc. Courtesy of Avco Embassy Pictures Corporation and Lawrence Turman and with the permission of Buck Henry.

They Shoot Horses, Don't They? screenplay by James Poe and Robert E. Thompson. (Based on the novel *They Shoot Horses, Don't They?* by Horace McCoy.) Copyright 1969 ABC Pictures Corporation. Reprinted with the permission of Robert E. Thompson.

Midnight Cowboy screenplay by Waldo Salt. (Based on the novel *Midnight Cowboy* by James Leo Herlihy.) Copyright 1969 Jerome Hellman Productions, Inc. All rights reserved. Released through United Artists Corporation. Courtesy of United Artists Corporation and with the permission of Waldo Salt.

Five Easy Pieces screenplay by Adrien Joyce. (Based on a story by Bob Rafelson and Adrien Joyce.) Copyright 1970 Five Easy Pieces Productions, Inc. Courtesy of Columbia Pictures Corporation and with the permission of Adrien Joyce.

Klute screenplay by Andy Lewis and Dave Lewis. Copyright 1971 Warner Brothers, Inc. All rights reserved. Courtesy of Warner Brothers, Inc. and with the permission of Andy Lewis and Dave Lewis.

Personal Acknowledgments

Most of the scenes in this book have never before been published, and there has never before been any anthology of acting scenes from filmscripts. That this collection exists is the result of the faith, help, and good-will of many people.

In the beginning, there were the film libraries. I particularly thank Anne Schlosser at the American Film Institute, Robert Knutsen at the Special Collections at the University of Southern California, and Carol Epstein at the Academy of Motion Picture Arts and Sciences, without whose kind attentions it would not have been possible to move beyond the initial period of research.

Then came the legal departments of the studios. They were asked to bear the brunt of an enormous labor of agreements and permissions, and all for the benefit of the actor who trains. It is one thing for me to believe that in the long run everyone in an audience will benefit from the actors having had access to this material in scene study class; it is quite another thing for the studio legal departments to be expected to see it this way. Without their time and energy, no such collection of film scenes could ever have been published.

Then came those individuals at Bantam Books whose contributions were essential: Toni Burbank, who originally said "yes;" Charles Bloch, who "takes care of business" with a grace that seems to me like art; LuAnn Walther, from whom I learned what it is that an editor does: her patience and clarity of thought and language, not to mention her belief in the purpose of this project, permeates the entire volume. The work of their associates—Jonathan Skipp, Sue Terry, Nancy Kenney, Lisa Mandel, and Kim Trattner—corralled endless aspects from out of chaos into the realm of the manageable. Jennifer Atkinson was responsible for unifying the multiple forms of scripts and notes into the orderly procession in which they appear.

There are those individuals whose contributions, like air, are both invisible and absolutely vital to the life of this collection. Eva Mekler and Michael Schulman originally set my thinking along the path on which the idea for this book first arose. Eileen Dunne, Karen Green Rosin, and Charles Rosin never lost sight of that path, helping me to keep track of my purpose and my prose when both would wander. Linda Lichter and Ken Sherman brought the idea to the publisher. Filmmakers Kathy Levitt, John Carnochan, Jane Crawford, and Robert Fiore extended a

476

hospitality that enabled me to complete this work. It was from screen-writer Jane Hancock that I have learned what it actually comes to mean to "believe in the work." Since the word "persistence" has been so repeatedly applied to what it took to bring this book to the actor in class, my parents Shirley and Harold must be mentioned, as I suspect I picked it up from them.

And finally, I thank the screenwriters who have provided us with the characters in these pages, characters who have often so profoundly penetrated into our personal and collective mythologies that we have shaped our selves and our lives around them. And I also thank the actors with whom I take and teach class, because it is they who have provided me with something worth doing.

—J.K.

ABOUT THE EDITOR

JOSHUA KARTON took honors in literature and drama at the Universities of California and Edinburgh before training as an actor at the American Conservatory Theatre. He returned there to teach, after designing and directing the film and video exhibits of the Bicentennial *Theatrical Evolution 1776–1976* (which received the 1976 New York Drama Desk Award) and after serving as program consultant for the television show *Forever Fernwood*. He is now a director of Los Angeles's Free Association Theatre performing, teaching, developing scripts, and creating curricula for its education programs as well as editing *Filmscenes and Monologues for Actors, Volume II*.

DISCOVER
THE DRAMA OF LIFE
IN THE LIFE OF DRAMA